Money, Myths, and Change

Worlds of Desire: The Chicago Series on Sexuality, Gender, and Culture
Edited by Gilbert Herdt

ALSO IN THE SERIES:

M. V. Lee Badgett

Money,
Myths,
AND
Change

*The Economic Lives
of Lesbians and
Gay Men*

■

THE UNIVERSITY OF CHICAGO PRESS
CHICAGO AND LONDON

M. V. LEE BADGETT is assistant professor of economics at the University of Massachusetts at Amherst. She received a Ph.D. in economics from the University of California at Berkeley. She also serves as research director of the Institute for Gay and Lesbian Strategic Studies.

Parts of chapter 2 appeared in "The Wage Effects of Sexual Orientation Discrimination," *Industrial Relations Review* 48, no. 4 (July 1995): 726–39. Used by permission.

Parts of chapter 3 appeared in "Choices and Chances: Is Coming Out at Work a Rational Choice?" in *Queer Studies: A Multicultural Anthology,* edited by Mickey Eliason and Brett Beemyn (New York: New York University Press, 1966). Used by permission.

Chapter 9 is based on "Thinking Homo/Economically," in *Overcoming Heterosexism and Homophobia: Strategies That Work,* edited by Walter L. Williams and James Sears (New York: Columbia University Press, 1997). © 1977 Columbia University Press. Reprinted with the permission of the publisher.

The University of Chicago Press, Chicago 60637
The University of Chicago Press, Ltd., London
© 2001 by The University of Chicago
All rights reserved. Published 2001
Printed in the United States of America
10 09 08 07 06 05 04 03 02 01   1 2 3 4 5

ISBN: 0-226-03400-3 (cloth)

Library of Congress Cataloging-in-Publication Data

Badgett, Mary Virginia Lee.
  Money, myths, and change : the economic lives of lesbians and gay men
/ M.V. Lee Badgett.
     p. cm. — (Worlds of desire)
Includes bibliographical references and index.
  ISBN 0-226-03400-3
  1. Gays—Economic conditions. 2. Homosexuality—Economic aspects. I. Title.
II. Series.
  HQ76.25 .B33 2001
  305.9′0664—dc21

                                                           00-011126

⊗ The paper used in this publication meets the minimum requirements of the American National Standard for Information Sciences—Permanence of Paper for Printed Library Materials, ANSI Z39.48-1992.

For Rosa, Rio, Brigid, Owen, and Lucky

CONTENTS

TABLES

ACKNOWLEDGMENTS

When I began this "economist studies gay people" journey into uncharted territory in the early 1990s, I had no idea that my course would result in this book. I just saw many important and exciting questions but few answers. Fortunately, scholars and activists who had come before me had produced much insightful historical, sociological, legal, and psychological work for me to draw on as I began. Those pioneers had also helped to create the academic and political space that allowed me to pursue this research, and I am very grateful for their courageous efforts.

Equally important were the individuals who directly encouraged me and helped me get started. In particular, the support of Jeffrey Escoffier, Jim Woods, Bill Dickens, Lisa D. Moore, Katie King, Bob Anderson, Rhonda Williams, Katherine Larson, and Richard Cornwall was essential early on for thinking through difficult questions and for maintaining my sense of professional connection and sanity. Over the years, I have also been lucky to have received suggestions, ideas, and much support from Mary C. King, Nancy Folbre, Lisa Saunders, Elizabeth Silver, Greg Herek, Prue Hyman, Susannah MacKaye, Marlene Kim, Cathy Weinberger, Patricia Connelly, and Anne Habiby. Nancy Cunningham was a wonderful collaborator on the study of giving and volunteering in the gay, lesbian, bisexual, and transgendered communities described in chapter 8.

I am very grateful to Nancy Folbre, Mary King, David Kirp, Lisa Saunders, Grant Lukenbill, Gil Herdt, Richard Cornwall, Carol Heim, and two anonymous referees for reading earlier versions of this manuscript. They offered wonderful advice, even though I couldn't use it all. Many people have offered helpful comments on articles that influenced this book. Gil Herdt and Doug Mitchell have been both supportive and exceedingly patient editors, which I greatly appreciate!

Many other people provided helpful comments on pieces of this work at conferences and in seminars and courses. In particular, I benefited greatly from thinking through issues with my students at the University of

Massachusetts-Amherst, the University of Maryland, and Yale University. My work with the Institute for Gay and Lesbian Strategic Studies has been energizing and intellectually stimulating, mainly because of people like Greg Scott, Ann Northrop, J. B. Collier, and Walter Williams. My colleagues in the Five College Sexuality Seminar, Barbara Cruikshank, Lisa Henderson, Margaret Hunt, Janice Irvine, Lynn Morgan, Jackie Urla, and Nancy Whittier, also provided helpful feedback and an important intellectual community.

I am very grateful to the Wayne Placek Fund of the American Psychological Foundation for supporting my work on incomes and discrimination. The Aspen Institute, the National Society for Fund-Raising Executives, American Airlines, and Pacific Bell provided support for the study of giving and volunteering. The support of those funders and of the Center for Public Policy and Administration at the University of Massachusetts made it possible to work with several wonderful research assistants. I thank Eric Carzon, Emily Jongkind, Aaron Harsch, Melanie Cahill, Billy Harris, and Stephanie Eckman for their hard work and contributions to this book. Thanks also go to Maria Rigas for her careful editing and to Robie Grant for the index

My parents and siblings have long provided crucial support for my career. I could not have finished this book without the love and forbearance of Elizabeth Silver and the quiet company of our dog Squirt. I am grateful for my family's support.

ONE

Introduction: Meeting the Myths

Are the economic decisions made by gay people different in some way from those made by heterosexual people? Do lesbian, gay, and bisexual people make economic decisions differently? Do they face different constraints from heterosexual people? How do gay people's standard of living compare with heterosexual individuals' and families' standard of living?

These questions are hard to answer because we know very little about the economic position of lesbian, gay, and bisexual people. Social stigma, violence, and discrimination have fostered a strategy of invisibility for many gay people, and that invisibility has made the lives of the broad range of gay people difficult to study. The combination of gay invisibility and selectively generated information has instead fostered the spread of a number of misleading myths about where and how lesbian, gay, and bisexual people fit in economy.

The myth of privilege: Lesbians and gay men make up an affluent, well-educated, professional elite, occupying positions of power and influence in the workplace and society at large. Many gay people in the United States are wealthy and influential: President Clinton's friend David Mixner, media mogul David Geffen; wealthy philanthropist and U.S. Ambassador to Luxembourg James Hormel; popular singer k.d. lang; and actor Ellen DeGeneres. Magazines feature cover stories on high-level corporate or political officials who are lesbian or gay. Artists publicly mourn the devastating losses to the arts communities from the HIV epidemic, including well-known gay artists such as Keith Haring and Robert Mapplethorpe.

The DINK (double income no kids) myth: Gay people have no family responsibilities to hamper their job advancement or accumulation of wealth. With no children to support or to save for, gay couples have twice as much income to spend on themselves. Indeed, some marketing surveys of lesbians and gay men show household incomes that are much higher than the typical U.S. household. As a result of this financial freedom, gay couples can afford homes in chic neighborhoods and make large contributions to support their political groups.

The myth of protective invisibility: Unlike other minority groups, gay people can avoid the effects of social stigma by hiding their homosexuality. Women and ethnic minorities, on the other hand, are easily identified and have been clearly singled out for unfair treatment in the past (and even today, many would argue). If gay people choose to be indiscreet and "flaunt" their homosexuality, they must face the social disapproval that is otherwise easily avoided.

The myth of the conspicuous consumer: Gay people are hedonistic and consumption-oriented, an ideal niche market for upscale products. Gay magazines and newspapers promote their readers to advertisers as an ideal market, and liquor companies, travel agencies, and bottled water companies target ads at gay consumers.

These are not the only stereotypes about lesbian and gay people. Many other now discredited myths and stereotypes have circulated widely over the years: gay people are child molesters, predatory, promiscuous, and mentally ill. But the economic myths, with their mixture of potentially positive and negative images, constitute a new challenge to social scientists, to the U.S. public, and to gay people and their political allies. Exploring the actual economic position of gay and lesbian people requires meeting these myths head-on.

The Origins of the Economic Myths

Where do the myths come from? Like many stereotypes, these myths often start with some observations about particular gay and lesbian people and then overgeneralize and overextend their reach. Some of the myths have been around as long as gay people have been noticed by the larger society. The myth of privilege and affluence has been around at least since ancient Roman times, when writers claimed that homosexuality was a weakness of the upper classes (Boswell 1980, 56). For many decades, the best known lesbian and gay people were part of a cultural elite, including artists and intellectuals such as Oscar Wilde, John Maynard Keynes, Walt Whitman, and Gertrude Stein, a fact that backed up the ancient claims.

Although the modern sources of the myths are complex, some of the blame for the promotion of the stereotypes certainly belongs to scholars who do not carefully interpret their findings. Early studies of lesbian and gay people—even sympathetic ones like Alfred Kinsey's—used samples of gay people who were not typical of gay people as a whole, which often skewed the socioeconomic status of those in the survey (see Kinsey et al. 1948, 105–9). In spite of increased skepticism about the current applicability of those early studies and a growing recognition of the variation in economic situations within the gay and lesbian communities, studies using biased samples persist. Recent marketing studies that are used to actively support myths often come from readers of gay magazines and newspapers, a group that is no more representative of the whole gay community than readers of the *New York Times* or *USA Today* are representative of people in the United States as a whole.

Clearly, gay people are hard to study. Even defining whom we should study, that is, which people are "gay" or "lesbian," has caused a heated debate in political and social arenas. One older critique of the lumping together of lesbians and gay men points to the very different experiences of men and women in our societies, differences that will mean that the lives of gay men and lesbians may be more different than similar. Looking at the research on economic differences between men and women, discussed in chapter 2, reveals many good reasons to believe that gender is at least as important as sexual orientation in determining a person's economic position. Because of those differences, I distinguish between lesbians and gay men when necessary in order to consider not just the impact of gender but to think about the interactions between the categories of gender and sexual orientation. When such distinctions are less important, I use the term "gay" to refer to both groups collectively.

More recently, the challenges to boundaries have expanded. Are bisexual people who have both male *and* female sex partners and intimate relationships part of the lesbian and/or gay community? What about those people whose biological sex at birth does not match their later gender identity? The development of a bisexual identity and of transgender and transsexual identities also pose difficulties for the researcher. To the extent that the larger society does not recognize the subtle differences between these groups, the distinctions between the economic experiences of gay, bisexual, transgendered, and transsexual people will be relatively small. I suspect, however, that as theorizing and empirical research related to these other categories progresses, distinctions will emerge in experiences among the groups delineated by other sexual and gender identities. Certainly, bisexual, transgendered, and transsexual people have options and decisions to make that are different from those faced by gay men and lesbians.

In this book, then, I focus primarily on the experiences of people who can by some definition be considered gay or lesbian. Given the broad range of dimensions of sexuality and gender identity, a categorization of people based primarily on the erotic attraction to those of the same sex is necessarily a crude one, but the crudeness is balanced, I believe, by the important analytical and empirical insights that this relatively simple cate-gorization offers. Lesbians and gay men face distinctive challenges as workers, consumers, and family members.

I should also note at this point that defining my focus on sexual orien-tation led me away from an in-depth discussion of the HIV/AIDS epidemic and its full impact on the economics of the gay community. Such a topic would be a worthy subject of its own book. The epidemic appears throughout my discussion, of course, since HIV has greatly influenced gay people's position in the workplace, family, marketplace, and society at large. I have not covered the many other ways that HIV has affected the gay economy, including the economics of health, health care, politics, and knowledge. For analytical purposes, I have set those subjects aside be-cause I wanted to avoid a disproportionate focus on gay men and, more significantly, because the issues raised here for lesbians and gay men pre-date—and may even postdate—the HIV/AIDS epidemic.

Defining the book's boundary around the sexual orientation of gay men and lesbians does not address exactly what "gay" or "lesbian" means, how-ever. Does it mean someone who engages in same-sex sexual behavior? Someone who fantasizes about such acts? Someone who will identify him-self or herself as gay or lesbian? Historians and anthropologists have shown that sexual activity between two people of the same sex has oc-curred throughout history and in many (if not all) cultures, but the social *meaning* and interpretation of that behavior has varied considerably. In ancient Greece, for example, sexual relations between two men were ac-ceptable under certain circumstances related to the class status of those involved and to the actual role taken by each man during the act. Histori-ans continue to debate to what extent we should call such men "gay" from a modern perspective (see articles in Stein 1990). Even today, in some cul-tures a man who is always the insertive partner in same-sex anal inter-course is still considered heterosexual (Almaguer 1991).

A recent study of sexual behavior in the United States demonstrates that while some people could be measured as "gay" by all possible definitions involving behavior, desire, and self-identity, others might engage in or have some desire to engage in same-sex sexual behavior but would not call themselves "gay" (Laumann et al. 1994). People classified as "gay" under any of those three definitions could face social stigma and, therefore, so-cial sanctions, but researchers must be conscious of potentially differen-tial effects. A fantasy that is never acted upon is not likely to have the same social consequences as publicly identifying oneself as gay.

Another tough question is how to find gay people, however defined, when those characteristics are not directly observable. Relying on self-reported behavior or identity means that if some people do not answer survey questions honestly, as might happen if closeted survey respondents fear discovery by a boss or family member, then survey results are suspect. Just as important, the places that researchers can relatively easily find gay people, such as gay bars, gay organizations, or gay newspaper readerships, might attract a group of gay people who are quite different from other people also defined as gay by the same kind of definition but who do not congregate in the same social spaces. Surveys of those groups of gay people might be biased in the sense that the people surveyed are wealthier or less likely to have children than the average gay person.

Survey bias is the starting point of a critique of the economic myths outlined above. This critique, which focuses on who was surveyed to generate "findings," is neither subtle nor startling for social scientists, who are conscious of the pitfalls in studying smaller subgroups to learn something about a larger group. (Ideally, the subgroups studied are chosen at random from the larger population, allowing the description of the smaller group to be applied to the larger group.)

Given the difficulties in studying lesbians and gay men, one might reasonably ask whether it is worth the trouble, especially in an economic context where we want to make some generalizations about *all* gay people, and perhaps even all *heterosexual* people, too. One answer is that the difficulties are decreasing as some recent surveys, discussed throughout this book, now provide a better picture of the range of experiences of gay people. Another answer to that challenge is that the myths themselves offer answers—although flawed ones—to the kinds of questions that social scientists should ask as they seek to understand the economic and social conditions of lesbians' and gay men's lives. Extending academic attention to the economic situation of lesbians and gay men is logical from an academic perspective, as economists and sociologists, in particular, try to understand the role of other social categories, such as race or gender, within the economy. The value of economic information has been heightened by ongoing political controversy over the legal standing of gay people, as policymakers, judges, and voters wrestle with public policy debates and lawsuits.

Rather than assuming that gay and lesbian people are economically distinct from heterosexuals in the sense implied by the myths, this book starts with a simpler approach that assumes that lesbian, gay, and bisexual people have the same basic economic needs as heterosexual Americans: providing for the material necessities of life, such as food, clothing, health care, and shelter for themselves and, perhaps, for children, as well as providing other culturally appropriate and necessary items and services. Gay people might use some or all of the same strategies for producing and acquiring goods and services as heterosexual people use, such as working for pay, doing housework, caring for children, and pooling resources with significant others. Studying these ends and means from an economic perspective might show that gay people do, in fact, have different income and employment outcomes, for instance. But economic inquiry also makes it possible to distinguish a simple empirical question about outcomes—*are* gay people's economic lives different—from a more interesting and more complex question about processes—*why* are they different?

Economics and Sexual Orientation

Until recently, economists have paid almost no attention to gay and lesbian people, and certainly not the kind of sustained attention necessary to provide useful insights. Within other academic disciplines, though, most notably history, psychology, sociology, and the humanities more generally, lesbian and gay studies has become a lively and exciting field. Academics from these other disciplines, as well as the occasional economist, have found economic factors to be quite important in understanding the development of a gay or lesbian identity in twentieth-century United States.

Some relatively early studies of gay and lesbian history suggest that modern "gay" and "lesbian" identities were influenced by economic circumstances and market forces. John D'Emilio's historical analysis of the United States, for instance, connects the rise of the gay community with the emergence of modern capitalism. The development of markets and of increasing wage labor in the nineteenth century led to the weakening of individuals' economic reliance on household production and their families (D'Emilio 1984). The loosening of family ties, the urbanization of the population, and the increasing separation of sex from procreation allowed the creation of a social space for those erotically attracted to people of the same sex, thus promoting the development of a new sense of social identity. Historian George Chauncey's account of the development of New York's gay world demonstrates how such space was created in the city's bars, bathhouses, restaurants, and boardinghouses in the late-nineteenth and early-twentieth centuries (Chauncey 1994).

In her analysis of the separation of men's and women's economic roles and occupations, economic historian Julie Matthaei draws similar ties between the economy and the development of modern gay and lesbian identities. The segregation of men and women in different economic spheres promoted contact and close ties among people of the same sex. For women in the twentieth century, the expansion of women's jobs and education created an economic role for women outside of the family and contributed to the development of lesbianism in two ways (Matthaei 1995, 17). First, education and work restricted women's marriage options by making those with jobs less desirable as wives. Second, and perhaps more important, these economic opportunities provided the possibility of economic independence, a crucial precondition for the privacy and material support necessary for women to live together without men.

All of these historical analyses suggest that what it means to be gay or lesbian in the United States in the twentieth century has been shaped by a broad social context that includes economic development. These studies have sketched out a context for thinking about the economics of being gay. But they have little to say about the role of lesbians and gay men within the contemporary economy and less about the impact of the economy on the lives of today's lesbians and gay men.

Variations in Modern Economic Life

Economists have only recently begun to consider the importance of social characteristics such as race, ethnicity, and gender, creating analytical approaches that may be applicable to sexual orientation, as well. The key issue economists have addressed is understanding why members of different social groups—men and women, white people and black people, gay people and heterosexual people—come to have such divergent roles and experiences in economic activities. Those differences are evident in many aspects of life, even in activities that do not immediately strike one as being related to the economy or as being the source of (or evidence of) differences related to sexual orientation.

But from the second our alarm clocks rouse us to start a new day, each moment is full of potential economic significance and is influenced by our gender, ethnic, and sexual orientation identities. Consider the morning activities evident in different households, for example. In my own home, I shower and dress, then focus my attention on walking the dog, making coffee, fixing breakfast, planning the day with my partner, and reading the newspaper. In the next town over, my friends Donna and Maria wake up their two young children to get them dressed, fed, and off to school. Another gay couple around the corner, Robert and Jim, spend a few minutes in their kitchen over coffee coordinating the use of their car, and making decisions about who will stop by the grocery store on the way home that evening and who will make dinner. Doug and Sarah compare schedules before Sarah gets their daughter in the car to drop her off at daycare. The final stage in each morning routine is usually the step out the door to head to work or, in Maria's case, to go to school.

Most people would clearly see the last step as an "economic" one that varies greatly from person to person and perhaps from group to group: we go to work to provide the money we need for food, clothing, shelter, daycare, etc., or we attend school to improve our future employment prospects. Grocery shopping also obviously involves a market transaction in which we exchange money for food items. The points where people and money come together, whether in a checkout line at the grocery store or on payday at a workplace, are obviously points of potential divergence by race, gender, or other group. On one level, the activities described in the previous paragraph seem quite similar across households, but on another level one can easily imagine the possible impact of an individual's cultural background and social status—perhaps including sexual orientation—on their tastes for particular consumer goods or participation in the paid labor force.

From an economist's perspective, the other routine aspects of our mornings are also economic in nature. From milk, cereal, water, coffee beans, electricity, appliances, and our own time and energy, we produce breakfast. Raising children involves parents' time and money, perhaps including payments for education or child care, not to mention love and sacrifice. The use we get from our past purchases of expensive assets like cars or houses might also involve the efficient sharing of those items with others. In households with more than one person, sharing also involves deciding how to use assets and time and who will use them to improve the well-being of the household's members. Economic decisions such as who does what within a household may very well depend on the sex or sexual orientation of the individuals involved, for instance.

From an economist's perspective, all of those tasks—producing meals, allocating time, using assets—are "economic" tasks not just because of the money and time involved, but because their outcomes define our material well-being. They are also "economic" because people are likely to use economic factors in their decision-making. This might mean a rational process of comparing possible uses of household members' time and choosing the one that adds the most to well-being in some sense. Or "economic" could mean acting with an awareness of constraints, whether time- or money-related. If gay people and heterosexual people (or men and women, or white people and black people) make decisions in different ways, have different ideas about the proper duties for men and women (or other social norms), form distinctive families, or face different constraints, then we would find very different outcomes by sexual orientation in whatever economic role we examine, including consumer, producer, investor, or family roles.

Difference can easily become disadvantage. Collusion among relatively powerful individuals who have negative attitudes about members of other social groups might limit access to jobs or particular housing markets for people in disfavored groups, for example. The social nature of the economy means that what we call discrimination is possible or even likely if members of dominant groups, say heterosexuals, have a distaste for working with or employing lesbian, gay, or bisexual people.[1] Distaste might be the product of social norms, or rules about how members of a society should behave, that forbid certain kinds of sexual practice or that define appropriate affectional and sexual partners as those of the opposite sex. The economic impact of being seen as a member of a disfavored group can be exacerbated when economically related institutions,[2] such as employers' health care plans or legal definitions of marriage, either deliberately or incidentally exclude certain kinds of people.

This book draws from several economic traditions to develop a more complex view of how lesbians' and gay men's unequal economic position is constructed. On one level, the analysis here takes into account the market processes and incentives that shape individuals' and firms' decision-making, which is what most people think of when they hear "economics." In addition, the analysis considers how social norms about gender and sexuality, public policies related to the workplace and family, collective action by members of privileged and disadvantaged groups, and economic institutions such as employers' compensation practices constrain gay people and shape their economic decisions and positions. Historical studies reveal that those norms and institutions vary over time and are not set in stone, suggesting the need to consider the complex set of social, political, and economic forces that influence norms and institutions. They may also be the products of or shaped by collective action, and those related to gay and lesbian people have at different times been shaped by the collective efforts of heterosexuals and, more recently, by gay people themselves. Any account of the economic position of gay people in the workplace, consumer marketplace, or family that ignores the influence of norms, institutions, and collective action misses important influences on the economics of being gay.

Another important question for economics asks why group differences emerge in the first place. What role does the economy, or more specifically, capitalism, play in creating the divisions between races, ethnic groups, or sexual orientations? Economists have struggled to explain *why* such dynamics related to race or gender might occur. Some economists assert a psychological attitude of racism or sexism and consider the impact of those attitudes. Others note the potential advantage to creating an "out group" that can be placed at a competitive disadvantage or can be assigned certain economic roles (as in assigning women childrearing responsibilities). Why would engaging in certain sexual practices come to define not just individuals but groups, and why would one group, say heterosexuals, want to dominate another group, say gay people, in political and economic terms? While this book does not attempt to answer these questions about the creation of categories directly, at the very least it should help to understand why those categorizations of people by sexuality are perpetuated through economic forces and why they are not easily changed.

Workplace Discrimination and Sexuality

The next three chapters of the book develop the issue of discrimination and intergroup relations in the context of lesbians' and gay men's jobs and careers. Chapter 2 examines the myth of gay privilege from the workplace perspective with a close look at the earnings of gay people and the impact of discrimination on those earnings. Study after study has demonstrated that women and people of color earn less than white men, most likely as a result of employment discrimination. Is a similar process at work for lesbians and gay men? Recent surveys that fulfill basic statistical requirements allow detailed statistical comparisons that contradict the myth of gay affluence. Rather than constituting an economic elite, as suggested by marketing surveys, academic studies show that gay men actually earn less than heterosexual men with the same education, experience, and residential characteristics, and lesbians earn no more than comparable heterosexual women (but far less than heterosexual men).

Those findings undermine the myth of gay affluence and shift our attention toward understanding why gay men and lesbians are compensated unequally. The financial penalty for being gay is evidence of systematic employment discrimination. As chapter 2 discusses in more detail, economists' dominant explanation is the existence of employers' distaste for hiring certain groups of people. Economists like Nobel laureate Gary Becker (1971) argue that, given enough market competition, market forces should erode the practice of discrimination, if not the actual discriminatory impulse. Employers who discriminate lower the productivity of their workforce, since by definition they hire the less productive person from the favored group. An employer who does not discriminate, then, should be able to earn higher profits than discriminating competitors, allowing greater growth and eventually driving the less profitable discriminating companies out of business. The implications of this theory for public policy are clear: forget nondiscrimination laws and let the market wear away discrimination. Closely examining the plausibility of this model of discrimination is essential for the discussion of public policy taken up in chapter 7.

Economists have also suggested other rationales for discrimination. Some theories shift attention away from individuals' attitudes about other groups as a cause of discrimination and toward collective attempts to monopolize particular economic roles and positions, especially those with high wages or employment stability. From this perspective, members of dominant groups have a personal financial stake in preserving an economic hierarchy. If this is the case, then competitive pressures might not wear discriminating companies down completely, since there is too little competition in some industries and because chronic unemployment gives companies access to many productive workers from favored groups. These alternative explanations of discrimination, developed further in chapter 2, point to collective action and social norms as important influences on gay people's position in the labor market. Norms about the proper behavior of men and women may influence the treatment and economic choices of gay men and lesbians, who by definition do not conform to what is considered proper behavior for men and women. At various times and in different contexts, collective action to enforce social norms related to gender and sexuality and to preserve economic hierarchies have resulted in laws and policies that require or allow discrimination against gay people.

In a context of potential discrimination and no policy protection, disclosing one's gay sexual orientation at work involves clear economic risks. Chapter 3 presents the ethical and social aspects that other researchers have considered in the context of disclosure and adds an economic angle by comparing the potential economic costs and benefits of being out at work. Chapter 3 also takes on the myth of invisibility, which blames gay people's openness for any discrimination that occurs. Public opinion polls suggest that Americans do not want gay people to disclose their sexual orientation. In the workplace context, though, discouraging disclosure treats gay people unequally since heterosexuals disclose their sexual orientation in many ways. Furthermore, the supposedly protective cloak of invisibility does not protect gay workers who must consciously and actively hide their sexuality at the cost of important social contact that could increase productivity and enhance the likelihood of promotion. On a larger scale, "coming out" has a potentially huge economic impact if closeted gay workers must strategize and actively hide their sexual orientation, reducing not only their productivity but the economy's overall output. Thus, policies that encourage gay people to hide their sexual orientation have clear social consequences.

One of the most obvious examples of workplace inequality for gay people is found in employers' fringe benefits practices that cover spouses and children of employees. Chapter 4 shows how these institutional practices discriminate against employees who have same-sex partners. Since most people younger than 65 with health insurance in the United States receive it through their own employer or a family member's employer, this form of discrimination creates a huge disadvantage for lesbian and gay people and their families. Employers have resisted attempts to extend benefits to gay employees' same-sex domestic partners, citing the fear of large increases in compensation costs. The very real economic concerns have proven to be less than compelling, as the experience of employers who offer benefits to domestic partners is that surprisingly few employees enroll partners and those partners do not generate high health care expenditures.

Largely at the instigation of gay and lesbian employees, many companies are reforming their compensation practices, and hundreds of employers now provide health care benefits to the domestic partners of gay and lesbian employees. Chapter 4 includes a discussion of the reasons for this profound and rapid shift, which accelerated in the 1990s. An analysis of the provision of health care benefits in their historical and economic context suggests that evolving norms related to compensation fairness, increasing labor market competition for workers, and gay employee organizations were major factors in employers' policy changes.

Gay Consumerism

The wooing of the gay consumer dollar, described in chapter 5, appears to be on a similar acceleration path as the extension of health care benefits.

Corporate interest in attracting gay customers has increased dramatically. Companies place ads in gay magazines, include gay characters in mainstream media ads, and customize their products for gay people's needs. A look back through gay economic history suggests that while the high level of attention to the gay market is new, a gay market has been around for a long time. The newest wave of attention to this market appears to represent the combination of several trends, including the continued loosening of legal restrictions on gay people and their activities, the heightened visibility of gay people as a result of the AIDS epidemic, the conscious "desexualization" of gay people by AIDS activists, the development of a cadre of knowledgeable gay marketers, and increased competitive pressure on U.S. corporations.

Much of the hype about the "gay marketing moment," as some have called it, centers on three of the four myths (the DINK, affluence, and conspicuous consumption myths), raising questions about the long-term prospects of the interest in the gay market. Chapter 5 recalls the findings contradicting the myth of affluence, and data on family income bolster that earlier conclusion. In some surveys, only gay men are significantly less likely than heterosexual people to have children in their home, suggesting that gay male couples *might* fit the DINK mythical image of two incomes. But the image of the gay conspicuous consumer is built on a myth that gay consumers are fundamentally different in their product interests, as well, an assumption with little strong supporting evidence as yet.

Overall, the gay market attention brings some benefits for the gay community since it attracts financial support to some crucial media and organizational institutions. But it also comes with some potential drawbacks, if increased competition for the gay market damages or destroys existing gay businesses. More ominously, political rhetoric suggests that the hedonistic consumer image leads to a distancing of the gay community from the larger U.S. populace.

Lesbian and Gay Family Economics

One positive side effect of the efforts to convince employers to recognize lesbian and gay employees' domestic partners—and perhaps even of the interest in gay consumer households—is the increased visibility of gay families, the topic of chapter 6. While the labor market and consumer marketplace are clearly sites of economic activity, the family often seems like a purely social or cultural structure. Economists see important production, consumption, and investment activities taking place within families and households, however. Purchases of many goods, such as houses, cars, and food, are often made for the general use of families rather than for only one individual. Further production of raw ingredients brought home from the grocery store is needed to make a meal for family members. And reproduction obviously plays an important part in creating the labor force of the next generation.

What might be less obvious is the economic reasoning behind family-related decisions. Getting married and having children could be the result of a kind of cost-benefit decision, for example. Much of chapter 6 focuses on how families combine the money and time from household members to produce goods and services, a complex decision subject to many influences. Married couples often divide family work in a simple way: the husband goes into the paid labor force and the wife stays at home raising kids and doing the housework. This particular division of labor could be an efficient allocation of each person's time to his or her most productive role. Or perhaps the traditional division of labor in married couples is the result of social norms about the proper family duties for men and women and has little to do with economic efficiency. Public policies also influence decisions about division of household labor by altering the costs or benefits of marriage and specialization.

In thinking about gay and lesbian families, similar sorts of questions arise—often in a public policy context—about why they form and dissolve, why they do or do not include children, and how they share or divide up work responsibilities. Anthropologists like Kath Weston and sociologists like Philip Blumstein and Pepper Schwartz have explored in detail some of the ways that lesbians' and gay men's families are structured, both in more traditional couples and in larger familial networks. Economists, though, have given little thought either to the similarities or the differences between gay and heterosexual families, even though comparisons could have potentially useful implications for understanding how and why *all* families are organized the way they are.

Differences in the relevance of gender norms and of access to legal and social institutions, most notably the inability to legally marry, could result in important differences among family types in their economic welfare and their economic decisions. So in addition to a more conceptual analysis, chapter 6 offers a glimpse into the economic realities of gay men's and lesbians' families based on both qualitative and quantitative studies. Overall, the picture that emerges is not one of gay people unencumbered by family responsibilities and possessing high discretionary incomes to spend on themselves. A more complete view of gay family life includes raising children and developing committed adult partnerships to create an economic family unit no less influential in the economic lives of individual gay people than are marriages for heterosexual people. In addition, the many ways that gay, lesbian, and bisexual people organize their family lives may provide helpful models to heterosexuals who increasingly face the kind of uncertainty and stress in providing for their families that gay people have long lived with.

Implications for Policy Changes and Economic Strategies

The next five chapters show that similar influences shape gay and lesbian people's positions as consumers, workers, and family members. Market forces, the competitive pressures on firms created by their unending search for profit-making opportunities, appear to have been as least partly responsible for the increased visibility of gay and lesbian consumers, and competitive pressures in hiring skilled workers appear to have promoted the advancement of domestic partner benefits. Changes in social norms related to gender roles and sexual behavior have made employers, voters, and policymakers more willing to enact progressive and inclusive policies. Collective action by gay, lesbian, and bisexual people has hastened other forces of change, pushing back repressive policies and promoting progressive ones. As a result, the legacy of public policies that limited gay people's economic position has been eroded.

Despite the progress that has occurred, public policy continues to limit gay people's attainment of economic equality. Workplace discrimination puts lesbians and gay men at an economic disadvantage, a disadvantage that can be measured in dollars and cents as well as in psychological terms. The lack of access to the legal institutions that support family life, particularly legal marriage, also adds to gay people's economic burden. They must often pay hundreds or even thousands of dollars to lawyers to simulate (imperfectly) what two heterosexual people and a ten-dollar marriage license can achieve overnight: a legally recognized family relationship. That legal relationship also comes with a host of monetary benefits that help heterosexual families raise children, plan for retirement, receive health care, and weather financial crises, among other things.

Gay people have responded to these economic stresses by organizing through the traditional political process, arguing for changes in public policy that would require nondiscrimination against gay individuals and their families. Chapters 7 and 8 shift my use of economic analysis to document and analyze inequality for gay people toward making recommendations about whether and how to create policies of equality. Political efforts to change policies have so far used economic analysis to a very limited degree. For instance, economists (and others) document the existence of discrimination and its harm to justify adding sexual orientation to anti-discrimination laws. Domestic partnership debates in the public and private sectors involve comparisons of financial costs and benefits.

But traditional economic analysis of public policies focuses on creating remedies when free markets fail to provide the socially desirable or "efficient" levels of particular goods and services. I consider the importance of promoting efficiency in chapter 7's analysis of policies to remedy workplace- and family-related economic inequality, but I go beyond efficiency to include other desirable social policy goals when comparing several possible policy approaches to gay issues. Adding other policy priorities, such as meeting basic human needs, encouraging caring labor, and promoting justice, situates what are often considered liberal gay and lesbian concerns in a broader framework that sees specific policy goals as steps toward a more progressive policy agenda. In this framework, national policies that forbid sexual orientation discrimination in employment and state-level policies that allow same-sex couples to marry, for example, promote efficiency, equity, and meeting basic needs.

If, as I argue, the policies analyzed in chapters 7 and 8 are worthy goals, how will political change come about? In the 1990s, gay political activism is as likely to occur in the marketplace as in traditional political contexts. Gay, lesbian, and bisexual people have fought economic inequality by using their economic power as workers, consumers, and investors to put pressure on corporations and other employers. In chapter 9 I look closely at several forms of collective economic action—workplace activism, consumer boycotts, and investor pressure—and their impact on gay people's economic well-being. Consideration of both the potential direct gains from economic activism and the larger benefits of organizing in different economic contexts suggests that while consumer and investor activism can contribute to pressure on employers, workplace activism holds greater potential for transformative social and economic change.

Concerns about Methodology and Political Bias

The inquiry in the book makes use of many traditions of economic analysis, drawing from mainstream market models as well as alternative approaches that have incorporated social norms and institutions into explanations of economic outcomes. I am telling a complicated story that describes and explains the economic position of lesbians and gay men but also places some of the blame for gay people's inequality on unfair political choices and public policies. The fact that I am a lesbian who participates in debates about public policy decisions and business practices might appear to further complicate the sketching out of this economic-political portrait—I have a political and personal stake in what that picture looks like.

Some economists try to sidestep speculation about their personal interests by asserting a difference between *positive* economics, or the search for a value-neutral understanding of how the world works, and *normative* economics, which asks whether the workings of the economy and its outcomes are desirable or whether they should be changed. The obvious problem with this distinction is that economists are human beings who cannot step outside of what they are studying to achieve a neutral and objective perspective. Individual human experiences, personal self-interest, or social position may influence the "scientific" process in many ways, shaping the substance and nature of the questions asked or the interpretation of empirical observations.

Critiques of science and the bombardment of Americans with seemingly contradictory "facts" about issues have encouraged a cynicism about the ability of academics to offer unbiased and credible insights into public issues. This book adds to the amount—and quality, I believe—of the information that concerned people must assimilate as they make important decisions about the kind of world they want to live in and the kinds of policies they will support with their time, votes, money, and heart. And the picture presented here challenges some of the conventional wisdom about the positions and roles of lesbian and gay people in the modern economy. Does this picture reflect my personal political agenda, or is it a credible account of how and why lesbians and gay men differ economically from heterosexual people?

I readily admit to having political opinions that inform some of my personal decisions about where to spend my own time and money. The legal, social, and economic equality of lesbians and gay men is a goal that I support. But the paths to that end are many and uncertain, in my opinion.

It is conceivable that particular portraits of the economic position of gay people might favor following one path or another in political activism. And some academic expert might want to create the most useful picture to further a particular political goal. On the other hand, a whole industry of "spin doctors" constructs political arguments to fit whatever empirical findings are at hand to a preexisting ideological framework. While that is a cynical comment about the role of academic information in political discourse, it provides, ironically, a different basis for thinking about the role and neutrality of academic research.

Consider one example from biological academic research on the causes of homosexuality. Recent scientific research has found evidence suggesting a genetic link to homosexuality (see Hamer and LeVay 1994). Is that helpful or harmful to the political cause of lesbian and gay people? Some gay people would argue that such a finding is essential to winning basic civil rights through the political and judicial system. Establishing a genetic link would mean that sexual orientation is an immutable characteristic, or something that an individual cannot change.[3] Other gay people would argue, however, that finding a genetic link increases the likelihood that a genetic test could be developed to identify fetuses that would eventually develop into gay adults. Such a test could allow prospective parents to abort their future gay offspring, providing an entirely new and frightening social and legal outlet for antigay activism. John D'Emilio points out that the prevalence of the immutability argument did not prevent Nazi persecution of gays in the 1930s and 1940s (D'Emilio 1992, 187). In the broader scheme of political life, it is not clear which research conclusion—finding a genetic link or finding evidence that no such close link exists—would be more advantageous to the interests of gay people.

Consider another example addressed in this book. Would it be more politically useful to find that gay people are relatively affluent or to find that they earn less than comparable heterosexual people? Some gay activists argue that an image of affluence is politically useful in many contexts, such as in threats of boycotts or in encouraging companies to develop gay-friendly employment policies with the reward of attracting a lucrative market. Other gay activists argue that an affluent group attracts little sympathy when claiming discrimination, undermining efforts to gain legal protection from employment discrimination, for instance. Under such circumstances, which conclusion should an economist look for—that gay people have higher or lower incomes than does the typical heterosexual? There is no obvious politically preferable answer.

I started my research on the economic impact of sexual orientation with what appeared to be an empirical puzzle. Marketing surveys showed high incomes for lesbians and gay men, while other evidence suggested that gay employees faced employment discrimination, which for women and people of color typically results in *lower* incomes. Not knowing how this puzzle would be reconciled, I plunged into the research with growing curiosity. What I did know and expect was close scrutiny and discussion from my fellow researchers in various social sciences. The lengthy academic process of discussion, comments, and recommendations makes for long publication lags, but at its best, the process promotes careful and rigorous scholarship and reveals potential alternative interpretations or key assumptions and values embedded in the project that should be made transparent to the reader.

Proceeding with openness and respect for debate and disagreement, then, might be the best or even the only way of avoiding distortions in research on topics as controversial as those surrounding lesbians and gay men. I believe it is the responsibility of the researcher to present findings, theories, and assumptions as clearly and openly as possible to make the analysis transparent to readers so that they may judge for themselves. I also believe that is the responsibility of critics to go beyond the sexual orientation of the researcher and to critique arguments on their own terms. In the end, we all are responsible for our own thinking and for the analytical judgments necessary to make decisions in our own economic, social, and political lives.

The Economic Penalty for Being Gay

When Dan Miller's boss found out that Dan was gay, his stellar work record as an accountant did not stop his boss from firing Dan. The boss later admitted that his decision to fire Dan was simple: "[H]is being a homosexual was the issue."[1]

After four years of excellent performance reviews, Cracker Barrel Old Country Store cook Cheryl Summerville, a lesbian, was suddenly dismissed after the CEO of Cracker Barrel explicitly directed managers to fire all gay employees.[2]

For years Postal Service employee Ernest Dillon endured antigay slurs, threats, and physical violence from coworkers who suspected that Dillon was gay. Despite numerous appeals to supervisors and even to the federal court system, the harassment only ended when Dillon got a job at a different post office branch.

Roger Crow, an administrator of an Iowa home for the mentally disabled, was quoted in a local newspaper as boasting that he had fired several gay and lesbian employees. Those fired included "at least three, excuse my French, faggots working here, and I had at least three dykes working here," who did not fit with the "atmosphere that [he] want[ed] to project."[3]

Dan Miller, Cheryl Summerville, and Ernest Dillon are examples of a handful of people who have publicly reported their stories of antigay workplace discrimination. In each of those cases, including the employees fired in Iowa, the employee experiencing discrimination had no legal recourse, since neither federal law nor state law in thirty-nine states prohibits employment discrimination based on sexual orientation. Only 25 percent of the nation's workforce (or 24 percent of the population) in eleven states—California, Hawaii, Wisconsin, Minnesota, New Jersey, Connecticut, Vermont, Rhode Island, Massachusetts, Nevada, and New Hampshire, as well as the District of Columbia—are covered by state laws against sexual orientation discrimination by private employers. Including the 106 cities and counties that also prohibit sexual orientation discrimination by private employers adds another 14 percent of the U.S. population; this puts the total amount of the population protected by a private sector nondiscrimination law at 39 percent (van der Meide 2000, 11). In May 1998, President Bill Clinton added sexual orientation to the list of protected characteristics in Executive Order 11478, covering 1.8 million civilian employees in the federal government.[4] In several states, executive orders provide similar protection for state employees.

Overall, though, the absence of explicit laws against sexual orientation discrimination for most workers has led to an escalating public debate about the expansion of civil rights laws in other states or at the federal level. This debate has prompted much interest in antigay discrimination, including some tough questions about how common discrimination against gay people is and what its economic impact might be. The myth of gay affluence pops up right in the middle of the political debates, fueling skepticism about gay activists' claims. In Congressional testimony, law professor Joseph Broadus concluded that gay people's high incomes contradict the call for legal protection against discrimination: "This is not the profile of a group in need of special civil rights legislation. . . . It is the profile of an elite" (Broadus 1994). The challenge behind the myth of affluence, plus a tradition of academic interest in discrimination, has generated new attempts to understand the experiences of lesbian, gay, bisexual, and heterosexual people in the workplace.

Work matters in many contexts and for many reasons. Our earnings power largely determines our economic position (in addition to the income some receive from wealth, or stock of assets), and work also confers social status. Finding and keeping a job that pays enough to reach a desired standard of living is an important challenge for all workers in a market-driven economy.

Many different factors influence individuals' employment success, such as levels of education and experience, their union membership, particular job skills, and place of residence. Other factors, in and of themselves unrelated to an employee's work performance, also influence labor market outcomes; these factors include race, ethnicity, and gender, among others. These characteristics are often related, as when the social factors—race, ethnicity, and gender—influence the more direct economic characteristics—education, experience, skills, and location. For instance, the migration of black workers from the South to northern cities after World War II opened up opportunities for better paying jobs (Smith and Welch 1986), while housing discrimination and segregated school systems perpetuated unequal access to higher quality schooling in both the North and the South. Many causal links can be drawn between the social factors, economic factors, and outcomes, but the links all have one connection in common: discrimination, whether in educational opportunities, housing, or employment.

Discrimination, or the unequal treatment of otherwise similarly skilled individuals based on their group membership, diminishes the economic position of members of the group. Since this effect is so clear in the labor market histories of women and people of color, labor economists and others concerned about discrimination expect a similar effect when analyzing discrimination against other groups, such as people with disabilities or gay people. Because of this expectation, the myth that gay people constitute a privileged, well-paid, professional elite raises questions about the actual existence of discrimination against gay people in the labor market. If gay people are treated badly in the workplace, this argument goes, then why aren't they worse off economically than heterosexuals? Given the controversy surrounding marketing surveys of lesbians and gay men that show higher than average incomes, a broader version of this question gives us a better starting point: Are lesbians and gay men economically worse off than heterosexuals as a result of discrimination?

This chapter approaches that question by starting with a close look at the marketing surveys. An analysis of them reveals serious flaws and shows that these surveys inflate the incomes of the typical lesbian or gay man. Evidence for the existence of employment discrimination comes from a variety of sources, including court cases, surveys of lesbians and gay men, and surveys of employer attitudes. I use the best available sources of income data for a statistical comparison of gay and heterosexual employees and show that gay men earn less than comparable heterosexuals, which is evidence of an economic penalty from discrimination. Connections between discrimination and economic status motivate a further exploration of how being gay might have economic consequences, so this chapter also includes an initial discussion of sexual orientation disclosure in the workplace—coming out at work—although chapter 3 will contain a more detailed analysis of this decision. Finally, the chapter offers some suggestions about why discrimination against lesbians and gay men might exist.

Data and Debate

The existence of discrimination against lesbian, gay, and bisexual people has been questioned in political debates. To counter gay activists' and their allies' contention that discrimination against gay people exists and should be outlawed, gay rights opponents assert that gay people are, in fact, a privileged elite and are economically unharmed by whatever private bias might exist. Surveys of lesbians and gay men in the late 1980s and early 1990s seemed to support an image of gay privilege and affluence. In one widely cited survey by the Simmons Market Research Bureau, the average gay respondent's individual income (including both men and women) was $36,900, which was much higher than even the 1988 U.S. median income for men working full-time and full-year, $27,342. Surveys by a market research company called Overlooked Opinions also found that gay men and lesbians were quite affluent, both as individuals and as households (Lukenbill 1995).

Interest in these surveys increased after the *Wall Street Journal* publicized the Simmons study in 1991. Explanations for gay people's apparently high incomes vary. Some argue that without family responsibilities, gay people are free to work long hours and rapidly advance their careers. Others with some sympathy to the problems of gay people in the workplace point to the possibility that gay people work harder to overcome the effects of stigma and to deflect or preempt any doubts about their sexuality (see Woods 1993, for evidence of this effect). Or, an alternative assumption consistent with the survey data might be that homosexuality is a pastime of the idle, decadent, upper economic strata, an argument almost as old as homosexuality itself (Boswell 1980).

Regardless of the explanation, many have been quick to use these numbers to bolster arguments both for and against proposals to outlaw discrimination based on sexual orientation, as well as to further positions on other social and economic issues. Gay rights opponents such as Joseph Broadus, quoted above, often refer to the allegedly high incomes of gays to argue against civil rights protections in numerous legislative hearings across the country. U.S. Supreme Court Justice Antonin Scalia referred to the same data to conclude that "those who engage in homosexual conduct tend to . . . have high disposable income" and, therefore, disproportionate political power (Scalia 1996).

On the other side, though, advocates of gay civil rights laws sometimes use the surveys as evidence of the gay community's economic clout and its ability to function successfully in a hostile world. Gay employee groups tout the affluent gay market as an enticement to get their employers to offer domestic partner benefits and to use gay-positive marketing images. And gay marketers use their surveys to sell advertising space and other marketing services to corporations anxious to find new affluent niche markets for their products.

Readers of mainstream media are bombarded with this message of affluence from columnists and political figures, and the message seems to get through. The Reverend Lou Sheldon, a conservative Christian leader, exclaims, "I mean homosexuals have high incomes, they have high levels of education; they're owners of major credit cards. There was a survey done. So you're not talking about poor people, homeless people living under a bridge" (Moxley 2000). Syndicated columnist Suzanne Fields proclaims, ". . . [M]any homosexuals have large disposable incomes to spend on themselves to define the trendy." (Fields 2000). Lino Rizzi, a local real estate investor in Vallejo, California, expresses delight at the influx of gay people into his neighborhood: "Gays take better care of their property, they have more disposable income" (Heredia 2000). Lesbian comedian and educator Suzanne Westenhoefer tells a high school student who is uncomfortable with gay people, "Gay men have more money than you. . . .Wouldn't it be more fun to be comfortable with gays?" (Gruson 1993). Journalists regularly trot out this fascinating but misleading story of affluence in articles about corporate interest in the gay market, a trend discussed in detail in chapter 5.

Some of the "explanations" for high incomes are tied to other economic myths about gay people's lives addressed elsewhere in this book, and the various uses of the Simmons and Overlooked Opinions surveys for political and marketing purposes also suggest a self-serving aspect to the acceptance of those numbers as "facts." But what makes this image of affluence mythical is not the popularity of the marketing survey results or even its historical roots, but rather the unexamined and problematic nature of the numbers themselves: the marketing surveys that find high gay incomes are tainted by serious biases in the selection of the people surveyed.

Researchers often want to learn something about a larger group of people by studying a much smaller sample of that group. To be able to generalize findings from the smaller group, the researcher must take care to choose a sample that is truly representative of the larger population. The standard way to do this is to choose respondents randomly so that every sample member has a known probability of being chosen—for a "probability" sample—or even the *same* chance of being chosen—a truly "random" sample. If the researcher uses a nonrandom sample, then biased findings are not unlikely, especially if the sample is chosen using one of the variables of interest, such as age, education, or income.

All of the marketing surveys that show high incomes suffer from a sample selection bias that would naturally attract respondents with higher than average incomes. The Simmons Market Research Bureau placed surveys in lesbian and gay magazines and newspapers, which some readers answered and returned to Simmons. This sample resulting from such a survey could be biased for at least two reasons. First, those responding might not be typical of gay newspaper readers, since those answering might be more interested in surveys, perhaps because of a higher level of education, which in turn would make respondents a relatively high-income group compared with other readers of the same newspaper.

Second, and more important, readers of gay newspapers are not likely to be typical of gay people as a whole. It is well known that, in general, readers of magazines and newspapers tend to be better educated and have higher incomes and are, therefore, not representative of the larger society. For instance, women who read *USA Today,* a newspaper with a national circulation, earned an average of $17,776 in 1989 compared with the national average of $9,624 for women (Simmons 1989; Badgett 1997b). Male readers earned $29,428, almost 50 percent more than the national average of $19,893 for men.

Consider a different example of African Americans, a group known to earn less than the average American, at least in part because of discrimination. A 1989 Simmons study of readers of *Ebony, Jet,* and *Essence* magazines, all of which are targeted at African Americans, showed that their readers had incomes comparable to (for men) or higher than (for women) the typical U.S. worker. Using government-collected statistics, of course, shows how atypical the magazine readers are, since in 1989 those readers earned 42–81 percent more than the average African American (Simmons 1989; Badgett 1997b). No legitimate economist would ever use data from national publications to study the general economic status of Americans; likewise, it would not be appropriate to describe all gay men and lesbians based on readers of *The Advocate* or *The Washington Blade,* two popular weekly gay publications.

Overlooked Opinions surveys are also biased toward finding people with higher incomes. Their respondents come from a large list of gay and lesbian people compiled through many sources, including magazine readers and those attending certain gay events, such as the March on Washington in 1993 or gay pride festivals. Aside from the obvious big problem with surveying magazine readers, attending some events (such as the March on Washington) requires the kind of economic resources that people with higher incomes are more likely to have, again pushing up the average income of those in the sample and skewing the economic portrait of gay America. Other recent surveys use data from political organizations, mail order houses, and gay credit card companies (PR Newswire 1997).

Sometimes these market researchers admit that their samples are not representative of all gay and lesbian people in the United States. And the problems with these surveys do not mean that there are not some affluent lesbians and gay men who constitute an attractive potential market for some products, an important distinction taken up further in chapter 5. What the marketing surveys may accurately tell potential advertisers is that there are at least some affluent gay people and that those affluent people read a particular gay magazine or that a marketing company has a mailing list of affluent gay and lesbian individuals. What the marketing surveys cannot tell advertisers or anyone else is that on average *all* gay and lesbian people earn high incomes.

Evidence of Discrimination

The impression given by the marketing surveys that gay people are a privileged elite unaffected by discrimination is contradicted by evidence of employment discrimination from several other sources. A 1987 survey of 191 Alaskan employers found that 27 percent of them would not hire, 26 percent would not promote, and 18 percent would fire an employee that they had "reason to believe" was gay (Brause 1989). One experiment clearly demonstrates the potential harm resulting from employers' antigay attitudes and intentions. Barry Adam (1981) sent out two identical resumes for hypothetical pairs of Canadian law students in applications for internships, labeling one of the pair as "gay" by including the phrase, "Active in Gay People's Alliance." The gay-labeled resumes received fewer interview offers than the nongay-labeled resumes, leading Adam to infer discrimination by the prospective employers.

Some other evidence exists that the potential for discrimination suggested by those studies has become a reality and is widespread. In surveys of lesbians and gay men, many respondents report experiences of discrimination in hiring, firing, promotion, and workplace harassment (Levine 1980; Levine and Leonard 1984; Badgett, Donnelly, and Kibbe 1992; Badgett 1997c). Table 1 presents findings from selected studies. Depending on the time and place, from 16 to 30 percent of gay and lesbian people surveyed report an experience of discrimination at some point in their work histories.

With the exception of the 1989 *San Francisco Examiner* surveys, these are self-reports based almost entirely on what are known as "convenience" samples (where responses are gathered through various institutions, such as gay bars or political groups), so careful interpretation is necessary. We cannot know how valid all of those discrimination reports are. For several reasons, those surveys do not tell us how prevalent discrimination against gay employees is nor what the economic effects might

Table 1 Findings from Surveys on Self-Reported Employment Discrimination

Survey Name	Percentage Experiencing Discrimination		Number of Respondents
	Ever	In last year	
National sample, *San Francisco Examiner*, 1989	16		400
San Francisco Bay Area, 1989	28		400
New Orleans, 1989	22		400
Boston, 1983	20		1,340
Philadelphia, 1993			3,759
Men	30	14	
Women	27	13	
Louisville, KY, 1992	30		616
Sacramento, CA, 1994–95		16	2,300

Sources: Badgett, Donnelly, and Kibbe 1992; Badgett 1997c.

be. On one hand, since those who say they have experienced discrimination were probably more likely to answer the survey, the surveys might make discrimination seem more common than the true overall rate of discrimination. On the other hand, some discriminatory acts might go unnoticed or be attributed to nondiscriminatory reasons by unsuspecting gay employees, so the reported rate could be too low. But even though the true overall rate of discrimination among lesbian and gay people is impossible to measure in these surveys, the self-reported experiences provide further evidence of the likely existence of workplace discrimination against at least some lesbians and gay men.

A couple of recent surveys also find that heterosexual workers have witnessed antigay discrimination, adding to the credibility of the claims made by gay people. In a 1993 study of Los Angeles lawyers, 24 percent of heterosexual women and 17 percent of heterosexual men report that they have experienced or witnessed antigay discrimination (Los Angeles County Bar Association Committee on Sexual Orientation Bias 1994). Between 11 and 14 percent of 343 heterosexual political scientists surveyed have witnessed discrimination against gay people in hiring, reappointment, or tenure decisions (Committee on the Status of Lesbians and Gays in the Profession 1995).

Discrimination and the Economic Penalty for Being Gay

Given this evidence of workplace discrimination, then, the claim that lesbians and gay men earn more money than heterosexuals is even more puzzling. Many studies show that discrimination against women and people of color *reduces* their incomes compared with those of men and whites with similar characteristics. Discrimination could affect income because a boss pays a gay worker less than he pays heterosexual workers in the same jobs. Lower rates of promotion would lead to lower than expected earnings for gay employees. Or difficulty finding a job because of hiring discrimination might force a lesbian to take the first job available, even if it paid less than other jobs for which she might be qualified. So discrimination itself is likely to lead to *lower* incomes for gay and lesbian people compared with what a similarly qualified heterosexual employee earns.

Since researchers rarely get to observe workplace interactions and decision-making firsthand to look for evidence of discrimination, analysis of data on individuals' incomes from large-scale data sets is the most common method of studying discrimination. (This approach also neatly connects with the main issue raised by the marketing surveys in debates over gay civil rights laws.) The beginning of this chapter noted that job earnings depend on a number of factors, including an individual's gender, race, training, education, experience, place of residence, occupation, and industry. Social scientists assess the impact of discrimination based on race and gender by comparing the incomes of people who are similar in the other important ways and then looking for differences between men and women, for instance. If women are paid less than men who have the same job-related characteristics, we could infer that women are treated differently from men by employers and that some systematic discrimination against women has probably occurred. In the same way, to assess the impact of sexual orientation discrimination, we want to compare similarly qualified gay and heterosexual workers.

In principle, this is a fairly simple and intuitive exercise, although in practice some further considerations (discussed below) are necessary when interpreting the results of statistical procedures designed to make such comparisons. In carrying out an analysis of incomes, the first challenge is to find a source of data that is not biased and has information on survey respondents' economic status and sexual orientation. This is not a simple matter, but several recent surveys of probability samples make a better analysis possible. Although these data sets contain fewer gay people than the marketing surveys discussed above, they will present a more accurate comparison picture because they are statistically unbiased.

The National Opinion Research Center (NORC) at the University of Chicago has been conducting the nationally representative General Social Survey (GSS) over the past two decades to assess social and political attitudes of the general public. In the late 1980s, the GSS began including questions on past sexual behavior, asking both men and women how many sex partners, both male and female, they have had since the age of eighteen. This study includes data from the 1989–1991, 1993, and 1994 surveys. This information on sexual behavior allows a categorization of people based on their *behavioral* sexual orientation.

A second data source is the 1992 National Health and Social Life Survey (NHSLS), also conducted by NORC (see Laumann et al. 1994). This survey of 3,432 individuals focused specifically on questions related to sexuality, including many of the same behavioral, demographic, and economic questions used in the GSS. In addition, the NHSLS contained more detailed questions on what the investigators termed "same-gender sexuality," with one question on self-identified sexual orientation and another set of questions identical to the GSS questions on sex of partners.

Combining the two data sets gives a total of 12,456 respondents, dropping to 4,616 when considering only full-time workers with no missing data. Of full-time workers, 4.3 percent of women and 4.0 percent of men had at least one same-sex partner.

Several issues related to using these data sets quickly come to mind. How accurate and honest are people in answering these questions? How important is the definition of "sexual orientation" as compared with either behavior or identity? And doesn't a gay worker's vulnerability to discrimination depend on whether bosses and coworkers know the worker's sexual orientation?

Researchers using survey data are always concerned about respondents' "misreporting" of information, especially with respect to information about stigmatized characteristics. The stigma related to having an abortion or working illegally in the United States makes collecting statistics on abortion or illegal immigration very difficult, and numbers on sexual orientation and behavior suffer from the same problem. So although many of the questions on the GSS and NHSLS were asked directly by trained interviewers, the questions on sexuality were posed in way designed to make respondents feel more comfortable answering truthfully. The questions on sexual behavior on the GSS were contained on a self-administered questionnaire and were accompanied by a reassurance that all answers were confidential and that honest answers were important for research on the AIDS epidemic. In the NHSLS, interviewers asked some questions directly but the questions used in this analysis were asked on self-administered questionnaires. This kind of confidentiality makes it more likely that respondents will answer truthfully.

Still, one could reasonably question using sexual behavior to measure sexual orientation, since the two concepts could have very different social meanings and workplace consequences. As mentioned in chapter 1, the sexual orientation definition issue has provoked a heated theoretical debate about how to think about the meaning of sexual orientation and who we think of as being "gay." The use of different measures of "same-gender sexuality" in the NHSLS demonstrates that the categories of same-sex erotic attraction, same-sex sexual behavior, and gay/lesbian/bisexual identities (all of which were self-reported) do not completely overlap (Laumann et al. 1994). For example, some people engage in homosexual behavior but do not identify themselves as gay or lesbian, although some correlation between behavior and identity clearly exists. Definitions used in surveys will matter, then, in identifying the group of "gay" employees to compare with the group identified as "heterosexuals."

The use of behavior to categorize individuals might not be much of a problem, however, depending on how the categories "heterosexual" and "gay/lesbian" are constructed. The simplest way to categorize people would be to label as gay or lesbian those who have ever had a same-sex partner. Since bisexual people will also fall into that category using the behavioral measure, this analysis compares heterosexual people with gay, lesbian, or bisexual people. Unfortunately, the data allow no way to know whether having a same-sex partner was recent or frequent, obviously a disadvantage in identifying a characteristic thought to have some social and economic influence over a lifetime and career. But a second categorization that might capture the usualness of same-sex partners is to compare the number of same-sex partners to the number of opposite-sex partners. If someone has had at least as many same-sex as opposite-sex partners, it seems unlikely that he or she would have a strictly heterosexual orientation. In the combined GSS/NHSLS data for full-time workers, 2.6 percent of women and 2.7 percent of men had at least as many same-sex as opposite-sex partners.

The more complete set of options in the NHSLS allows a comparison of the two definitions to measures of self-identified sexual orientation for the 1992 survey respondents. Of the people who have had one or more same-sex partners, 46.3 percent (fifty individuals) classified themselves as heterosexual, suggesting a poor match between the simple classification by behavior and self-identity.[5] Of the people in the NHSLS with at least as many same-sex as opposite-sex partners, however, only 15.7 percent considered themselves heterosexual, while 56.9 percent considered themselves "homosexual," 11.8 percent called themselves "bisexual," and 13.7 percent considered themselves "something else." Clearly the second definition eliminates most of those individuals who consider themselves heterosexual despite having same-sex partners in their past. Although the sample sizes are small in the NHSLS alone, this comparison strongly suggests that the second categorization comparing numbers of same-sex and opposite-sex partners is a much better match for self-identified sexual orientation than the first categorization.

The theoretical debate over the relationship of behavior to identity has important research and policy implications,[6] but it might not be necessary to come down on one side or the other in studying workplace discrimination. First, for a gay worker, the perceptions of heterosexual coworkers are probably more important in the workplace than a particular self-understanding of what it means to be gay, and it is not clear how much of a distinction most heterosexuals would make between behavior and identity. Second, public opinion surveys show that many people in the United States have moral objections to same-sex sexual behavior (Yang 1997). Sexual acts between two people of the same sex are still illegal in eighteen states (van der Meide 2000, 14), suggesting that same-sex behavior as well as identity are subject to social sanctions and are, therefore, useful ways of categorizing and comparing people in discrimination studies.

A more important difference between the two definitions of sexual orientation might arise if self-identified gay people are more likely to disclose their sexual orientation at work. Since "coming out" usually involves publicly attaching a label or identity to oneself, disclosure requires some sense of self-identity. Even if identity is more likely to result in discrimination because it is more likely to be disclosed, the potential for involuntary disclosure of same-sex sexual behavior still makes people who are only behaviorally gay or lesbian vulnerable to discrimination.

The issue of disclosure is, itself, an important one to think about in the context of workplace discrimination and of income differences between heterosexual and gay people and is developed in depth in chapter 3. Obviously, for coworkers or supervisors to take some *direct* discriminatory action, they must have some idea—based on an assumption, guess, or explicit disclosure that might be either voluntary or involuntary—that a particular employee is gay. Thus revealed, a gay employee might be fired or denied a promotion, likely resulting in a lower income than he or she would have received if presumed to be heterosexual.

Even if a lesbian employee keeps her sexual orientation secret, though, she may still find herself at an economic disadvantage resulting in lower incomes if (1) she must avoid career-advancing social situations with coworkers that might raise questions about her presumed heterosexuality, (2) she finds it difficult to work closely with curious coworkers, or (3) she becomes alienated as a result of the pressures of remaining closeted and is absent frequently or changes jobs often. Any of those circumstances would tend to reduce her likely earnings, but each of them is related to a work environment that the lesbian employee finds hostile to her homosexuality rather than to some intrinsic productive characteristic of the employee herself. This distinction suggests that a form of *indirect discrimination* could operate if a gay person is not out at work (see Badgett 1995b).

An alternative possibility is that the closeted lesbian might work harder to avoid close scrutiny or to assuage her fears of discovery. In that case, she might actually end up being more productive and earning more than she would have otherwise. (But if she works harder than the typical heterosexual in the same kind of job to compensate for a potential stigma and is earning the same salary as heterosexual coworkers, we would probably consider that unfair since her extra effort should result in earning *more* than her coworkers.) At this stage of research on sexual orientation in the workplace, it is impossible to know how many gay employees would fall into the two different groups of closeted gay people or even if on average the wage effects of the two groups cancel each other out in the larger labor market.

Overall, then, while disclosure might be necessary for *direct* discrimination, even nondisclosure might be associated with a kind of *indirect* discrimination that is related to the work environment rather than to the gay worker's actual abilities and will also have negative economic consequences for the employee. If we knew which people classified as gay, lesbian, or bisexual are out at their workplaces in the combined GSS/ NHSLS data, we could try to separate the economic effects of direct and indirect discrimination. Since that information is unavailable, lumping all gay workers together will necessarily mix the effects of direct and indirect discrimination.

If we combine this source of imprecision with the fact that not all people will answer truthfully, we should pause to ask whether the resulting comparison of "gay men and lesbians" with "heterosexuals" will have any useful outcome. In the end, the meaning of the comparison depends on the question asked. If the question is, "What is the effect of direct discrimination?" then this exercise will not give us a very precise answer since the effects of indirect discrimination are mixed in. From a policy perspective, however, we might want to know about *both* effects. In fact, the income difference that we observe might be an underestimate of the true difference from direct discrimination if those expecting the biggest income losses are the ones who do not come out at work. If those people were to come out and experience direct discrimination, then we would see an even larger average earnings loss from being gay.

If the question is, "Are gay people better off economically than heterosexuals?" then we will get a good answer as long as a large percentage of gay people do not misreport their behavior or identity (in the case of the NHSLS) to interviewers. For either question, misreporting will tend to narrow the difference observed between the two groups since the group of gay employees being shifted into the "heterosexual" definition is likely to have lower incomes because of direct and/or indirect discrimination. So we will necessarily have an underestimate of direct discrimination given the imperfect data, but from a statistical perspective, this kind of bias is a conservative one that pushes *against* finding an earnings penalty for being gay, making any differences that we find more believable even if imprecisely measured or underestimated.

Making a Detailed Comparison

As noted above, many factors influence an individual's earnings. Some of those factors, such as productivity, skills, or experience, reflect the kinds of qualities that economists think employers care about most from a profit-making perspective. Unfortunately, neither survey contains information on individuals' actual productivity or experience, so this analysis uses proxies for productivity such as education (which should increase productivity) and potential experience, represented by the respondent's age.[7] Other factors that have been shown to affect earnings, such as race, sex, and geographic location, reflect the social reality of discrimination and economic variation in cost of living rather than the productive potential of an employee. To look for differences in earnings that might arise from sexual orientation discrimination, then, we must sort out the effects of these other factors, as well.

Social scientists faced the same challenge in studying race and sex discrimination and adapted some statistical techniques for this purpose that can be used to look for sexual orientation discrimination. The basic technique, known as multiple regression, allows us to look at the difference in earnings between gay workers and heterosexual workers holding all of those other factors constant. In other words, controlling for those other influences means that we are comparing the average earnings of gay men with a college degree, ten years of work experience, and who live in a large city with the average earnings of heterosexual men with a college degree, ten years of work experience, and who live in a large city, for example.

More technical details are outlined in the appendix to this chapter. The most important thing to know is that the variables controlled for were education, race, urban residence, age, geographic region, marital status, and occupation. To take into account the fact that full-time and part-time workers will have very different incomes both because of the number of hours worked and because part-time workers often receive lower hourly wages, only full-time workers are included in the statistical procedures. Because men and women have very different labor market experiences, the samples are separated by sex before analyzing the data. The sexual orientation variable counts as lesbian, gay, or bisexual only those who have had *at least as many* same-sex partners as opposite-sex partners. (Using the broader definition, having had one or more same-sex partners, makes virtually no difference in the results, however.)

The average lesbian/bisexual woman in this sample earns $21,331 per year (in 1991 dollars), 8 percent more than the average heterosexual woman, who earns $19,738 per year. Lesbian/bisexual women are more likely to have a college degree and live in a large urban area and are a bit younger, on average. (Table 2, located in the appendix, shows the averages for these and other characteristics.) Gay/bisexual men earn $21,258 compared with heterosexual men, who earn $28,680 per year, a 35 percent difference. The gay/bisexual men, like lesbians, had more education than heterosexual men, were younger, and were more likely to live in urban areas. The differences in education and other characteristics by sexual orientation demonstrate the importance of going beyond average incomes. Higher levels of education and living in urban areas would usually increase earnings of gay people, but being younger tends to reduce their average income compared with that of an older group.

After taking the differences in characteristics into account, lesbian/bisexual women earn 11 percent more than heterosexual women. The difference is not statistically significant, however, which means that in this sample we cannot be certain of the true difference in income, and an income comparison of a different group of women might show very different results. The best guess is that lesbians earn 11 percent more, but the likely range implied by the "margin of error" (or two times the standard error of the coefficients, to be more precise) in this analysis is that lesbians' income ranges from 10 percent below to 39 percent above heterosexual women's earnings. The best way to resolve the uncertainty would be to survey many more women in the future.

Gay/bisexual men, however, still earn 17 percent less than heterosexual men with the same education, age, race, location, and occupation.

(The range suggested by the margin of error is from 1 percent less to 30 percent less, so we can also have confidence in a statistical sense that gay men really earn less than heterosexual men.) The fact that the difference in average earnings between gay/bisexual men and heterosexual men falls from 35 percent to 17 percent after controlling for other factors influencing income suggests that about half of the difference in average earnings results from gay men's different characteristics. The technical appendix presents the full findings from the regressions.

The other half of the earnings difference between gay/bisexual men and heterosexual men is not explained by their different characteristics, however. Many economists and sociologists argue that this unexplained difference is caused by discrimination. Exactly which kind of employer action—in the context of promotions, in initial hiring, or in other compensation decisions, for instance—causes this earnings penalty is not clear, however.

To interpret gay men's lower incomes as evidence of discrimination requires some assumptions about possible differences between the two groups that are not captured by the information used in the statistical procedure. In particular, if gay men and heterosexual men differ in their workplace efficiency in ways that are not measured by the information in the survey, then the wage gap observed here might reflect the unmeasured difference instead of discrimination. This is a common concern in studies of discrimination by race or gender. For instance, some economists would argue that a similar analysis comparing white men and black men would overestimate the impact of discrimination since black men might attend generally poorer quality public schools, resulting in lower unmeasured skills for African American men (Juhn, Murphy, and Pierce 1991).

In the case of gay men, though, the usual sources of unobserved differences—schooling quality, actual labor force experience, or other factors related to ability—are not likely to vary systematically by sexual orientation. No good arguments exist about why gay men might have received inferior schooling, and for every anecdote about school-age trauma related to sexual orientation, another story exists to suggest that some young gay people become overachievers to compensate for their feelings of alienation (e.g., Reid [Tobias] 1973). A study by Black, Gates, Sanders, and Taylor (2000) suggests that gay men's backgrounds are quite similar to heterosexual men's backgrounds as measured by the educational attainment of their fathers. This reinforces the idea that unobservable factors are not likely to account for gay men's lower earnings.

These findings match the findings of two earlier studies, one using just the earlier years (and, therefore, a smaller data set) from the GSS (Badgett 1995b)[8] and one using a very different source of data from the 1990 U.S. Census of Population (Klawitter and Flatt 1998). The 1990 Census allowed individuals to identify themselves as an "unmarried partner" to the household's reference person, an option added to the list of possible relationships that also includes spouse, child, other family relationships, and roommates or boarders, for instance. No other questions asked more specifically about sexual orientation, but having an "unmarried partner" of the same sex would appear to be a measure of social behavior analogous to the GSS/NHSLS sexual behavior measure.

One advantage of using the census data is the large sample size available to Klawitter and Flatt, including roughly 14,500 same-sex unmarried partner couples. Two disadvantages were the exclusion of single people, whose sexual orientation obviously could not be inferred by matching them to a partner, and the suspicion that the very low use of the "unmarried partner" option means that many couples did not identify themselves as such, either out of fear of disclosure to the federal government or because they did not understand the option. Only one-fifth of one percent (0.2 percent) of households in the United States reported same-sex unmarried partners.

Despite those concerns, the census findings match the GSS findings quite closely. The Klawitter and Flatt study compared people in married and unmarried opposite-sex couples with people in same-sex couples. They found that men in same-sex couples earned from 13 to 31 percent less than men in married couples, depending on where they lived.[9] Women in same-sex relationships who worked full-time, on the other hand, had no statistically significant difference in earnings compared to married women who worked full-time.

Two other studies using the GSS and NHLS data sets and similar statistical methods but somewhat different categorizations of sexual orientation confirm the large earnings disadvantage for gay men but find larger incomes for lesbians.[10] John Blandford's analysis shows a 30–32 percent wage penalty for unmarried gay/bisexual men, while unmarried lesbian/bisexual women earn 17–23 percent more than married heterosexual women (Blandford 2000). The work by Black et al. (1998) finds a somewhat smaller penalty for gay men but a similar earnings advantage for lesbians.

Given these findings, one obvious question is why these studies find that gay/bisexual men appear to face sexual orientation discrimination but lesbian/bisexual women do not, at least as measured by income gaps. Several factors could explain the difference, although sorting them out empirically is impossible with the existing data. For instance, since the Americans with Disabilities Act outlaws discrimination against people who have or are suspected of having AIDS, employers might (legally) discriminate more against gay men, whom employers might assume are likely to contract HIV. Since cases of AIDS among lesbians are much rarer, this would lead to discrimination against gay men but not against lesbians. Or perhaps heterosexual men see gay men as a greater threat to masculinity in the workplace than are lesbians, generating a greater dislike of gay men and greater discrimination. Studies show that heterosexual men have more negative attitudes toward gay men than they do toward lesbians (Herek 1991; Kite and Whitley 1996).

Instead, employers might see lesbians (even those who are not out at work) as being more like heterosexual men in their work commitment and their independence from family-related career impediments. (Lesbians with partners who are not out would need to hide details of their family life.) A lesbian would not have a male partner whose career comes first and who might encourage her to leave her job and have children. Lesbians might even have greater levels of workplace experience and commitment than heterosexual women, but those wage-enhancing differences are not observed in the data sets available. (Both Blandford [2000] and Black et al. [1998] favor this labor force attachment explanation.) Our imperfect measures might then cover up the fact that lesbians would be expected to earn more than heterosexual women. Or finally, the fact that lesbians might be less likely to come out at work, as revealed in some survey data, could result in lower levels of direct discrimination, reducing the measured wage difference from heterosexual women. For instance, a 1989 survey of a random sample of lesbians and gay men found that 62 percent of gay men but only 33 percent of lesbians answered yes when asked, "Have you told your co-workers about your sexual orientation?" (Badgett 1996b).

To sum up, evidence of discrimination is clear in the data for gay and bisexual men. Any discrimination against lesbian and bisexual women is not evident in the earnings comparisons with heterosexual women, although the survey evidence mentioned above suggests that lesbians perceive themselves to have been victims of discrimination. Discrimination against lesbians might take some other less obvious form or might be clearer if we could better measure certain key variables. Or perhaps, lesbians' main labor market disadvantage is from being female.

Why Does Discrimination Exist?

One enduring puzzle for economists and other students of discrimination is explaining why the kind of workplace discrimination implied by the income comparisons exists and persists. On one level, the answer might seem to be obvious: members of more powerful groups dislike members of certain other groups, and that dislike is translated into discrimination by employers or coworkers. Certainly, evidence of the dislike of gay people abounds in the United States.

One extensive analysis of public opinion poll data reveals that, despite a general trend toward more positive attitudes toward lesbians and gay men, many people in the United States continue to express reservations and negative feelings about lesbians and gay men (Yang 1997). For instance, the National Election Studies ask respondents to use a "feeling thermometer" (scaled from 0 to 100) to express opinions about different groups, with ratings below 50 expressing "colder" or less favorable opinions. In 1996, the average rating for gay men and lesbians was 40, indicating general disfavor, a rating that was lower than that of all other groups except for "illegal immigrants" (Yang 1997, n. 18). Similarly, half of those surveyed in a 1996 Gallup Poll did not consider homosexuality "an acceptable alternative lifestyle," and 56 percent questioned in the 1996 GSS believed that sexual relations between two adults of the same sex are "always wrong" (Yang 1997, 21–22).

Other survey evidence provides a more positive picture with respect to workplace issues, in particular. Both a 1996 Gallup Poll and a 1997 Princeton Survey Research Associates survey found that 84 percent of those polled believed gay people should have equal rights to job opportunities (Yang 1997, 7). When asked by the National Election Studies whether laws should protect gay people against job discrimination, 68 percent of women and 59 percent of men said they favored protective legislation (Yang 1997, 9). Of the 818 adults surveyed in a national 1993 *Washington Post* poll, 69 percent said that they "feel comfortable" working with a gay person (Warden 1993).

Although the majority of Americans might be relatively liberal or tolerant with respect to gay people in the workplace, these polls also identify a sizable number of people who are not comfortable with or accepting of gay people in the workplace. (And even those individuals expressing more liberal attitudes might not act in accord with their principles.) Is the group of intolerant workers large enough to change the job and earnings prospects of lesbians and gay men? Not all of the bosses or coworkers of Dan

Miller, Cheryl Summerville, or Ernest Dillon acted in a hostile and antigay manner. A minority of supervisors and employees—even a small minority—could be large enough to result in discriminatory behavior ranging from publicly telling a fag joke, which creates an intimidating and hostile climate for gay employees, to actually firing a gay employee or directly harassing a lesbian coworker.

Personal attitudes are closely related to one prominent theory of discrimination in the labor market, developed by economist Gary Becker (Becker 1971). Becker starts from the existence of employers' and employees' negative attitudes toward members of a particular group. In his model, some employers who are members of dominant groups might have some distaste for employing members of some different group unless the disliked employees can be paid less. The lower wage compensates the employer for the negative effect on his or her well-being from hiring the disliked employees. In a variation of this theory, coworkers might have a similar preference for discrimination, leading an employer (even one without the discriminatory preference) to either hire fewer out-group members or to pay the out-group members less so that the workers with the taste for discrimination can be paid more, again as compensation for having to work with disliked people. Either way, the discriminatory attitudes lead to members of one group being paid less than another, even though members of both groups are equally productive in the workplace.[11]

In general, unfortunately, economists leave the origins of the discriminatory tastes largely unexamined (see, for example, a critique in Reich 1980). Some seemingly obvious explanations are not very helpful, either. For instance, antigay attitudes could be thought of as a response to an evolutionary imperative to reproduce. Homosexual behavior could be stigmatized because it is seen as a threat to the survival of the species or of a given culture. While it is certainly true that sexual acts between two people of the same sex will not lead to pregnancy, this argument relies on an unnecessary assumption that an individual's sexual behavior will be exclusively with someone of the same sex and that a large proportion of individuals in any given society (and especially women) will be so exclusively engaged that the birthrate plummets. Engaging in sexual behavior with someone of the same sex does not preclude or even necessarily reduce behavior with a higher probability of conception, suggesting that an argument for an evolutionary imperative to prohibit homosexual behavior is illogical (Boswell 1980, 8). Even in the United States today, for example, avowed lesbians who usually have only female sex partners may become pregnant through voluntary sexual intercourse with men or through alternative insemination procedures, suggesting that neither the desire nor the ability to bear and raise children is absent—or perhaps even reduced—in homosexuals. Sociobiologist E. O. Wilson argues, instead, that homosexuality might be genetically associated with altruism, a desirable characteristic that could improve evolutionary fitness if homosexuals helped their close relatives to raise more children (Wilson 1978, 144). Finally, anthropologists have found that homosexual behavior has been accepted and perhaps even highly valued in some cultures, such as in some Native American cultures (Williams 1978), which would seem unlikely if such behavior truly threatened the survival of a culture.

Another possibility is that antigay attitudes result from religious teachings and beliefs. John Boswell's study of the first fourteen centuries of Christianity suggests that Christian ideology was the conduit—not the source—of intolerance for people with an erotic attachment to people of their same sex (Boswell 1980). He hypothesizes that the shift from the relative tolerance of early imperial Rome to the more gay-oppressive early Middle Ages was related to the ruralization of Roman civilization (where ruralization tended to be accompanied by more rigid sexual norms) and the increased absolutism and regulation of personal life by the Roman government (Boswell 1980, 119–121). A shift back toward greater tolerance in the tenth through twelfth centuries appears to have been related to the revival of urban life (increasing tolerance), and yet another shift toward intolerance in the thirteenth century was tied to the rise of a more powerful and absolutist government that legislated against homosexuality. In that last period, the fate of gay people was closely linked with the ill treatment of Jews, Muslims, usurers, and heretics, although the underlying causes of hostility were usually not clear.

The work of Boswell and other scholars demonstrates that the existence of antigay attitudes is not universal across time and place. Even before the recent improvements in attitudes toward gay people in the United States (as shown in the survey data discussed above), in the early part of the twentieth century attitudes also appeared to be relatively tolerant compared with those of the middle part of the century. Historian George Chauncey finds that an extensive and visible gay subculture existed and thrived in New York in the early twentieth century. Men in certain class and ethnic groups, particularly unmarried male immigrants, could engage in sex with other men without being labeled "abnormal." Over time, however, "normality" came to exclude the possibility of homosexual behavior, generating a public concern about the threat of homosexuality that led to increasing oppression of public gay life. Chauncey dates the shift toward intolerance of homosexuality from the 1930s and connects it to a crisis in gender arrangements and, in particular, to a crisis in "masculinity." The growing middle-class economic reliance on sedentary and subordinate work within the context of corporate bureaucracies threatened middle class men's sense of masculinity, as did women's challenges to male control over public spaces (Chauncey 1994, 111).

> The revulsion against gay life in the early 1930s was part of a larger reaction to the perceived "excesses" of the Prohibition years and the blurring of the boundaries between acceptable and unacceptable public sociability. But it also reflected the crisis in gender arrangements precipitated by the Depression. As many men lost their jobs, their status as breadwinners and their sense of mastery over their own futures, the central tenets undergirding their gender status, were threatened. (Chauncey 1994, 353)

The crackdown on public gay life that began in earnest in the 1930s thus reflected a *shift* in attitudes toward homosexuality, not simply a continuation of historically stable attitudes.

The historical research suggests that negative attitudes toward gay people cannot simply be assumed and must instead be explained within their broader social, economic, and cultural contexts. An alternative and more social scientific approach would be to examine the functions served by antigay attitudes, some of which are evident in the historical research.

Gregory M. Herek (1991) examines these attitudes within a modern context and offers several explanations for negative attitudes toward gays and lesbians (or prejudice). Herek finds that prejudice may serve several important psychological functions. Prejudging group members might help someone "in making sense of her or his previous interactions with gay people and provid[ing] a guide for future behavior," an "experiential-schematic" function. Negative attitudes could increase the holder's self-esteem either through expressing his or her core values or by affirming membership in a social group, a "self-expressive" function. Or they might allow an individual to reduce anxiety and conflict about their own sense of sexuality or gender, an "ego-defensive" function.

Although Herek's framework is helpful in understanding antigay prejudice, it does not explain why categorizations of individuals by their sexual orientation arise and become psychologically salient in fulfilling those functions, nor does it explain how attitudes might be manifested in discriminatory behavior in the workplace. That link between attitudes and behavior is one yet to be explored by economists, but social psychologists acknowledge the complicated relationship between the existence of attitudes toward a group and behavior that reflects those attitudes. In the context of the debate over allowing gay people to serve openly in the military, for example, Robert MacCoun (RAND 1993) traces the links between attitudes and behavior. He shows that a complex web of factors influences behavior, which are detailed in the next chapter. Those intervening factors could discourage even a highly prejudiced individual from acting on that prejudice in the workplace. Herek's functionalist framework for antigay attitudes does, however, provide a link between what is unexamined in Becker's work—the existence of and rationale for negative attitudes toward some group—with other economic theories of discrimination.

Other economists have argued that discriminatory behavior is not a simple outcome derived from some arbitrary "taste" or attitude but, in fact, serves some important economic functions for members of more powerful groups. Heidi Hartmann (1981) maintains that men's harassment and discrimination in the workplace promotes men's interests in having women provide services for men and their children in the home, an interest that Rhonda Gottlieb (1984) also connects to the ideological and political repression of gay men and lesbians that is designed to preserve what Adrienne Rich has called "compulsory heterosexuality."

In thinking about the connection between antigay attitudes and discrimination, then, we also should consider whether the attitudes and behavior serve an important economic purpose in addition to a psychological purpose. Discrimination could be a way for heterosexuals to monopolize jobs or to assign less desirable jobs to certain groups. Some economists theorize that discrimination is an outcome of job competition between different racial and ethnic groups, where powerful groups can reserve good jobs for their own members by creating exclusionary barriers for members of less powerful groups (Hill 1984; Darity and Williams 1985; Shulman 1991). According to this theory, discrimination against disadvantaged groups is greatest when the threat to the economic position of more powerful groups is strongest, as when unemployment rates climb during a recession or as income inequality increases (as it did over the last three decades of the twentieth century).

While discrimination might have the effect of reserving jobs for some groups, historical research has not shown heterosexuals engaging in the kind of concerted collective action to exclude gay people that, say, some white trade unionists promoted to keep blacks out of certain jobs in the first half of the twentieth century (see Hill 1984 or Spero and Harris 1968, for examples). Historically, gay-specific exclusionary policies were certainly in existence in federal government employment from the 1940s at least through the 1960s (D'Emilio 1983), for instance, or in elementary school teaching, even to the present day in many places. In these cases, though, the prohibition of gay people was usually based on more generalized norms of sexual morality and concern that gay people would somehow either betray the trust of the government or would endanger the well-being of children (concerns that were not justified in practice), suggesting that the exclusionary impulse was not directly related to a desire to monopolize jobs for heterosexuals. At the same time, however, such exclusions could certainly have the *effect* of monopolizing positions for heterosexuals, although it seems more likely that those exclusions simply force gay people into hiding their sexual orientations. Once the effect is institutionalized in a given distribution of jobs and income, the fear of additional competition might reduce some heterosexuals' willingness to stop discriminating.

We can also see the potential influence of heterosexual people's competitive concerns in two gay-related policy contexts, as the job competition theory would predict. First, toward the end of the 1992 recession, Coloradans voted in a state constitutional amendment that would repeal any existing local or state law that outlawed sexual orientation discrimination and would prohibit the passage of future nondiscrimination laws.[12] An editor of a prominent Colorado newspaper argued that this vote did not reflect antigay attitudes but instead, Coloradans' "simmering resentment concerning preferential treatment of previously protected groups, and the public's resolve not to enlarge the list" (Carroll 1992). A second possible example of the competitive dynamic comes from the military context, when in times of great need for service members, such as the Gulf War in 1991, the armed forces have been willing to overlook or delay actions against gay service members (Lambert 1991). But later in the 1990s during the continued shrinking of the military, dismissals for homosexuality began to increase after the "Don't Ask, Don't Tell, Don't Pursue" policy was codified (Servicemembers Legal Defense Network, 1999).

Another economic rationale for discrimination is that employers might even promote competition between groups to keep workers of different groups from banding together and demanding higher wages from employers (Reich 1981). This theory of discrimination that involves an employer's active exacerbation of group conflict within its workforce (the "divide and conquer" model) would also seem to be less applicable in explaining antigay discrimination. First, the relative invisibility of sexual orientation as a defining characteristic would make it difficult, if not impossible, for an employer to consciously exploit differences in sexual orientation among workers. And second, if this model of discrimination has any current or historical relevance, employers have had and continue to have numerous other sources of divisive angles along which to split employees, such as gender, race, and ethnicity. An attempt to further divide a workforce by exploiting dislike of a relatively small group of lesbian and gay people could even backfire if that dislike became a unifying force among heterosexual workers who would otherwise be divided.

Finally, discrimination could be a profit-maximizing strategy for employers because of the information that sexual orientation provides about a worker's productivity, but this possible explanation is also unsatisfactory for explaining antigay discrimination. Employers could benefit from "statistical discrimination" against individuals in a group if membership in the group gives employers information about how well individuals perform job duties (Aigner and Cain 1977). In this model of discrimination, profits rise as employers use statistical discrimination to hire a more highly skilled work force. Statistical discrimination is mainly relevant for employment decisions such as hiring, in which an employer has imperfect information about an applicant's abilities and intentions but knows that the applicant is a member of a group that has, on average, different levels of productive characteristics. The employer can then use that information to make hiring decisions.

In the case of most gay applicants, though, it seems reasonable to suppose that an employer would not know the applicant's sexual orientation, making distinctions on that basis impossible. Equally important is the fact that it is hard to imagine a productive characteristic that could be related to sexual orientation. In statistical discrimination against women, for instance, employers might assert that women, on average, have higher turnover rates compared with men because of their family responsibilities, making even apparently qualified individual women less attractive than male candidates.[13] In a culture in which gay people and heterosexual people are raised in the same neighborhoods, the same families, and the same schools, it is difficult to come up with a convincing argument for assuming that gay people are somehow less productive on average than heterosexual people. In fact, as noted above, stereotypes of female workers as unreliable because of family responsibilities could work in lesbians' favor (see Friskopp and Silverstein 1995). (The fact that sexual orientation does not appear on lesbians' résumés to encourage privileged treatment, however, suggests that those gains do not occur and that lesbians still fear discrimination.) On the other hand, employers might be concerned that gay men are more likely to be HIV-infected than heterosexual men and will, therefore, have higher rates of absenteeism or turnover, but such concerns should be of little relevance for attitudes related to lesbians.

Virtually no research exists on the issue of qualifications, but one intriguing study by the military compared servicemembers dismissed for homosexuality with others recruited at the same time (1983) with respect to past school problems, drug and alcohol use, job experience, criminal felonies, and Armed Forces Qualification Test (AFQT) scores (see Dyer 1990).[14] Overall, with the exception of the measure of quantity of drug and alcohol use, those dismissed for homosexuality showed comparable or higher levels of social adjustment when compared with that of the average recruit. The AFQT provides a measure of cognitive ability, which is likely to capture at least some component of skill valuable to the military and other employers. From that perspective, both the men and women dismissed for homosexuality had higher average scores than did either heterosexual men or women, suggesting that the use of sexual orientation as a screening criterion for job-related ability should work *in favor* of gay applicants, not against them.

Economic theories can also help to explain what should be done about antigay discrimination. Chapter 7 examines in detail whether discrimination is likely to go away on its own—economic theory suggests not—and what, then, should be done. The current public policy in thirty-nine states and at the federal level allows discrimination against gay men and lesbians to occur openly and legally by employers. An obvious first step explored in that chapter is a blanket prohibition on discrimination. Figuring out other ways of eliminating workplace discrimination and prejudice will be incomplete until we know more about the origins of prejudice and discrimination.

Conclusions about Discrimination

Ironically, the easiest question related to sexual orientation employment discrimination is the one that at first seemed the hardest. All sorts of evidence, from anecdotal accounts and surveys to income studies, clearly demonstrates that workplace discrimination is alive and well. The myth of gay affluence does *not* accurately characterize the earnings record of lesbians and gay men. The expected harm from discrimination is also evident: gay and bisexual men earn from 17 percent to 28 percent less than similarly qualified heterosexual men (from a range of studies), and while the average lesbian's and bisexual woman's earnings appear to be no lower than those of comparable heterosexual women, lesbians are vulnerable to job and income loss from discrimination. Lower earnings and economic vulnerability in this case are not based on a difference in the abilities or performance of gay people, suggesting that discrimination makes little economic sense from the perspective of employers.

The truly difficult question is explaining *why*. Economists have offered numerous possible reasons for employers to discriminate. Some reasons, like the taste for discrimination model, assume the prior existence of anti-gay attitudes or social norms that lead employers to indulge their irrational prejudices at the cost of profits, but those attitudes and norms are assumed rather than explained. Other explanations argue that discrimination is a profit-enhancing strategy for employers, but available historical evidence and some early quantitative data suggest that those explanations are not adequate, either.

Our understanding of the forms that discrimination takes against lesbian, gay, and bisexual people is obviously at an early stage, so perhaps it is not surprising that our ability to explain *why* discrimination occurs is so rudimentary. Our search for the more specific effects and rationales will be aided by insights from economics, however. Thinking about the economic reasons for discrimination highlights the role of market incentives in creating and perpetuating discrimination. An economic approach can also incorporate the idea that attitudes are not necessarily noneconomic cultural artifacts but are perhaps greatly influenced by economic conditions (such as the unemployment rate) and market competitive dynamics. Coalitions of heterosexuals, whether employers or fellow employees, can also greatly influence the position of gay people in the workplace and, therefore, the level of inequality that gay people experience.

Other social scientists studying antigay discrimination are equally unable to explain the source of social norms against homosexuality and attitudes against lesbians and gay men that provide the crucial ingredients for discrimination. Once antigay attitudes and actions exist to serve some social or psychological purpose, economic theory can help explain why their perpetuation might serve to improve jobs and opportunities available to heterosexual people, but at least right now there is little reason to see those economic motivations as the *origins* of the sort of antigay prejudice evident in opinion surveys.

One possible explanation for the difficulty in understanding antigay discrimination is that theories of discrimination were designed to explain either race or sex discrimination. Perhaps sexuality presents unique workplace concerns, in which case antigay discrimination might require an

independent approach. Sexual orientation is not an observable characteristic of an individual, as sex and race usually are, a situation that suggests
the need for a more tailored approach that incorporates gay invisibility.
This chapter's analysis of discrimination included a preliminary consideration of disclosure of sexual orientation within the workplace. Further investigation of the coming out decision in the next chapter will help to focus on sources of workplace disadvantage and will suggest that sexuality
itself is another source of tension and conflict between gay and heterosexual people in the workplace.

Technical Appendix

Some specific comments on the data are in order. First, both the GSS and
NHSLS report earnings categories for the respondent's total earnings from
the respondent's listed occupation in the previous year rather than the actual level of earnings. To create comparable earnings variables for the two
data sets, each respondent was assigned an earnings level corresponding
to the midpoint of the range reported in the survey, which was then ad-
justed for inflation across years using the Consumer Price Index. Second,
because the NHSLS only reported educational degrees rather than years of
education, a potential labor market experience variable could not be constructed (the typical potential experience variable is age minus years of education), so age was used as a less precise proxy for labor market experience in the regressions. Third, since annual earnings depend on whether
one works full-time or part-time, this study only uses full-time workers. Finally, because certain subgroups of the population were oversampled in
the NHSLS, sampling weights provided by NORC were used for NHSLS respondents and a weight of 1 was assigned to GSS respondents in the
pooled sample to calculate the regressions and means presented below.

Table 2 presents the means of the variables used in the analysis of earnings. As noted in this chapter, the statistical technique used for both data
sets to compare earnings is multiple regression, or ordinary least squares.
As is usual in studies of wages, the dependent variable is the log of earnings. Table 3 presents the actual coefficients resulting from the regressions. The first two columns of numbers present the results for women,
and the next two, for men. The first specification for both men and
women does not include occupational variables, but the second does take
into account occupations. A positive coefficient means that the characteristic increases earnings, and a negative coefficient means that the characteristic tends to decrease earnings. Asterisks denote whether a coefficient
is statistically different from zero.

The coefficient on the variable for being lesbian, gay, or bisexual shows the earnings difference related to sexual orientation. The coefficient can be translated into the percentage difference in wages with the equation $e^b - 1$, where b is the coefficient. For example, the coefficient of -0.19 for being a gay or bisexual man implies that gay men earn 17 percent less than heterosexual men with the same characteristics.

Table 2 Variable Means in the Combined GSS/NHSLS Sample

	Lesbian/ Bisexual Women	Heterosexual Women	Gay/Bisexual Men	Heterosexual Men
Earnings (dollars)	21,331	19,738	21,258	28,680
	(12,013)	(11,766)	(15,315)	(16,774)
No high school degree	13.9%	7.4%	7.5%	10.2%
High school degree	28.6%	46.5%	41.7%	42.7%
Some college	15.8%	17.0%	13.1%	17.6%
College degree	29.2%	20.9%	18.7%	19.2%
Graduate degree	12.5%	8.3%	19.0%	10.3%
Never married	56.4%	18.7%	75.0%	19.4%
White	82.2%	82.5%	87.3%	87.0%
Big SMSA	77.1%	53.0%	60.5%	48.9%
Northeast	10.3%	16.5%	22.2%	17.5%
Midwest	23.3%	26.4%	16.1%	27.5%
West	26.6%	21.1%	30.2%	20.0%
South	39.8%	36.1%	31.5%	35.1%
Age	35.2	38.6	34.2	38.9
	(7.4)	(10.3)	(9.6)	(11.0)
Manager	8.8%	15.7%	18.3%	15.6%
Professional/technical	42.7%	23.9%	31.2%	17.9%
Craft/operative	11.4%	11.8%	17.8%	41.5%
Clerical/sales	16.3%	37.2%	24.9%	17.0%
Service	20.7%	11.4%	7.7%	8.1%
N	53	1935	70	2558

Note: Standard errors are in parentheses.

Table 3 Coefficients from Multiple Regression
(log of earnings as dependent-variable)

	Women			Men		
	LGB (1)	LGB (2)	LGB (2)	LGB (1)	LGB (2)	LGB (2)
Intercept	8.77**	8.77**	8.42**	9.03**	9.03**	8.99**
	(0.08)	(0.08)	(0.08)	(0.07)	(0.07)	(0.08)
LGB	0.03	0.04	0.11	−0.14**	−0.16**	−0.19**
	(0.08)	(0.11)	(0.11)	(0.06)	(0.08)	(0.08)
Some college	0.14**	0.14**	0.06	0.09**	0.09**	0.07**
	(0.04)	(0.04)	(0.04)	(0.03)	(0.03)	(0.03)
College degree	0.45**	0.45**	0.30**	0.37**	0.37**	0.29**
	(0.04)	(0.04)	(0.04)	(0.03)	(0.03)	(0.04)
Graduate degree	0.68**	0.68**	0.49**	0.53**	0.53**	0.41**
	(0.06)	(0.06)	(0.06)	(0.04)	(0.04)	(0.05)
Never married	0.01	0.01	0.01	−0.32**	−0.32**	−0.32**
	(0.04)	(0.04)	(0.04)	(0.03)	(0.03)	(0.03)
White	0.04	0.04	−0.00	0.16**	0.16**	0.15**
	(0.04)	(0.04)	(0.04)	(0.04)	(0.04)	(0.04)
Big SMSA	0.17**	0.17**	0.15**	0.18**	0.18**	0.17**
	(0.03)	(0.03)	(0.03)	(0.03)	(0.03)	(0.03)
Northeast	0.11**	0.11**	0.11**	0.19**	0.19**	0.19**
	(0.05)	(0.05)	(0.05)	(0.04)	(0.04)	(0.04)
Midwest	0.05	0.05	0.06*	0.14**	0.14**	0.14**
	(0.04)	(0.04)	(0.04)	(0.03)	(0.03)	(0.03)
West	0.08*	0.08**	0.08*	0.09**	0.09**	0.08**
	(0.04)	(0.04)	(0.04)	(0.03)	(0.03)	(0.03)
Age	0.01**	0.01**	0.01**	0.02**	0.02**	0.02**
	(0.00)	(0.00)	(0.00)	(0.00)	(0.00)	(0.00)
Manager			0.71**			0.26**
			(0.06)			(0.05)
Professional/ technical			0.66**			0.22**
			(0.06)			(0.06)
Craft/ operational			0.34**			0.06
			(0.06)			(0.05)
Clerical/sales			0.54**			0.09*
			(0.05)			(0.05)
Adj. R-squared	0.162	0.162	0.229	0.255	0.255	0.265
N	1987	1987	1987	2627	2627	2627

Note: ** denotes statistically significant at 5 percent level; * denotes significant at 1 percent level. The omitted category is having a high school degree or less education, living in the South, in a service occupation

THREE

The Costs of the Closet

I don't think the firm would care if a lawyer *was* gay, but would care if he/she was *openly gay* at the office, social events, etc.

There is a strong culture of conformity—of not sticking out. For gays and lesbians, that means we must keep our personal life private. But, in our work reviews, we get criticized for being private and quiet.
Los Angeles County Bar Association Committee on Sexual
Orientation Bias, Report (22 June 1994)

The fact that sexual orientation is not an easily observable characteristic, unlike race and gender, for instance, suggests a seemingly obvious strategy for avoiding discrimination and marginalization. Why didn't Dan Miller and Cheryl Summerville simply avoid telling the world and their employers that they were gay? Coworker ignorance, if not bliss for gay employees, at least ought to provide shelter in most workplaces, according to the myth of protective invisibility. Dan and Cheryl might still have their jobs had they not been known to be gay. The fact that they came out despite the obvious potential consequences hints at the importance and value of being openly gay; the fact that they were punished for being openly gay reveals the very unequal position in which gay people find themselves.

One decision faced in any given social situation by a gay man or lesbian, whether interacting with coworkers, neighbors, or family concerns this issue of disclosure. The complexity of the decision-making process and the potential consequences of disclosure make it an ongoing effort that is difficult to describe adequately, even when limiting the discussion to the workplace. Because one very real potential consequence is discrimination, the workplace disclosure decision includes a clear economic element that situates coming out within the scope of this book. Sorting out the determinants of disclosure requires an understanding of the social norms related to sexuality in the workplace, the role of collective action in motivating and facilitating disclosure, and the role of rational and self-interested calculation in coming out. An additional question, which is rarely brought up in discussions of disclosure, asks whether public and

private policies should encourage gay people to come out in the workplace and how policy could encourage coming out. These pieces of the
coming out process and decision are explored in this chapter.

Coming out is the subject of a large social science literature. This chapter draws on the subset of past research that not only focuses on the workplace but also situates coming out within a broader analysis of how workplaces structure sexuality and how sexuality might structure workplaces.
This literature (discussed below) suggests that the mere existence of the
myth that invisibility protects gay men and lesbians from discrimination reflects both a double standard that puts gay people at a disadvantage and a
profound discomfort with the idea of sexuality in the workplace. This
double standard and the discomfort define a set of norms or rules for the
workplace about appropriate expressions and behavior related to sexuality, providing a more sexuality-specific context for analyzing discrimination against gay people in the workplace.

The double standard emerges most clearly when recognizing that heterosexual employees frequently disclose their heterosexuality, and they do
so without conscious decision-making about its consequences—mainly because the consequences are unlikely to be negative. Displays of heterosexuality abound: pregnant women, spousal benefits, employees on parental leave, kids at company picnics, and wedding showers for coworkers
are all tangible signs of many workers' underlying heterosexual orientation. When Don DeMuth, Dan Miller's boss (an example of a discriminatory boss from chapter 2), introduced his wife to Dan, he probably did
not think of those actions as "coming out" as heterosexual. But Dan never
introduced his own partner to Don, knowing that Don disapproved of
homosexuality.

The social norm that discourages disclosure of homosexuality can also
be expressed more directly. When surveyed in 1993, 37 percent of Americans preferred that gay people not disclose their sexual orientation
(Moore 1993).[1] Some object to the introduction of private lives, often
characterized as "what someone does in bed," into a public space, the
workplace. Others might simply be reacting to a basic dislike of gay
people, but a dislike that can remain latent if the sexual orientation of
one's coworkers is unknown.

Within the workplace social setting, a gay or lesbian employee must
choose how much—if anything—he or she will reveal about being gay. In
analyzing the choice to conceal or disclose one's sexual orientation, the rationality of a strategy depends on a number of assumptions, which this
chapter examines. One key question asks how protective invisibility could

be. The possibility of involuntary disclosure, of active employer efforts to identify gay employees, and of economic penalties associated with the closet all suggest that the closet is not the safe economic haven that some would assume.

Nevertheless, given the stigma associated with being gay, it is not surprising that in surveys of lesbians and gay men anywhere from 28 to 72 percent report that they use a concealment strategy to avoid discrimination (Badgett, Donnelly, and Kibbe 1992). What is more surprising, perhaps, is that despite the stigma and possible negative repercussions, many gay people come out in the workplace. Why would they do this? One way to think about it is as an economic decision-making process in which people rationally weigh the costs and benefits of coming out. The costs are more obviously monetary than the benefits, since discrimination generally involves a financial loss of some kind. The personal benefits, while more amorphous, might be psychological, political, or social.

But the issue of workplace disclosure has broader ramifications that transcend the personal considerations of individual lesbians and gay men. On a political and social level, many people consider coming out to be the most important strategy for social change with regard to the legal and social position of gay people, pointing out that people who know a lesbian or gay man tend to have much more favorable attitudes about gay people (Herek and Glunt 1993; Herek and Capitanio 1996). Events like the annual National Coming Out Day in October have begun to institutionalize this strategy, encouraging lesbian, gay, and bisexual people to "take the next step" in revealing their sexual orientation. On an economic level, the distracting effort required to maintain a secret or to manage a stigmatized identity, in Goffman's language (Goffman 1963), and the inhibiting effect of being closeted surely diminishes the productivity and effectiveness of lesbian, gay, bisexual, and heterosexual people in the workplace, however difficult it might be to quantify such effects. Coming out on a large scale could have a positive economic impact, assuming that heterosexual workers and employers do not respond in a universally negative and discriminatory way. From this perspective, encouraging gay workers to stay in the closet may be a socially costly course of action.

Why Is Coming Out in the Workplace So Threatening?

The previous chapter asked why negative attitudes toward lesbians and gay men would exist and argued that such attitudes are not easily explained. Negative attitudes could be the source of employment discrimination against gay people, or discrimination might exist because being openly gay has a particularly threatening effect on the workplace, leading to the development of economic sanctions and norms (or social rules) against open expressions of being gay. A gay man's or lesbian's coming out at work could inspire a negative reaction based on a perceived threat or disruption that is specific to the workplace. In other words, invisibility might be protective, placing the responsibility for discrimination on the actions of people who publicly reveal their homosexuality or bisexuality.

Joanna Brewis and Christopher Grey describe two strains of thought that characterize all forms of sexuality as dangerous within the workplace, both to employers and to at least some employees. The "modernist-masculinist" viewpoint distinguishes between the corporate organization's existence in the public sphere and sexuality's existence within the private sphere. Separation of the two spheres is key to the operation of the rational corporation: "The expulsion of sexuality from the organization, the drawing of lines between public and private, is characterized as essential to the efficiency of operations. Emotion, sex and intimacy are to remain at home . . . " (Brewis and Grey 1994, 69). What Brewis and Grey characterize as "modernist-feminist" thought similarly denies sexuality a legitimate role in the workplace: "Sex at work is unacceptable because sex cannot be untainted by power in such an inherently unbalanced situation" (Brewis and Grey 1994,70). Openly acknowledging sexuality in the workplace is dangerous because it threatens efficiency, from one perspective, and threatens women's position, from the other perspective.

Using the "modernist-masculinist" view as his reference point, James D. Woods argues that sexuality is viewed as posing a threat to "the legitimacy of bureaucratic authority" and to the impartiality at the heart of corporate America (Woods 1993, 32). In such a context the presence of gay men (and, presumably, of lesbians) violates the organizational "asexual imperative" (36), generating tension, hostility, and suspicion toward openly gay men. Marny Hall (1989, 135) points out that lesbians, both as women as well as members of a sexually defined minority, represent a similar threat of disruption.

While the corporate concern with repressing sexuality is, at least at face value, a universal concern applying to gay and straight alike, clearly sanctions against overt evidence of sexuality are unevenly applied. Woods catalogs the ever-present workplace displays of heterosexuality, such as family pictures, wedding rings, or family-oriented social events, as well as more overtly sexual situations, such as intraoffice dating or sexual jokes. But in those situations he notes that the "heterosexual values and behaviors have been cloaked. They are perceived as belonging to categories other than sexuality and thus remain invisible *as sexuality,*" (58) being interpreted instead as signs of kinship or social roles, for example. Merely coming out as gay, however, can generate concerns that a gay person is inappropriately "flaunting" or "making an issue" of his or her homosexuality. Or, as Hall puts it, "the person known to be homosexual must do nothing in particular in order to be perceived in terms of excessive eroticism" (Hall 1989, 124).

The double standard and the hostile reaction to gay people, Woods argues, is rooted in heterosexism: "The traditional white-collar workplace is 'heterosexist' in the sense that it structurally and ideologically promotes a particular model of heterosexuality while penalizing, hiding, or otherwise 'symbolically annihilating' its alternatives" (9). Ideology, then, supplies another motive for workplace inequality—heterosexuality is better than homosexuality. Power (or "cultural authority," as Woods puts it) allows heterosexuals to impose a sexual double standard in the workplace by labeling heterosexual institutions, values, and behavior as asexual social roles but labeling gay relationships and behavior as sexual. The power to label makes expressions of heterosexuality benign while expressions of homosexuality are defined as threatening the very stability of the capitalist enterprise.

Even without a satisfying explanation for the origins of a heterosexist double standard, an organizational focus combined with an ideological preference for heterosexuality helps to define economic rationales for antigay discrimination. For employers, antigay discrimination might be less related to an employer's own prejudices (as in Gary Becker's theory of discrimination discussed in chapter 2) and more closely related to concerns about undermining employers' carefully constructed organizational structures. Economists who have studied the historical development of employment structures note that many companies rely on the existence and acceptance of impersonal, seemingly objective rules and procedures for hiring, promotion, evaluation, and compensation to maintain an adequately productive workforce.[2] The system of rules legitimates the hierarchy necessary for carrying out the company's profit-driven activities and reduces the importance of personal relationships between coworkers or between bosses and subordinates that might interfere with the firm's mission.

Perhaps employers fear that gay people's disclosure would open the floodgates of sexual expression among all employees, leading to the breakdown of corporate hierarchical authority as subordinates seduce supervisors or as higher level employees engage in behavior that exposes the company to sexual harassment lawsuits. Heightened awareness of sexual attraction in the workplace might distract workers and directly threaten productivity. Under these circumstances, even employers with relatively positive attitudes about lesbians and gay men might still discriminate to eliminate what employers might perceive as a threat to organizational integrity.

For coworkers, gay employees' coming out might intensify already openly antigay sentiment or could arouse latent antigay attitudes, creating a situation in which gay workers are harassed or ostracized in the workplace. Even more subtly expressed discomfort could lead to lower productivity for the workplace as a whole if heterosexual workers do not interact with their openly gay colleagues in a way that maximizes efficiency. This effect of disclosure calls to mind Becker's theory that roots employer discrimination in coworkers' negative attitudes, a theory extended by Finis Welch to show how integration could have an adverse effect on productivity in the presence of prejudice (Welch 1967). This threat to productivity would also rationalize employers' desire to avoid hiring or to remove openly gay people from the workplace.

Under the circumstances presented in an organizationally rooted economic model, an effective employer strategy for dealing with gay employees appears to be "Don't ask, don't tell": closeted gay employees do not threaten the profit-maximizing enterprise, but those who insist on coming out might. Economic incentives—mainly the threat of discrimination— enforce such a strategy, aided by the fact that "Don't ask/don't tell" is inscribed in workplace norms. These socially recognized expectations about behavior appear to be internalized by gay workers themselves in many cases, adding to the power of the economic threat. The men Woods describes "have largely bought the conventional wisdom that a man must be a consummate professional, that like his straight peers, he must be 'asexual' at work" (Woods 1993, 71). Similarly, Friskopp and Silverstein note that many of the gay and lesbian Harvard Business School graduates they studied "wished that all personal subjects could be declared out of bounds at work" (Friskopp and Silverstein 1995, 129). Decisions about coming out will likely be shaped by internalized social norms as well as by the negative sanctions imposed for violations of externalized norms.

Can Concealment Work?

Examining motives from all perspectives—employers, coworkers, and gay and lesbian employees alike—appears to support the idea that invisibility is a protective shield against discrimination. Practical questions remain about the meaning and effectiveness of a strategy of concealment, however. In the simplistic view characterized by the myth of invisibility, nondisclosure is as simple as silence. Just as someone might never admit to coworkers, "I can't sleep without my teddy bear," a lesbian need never say, "I am a lesbian." Even if related subjects arise in a normal workplace conversation on insomnia or gay rights, for instance, the individual has a choice of whether to reveal such personal information and can easily withhold it if it might lead to ridicule or discrimination. As long as the words are not spoken, the knowledge that someone is gay or lesbian does not exist, in this view.

Woods's analysis of workplace disclosure argues that "coming out" is less a simple dichotomous choice—being in or out—and more of a process of "managing" a stigmatized identity. In his study based on interviews with over seventy gay men in professional and managerial jobs in 1990 and 1991, Woods explores the complex strategies used by his respondents to manage the stigma of being gay. He identifies three basic strategies: counterfeiting a heterosexual identity, avoiding situations or discussions that would reveal any sexual identity, and integrating "authentic expression[s] of a man's sexuality" into the social setting of the workplace (Woods 1993). Passive silence was not a viable option for those gay men, since the counterfeiting strategy requires active effort by definition, and even the avoidance strategy involves some active effort to foresee, plan, deflect, and maneuver around potentially revealing situations and conversations.

In her in-depth interviews with thirteen lesbians, Hall finds that even lesbians who had come out in the workplace to some people continued to use nondisclosure as an identity management strategy. Her respondents used several strategies to avoid the moral bind that many felt themselves to be in, including partial disclosure of personal information (of weekend activities with a roommate, for instance, who was actually a lover), avoidance of personal situations, and the cultivation of a distracting image of "differentness" (for instance, as a feminist) (Hall 1989,137). As with the gay men in Woods's study, nondisclosure was an active strategy, not a passive one.

Another problem with the simple view of gay invisibility through nondisclosure is the assumption that the decision is purely in the hands of the gay worker. Some public policies have sought and continue to seek out closeted gay men and lesbians. The history of the military ban on homosexuality, which is full of active efforts (often termed "witch hunts") to find and dismiss gay servicemembers (see, e.g., Shilts 1993), demonstrates the obvious problems with that assumption. Similarly, active efforts to discover and fire gay employees were common in the federal government at least through the 1960s (Johnson 1994–95).

Even when companies and other employers are uninterested in identifying gay workers, one individual either inside or outside the organization can spread information or rumors about the homosexuality of an employee. Or else military records, arrest records, or media coverage of gay events can reveal or create perceptions of employees' sexual orientations. Dan Miller's boss learned of Dan's homosexuality when Dan was briefly interviewed on television about a local gay political issue. Thus the prospect of involuntary disclosure further undermines the usefulness of a strategy of nondisclosure.

And finally, the true value of nondisclosure—at least in an economic context—must lie in its ability to protect a gay man or lesbian from the kind of workplace disadvantage that occurs in the case of a discriminatory firing or demotion. Even with complete nondisclosure, the protection from invisibility is doubtful. As I argue in chapter 2 in my discussion of "indirect discrimination," ethnographic evidence suggests that the kind of effort required to prevent disclosure might also inhibit the workplace performance and value of a worker. Woods points out that counterfeiting and avoidance, in particular, are costly strategies for gay men, reducing the individual's self-esteem, depth of friendships, and loyalty and increasing his stress level. Increased absenteeism and turnover might result from these personal impacts of nondisclosure, increasing employers' costs and unwillingness to promote even a closeted gay man or lesbian. The personal consequences of the closet may also reduce workplace effectiveness, especially where close working relationships are necessary, which is also costly for employers and could result in fewer promotions and raises and more dismissals for closeted gay employees.

In their study of Harvard Business School graduates, Friskopp and Silverstein find further evidence of the costs of the closet to the lesbian or gay worker. Generally speaking, their high-level white-collar interviewees who reported experiences of personal discrimination were those who were relatively closeted on the job: "None of those who had been personally discriminated against were openly gay. Rather, we found repeatedly, it was closeted gay people who told us they suspected they were discriminated against because they didn't fit" (72). The lack of fit results partly from the social isolation often involved in remaining closeted and perhaps partly from the status of being an unmarried person (106). The experiences of Harvard graduates demonstrate that nondisclosure is no guarantee of smooth sailing through a career, even for those in the economic elite. Like the emperor's new clothes, the shield of invisibility provides little protection.

If the closet is not a safe haven from the prospect of employment discrimination, then gay employees make decisions along a spectrum anchored by two economically threatening positions: at one end is full concealment, and at the other, a strategy of openness. Risk exists all along the spectrum, as interviews with lesbians and gay employees make clear, but accurately assessing which end poses the bigger economic risk is difficult and likely changes over time as public opinion about gay people shifts, for instance. Friskopp and Silverstein claim that openness is less risky than concealment, giving gay employees a chance to educate their bosses and coworkers and to overcome the heterosexism present in the workplace. In their opinion, the closet is a bigger cause of workplace disadvantage than is being out.[3] For the men in Woods's study, however, adopting an integration strategy does not result in open acceptance: "Even when a man is well received, he is defined by his difference. . . . By definition tokens are not peers" (Woods 1993, 216–17). Woods is more convincing in concluding that coming out places gay men (and presumably lesbians) in the same visible and vulnerable position faced by women, people of color, and other stigmatized groups—a position, in other words, that is characterized by many workplace and career challenges not faced by heterosexual people. Overall, while the heterosexism apparent in corporate culture suggests that disclosure of the presence of gay employees is not a necessary condition for antigay expressions, the ethnographic evidence suggests that disclosure heightens the potential for homophobic reaction, whether the disclosure is actual or perceived, voluntary or involuntary.

The Choice to Disclose—Is It Rational?

Acknowledging the risks of both disclosure and nondisclosure complicates the decision-making process for lesbian and gay employees. Some elements of the disclosure decision have been explored by other researchers. Beth Schneider argues that lesbians' disclosure and their amount or quality of social contact with coworkers are interrelated, with more social workplaces encouraging disclosure (Schneider 1986). The studies by both Woods and by Friskopp and Silverstein identify forces that push lesbians and gay men in the direction of being more open about their sexuality, including the demands of workplace friendships and networks, attempts to change an unfair situation, or responses to personal crises (Friskopp and Silverstein 1995, 218–21).

A Model of Rational Disclosure. None of the studies discussed above were designed specifically to capture the economic elements of disclosure, but employment discrimination was clearly a driving fear behind workers' nondisclosure in all three studies. The connection between disclosure and discrimination—the possibility of employment or wage loss—suggests powerful economic incentives at work in gay and lesbian workers' disclosure choices. Economic reasoning emerges in the voluntary decision to disclose one's sexual orientation in the workplace, as gay workers seek both income and disclosure. An individual's weighing of the potential economic risk does not mean that psychological, social, political, or ethical factors do not influence a gay worker's decision to disclose her or his sexual orientation. The discussion above suggests that gay workers' own opinions about the value of disclosure will be influenced by the hostility to gay people that is embodied in workplace norms and policy environments. Rather, highlighting the elements of the kind of decision-making that economists classify as "rational" is important, not simply because of a belief in rational, purposive behavior, but because of the implications of such behavior for research, politics, and policy-making.

One way of thinking about disclosure as a rational choice is as a cost-benefit decision: if the benefits of disclosure outweigh the costs, then gay workers will disclose their sexual orientation. A more subtle decision-making process can be simulated by thinking about workers' choices from among various combinations of income and disclosure, each of which gives the worker some level of satisfaction (or utility, as it is known in economic models). Individuals' preferences for disclosure may vary with a gay man's or lesbian's political and ethical beliefs and with the psychological costs to self-esteem of nondisclosure, or "passing" as heterosexual. The psychological need for disclosure is likely to increase with the sociability of the workplace (Schneider 1986) and the need for social interaction for career advancement. Gay workers are assumed to want both more income and more disclosure, and therefore they may be willing to give up some of one for the other.

At work, a tradeoff between the two is necessary because the risk associated with disclosure becomes a possible loss in income resulting from discrimination once the stigmatized sexual orientation is revealed. In other words, gay people "buy" disclosure and pay for it with the risk of income loss. Given the risks involved in each worker's particular circumstances, gay workers choose the available combination of disclosure and

income that provides the greatest satisfaction. To summarize this rational
choice model, the disclosure decision involves workers weighing their
preferences for income and disclosure and making their decision knowing
that disclosure might result in a lower income.[4]

The strategy for testing this way of thinking about disclosure in the real
world involves comparing the workplace decisions about coming out for
people who are similar in some characteristics that might influence preferences for disclosure (race, age, sex, and some workplace characteristics) but face different tradeoffs of income and disclosure, either because
of different levels of apparent discrimination risk or different incomes. If
factors affecting the riskiness of the choice are important determinants of
individuals' disclosure decisions, then individuals are likely to be engaging
in the sort of decision-making that economists call "rational."

Data Description and Measurement Issues. Data for this study come
from mailed in responses to a survey published in the spring 1992 edition
of *Out/Look* magazine, a National Lesbian and Gay Quarterly published in
San Francisco. This particular survey, *Out/Look Survey #16,* was one of a
regular series of surveys published in the magazine. Out of a circulation of
approximately 12,000,[5] 322 people returned surveys, resulting in a response rate of approximately 2.6 percent. Of those 322 respondents, 284
answered all of the questions needed for this study.

While *Out/Look* reader surveys are clearly not a random sample of lesbian, gay, and bisexual people in the United States, the direction of bias related to disclosure is fairly obvious. The survey asks, "Are you 'out' to other
coworkers?" and "Are you 'out' to your immediate boss?" Table 4 describes the disclosure characteristics of the sample. Only a few respondents (6.5 percent) report complete nondisclosure. Comparing this figure with the only known disclosure rate from a national random sample
of gay, lesbian, and bisexual people shows that the *Out/Look* group is
unusually open in the workplace. A 1989 survey by Teichner Associates
for the *San Francisco Examiner* found four hundred gay and lesbian individuals through random-digit dialing. In the Teichner survey, 54 percent
of respondents (89 percent of whom were employed) answered yes to the
question, "Have you told your coworkers about your sexual orientation?"
If we assume that the Teichner survey respondents considered the yes-no
answer possibilities to mean either being out to at least one coworker
(yes) or being out to zero coworkers (no), then the *Out/Look* respondents are only one-seventh as likely to be complete nondisclosers to a
coworker.

Table 4 shows that the degree of disclosure varies greatly among the

Out/Look respondents, even though this is a relatively "out" sample. As Woods points out, disclosure is not an all-or-nothing process. Almost two-thirds of the respondents have disclosed their sexual orientation to the majority of their coworkers, and slightly more have come out to their immediate supervisors. While the *Out/Look* sample is biased toward workers who have already disclosed their sexuality, it is not clear how biased it may be toward *highly* disclosing gay workers. Other sources of bias are also possible: this is a very well-educated group, and readers of this magazine probably share the magazine's left-of-center political perspective. Those two factors might explain the high degree of disclosure overall, if *Out/Look* readers are politically motivated to come out. However, the degree of disclosure varies enough between people to draw out the influence of other characteristics within this very out group.

The nature of this sample raises other issues, too. In their analysis of a different survey of *Out/Look* readers, Kenneth Sherrill, Scott Sawyer, and Stanley Segal (1991) find that *Out/Look* readers are not only relatively liberal/radical but are also members of what they characterize as the "intelligentsia." If such a group was predisposed to rational or analytical decision-making, this sample would be biased in favor of finding evidence of rational deliberation. In other words, the *Out/Look* readers' disclosure choices might not be representative of the decisions and decision-making processes of other lesbian, gay, and bisexual workers. This possibility will be considered further below.

Another issue with this data set concerns the causal connections between the factors that might influence disclosure. The time frame for all of the questions used in this study was in the present, which means that a person might have come out *after* some of the workplace factors changed to their present condition. In that case, we cannot infer that the presence of some characteristic *caused* a worker to come out. Instead, the workplace might have changed to its current condition after the worker came out. The statistical technique used here is more properly interpreted as uncovering *correlations* (or statistical relationships) between variables that are suggestive but not hard evidence for *causal* links between the variables. The uniqueness and depth of the questionnaire makes this a valuable data set, nonetheless.

The *Out/Look* readers responding to the survey give several reasons for their disclosure, such as maintaining personal ethics (i.e., honesty), changing attitudes (i.e., education of coworkers), and reducing deceptive effort, that reveal a clear preference for being out at work (see bottom half of Table 4). The *Out/Look* questions also include information about other

Table 4 Workplace Disclosure and Factors Related to Disclosure

Are you "out" to other coworkers?	
All of them	38.8%
Most of them	24.8%
Some of them	17.7%
Few of them	12.1%
None of them	6.5%
Are you "out" to your immediate boss?	
Yes	68.3%
No	15.5%
Not sure	12.7%
No answer	3.4%
Which factors influenced your decision to come out?	
(percentage indicating that the factor had an influence)	
Include spouse/lover in company events	24.8%
Improve relationships with boss or coworkers	28.6%
Educate coworkers	57.1%
Help change company policy about lesbians and gays	22.4%
Feel more honest	83.9%
Avoid hassle of misleading coworkers	61.8%

Source: Author's calculations from *Out/Look* survey

factors that might have influenced a respondent's internal valuation of (i.e., preferences for) disclosure:

Age: Younger workers who entered the workforce after the emergence of the gay liberation/civil rights movements might be more committed to coming out as a political statement. The average age of sample participants is 35.2 years.

Sex: Occupational segregation and other gendered features of labor markets might change women's preferences for disclosure. In this sample, 56 percent of respondents are women. Other research suggests that lesbians are less likely to be out at work than are men (Badgett 1996b).

Race or ethnicity: This would measure cultural variation in preferences for disclosure, as well as racially motivated differences in labor market treatment and outcomes, but the predicted effects are not clear. As with women, people of color face a different workplace environment and additional challenges related to racial discrimination that might make them more or less likely to come out than a white male worker. The *Out/Look* sample contains 8.5 percent people of color.

HIV status: HIV-positive workers might require some accommodations by employers in case of illness and would, therefore, be more likely to be "out" about being HIV-infected. Only 6 percent of the respondents report being HIV-positive or having an AIDS diagnosis.

Education: College-educated workers might have had more contact with gay social and political organizations that strongly advocate coming out. This is a well-educated sample, with 85.2 percent of respondents having at least a college degree.

In addition to those preference-related factors, the survey collects information on the respondents' workplace situations, providing some information that Schneider identifies as related to the social closeness of coworkers (the distribution of these characteristics is detailed in Table 5):

> *Size of office:* Smaller offices, defined here as having fewer than twenty-five employees, might demand more closeness.
> *Occupation:* Managerial or professional work may require social interaction for advancement.
> *Type of employer:* Those who are self-employed or work for a nonprofit organization might work in more liberal climates, obviously depending on the organization's mission.
> *Supervision responsibilities:* These may inhibit social closeness with subordinates. The need for social closeness could inspire more coming out to cement social relationships, or it could inhibit coming out if coworkers are thought to be homophobic.

And finally, several other variables provide some information that workers could use to assess the riskiness of a coming out decision: (1) having out gay coworkers, (2) seeing out coworkers being treated equitably, and (3) being part of a company with a policy prohibiting sexual orientation discrimination. All of these factors might cause a gay worker to expect fewer negative sanctions for coming out, leading to more disclosure.

The survey also asks for respondents' income (from all sources), but the potential impact of past disclosures and discrimination on current income make interpretation of the measured income effect difficult.[6] Aside from the measurement issue, income could have very different effects on the coming out decision. High-income workers potentially have more to lose, but they might also have more workplace authority to suppress negative peer and subordinate reactions following disclosure. Unfortunately, the survey did not ask questions about the respondent's ability to find another job or what his or her alternative income might be if discrimination occurs. If someone could easily find another job with the same income, the risk of income loss from discrimination might be low.

Finally, measuring the degree of disclosure (the "dependent variable" in the model) is not a simple matter. Disclosure can be either/or at the individual level: someone either knows or does not know that a coworker identifies as gay or lesbian. (But as noted above, disclosure may be involuntary or may be suspected, disrupting the idea of "knowing.") The overall level of a gay worker's disclosure could be thought of as the result of a series of one-on-one disclosure decisions, or it could be measured continuously as the number of coworkers who know the gay worker's sexual orientation. But at a certain point, if enough people know that someone is gay, then other coworkers are likely to find out indirectly. Having reached some threshold of general knowledge, we could think of the lesbian or gay worker as using a form of the strategy that Woods calls "integration" (Woods 1993, 173), which could also be captured with an in/out variable. Although the questions on the *Out/Look* survey define several categories of disclosure rather than just "in" or "out" of the closet, the questions allow a simple distinction between respondents who are out to all or most coworkers and those who are out to some, few, or none of their coworkers.

Results. The basic statistical technique (the probit procedure in the LIMDEP statistical package) sorts out the effects of the worker's characteristics and the workplace characteristics on the probability of a worker being out at work to most or all of his or her coworkers. The coefficients from the procedure measure the separate effect of each variable while holding all other variables constant. Table 5 presents the average values of the variables for the sample in the first column (some of which were discussed above), the third column presents the raw coefficients from the statistical procedure, and the second column gives the effects of each explanatory variable on the probability of a respondent being out to most or all coworkers. The footnotes on the coefficients in the third column indicate that the variable had a statistically significant effect on disclosure. With this statistical technique, figuring out the variables' effects on the probability of being out requires some reference person. For this procedure, the reference or "typical" person is a white, thirty-five-year-old lesbian with a college education who is working in a managerial/professional position for a company in a large office and making approximately $40,000. The second column shows the variables' impact on the probability of that reference person being out, but the general size and direction of the effect would be similar for other reference people, as well.

The results clearly point out several characteristics that influence gay workers' disclosure decisions. Only one variable, race, stands out as reducing the probability of disclosure: gay white workers are less likely to disclose their sexual orientation at work. The second column shows that a lesbian or gay man of color with the same reference person characteristics listed above would be 22 percent more likely than a white lesbian or gay man to disclose her sexual orientation. This difference probably

Table 5 Variable Means and Effects on Probability of Disclosure

Variable	Mean or Percent (standard deviation)	Effect of Variable on Probability of Coming Out[a]	Probit Coefficient (t-statistic)[b]
Out to most or all coworkers	62.3%		
Constant			0.46 (0.9)
Income	$41,623	-1.7×10^{-7}	-0.54×10^{-6}
	(38,244)		(0.2)
Female	56.0%	−0.07	−0.24 (1.3)
White	91.5%	−0.22	−0.70[c] (2.1)
Age (years)	35.2 (10.4)	−0.002	−0.01 (0.7)
Education:			
high school	12.3%		
college graduate	42.6%	0.10	0.32 (1.2)
trade/vocational	2.5%	0.16	0.53 (0.9)
graduate degree	42.6%	0.08	0.25 (0.5)
HIV-positive or AIDS	6.0%	0.06	0.21 (0.5)
Company has			
nondiscrimination policy	45.4%	0.21	0.69[c] (4.0)
Out coworkers	66.5%	0.01	0.02 (0.1)
Out coworkers treated fairly	53.9%	0.18	0.59[c] (2.4)
Managerial or professional job	65.5%	−0.04	−0.15 (0.8)
Works in office with			
more than 24 employees	46.8%	0.01	0.02 (0.1)
Supervise more than three			
employees	15.8%	−0.09	−0.28 (1.2)
Type of employer:			
self-employed	7.4%	0.09	0.28 (0.8)
not-for-profit	17.6%	0.15	0.48[d] (1.8)
company	33.5%		
educational institution	22.5%	0.12	0.39 (1.6)
government/military/other	19.0%	0.03	0.09 (0.4)
N	284		

[a]Effects on the probability of disclosure are calculated for a white woman with a college degree who works in a large corporate office.

[b]Dependent variable in the probit model is whether respondent is out to most or all coworkers. The probit coefficient was not calculated for respondents with less than a college degree who worked for a company. Their disclosure probability is captured by the constant.

[c]Statistically significant at a 5 percent level.

[d]Statistically significant at a 10 percent level.

results from the very small number (24) or selective sample of people of color, although it could also reflect more subtle choices of supportive workplaces by people of color than this study can pick up. None of the other variables with negative coefficients were statistically significant.

Most important, two of the risk variables and one workplace variable had large positive effects on disclosure. Gay workers who have seen out gay coworkers treated as well as or better than other coworkers and workers whose employer has a sexual orientation nondiscrimination policy are much more likely to disclose their sexual orientation. Being covered by a nondiscrimination policy increases the reference person's probability of disclosure by 21 percent, and having out gay coworkers who are treated fairly increases the probability by 18 percent. Gay workers employed in a not-for-profit organization are also more likely to disclose, perhaps because of a more liberal atmosphere.

Overall, the number crunching provides strong support for the idea that gay and lesbian workers in this sample are exercising rational decision-making since they are more likely to come out when the economic risk is lower. The influence of the risk variables for this group of lesbians and gay men suggests that some of the other factors related to the workplace social environment, such as the size of workplace and supervisory responsibilities, may not be as important in the disclosure decision.

As noted above, it may not be appropriate to generalize findings from a small, self-selected group of gay workers to the larger population of gay workers. Furthermore, we cannot tell if the policies and coworker situations were in place before the worker's disclosure decision, so the causal links are unclear. For instance, instead of employer policies encouraging gay workers to come out, openly gay workers might be more likely to convince their employers to adopt nondiscrimination policies. Regardless of causation or representativeness, however, the findings clearly demonstrate links between disclosure and risk characteristics that were only speculative previously and those links are crucial for the following purposes.

First, as alluded to in the last chapter, economists and other social scientists studying the workplace effects of sexual orientation must consider disclosure to separate out the effects of direct discrimination against employees known or thought to be gay from the indirect discrimination that gay and lesbian employees might experience when they remain in the closet. Incorporating the disclosure decision in comparisons of income by sexual orientation, for instance, will require more subtle statistical techniques. Unfortunately, we do not have data that would allow consideration of disclosure and income determination simultaneously, but this chapter's findings suggest that we should collect information on workplace characteristics and disclosure as well as the more typical economic variables in future surveys.

Second, lesbian and gay workplace activists (and other political activists) should continue to question the disclosure decision more closely.

The potential ambiguity of the causal links at work in this study could mean that either nondiscrimination policies have encouraged disclosure or that disclosure has encouraged the adoption of nondiscrimination policies. But activists must deal with difficulties in both directions, and this study suggests that either or both of the following arguments could be true: (1) Employers who argue that sexual orientation nondiscrimination policies are unnecessary and will not help gay workers are ignoring the negative effects of the lack of policy protection on the disclosure decisions (and possibly the psychological well-being) of their gay employees. (2) Closeted gay employees who come out can make a difference, both in promoting favorable employment policies and in serving as a positive example to their coworkers. Chapter 9 will return to this issue of workplace disclosure and collective action as an element of political strategy.

The debate over public nondiscrimination policies also touches on the issue of disclosure. For instance, some legislators do not see the need for gay civil rights laws because "there are no gay people in my district." Given the findings of this chapter, those legislators might begin to realize that the very lack of legal protection for lesbian and gay people probably explains their invisibility and apparent absence.

The disclosure issue often arises in another context in policy debates: the disclosure-discrimination connection appears to distinguish sexual orientation discrimination from race or sex discrimination, since for most women or people of color, sex and race are characteristics that cannot be hidden. Given this restatement of the myth of protective invisibility, one might conclude that equal workplace treatment (i.e., eliminating sexual orientation discrimination) is as simple as encouraging gay workers to resist the temptation to disclose their sexual orientations. This conclusion would be wrong since it allows heterosexuals to disclose their sexual orientation but not homosexuals or bisexuals—a classic case of differential (i.e., discriminatory) treatment based on sexual orientation. And as earlier parts of this chapter suggest, of course, nondisclosure is far from simple.

Overall, the results from this analysis suggest that disclosure is a complex and weighty decision, even for individuals who are highly educated and earning relatively high incomes. When many lesbian and gay workers choose to be more open about their sexual orientation, it suggests that they value disclosure enough to override the fear or expectation of discrimination and the internalized norms about sexuality in the workplace. Pursuing policies of nondiscrimination would improve the well-being—and perhaps the productivity—of lesbian, gay, and bisexual workers by allowing and encouraging them to take the important step of coming out at work.

Larger Economic Effects of Coming Out— Raising or Reducing Productivity?

The economic model of coming out presented in the previous section implies that individual gay men and lesbians make decisions based mainly on their own perceived interests and workplace situations.[7] Given a particular workplace environment, the amount of income (or advancement probability) risked, the perceived probability of discrimination, and the nonpecuniary costs and benefits of disclosure, the choices made by gay workers reflect their individual best interests. While this approach to thinking about economic behavior is a common one in economics, an equally common concern is whether the outcomes of an individual decision-making process are best for the overall well-being of a society and economy. Looking for unintended social consequences of individual decisions—known to economists as "externalities"—further situates the economic decision-making process in the social and political realm.

Many examples of externalities are negative, such as the social costs imposed when a company generates electricity as a profit-making and socially beneficial venture but also emits hazardous air pollutants in the process. Other externalities are positive, such as the beneficial social effects of universal education for individuals. In coming out in the workplace, two social benefits are not fully experienced by the individual worker. The first and simplest benefit is that workers who come out influence their fellow workers' decisions. The quantitative analysis of coming out suggests that seeing out gay coworkers treated fairly increases the probability that other workers will come out.

Second, the in-depth interviews conducted by Woods, Hall, and Friskopp and Silverstein all suggest that the strategy of nondisclosure involves a negative economic effect not taken into account by gay employees, namely, the productivity cost of nondisclosure that is not reflected in the earnings of the gay worker.[8] Woods (1993) points out that counterfeiting and avoidance, in particular, are costly strategies for gay men and their employers, with costs to the individual's self-esteem, stress level, and friendships and to the employer's ability to evoke loyalty and effort from gay employees. Similarly, Friskopp and Silverstein (1995) identify several ways that their respondents' nondisclosure hurt productivity and employers. If applicants omit credentials and skills from resumes related to gay or AIDS-related organizations, employers lose information and the ability to recognize able leaders and highly qualified employees. Being closeted inhibits teamwork among employees, and the stress of the closet reduces morale.

While quantifying the productivity impact of the closet is not possible, a simple example illustrates the potential cost to employers and the economy as a whole. Even spending only five minutes a day managing the requirements of remaining closeted means that 1 percent of gay and lesbian employees' work time is lost, an amount that seems small but could mean millions or even billions of dollars in lost economic output over the course of any given year. Add to that the lost training costs incurred by employers who face higher turnover because of the closet and the reduction in energy and effort from demoralized gay workers, and it is clear that while the decision to be closeted might make sense for an individual gay worker, for a single company or for society as a whole it could be quite costly with no apparent offsetting economic benefits. In other words, the net benefits of coming out might be positive in a social sense but negative in an individual sense.

That hypothetical calculation might even underestimate the productive benefits of disclosure. Jonathan Rottenberg, business consultant and the founder of the Boston Computer Society, suggests that the skills learned in the process of coming out improved his workplace productivity: "I feel that the process of coming to terms with being gay and talking with people about it and not backing down from it has done more to build my capabilities as a consultant than almost anything else that I have done so far" (Friskopp and Silverstein 1995, 207).

Of course, the larger impact of coming out could instead generate a negative impact if coming out generates hostility and resistance among coworkers. As discussed earlier in the chapter, this very real possibility seemed to create a rationale for employers' antigay discrimination or at least for their preference for nondisclosure. If heterosexual workers' productivity falls when gay workers come out, employers (and the larger society) have no incentive to encourage disclosure. In Gary Becker's economic theory of coworker discrimination, segregation of groups of employees is sufficient to avoid productivity-reducing friction that induces employers to pay one group less.[9] Given the relatively small size and diversity of the gay population, though, segregation is not likely to be an effective strategy in this case. Becker's approach to thinking about coworker discrimination leaves out two important considerations, however: the employer's ability to manage and changing employee attitudes over time.

Employers' experiences with other sexuality-related concerns suggest that they may be able to manage the negative reactions of coworkers. First, the double standard for disclosure implies that employers have already adapted to some expressions of employees' heterosexual orientation in the form of family-oriented benefits or in lunchtime baby or wedding showers. Employers have begun to develop policies to manage even more explicit expressions of heterosexuality, such as interoffice heterosexual dating, for instance. A recent survey by the Society for Human Resource Management finds that 87 percent of companies surveyed allow romantic relationships among coworkers ("Office Dating Is Less of an Issue . . . ," 2000). Second, employers are learning how to manage explicit conflict related to sexuality in the workplace. The increasing presence and political savvy of women has led to a heightened concern about sexual harassment, usually perpetrated by heterosexual male employees. Employers have implemented policies that define and prohibit sexual harassment, educational programs about sexual harassment, and procedures for settling complaints about harassment. As mentioned earlier in the chapter, modern corporate reliance on rules and policies are designed to shape employee behavior in almost all matters related to the social and productive nature of the workplace.

Perhaps surprising, the example of the military provides further evidence that inappropriate reactions to people seen as sexualized, whether heterosexual women or lesbians and gay men, can be mitigated. Psychologists who have studied military unit cohesion, an analogous military concept to civilian employers' concerns about workers' ability to get along and to work productively, have identified a much more complex social context than that envisioned by economists. Robert MacCoun explains that task cohesion, or "a shared commitment among members to achieving a goal that requires the collective efforts of the group" (MacCoun 1996, 159), is more important in a group's performance than is social cohesion, that is, closeness and friendship among group members. Many environmental factors, some of which employers can control, tend to enhance cohesion, such as proximity, leadership, group size, successes, a shared threat, or personal similarities (which influence social cohesion more than task cohesion). Within this framework, employees' negative attitudes toward gay men and lesbians might not reduce productivity or behavior since other incentives exist to work cooperatively. Employers can influence prejudiced workers' behavior by creating sanctions for acting on negative attitudes, by having bosses set different normative examples, or by training workers to respond in a standard way to situations (MacCoun 1996, 168–71).

Responding to coworker reaction and conflict may take time, however. Thus, in the short run, some conflict between heterosexual and gay workers might exist and would either result in lower productivity or in more discrimination by employers who identify gay people as the troublemakers. Over time, heterosexual workers' negative attitudes might change as their openly gay colleagues educate, persuade, or demonstrate to them that homosexuality is not a barrier to being a good coworker. Research on attitudes toward lesbians and gay men finds that people who know a gay person tend to have more positive attitudes toward gay people in general (Herek and Capitanio 1996). As prejudiced heterosexuals get to know gay coworkers, the level of prejudice may diminish over time.

Assuming that workplaces do not collapse into permanent chaos once a gay or lesbian worker discloses his or her sexual orientation, more coming out by gay workers is likely to have a net positive impact on the economy as a whole over time. The unintended social consequences of coming out (positive net economic consequences over the long run) and of staying closeted (negative productivity consequences) suggest that there should be economic incentives to increase the level of disclosure among gay workers. The fact that those consequences of individual decisions are unintended means that they will probably not be part of an individual gay worker's decision-making process. In other words, the benefits taken into account by a gay man struggling with a coming out decision are *less than* the total actual benefits to society, reducing the likelihood that the benefits of coming out will outweigh the costs. As a result, too many gay men and lesbians will decide to remain closeted.

In analyzing other externalities, economists suggest that hurdles be removed and incentives added to encourage this socially beneficial behavior. How could the cost of coming out be reduced in order to encourage it? The model described above and the quantitative analysis suggest two possibilities. First, gay men and lesbians are making decisions based on the perceived risk of coming out, and in situations in which the risk appears to be lower (or actually is lower)—for instance, when the employer has a nondiscrimination policy—the degree of disclosure is higher. Thus, employers and governments can enact nondiscrimination policies as a means of encouraging disclosure. Second, employers could offer more direct incentives for coming out, such as domestic partner benefits. Those benefits could either act as a direct incentive to disclose that one has a partner or as an indirect indication that the risk of discrimination is low.

Of course, coming out is not always the result of a well thought out, individualized calculation for all gay, lesbian, and bisexual people. People might not act so deliberately, although even people who impulsively disclose their sexual orientation might have pondered the costs and benefits at an earlier point. Social norms that define discussions of gay people's family life and social life as off-limits in the workplace constrain the willingness and ability of gay men and lesbians to act according to a more "rational" calculation of the costs and benefits of coming out. Public policies that condone discrimination set up a decision-making environment that discourages coming out in the workplace. Even if coming out is not a purely individual decision, thinking about it in economic terms provides insights useful for future research and for policy analysis.

The economic decision-making process outlined here also helps to understand much of the collective action going on in the workplace and the dynamic behind the changes seen in corporate policies in the 1990s. The quantitative results described in this chapter suggest that coming out begets more coming out by coworkers. A more collective coming out by gay employees is often the precursor to organizing within the workplace for policy changes. The changes in policy won by activists can actually increase the benefits to coming out. The most prominent of these changes concerns domestic partner benefits, considered in chapter 4.

Compensation Discrimination, Revisited: Benefits

Equal pay for equal work. That slogan of the women's movement for work-place equality resonates with lesbian and gay employees who argue that their employers' benefits policies discriminate against gay employees with long-term, committed partners. The argument by gay employees is simple: since same-sex couples cannot legally marry in the United States, the same-sex "domestic partners" of lesbian, gay, or bisexual employees can never be eligible for health care and survivor pension benefits (or other benefits) provided by many employers to the spouses of employees. Raising the issue of a family's economic needs challenges the tendency to see gay and lesbian people as primarily single, as in the myth of conspicuous consumption, or as economically secure and independent, as in the DINK (double income no kids) myth.

Consider the situations of some of my own colleagues:

> Donna, a faculty member, and her partner have lived together for several years. They are jointly raising the partner's young children from a previous marriage. Donna's partner wants to return to school full-time, but finances and child care issues stand in the way.

> John and his partner have lived together for six years while John has been in graduate school. His graduate assistant's salary plus his partner's earnings allow them a comfortable but not lavish lifestyle.

While the two families might sound similar as loving committed relationships characterized by economic interdependence and shared responsibilities, only one is considered a family by John's and Donna's employer. John and his partner Susan married while John pursued his degree, making Susan eligible for coverage under John's university-provided health insurance. This coverage became especially important when Susan lost her job and her own employer-provided coverage. Donna teaches at the same university, but her partner Maria does not have access to the health insurance, tuition remission, and child care benefits provided by Donna's employer to legal spouses, since Donna and Maria are not—and cannot be—legally married. Donna and Maria hope for good health while Maria and her children remain uninsured.

Employers use family relationships to define employees' benefits with respect to family-related leave, retirement benefits, health care plans, relocation allowances, credit union memberships, and even company store discounts, among others. Health care benefits have been the biggest prize in the domestic partnership debate, though. On average, health care benefits for employees and their legally recognized family members account for 6 percent of compensation per hour in 1999 (U.S. Department of Labor, BLS 1999a). In 1994–95, 73 percent of full-time workers had all or part of their own and their family's medical care benefits paid for by their employer (Foster 1998). In the case of my friends, John receives over one thousand dollars in extra benefits, the value of which could be even more for Donna if she and Maria must instead purchase individual health insurance policies on the open market or simply cover out of pocket every health care expense incurred by Maria and their children. This compensation disparity provides much of the impetus for lesbian, gay, and bisexual employees' organizing in the workplace, which will be taken up more explicitly in chapter 9.

Addressing this inequity, many gay activists argue, is as simple as expanding eligibility for benefits to a gay employee's domestic partner who, like a legal spouse, shares a household and the necessities of life in a committed, long-term relationship with an employee. With their eyes on the bottom line, employers claim that such solutions are not so simple, raising labor costs and leading to administrative headaches. Some employers, particularly those in the public sector, situate the true source of the problem outside the employment context in state laws about who may marry. From that perspective, the issue is one of social policy rather than employment discrimination.

Other issues also arise. What about coverage for the opposite-sex domestic partners of unmarried employees? My friends Sarah and Doug faced this insurance problem, too, after they had lived together for over a decade, resisting legal marriage for philosophical reasons. When Doug switched to a freelance writing career, he lost his insurance and could not be covered by Sarah's university coverage.

But even covering all domestic partners will not eliminate the disparity in compensation for truly single employees. Workers who have neither a same-sex nor an opposite-sex partner or spouse are, in effect, paid less than their colleagues with families. In addition to that particular concern with equity, some argue that the real problem lies in the oddly decentralized and inadequate health care and pension systems for Americans. Why not take those issues on directly in a large-scale reform effort? Depending on who asks the question, the issue of employment benefits equity can become considerably more complex than equity for lesbian and gay employees, and equalizing lesbians' and gay men's status could result from several possible changes in public or private policy. In that context, the choice of a political strategy becomes an important decision for those pushing for change, a decision discussed in more detail in chapters 7 and 8.

This chapter focuses more narrowly on the benefits practices themselves, in particular, how and why employers provide health care benefits to their employees and to certain recognized family members, as well as why some employers now are offering benefits to domestic partners. Mainstream economists often neglect the impact of nonpecuniary compensation in their comparisons of the economic and employment status of members of different groups. In their view, fringe benefits are simply a somewhat different form of compensation, like wages offered in the form of health insurance (Kaufman 1994), without always considering how the structure of those benefits might influence labor market behavior and economic status.[1]

The 1990s were a period of enormous change, as groups of employees—mainly gay and lesbian employees—convinced their employers to recognize domestic partnerships in granting benefits. Getting an accurate count of the number is impossible, since employers are added to the list every day. A 1998 survey by KPMG found that 10 percent of companies surveyed offered health benefits to domestic partners. The Human Rights Campaign is one of several organizations tracking partner benefit developments, and their list of employers granting partner benefits included 865 private companies, state and local governments, nonprofit organizations, unions, colleges, and universities as of April 2000 (Human Rights Campaign 2000). They also listed 2,707 other (mostly smaller San Francisco–area employers) companies that have been certified as offering partner benefits by the San Francisco Human Rights Commission. Regardless of the specific number, the number has grown quickly from a handful in the early 1990s to thousands more today.

A look at the history of benefits shows that employers' benefit offerings have been influenced by employee collective action, competition for employees, existing wage ideologies, and public policy. Each of these same factors, in turn, has played a role in the accelerating growth of domestic partner benefits.

A Brief History of Employment Benefits

A useful starting point is to examine employers' decision-making about benefits. Why do employers offer benefits to employees at all, and beyond that, why extend those benefits to include some nonemployees? In the nineteenth and early twentieth centuries, employment benefits such as disability payments and pensions were viewed largely as paternalistic gestures that employers hoped would decrease employee turnover, increase worker efficiency, and prevent union organization (see Brody 1968; Brandes 1976; or Jacoby 1985). Some unions even started their own insurance plans to meet their members' needs (Brody 1968, 93). The Great Depression led this group of employers to cut back or eliminate their pension plans and similar benefits, ending the phase of labor-management relations known as "welfare capitalism."

During World War II, a rapidly improving economy led to fears of inflation, prompting government wage and price controls. As the nation's economy emerged from the Depression, though, employees and their unions wanted to see increases in their standard of living. The National War Labor Board was responsible for considering requests for wage increases and responded to pressure from unions (and even some employers) by allowing employers to offer insurance, pensions, and other benefits in lieu of more inflationary wage increases (Jacoby 1985, 266).

After the war, a key federal court decision in *Inland Steel v. NLRB* upheld a National Labor Relations Board ruling that pensions were one of the "conditions of employment" that were mandatory topics for collective bargaining (Greenough and King 1976, 64). This decision, along with growing demand from unions, led to a boom in offering benefits to employees in unionized companies (Jacoby 1985). Labor market competition (and often the desire to avoid unionization) contributed to the spread of these benefits throughout the union and nonunion sectors (see Vernon 1993; Foulkes 1980). And as many recent strikes illustrate, unions still fight to preserve employment benefits, as demonstrated by a strike against San Francisco Bay Area grocery stores by the United Food and Commercial Workers union (Beckett and Power 1995).

Gender, Wage Ideologies, and Benefits. But the question related to benefits for families remains. Why are some benefits created as part of employees' compensation extended to nonemployees who are spouses or children of employees? The history of providing family benefits is tied closely to gender-based justifications of compensation and, in particular, to the idea of the "family wage." Dating back to the nineteenth century, the family wage concept referred to the amount a man needed to earn to support not just himself but also his dependents, that is, his wife and children (see, in general, Kessler-Harris 1990; May 1982). Working women were presumed to have other sources of financial support from their working husbands or else were thought to have no other dependents, even though both assumptions were often false.

Early in this century, the family wage idea was used to justify paying women less than men, even when women performed the same jobs as men with equal productivity (Kessler-Harris 1990, 23). Similarly, benefits offered to men—life insurance, pensions, and paid vacations, for instance—were either not offered to women or were constructed in a way that made women rarely eligible to receive the benefits (Kessler-Harris 1990, 25). Since women did not need a wage beyond what was necessary for their own personal subsistence, from this perspective, employers apparently also believed that women did not need to provide financial security for themselves or for other family members through employer-provided benefits.

After World War II, the idea that women should be paid less than men because of women's lesser need for employment and wages was eventually replaced by a concept of fairness based on equal pay (and equal benefits) for equal work. The Equal Pay Act of 1963 codified this principle with respect to women. Title VII of the 1964 Civil Rights Act strengthened this emerging principle of paying people based on what they do rather than who they are, that is, not paying someone more for being male, for being white, or for being of a certain religion. Employers can no longer deny benefits to women when they are offered to men in the same jobs, although the fact that many women work part-time means that they often do not qualify for health or other benefits under gender-neutral employment policies.[2]

The Role of Public Policy in Promoting Benefits. Public policy related to the provision of benefits has undoubtedly played an important role in encouraging employers to extend benefits to employees and their legally recognized family members. In general, public policy related to benefits has focused on more structural issues: tax status, financial integrity, employee security, and benefits equity (between lower- and higher-paid employees) (see Greenough and King 1976, 59–67). For instance, although an employee's salary is subject to state and federal income tax, the money paid by an employer for health insurance for the employee and his or her family is *not* considered taxable income. The employer is also allowed to deduct the cost of wages *and* health care benefits from taxable earnings, reducing the company's taxes. This tax treatment of both employers' contributions and employees' benefits have made pensions and health insurance particularly desirable forms of compensation compared with actual direct wage payments. Public policy has also been involved from the public welfare angle, with the public plans for old age financial security—Old-Age and Survivors Insurance—and for health insurance for the poor and aged—Medicaid and Medicare—being designed not to replace private sector plans but to *supplement* those provided by employers (and, in the case of pensions, to supplement workers' savings). And occasionally the federal government has required benefits, such as unpaid family-related leave under the Family and Medical Leave Act, to promote important social goals.

Today, the influences of public policy and of labor market pressure for benefits are clear. In 1999, the cost of all benefits accounted for 27.5 percent of employers' labor costs for civilian workers in the United States (U.S. Department of Labor, BLS 1999a). The measured influence of employer provision of particular benefits varies somewhat, depending on the government survey. One study shows that 75 percent of workers were offered health care benefits by their own employer in 1996 (Cooper and Schone 1997). Another government survey finds that employers provided some kind of retirement plan for 57 percent of all employees in 1994–95, and health care benefits for 61 percent of employees (Foster 1998). More detailed data suggest that 41 percent of full-time workers with coverage had their own medical benefits fully paid for by their employers, and 28 percent had family health benefits fully paid for by employers (Foster 1998). (Employers partially financed health benefits for 36% of workers and 55% of their families.) Both surveys show that relying on employers to provide health insurance has resulted in some form of coverage for many people: 61.4 percent of people in the United States are covered by health insurance that is provided by their own employer or by a family member's employer (U.S. Bureau of the Census 1999a).

Further development of the general trend toward equity in employee compensation has been slow in the benefits area, since many employers still provide more benefits, that is, higher compensation, to married employees. Out of concern for both equity and cost containment, some employers now provide "cafeteria" or flexible benefit plans that give employees a set amount of money to spend on benefits, including family insurance coverage, for instance (Vernon 1993). These plans are growing in popularity but are not as common as the more traditional family-related plans, covering 34 percent of employees in 1994–95 (Foster 1998), which suggests that forces other than concerns about equity among employees must support the more common benefit policies.

Overall, public policy has usually allowed employers to choose both whether to offer benefits to *any* employees at all and whether benefits for any nonemployees should also be subsidized. In this decentralized decision-making context, gay and lesbian employees seeking benefits for domestic partners have mostly sidestepped the public policy setting, instead putting direct pressure on their employers to recognize and redress some of the perceived inequities in benefits plans.

Motivations for Seeking Expanded Access for Lesbians and Gay Men. Demands for fair treatment from all social institutions have been at the heart of the gay and lesbian equal rights movement for decades. But the exclusion of long-term gay partners from the economic benefits of marriage, including employer-provided benefits for spouses, gained particular saliency in the 1980s, fueled by the AIDS epidemic and the lesbian baby boom.

In the course of the AIDS epidemic, tragic scenarios highlighted the importance of recognition of partners. Homophobic family members refused entrance to hospital rooms to anguished men who sought to visit their sick or dying lovers. Partners of men who died without wills lost jointly purchased property to biological family members of the deceased. Men lost their health insurance but were ineligible for coverage under their partner's plan. As if holding a message written in invisible ink up to a candle, the epidemic revealed the larger economic and social meaning of the legal solitude of gay men involved in committed relationships.

For lesbians, much of the economic pressure came from happier circumstances but was also problematic. The practice of lesbians adopting or giving birth to children, usually through donor insemination, flourished in large metropolitan areas beginning in the 1980s (Weston 1992). Many lesbians and their partners (and perhaps other coparents) raised these children in the midst of an acute awareness that the economic supports available to other families were not available to lesbian-headed families. Most relevant, the nonbiological parent could not include her partner or even her partner's child for whom she assumed financial responsibility on her employer-provided health care coverage. In an era of escalating health care costs, the potential lack of coverage left lesbians and their families vulnerable to financial disaster.

These larger social trends intensified the need for recognition of long-term partners on many levels. David Chambers (1992) documents the important role of the AIDS epidemic in shaping both the form and the rhetoric of the movement to recognize domestic partners by cities and courts. Employers have also become potential organizing targets for lesbians and gay men. Gay and lesbian employees began first to question the exclusion of their partners from the benefits that help to support families in the United States, eventually taking those concerns and concrete proposals for change directly to their employers. A longer discussion of those organizing efforts is in chapter 9. The next section of this chapter covers the practical issues involved in equalizing compensation.

Practical Proposals, Practical Concerns

In a simple sense, lesbian and gay employees are asking their employers to treat employees' long-term partners and coparented children in the same way that the employer treats spouses and a couple's legal (i.e., adopted or biological) children. In practice, creating and implementing an equitable policy, though, requires careful consideration and handling of several important issues. The kind of relationship that has come to be recognized as a "domestic partnership" varies to some degree among employers, but many similarities have emerged out of the interaction of employees' proposals and employers' worries.

The biggest benefit at issue so far is health care benefits. The motivation for action by employees with unmarried partners is understandable given the fact that more than forty-three million people in the United States lack health insurance (U.S. Bureau of the Census 1999a), and most Americans under 65 with health insurance get it through an employer. And in an era when holding down health care costs has become a major concern for employers, companies' concerns about higher labor costs and the feasibility of administration are also understandable. These practical issues are the first hurdles for domestic partner advocates, and the concerns pop up in almost every company that considers covering domestic partners.

Defining a Domestic Partner. Employers' first concern is often how they would recognize a "domestic partner," since such relationships are not typically publicly defined or recorded. Although employers rarely ask for proof of marriage from their employees who sign up spouses, marriages are at least externally verifiable if necessary. While many gay employees prefer a similarly informal kind of declaration of partnership to employers, employers and insurance companies prefer tighter requirements to hold down the number of new enrollees and to ensure that the partner is not, for example, a casual acquaintance who is signing up because he or she is sick. As a result of these concerns, more specific and stringent definitions have developed:

> [A] domestic partnership is understood to be an intimate, committed relationship between two individuals of legal age who are financially and emotionally interdependent, share the same residence and intend to remain together indefinitely. (International Society of Certified Employee Benefit Specialists (ISCEBS) 1995)

> [T]wo individuals of the same gender who live together in a long-term relationship of indefinite duration, with an exclusive commitment similar to that of marriage, in which the partners agree to be financially responsible for each other's well-being and each others' debts to third parties. (Stanford University)

> Two adults of the same sex who have chosen to share their lives in an intimate and committed relationship, reside together, and share a mutual obligation of support for the basic necessities of life. (Hollywood Supports 1993)

Usually an employer requires a formal declaration of partnership, asking the employee and partner to sign an affidavit attesting to meeting certain criteria that define a domestic partnership. Although such criteria vary, common elements include some or all of the following (Badgett 1994; Hostetler and Pynes 1995):

(1) Minimum time requirements for duration of the partnership before a partner is eligible for benefits. Some declarations specify a time between partnerships if one is dissolved. These requirements are typically six months to a year (ISCEBS 1995).
(2) Evidence of financial interdependence, such as a joint checking account, shared assets, or shared debts.
(3) Sharing a residence, either rented or owned.
(4) Naming the partner in a will or as a beneficiary of life insurance or pension plans.
(5) Restrictions for the relationship, including exclusivity, no close blood relationship, and no current legal marriage to someone else.

Obviously, some of those requirements look similar to the lived reality of many marriages, but some exceed the legal requirements of marriage. For instance, the fact that partners must often cohabit for six months to a year before eligibility for some employers' benefits is much more restrictive than marriage. In many places, a heterosexual employee can get a marriage license one day, get married the next morning, and show up at the benefits office in the afternoon to sign up her husband for insurance. Also, some of the material requirements for establishing domestic partnerships are likely to be difficult for younger or lower-paid employees to meet. No research exists on how exclusionary such criteria prove to be in practice.

Increased Enrollment. Employers' insistence on the more stringent requirements is related to the other major concern—costs. In one survey of 459 employers, 56 percent of those not offering domestic partner benefits cited cost concerns as a "very important" factor, and another 29 percent said costs were a "somewhat important" factor (ISCEBS 1995). This has been a particularly worrisome issue with respect to health care benefits. One immediate source of higher costs comes from enrolling more people. Since no one knows how many employees are gay, much less partnered, the employers who offered benefits to domestic partners early on had to take a leap of faith that a manageably small number of employees would sign up. With time and accumulated experience, the knowledge gap to be bridged has closed, since most employers report that relatively few domestic partners enroll.

Table 6 shows the percentage of employees enrolling domestic partners at several different places of employment. For the most part, all different types of employers, whether private or public sector, see few domestic partners signing up for benefits, whether opposite-sex or same-sex. Typically, the rate of enrollment falls below 1 percent of all those employed. The exceptions tend to be western cities, such as Seattle (or Berkeley or West Hollywood), that might attract a less traditional workforce that includes both heterosexual and gay employees with domestic partners. Including opposite-sex partners usually results in higher enrollment rates. The examples in table 6 show enrollment rates for opposite-sex partners that are significantly higher than the proportions of employees who sign up same-sex partners.

At first glance, these small numbers seem odd for same-sex couples. Why would gay and lesbian employees work so hard to convince employers and then fail to take advantage of their success? Not knowing how many employees are gay and partnered means that we do not know how much lower enrollment is from its potential, but several reasons have been offered to explain the minuscule rates. Probably the biggest factor is the fact that employees' partners are also likely to be employed and to have their own employer-provided health benefits. As chapter 6 will discuss, studies of gay couples show high rates of labor force participation for *both* partners in a couple as well as a strong norm of equal participation in the paid labor force. Plus, unlike health care benefits for spouses, employer contributions for domestic partner benefits are considered taxable

**Table 6 Enrollment of Domestic Partners as Percentage
of Workers with Health Care Coverage**

	Total (percent)	Same-Sex (percent)	Opposite-Sex (percent)
Public Employers			
New York City (1)	1.2	N.a.	N.a.
New York State (1)	0.6	0.1	0.4
State of Vermont (1)	5.6	0.6	5.0
State of Oregon (1)	1.9	N.a.	N.a.
Private Employers			
Anthem Blue Cross			
Blue Shield (1)	0.2	0.2	Not eligible
Apple Computers (2)	0.6	0.6	Not eligible
BankBoston (1)	0.6	N.a.	N.a.
IBM (2)	Less than 1	Less than 1	Not eligible
ITT Hartford (1)	0.7*	N.a.	N.a.
Knight-Ridder			
Newspapers, Inc. (2)	0.4	0.4	Not eligible
New York Times Co. (2)	0.2	0.2	Not eligible
Xerox (1)	Less than 1	N.a.	N.a.

Note: N.a. means breakdown not available

Sources: (1) Author's contacts with employers, 1997–99; (2) National Lesbian & Gay Journalists Association (1999), 1997 data.

income, and the additional taxes will make the benefits less attractive. Another possible contributing factor to low rates is the closet. Some gay or lesbian employees will fear the public disclosure of their homosexuality as a result of signing up a partner, despite employers' assurances of confidentiality and the financial reward for coming out.

Even without signing up their partners, gay employees gain symbolically from their employers' recognition of domestic partners and might even gain in a larger social sense from an increased degree of openness about their relationships. Eligibility for partner benefits also comes with other potential benefits, including a sense of security should a partner lose his or her job and flexibility for making decisions about whether a partner can afford to leave a job to return to school, raise children, or become self-employed. As gay couples have time to adapt to their new possibilities, enrollments of partners might even increase slightly.

Fears of Fraud and AIDS. Employers also worry that higher costs from new enrollment will be exacerbated by high health care costs of those new enrollees. Whenever insurance coverage is optional (as it would be for partners but not employees in plans in which all employees are enrolled) and relatively inexpensive or subsidized, those with the biggest incentive to sign up will be those who are less healthy and expect to use the benefits often. This concern, known as "adverse selection," would be occurring if the domestic partners had higher-than-average medical expenses. Those higher expenses could cause insurance premiums to rise for *all* employees, potentially increasing the amount paid by the employer and any portion of the premium paid by employees themselves.

In particular, suddenly allowing employees to declare an unmarried partner raises the specter of gay men signing up their partners, friends, or even casual acquaintances who are HIV-infected. The strict criteria for establishing a partnership are partly designed to allay this fear. Again, experience has proven to be the best antidote to employers' concerns. Employers have not reported any problems with fraudulent registrations of partners. And in two studies of employers in the early 1990s (cited in Hostetler and Pynes 1995), no employers reported any AIDS cases among domestic partners. The earliest employers to provide partner benefits often had to agree to surcharges or other measures to protect insurance companies from unexpected losses from high costs for partners. For instance, the City of Berkeley, which began providing benefits to both same-sex and opposite-sex partners in 1985, had to pay a 2 percent fee to Kaiser Permanente. When no unusually high costs were reported for domestic partners in the first three years of the plan, Kaiser dropped the fee (Spencer's Research Reports on Employee Benefits 1992). The City of Seattle also had to pay a temporarily higher premium when first extending benefits to partners (Blanton 1993).

Inevitably, some employer will report that one or more covered domestic partners has AIDS. Other evidence suggests that even this inevitability is not something to fear as a widespread phenomenon. First, many of the employees signing up partners will be lesbians, who have lower rates of HIV infection than heterosexuals, which should hold down the number of HIV-infected partners even over the long term. Second, recent medical advances have resulted in HIV/AIDS treatment costs comparable to costs for other medical conditions or chronic illnesses. One study conducted before the introduction of the life-enhancing protease inhibitors estimated that the cost of caring for one person from the time of HIV infection until death was $119,000 (Hellinger 1998). The same researcher notes that protease inhibitors have increased the lifespan of people with AIDS, suggesting that drug costs may increase as such drugs are more widely used. But a cost-reducing effect comes from likely decreases in hospitalization costs. Also, compare HIV-related costs with the cost of treating certain birth defects that could occur for employees' children.

For instance, the cost of medical treatment for cerebral palsy averages $142,000 (Waitzman et al. 1994). Overall, the impact of covering a few people with AIDS would be no different from the implications of covering people who might develop other serious health conditions.

Insurance Company Resistance. Sometimes other barriers arise from regulators of the insurance industry and the conservatism of the insurance companies. In some places, state insurance commissions interpret regulations to prohibit benefits for partners, creating a major barrier to insurance companies that want to sell partner coverage. For instance, John Oxendine, the Georgia Insurance Commissioner, turned down the applications of insurers who wanted to provide partner coverage for local employers. The Commissioner argued that covering partners was contrary to the "moral and ethical fiber" of Georgians and only allowed domestic partner coverage when ordered by a Georgia court to do so in 1999 (Brown 1999). New York insurers were held back until 1993 when the New York State Insurance Department decided to reinterpret state law to allow insurers to cover domestic partners (Hewitt Associates 1994). This opened the door for Columbia University and the state of New York to provide partner benefits.

Sometimes insurance companies simply refuse to provide such coverage. This is not a barrier for large self-insured employers, but many smaller employers who must purchase coverage face insurance company resistance. In some cases, information and education have overcome insurance providers' objections, but not always. Even though Lotus Development Corporation was self-insured, the company that sold Lotus coverage for claims exceeding Lotus's self-insurance limit was reluctant to include domestic partners without a great deal of education by Lotus officials (Noble 1992). Sometimes an employer can offer benefits to partners in only some locations or through particular plans. For instance, Yale University only covers domestic partners in one of its health care plans run on its own campus. The San Francisco Human Rights Commission has developed a list of insurance carriers in each state that will provide partner coverage, listing at least four carriers per state (<www.hrc.org/worknet/dp/insure.pdf>).

Perhaps the best evidence that the resistance of insurance companies is declining is the fact that some insurers provide such benefits to their own employees. Kaiser Permanente of Northern California, Blue Cross/Blue Shield (in various locations), Harvard Pilgrim Health Care, Aetna, ITT Hartford, and Consumers United Insurance all offer health benefits to (at least some) partners of employees.

Tax Issues. Outside of the realm of antidiscrimination policy, other policy issues have also influenced the provision of partner benefits. In particular, the tax treatment of domestic partner benefits has been a barrier both to employers' willingness to offer partners benefits (ISCEBS survey) and to the principle of equal treatment. According to several private letter rulings provided by the Internal Revenue Service, unless the employee can claim her partner as a dependent under the Internal Revenue Service's very stringent criteria, the employer's contributions to the cost of any of the benefits is considered taxable income ("Letter Rulings" 1992). For employees with partners, the extra tax burden reduces the attractiveness of the benefit. At Lotus, for instance, employees with covered partners paid as much as an additional $1,350 in taxes (Hammonds 1991). For example, if partner benefits cost an employer an extra $250 per month, an employee gets an extra $3,000 per year in taxable income. A lesbian in the 28 percent tax bracket who puts a partner on her plan will add $840 to the income taxes she owes.

Fears of Backlash and Moral Objections. Another employer concern is backlash from customers. The form of backlash varies depending on the kind of business. For instance, it is hard to define exactly who the "customers" of universities are, but some college administrators fear a drop off of alumni donations or, in the case of public universities, adverse reactions from state legislatures. Profit-seeking businesses might fear consumer boycotts and loss of sales revenues.

The potential for backlash exists, but the probability is difficult to predict. Few cases have resulted in measurably negative consequences. Although some alumni have withdrawn their usual contributions in outrage over domestic partnership plans, other alumni have responded positively, especially lesbian and gay alumni, some of whom are now organized at particular colleges and universities. (A boycott of contributions to Carnegie Mellon by gay alumni showed that the threat can cut both ways [Lambda Alums 1996].)

Customers of profit-making firms have not had an obvious impact one way or the other. Opposition from some religious groups, angry letters from Florida legislators, and a vow by Southern Baptists to boycott Walt Disney Corporation after their decision to offer partner benefits all failed to intimidate Disney officials (Navarro 1995; Roberts 1995). The difficulties for adamant opponents of domestic partner policies are evident from the Apple Computer experience. When Apple sought economic development tax breaks for opening a new plant in Williamson County, Texas, the county board initially turned the company down because Apple offered domestic partner benefits. This political opposition to partner benefits could not hold up against the economic pressure to create more local jobs, however. Even then governor of Texas Ann Richards lobbied against the board's initial decision, and the board eventually agreed to provide the tax breaks.

The significance of moral objections comes from an unexpected source, too: from employers themselves. Economists typically see companies as profit-driven operations, with managers making decisions only in response to changes in production costs and sales revenues, remaining mostly unaffected by human emotion or moral sentiment.[3] But employers in the ISCEBS survey gave "moral objections" as one of the reasons for not offering domestic partner benefits, with 34 percent saying that was a "very important" factor in the decision (ISCEBS 1995). (The survey distinguished between "moral objections" and "employee backlash," suggesting that the respondents were referring to decision-makers' moral objections, not those of heterosexual employees.)

The Impact of Barriers. The barriers faced by employees seeking recognition of domestic partners are formidable, involving economic concerns and normative issues, empirical questions and theoretical predictions. Developing "answers" or reasoned responses to the questions that employers raise has kept many a gay employee-activist busy nights and weekends. The ability of reason and research to overcome employer objections is not likely to be automatic, especially since even activists admit that benefit costs are likely to rise at least somewhat and by an amount that can be difficult to predict precisely. In the face of risk, employers must have some other positive rationale for taking the step toward partner benefits.

Employer Motivations for Offering Partner Benefits

The history of employment benefits provides a helpful framework for analyzing the motives of employers who have overcome the barriers described above to offer spousal benefits to domestic partners. Several factors have influenced the development of benefits: collective action by employees, wage ideologies, public policy, and labor market competition. All four of these factors appear to be present in the motivations of the employers now recognizing domestic partners. These influences in the decision to offer benefits are apparent from employers' public statements about domestic partner benefits and from survey responses, and a close analysis of the kinds of employers offering these benefits reveals further motivations.

Collective Action. Employers are unlikely to have invented the idea of domestic partner benefits on their own without at least some prompting from employees. Logically, then, somebody must request such benefits to get employers to consider them. In some cases, this might be one or more individual requests to the company benefits office. In the ISCEBS survey, the driving force behind an employer's decision to offer partner benefits cited most often was "employee inquiries/requests," the response of 35 percent of the seventy-one companies. Another 6 percent listed collective bargaining as the driving force (ISCEBS 1995). Given the wording of the question, it is not clear to what extent such requests were part of a concerted effort by groups of lesbian and gay employees and to what extent they were individually motivated independent of group interest.

Unions, the traditional and legally recognized route of workplace collective action, have been involved in the domestic partner movement from the beginning. In 1982, the *Village Voice* was the first employer to agree to offer partner benefits as the result of negotiations with District 65/UAW (Frank and Holcomb 1990, 33). The city of Santa Cruz extended benefits to partners of city employees during their 1987 negotiations with the Service Employees International Union (SEIU) (Hewitt Associates 1991). The Lambda Legal Defense Fund compilation of employers offering benefits lists twenty-five unions that have negotiated such benefits for its members. Lesbian and gay union members have joined together within unions to push union leaders to bargain for sexual orientation nondiscrimination clauses and domestic partner benefits (Frank and Holcomb 1990).

Aside from the traditional forms of workplace collective action through unions, lesbian and gay employees are consciously organizing into their own workplace-focused groups, and that focus is often directed at benefits issues. (Chapter 9 discusses this phenomenon in more detail.) When writer Ed Mickens looked for the "100 Best Companies for Gay Men and Lesbians," he rated companies according to four criteria: having a nondiscrimination policy, providing benefits to same-sex domestic partners, including gay issues in diversity training, and recognizing a gay employee group. Of the one hundred companies singled out, forty-three had a formally organized group of lesbian and gay employees, and another nineteen had informal groups (Mickens 1994). A 1993 survey of Fortune 1000 and other companies by the National Gay and Lesbian Task Force uncovered thirty-nine formally recognized employee groups in 20 percent of responding companies (Baker, Strub, and Henning 1995). National conferences on lesbian and gay workplace organizing attract participants from hundreds of companies, many of whom are involved in organized groups. The gay employee groups may serve several functions for their members, such as being social and professional meeting places, but often these groups also take the lead in pressuring their companies to offer benefits to partners.

A case study of domestic partner benefits in higher education demonstrates the importance of collective action (Badgett 1994; Badgett 1995a). On numerous campuses, groups of lesbian, gay, bisexual, and sometimes heterosexual employees have organized into groups to plot strategies, collect information, lobby decision-makers, and publicize the need for policies to ensure fairness for lesbian, gay, and bisexual employees. Typically, the efforts first focus on securing an explicit policy of nondiscrimination on the basis of sexual orientation. Given that base, employee groups then shift their efforts to domestic partner benefits. Although not all such efforts have been successful, most of the successful efforts have followed a similar path.

External collective action has influenced public employers in cities with politically organized lesbian, gay, and bisexual communities (Gossett 1994). The city governments of San Francisco, New York, and Atlanta, for instance, faced organized pressure from the local gay community. In San Francisco, gay activists engineered a victory in a referendum on citywide registration of domestic partnerships in 1990, which paved the way for the Board of Supervisors to approve benefits for partners of city employees in 1991 (Chambers 1992). New York activists pressured Mayor David Dinkins to fulfill his campaign promise to grant benefits to partners (Finder 1993). Facing a tough reelection fight, Dinkins rushed through negotiations on partner benefits with the Municipal Labor Council (made up of city employee unions) to satisfy gay voters, thereby settling a lawsuit charging that the city's benefits policies discriminated against gay workers (*Washington Blade* 1993).

These examples demonstrate that collective pressure on employers to provide partner benefits can come from many sources: several individual employees, unions, organized gay employee groups, or gay political activists. The source might matter since each form implies different potential consequences for a resistant employer. A union could conceivably strike over an employer's refusal to give benefits to partners (although I know of no cases of this happening). Political activists could attempt a boycott of a private business or an overthrow of elected officials controlling public sector benefits. Gay employee groups are not legally recognized bargaining agents and could not strike without risking dismissal, but those groups' continual presence in the workplace allows for ongoing education and pressure on employers. Lesbian and gay employees can also "vote with their feet" by leaving the company, but this requires an attractive work alternative and falls more clearly under the labor market competition category discussed below. Whatever the source, some form of collective action appears to be a minimum requirement for employer consideration and, in at least some cases, collective action appears to be decisive.

Wage Ideologies. Perhaps because of the legislative and judicial successes of the civil rights movement and the women's movement, a guiding principle of modern wage setting appears to be equity. Evidence suggests that this general principle plays an important role in employer decision-making on the domestic partnership issue. In the ISCEBS survey, over half of the employers providing partner benefits report a driving force related to equity concerns: "corporate philosophy" (27 percent), "consistency with employer nondiscrimination policy" (25 percent), or "compensation/equity issues" (7 percent) (ISCEBS 1995).

In their public announcements of extension of benefits to partners, employers often cite an equity motivation. This motive concerns the treatment of either their lesbian and gay employees or their employees with nontraditional families, as the following quotations from company statements demonstrate:

> *"This is really a discrimination issue.* We realized that family structures are changing and want to respect this diversity." (Donna Goya, senior vice president of human resources, Levi Strauss & Co. [Ames 1992; emphasis added])

> Many of our employees are members of households of people who are committed to and financially responsible for each other. While many of these households are traditional families, many others are less traditional but *just as significant to the individuals involved.* In recognition of this fact, Sybase believes a more inclusive definition of "family" is appropriate for purposes of providing certain employee benefits. (Mark Hoffman, Sybase, Inc.[Hoffman 1992; emphasis added])

> By making this change, we are clearly underscoring our firm commitment to keeping Silicon Graphics a special place in terms of *our support for diversity* among our employees. *We are addressing the fact that state and federal laws do not provide same sex partners the possibility of legalizing their relationships through marriage.* This

prevents those employees who would choose the option to get married, if they could, from sharing their health and other benefits with their partners. (Ed McCracken, Silicon Graphics [McCracken 1992; emphasis added])

[The domestic partner policy] underscores MCA's ongoing *commitment to creating a work place free of discrimination by ensuring fair treatment* of all employees, regardless of sexual orientation. (Sidney J. Sheinberg, president, MCA Inc. [Jefferson 1992; emphasis added])

Since early in its history, Lotus has had a stated policy prohibiting discrimination based on sexual preference. Lotus recognizes that lesbian and gay employees do not have the choice to legalize permanent and exclusive relationships through marriage; thus, they cannot legally share financial, health and other benefits with their significant partners. For this reason, *in the interest of fairness and diversity* Lotus will recognize the significance of such relationships by including them in our policies and benefits. (Russ Campanello, vice president, human resources, Lotus Development Corp. [Campanello 1991; emphasis added])

While mainstream economists often argue that norms and ideologies play little role in important business decisions related to production costs such as employee compensation, we have already seen the presence of employers' moral objections among the barriers to gay employees' lobbying efforts. The fairness norm, therefore, has the potential to play a very important rhetorical role, counterbalancing moral objections to homosexuality expressed by employers or managerial decision-makers. With two or more competing norms, one of which (compensation equity) is often reinforced by explicit corporate or public policies, moral opposition to domestic partner benefits might be somewhat neutralized or muted, allowing more focus on some of the other arguments for and against a new policy.

Of course, employers might have many reasons for adopting a new benefits policy other than their publicly professed concern with equity, and some of those reasons may not be flattering to the employer if aired in public, such as the need to catch up with competitors. But the fact that many employers publicly cite a normative motive attests to the norm's power to legitimate business decisions, even if fairness is only part of the true underlying motivation.

Public Policy and Legal Pressure. Perhaps the biggest influence of public policy has been through its influence on widely held wage philosophies. In addition to the existence of federal, state, and local laws against discrimination based on sex, race, religion, and other factors, an increasing number of states and municipalities explicitly forbid employment discrimination based on sexual orientation. As noted in Chapter 2, state laws alone cover 24 percent of the U.S. population, with local laws in some large metropolitan areas covering many more. So far, though, these laws seem to have provided more normative than legal clout, highlighting the need for fair treatment of lesbian, gay, and bisexual employees.

Courts have been relatively consistent in deciding that traditional spousal benefits policies should not be considered sexual orientation discrimination. For instance, in *Phillips v. Wisconsin Personnel Commission*,[4] a Wisconsin state court ruled that the failure to provide spousal benefits to committed same-sex partners of employees did not constitute sexual orientation discrimination since partners of unmarried heterosexual employees were not eligible for benefits, either. While recognizing that same-sex marriages were not legal in Wisconsin (or anywhere in the U.S., for that matter) and that the lesbian bringing suit did not have the same options as an unmarried heterosexual with a partner, the court found that the decision about both the issues of benefits and of same-sex marriage were matters for the legislature, not the courts (see n. 8 of the decision).

Similarly, in *Rovira v. AT&T*, a lesbian sued her deceased partner's employer for death benefits provided to surviving spouses and children. A district court judge ruled in 1993 that AT&T's policy forbidding discrimination because of sexual orientation or marital status was only a guideline and not a contract. Further, the policy applied only to actual employees and did not cover their beneficiaries (Pines 1993). In a suit by the American Association of University Professors against Rutgers University, a New Jersey state court ruled that offering only spousal benefits was not illegal discrimination under that state's ban on sexual orientation discrimination (Lambda Legal Defense Fund 1999).

In the 1990s, a few other judicial bodies interpreted similar situations differently. In a 1993 ruling, the Vermont Labor Relations Board ruled that the University of Vermont violated its policy against sexual orientation discrimination in refusing to provide spousal benefits to domestic partners of gay employees.[5] The board found that while the policy granting benefits based on legal marriage did not specify sexual orientation, the policy clearly had a disproportionate impact on the ability of lesbian and gay employees' partners to receive the same benefits as spouses. A more recent decision by the Alaska Supreme Court found that the University of Alaska violated state law against marital status discrimination in its denial of benefits to same-sex partners.[6] The city of Seattle offered partner benefits after the city's Human Rights Department ruled that the city's benefits practices were discriminatory (Hewitt Associates 1991, 18).

The conflicting judicial interpretations of the issue suggest that policy pressure operating through the courts is not yet an important factor in the spread of partner benefits, since legal decisions do not consistently answer the question of whether sexual orientation nondiscrimination policies *require* domestic partner benefits. In fact, courts may not reach a consensus on this issue without more explicit language in civil rights legislation.[7]

The threat of a costly and embarrassing lawsuit might be influential in an employer's decision, though, even if the employer expects to win. But in the ISCEBS survey, only two employers said that the threat of legal action was a primary factor in their decision to provide partner benefits (ISCEBS 1995). It may be that the lawsuit threat simply adds to the weight of other arguments in favor of recognizing domestic partners. The Montefiore Medical Center responded to the threat of a lawsuit by implementing partner benefits. Activists at several universities said that they had effectively used the threat implied by the Vermont ruling (Badgett 1994). And, as mentioned earlier, employees of the city of New York received benefits as part of a settlement of a lawsuit by the Gay Teachers Association against the city's school board.[8] In both of those cases, though, other factors were also influential: the academic activists employed many other arguments, and the New York City workers benefited from then Mayor Dinkins's need for the gay vote in an upcoming election.

Governments have other tools available to use in influencing private employers. One is setting an example through benefits practices for government employees. New York, Oregon, California, Vermont, Washington, and Connecticut now provide health care benefits to all or most state employees' domestic partners. Fifty-four cities do so for city employees (van der Meide 2000, 85). However, a difficult policy barrier for cities' and other local municipalities' ability to give coverage to city employees' partners is the limitation on home rule and possible conflicts with the state government's authority over family definitions (see Gossett 1999, for a longer discussion of this issue in the context of gay rights laws). The city of Atlanta initially had its domestic partner coverage ruled unconstitutional until it changed coverage for domestic partners to coverage for "dependents," a term that the city defined in concordance with state law (*City of Atlanta v. Morgan*, 288 Ga. 586, 492, S.E.2d 193, 1997). The city of Boston was not so lucky, with the state's Supreme Judicial Court ruling that the city's partner coverage for its employees was inconsistent with state law (*Dennis Connors v. City of Boston*, SJC-07945, 1999).

Governments also have influence as customers of private sector businesses. Since 1997, the city of San Francisco has used the city's purchasing power to dramatically increase the number of employers offering partner benefits. San Francisco's Equal Benefits Provision (in chapter 12B of the city's administrative code) requires city contractors who provide benefits to spouses to provide equal benefits for domestic partners, both same-sex and opposite-sex. If contractors cannot convince insurance companies to cover partners or cannot equalize benefits for some other reason, the company must pay employees with partners the cash equivalent of the benefit (San Francisco Human Rights Commission 1998). Two years after the ordinance was implemented, over two thousand employers (mostly small local employers) had been certified by the city's Human Rights Commission as being in compliance with the law, or far more companies than had appeared on the lists of organizations tracking the spread of partner benefits. The law has some limited reach outside of San Francisco, as it requires nondiscrimination in benefits for any facility in San Francisco and in other company facilities performing work for a city contract. So far, a revised version of the city ordinance has held up against most legal challenges by the Air Transport Association of America.[9] Los Angeles and Seattle have enacted similar rules for city contractors.

Labor Market Competition. Employers' concerns about higher compensation costs are the kinds of arguments expected by economists, since an increase in costs per worker unmatched by an increase in productivity or lower costs elsewhere in production might lead to lower profits. That is essentially an argument directly related to the company's ability to compete in its *product* market. One possible reason that employers have overcome their fear of losing profits is the belief that gay and lesbian workers, in particular, might become more productive if their employers offer domestic partner benefits, giving a boost in morale and sense of fair treatment or reducing stress related to work-family issues. While that enhanced productivity argument might be attractive and even plausible, it is very difficult to demonstrate directly that higher productivity will offset higher costs and even more difficult to see this factor in employers' decisions. Future research is needed on this question.

Other economic arguments provide more empirically supportable hypotheses regarding employers' decisions to offer partner benefits. These arguments are related to the *labor* market within which an employer locates and hires its workforce. Within the labor market, an individual employer competes with other employers for the best workers. Then employers try to retain those valued workers, which generally involves keeping employees satisfied given the wages, benefits, and working conditions they could get from another employer. Hiring and training new employees can be costly, with estimates of hiring costs ranging from $3,310 to $6,359 (Thaler-Carter 1997) and annual average training costs of $305 (U.S. Department of Labor BLS 1996), giving firms a financial incentive to retain employees. Employers offering domestic partner benefits might be able to attract and retain better employees than an employer not offering such benefits. And while this kind of competitive advantage primarily depends on the number of lesbian and gay employees in the relevant labor pool, it is not inconceivable that some heterosexuals who value diversity in their workplaces will also be attracted to those employers.

Surprisingly, though, few employers in the ISCEBS survey report a competitive motivation for offering partner benefits: 7 percent cite as a driving force the "desire for leadership role in benefits innovation," and 13 percent give "competitive edge" as the main factor (ISCEBS 1995). On the other hand, over one-third of employers that do *not* offer domestic partner benefits suggest that the strongest influence on those employers in the future will be "increased competition to attract and retain employees." The difference in the motives of those we might consider "innovators," or the early providers of partner benefits, compared with the possible future providers suggests an interesting dynamic to the competitive process in the labor market: innovation in benefits by leaders may be motivated by many nonpecuniary factors, creating precedents that ultimately lead to competitive pressure on followers.

The best evidence for the role of competition comes from an analysis of the kinds of employers providing partner benefits. Using lists of private employers offering domestic partner benefits collected in 1999 by the Human Rights Campaign, Lambda Legal Defense and Education Fund, and Hollywood Supports, a master list of employers was compiled. From that list, more detailed information on 405 private sector employers was collected from electronic databases with information on companies.[10] Table 7 shows the number of employers in the for-profit industries found most often on the list. The percentages reflect the number of *employers* with partner benefits in a particular industry divided by the total number of companies providing such benefits. The employers vary considerably in size, so the percentages in the table do *not* reflect the percentage of employees covered.

The pattern in table 7 is clear. Almost half—48 percent—are in only six industries: insurance, computer equipment and programming, hospitals, newspapers and publishing, and legal services. Another factor defining

Table 7 Industry Composition of Employers Offering Domestic Partner Benefits (DPBs)

Industry	Number with DPBs	Percentage of Total
Insurance	18	4.4
Computer and Office Equipment	16	4.0
Hospitals	16	4.0
Newspapers, publishing	18	4.4
Computer programming	48	11.9
Legal services	80	19.8
Subtotal	196	48.4
Total	405	

labor markets is geography. For many kinds of jobs, employers will be competing most directly with other firms in the same city or region. Table 8 shows that over one-third of employers offering partner benefits are primarily located in seven cities. The city clustering, as well as the industry clustering, suggests that labor market competition might be a very important explanation in the spread of such benefits. Once one employer offers benefits for partners, others competing for similar workers must match those terms of compensation or risk losing valuable workers and job applicants.

In announcing the implementation of domestic partner benefits, many employers credit competitive pressure with leading to the policy change:

> This change is a result of research conducted by HR which looked at our current HR policies, programs, and benefit plans (which include coverage for spouses of Apple employees) and *what other companies are doing regarding covering domestic partners.* As a result of this research, we recommended . . . that Apple extend some of our policies and programs to cover domestic partners." (Kevin Sullivan, senior vice president, human resources, Apple Computer, Inc. [Sullivan 1992; emphasis added])

> Since its inception, Borland has realized that our people are our most valuable resource. Borland is able to produce outstanding software products and maintain the best customer service in the industry because *we hired and retained quality people.* This program, as well as other employee benefits, reflects this belief. (Philippe Kahn, CEO, Borland International, Inc. [Kahn 1992; emphasis added)

> *Our failure to provide these benefits puts us at a disadvantage* with other institutions with which we compete for outstanding faculty and

Table 8 Cities with Most Employers Offering Domestic Partner Benefits

City	State	Number with DPBs	Percentage of Total
Los Angeles	CA	18	4.4
San Francisco	CA	27	6.7
Chicago	IL	11	2.7
Boston	MA	12	3.0
Minneapolis-St. Paul	MN	10	2.5
New York City	NY	55	13.6
Washington	DC	18	4.4
Subtotal		151	37.3
Total		405	

staff. (Nannerl O. Keohane, president, Duke University [Keohane 1995; emphasis added])

The impact of competition on the spread of partner benefits among high-technology companies is striking. The presence of a professional organization of gay workers, "High-Tech Gays," and the relatively gay-tolerant atmosphere of the San Francisco Bay area probably adds to the competitive pressure. But the competitive threat has been exercised: after the software company Ask/Ingres was acquired by Computer Associates, the Ask/Ingres employees lost their domestic partner benefits. Reports indicate that the loss of partner benefits led to the mass resignation of over two hundred Ask engineers (Gay/Lesbian/Bisexual Corporate Letter 1995).

However, this pattern also implies some possible limits to the pressure from competition. The industries are highly competitive in their product markets, and employers are profit-conscious. All six industries require the hiring and retaining of some highly skilled workers, who are relatively scarce and whose efforts are central to the business, such as attorneys and software engineers. In businesses in which the skills requirements are more flexible and perhaps easily met with training, or in situations in which there is a relative glut of employees, competitive pressures might not be terribly effective in promoting the spread of domestic partner benefits.

Another pattern—the acceleration of announcements by employers through the 1990s—suggests that other economic factors were also present. The acceleration is obvious. In their 1991 report, benefit consultants Hewitt Associates listed eleven public sector employers and five private sector employers that provided partner benefits. Only three years later, the 1994 report by the same company listed seventy private employers, 44 colleges and universities, and 43 public employers that offered some form of partner benefits. (And more names have been added to those lists since 1994.) The Human Rights Campaign list in 2000 shows 865 employers offering partner benefits.[11] The number of companies offering domestic partner benefits is increasing at an increasing rate.

Two economic factors likely contributed to the acceleration. The first factor, the business cycle's booms and busts, affects the labor market by decreasing or increasing the number of unemployed people who want a job but cannot find one. Higher unemployment makes it easier for companies to find qualified workers and also makes it less likely that employees will quit to look for another job. So employers would not need to make extra efforts to retain or attract current workers during a recession, since many available workers want jobs and have less bargaining power. Low unemployment rates mean that employers have to work harder to find and hold onto employees. In the early 1990s, a recession hit the U.S. economy about the time that employers began considering or hearing about domestic partner benefits. The recovery (which began in the second half of 1992 as measured by unemployment rate increases) and prolonged economic boom would have reinforced any competitive pressure already felt by employers and would have boosted the number of employers offering partner benefits. The unemployment rate fell as low as 3.9 percent in 2000, the lowest rate since 1970.

The second factor concerns the pressure of rising health care costs. In the mid-1990s the rapid rise in employers' health care costs slowed and even fell slightly (Walker and Bergman 1998, 21). This important trend is apparently the result of several factors, including cost containment measures such as managed care, slower increases in health care costs in general, shifts in costs to employees, and lower numbers of employees receiving health insurance (U.S. Department of Labor, BLS 1996). The broader trends for employers reduced the risk of a massive cost increase from offering domestic partner benefits, since early adopters of partner benefits did not know how much enrollment would increase.

For at least some industries, then, the competitive conditions were in place for encouraging companies to offer benefits to employees' domestic partners by the mid-1990s. Positive pressure from other firms and lessening negative pressure from the business cycle and rising health care costs increased the likelihood of changing benefits practices.

Conclusions and Public Policy Dimensions

Any one of those four major influences on the spread of partner benefits alone would probably not be sufficient. Without employee requests or organized pressure, employers might not realize that gay and lesbian employees see spousal benefits as violations of a company's nondiscrimination pledge. Without an equity norm or fears of lawsuits, employers might not be willing to risk higher compensation costs. Without competitive pressure, the only companies taking the plunge might be atypical companies with equity-conscious CEOs, and so on. The various forces that have shaped U.S. employers' provision of benefits throughout this century form a set of swirling currents that—depending on where in the river employers start out—carry some toward the partner benefit side of the shore while the others float down the river until encountering some new current, perhaps when lesbian and gay employees organize a committee to research and lobby for partner benefits.

My friends Donna and John, who were mentioned at the beginning of the chapter, work for a large state university that is currently considering offering benefits to employees' partners. Progress through the layers of decision-making has been slow in a large bureaucratic organization. This university's strong equity policy, its vocal and increasingly well-organized gay employees, and its competition for staff and faculty with other campuses are the forces pushing against the barriers revealed in the course of deliberation: lack of information, risk of cost increases, and normative objections.

Several situations could shift the speed of domestic partnership adoption considerably, although the likelihood of any one of them occurring is small or unknown. For instance, universal medical coverage for Americans through significant national health care reform would dramatically reduce the cost to employers of treating domestic partners like spouses in benefits. Cost concerns are a major barrier to employer action right now, and health care costs are the core issue. Depending on its structure, universal coverage could significantly reduce the number of partners signing up for health care benefits.

If employers' health care costs start rising rapidly again in the absence of broader health care reform, convincing more employers to add domestic partners might become more difficult. Of course, employers' health care cost trends are difficult to predict, and only some of the factors influencing costs are under employers' control. But even rapidly rising costs might not halt the spread of domestic partner benefits. Those adopting new policies face less uncertainty about the magnitude of cost increases, since the small increase in enrollment is now well documented.

Another possibility, discussed further in a later chapter, is that marriages of same-sex couples will be legalized. Gay and lesbian employees would then have access to employer benefits for partners by getting married. If this happens, the rapid adoption of partner benefits could come to a screeching halt since pressure from two of the major forces behind these efforts are likely to disappear: lesbian and gay employee groups and the equity norm. Employers could then treat gay employees equally by treating legal spouses of gay employees in the same way that legal spouses of heterosexual employees are treated. The remaining employees with nontraditional families or unmarried partners might still want access to spousal benefits, of course. But the driving force from gay employee groups is likely to diminish significantly if, as many expect, gay couples choose to marry. Right now, individual heterosexual allies are more visible and present in the debate over partner benefits than is an organized presence from heterosexuals with domestic partners, even though those with opposite-sex partners have the most to gain (Badgett 1994).

Short of those dramatic social and economic changes, other more incremental policy changes could influence the adoption of partner policies. As noted above, explicitly including benefits in sexual orientation nondiscrimination laws would clearly put pressure on employers. Changing federal tax policies to exclude employers' subsidies of partner benefits from employees' taxable income would ease the way. Changing the allowable definitions of family in state insurance regulations and in federal laws regulating pensions would remove yet another policy barrier. Chapter 8 takes up policy considerations in more detail.

Even without such changes, the story of the spread of domestic partner benefits demonstrates the flexibility of employment compensation systems to respond to changing employee needs and pressures. Events of the 1990s have opened up both strategies and tactics for fighting workplace discrimination against gay employees, showing that discrimination can still be rooted out directly: if employers have the will, there's a way.

FIVE

Queer Conspicuous Consumption

There's one Traveler's Cheque for couples who sometimes see the world a bit differently.

Ad in *10 Percent*

Just out. There's a great vodka out on the shelf. . . . So no matter what label you're used to, join the growing crowd that has switched to SKYY Vodka, the Ultra Premium choice.

Ad in *10 Percent*

Yes-Man. Battle-Ax. Gold Digger. Gigolo. Black Sheep. Dumb Blonde. Girl-Next-Door. Labels belong on beer, not people. Bud Light.

Ad in *OUT,* June 1996

We've been together about three years. . . . This table included a leaf. A leaf means . . . staying together, commitment. We've got another leaf waiting when we really start getting along.

Two men in an Ikea television commercial, 1994

Readers of lesbian and gay-oriented magazines are getting used to advertisements from mainstream companies like the ones above, even though the appearance of these ads in gay publications is a fairly recent phenomenon. More recently, ads for toothpaste and pet food have appeared (Wilke 1998). Every now and then gay-themed ads show up in mainstream media, much to the surprise and delight of gay viewers, such as the Ikea ad showing two men discussing their relationship while shopping for a dining room table. (That ad was shown only after 10 P.M.) Other ads designed to appeal to gay consumers, like homoerotic Calvin Klein men's underwear ads or ads for butch and androgynous clothing styles for women, also appear in magazines and billboards viewed by heterosexual as well as homosexual consumers.

To some enthusiastic observers, this "gay marketing moment," as Amy Gluckman and Betsy Reed have dubbed it (Gluckman and Reed 1997), represents a "marketplace revolution" that will affect "corporate hiring practices in the workplace and even the commercial buying habits of heterosexual Americans" (Lukenbill 1995, 1). Other less enthusiastic observers worry that the new marketing trend will instead splinter or depoliticize the lesbian, gay, and bisexual community (Vaid 1995; Hyman 1995). Interest in the gay market has fueled the myth of conspicuous consumption, drawing attention to this economic side of gay and lesbian lives and often overshadowing attention to economic inequality faced by gay people.

Just as companies have begun to offer domestic partner benefits to employees as part of a complex but observable process involving economic, political, and ideological change, the apparently sudden corporate interest in the buying habits of gay and lesbian Americans is also not a mystery. The story is more complicated than the myth of conspicuous consumption would suggest, however, and the true novelty might instead be conspicuous marketing. In the twentieth century in particular, commercial institutions both within and outside the gay community have been integral in the development of a gay identity and community in the United States. This latest stage of commercialization is the result of a complex interaction between market forces, corporate marketing practices, gay collective action, less homophobic public policies, and the rise of the "professional homosexual."

A quick perusal of glossy gay magazines and many local gay newspapers provides convincing evidence that the current gay marketing moment is real. A closer look at the selling of the gay market in the third section of this chapter, however, reveals a shaky foundation of myths and incomplete information about gay people's economic power, buying habits, and household structures. In fact, the latest incarnation of the myth of affluence grew out of the gay marketing phenomenon. Put high incomes together with the assumption that gay people have few economic worries or dependents, and the DINK myth—double income no kids—emerges to further entice marketers. But as chapter 2 discussed and chapter 6 will further develop, the best available data on the demographics and economic status of gay people cast serious doubt on these myths, especially for lesbians. Exactly how much the gay market differs from the larger heterosexual market is still unclear.

Other tough questions ask what these marketing efforts mean. Is the marketing equally directed at gay men and lesbians? Can the "moment" be sustained if the gay population is shown to be basically similar to the heterosexual market in terms of family structure and incomes? Are the implications of the marketing attention positive or negative for gay people's lives? Will marketing to the gay community reduce workplace discrimination, introduce heterosexual consumers to more positive images of gay people, and provide financial support for gay media, organizations, and events? This chapter closes with speculation on the implications of the gay marketing efforts.

From Closet Consumption to Conspicuous Consumption

Where did the "gay marketing moment" come from? Economists view companies as profit-driven entities, constantly acting on opportunities to increase their profits. Logically, then, if money is to be made in marketing to the gay community, companies should do it, especially if markets are free enough from government regulation to allow companies to respond to profitable opportunities. Since the economy of the United States has been one of the least regulated modern economies, one might ask why it took so long for companies to begin to see the available opportunities in the gay, lesbian, and bisexual communities.

As many observers have noted, the historical emergence of a common identity and social movement among gay men and lesbians in the United States has long been related to commercial businesses, such as bars, bathhouses, and bookstores (Altman 1982; Chauncey 1994; D'Emilio 1984; Evans 1993; Peñaloza 1996; Vaid 1995). Such developments did not take place in a completely unfettered market situation, however, and government actions and reactions slowed the early growth of goods and services designed primarily for gay people. Developing social movements and political gains, in turn, affected the relationship of gay and lesbian people to the market (Peñaloza 1996; Evans 1993; Lukenbill 1995).

Using economic analysis to connect the theoretical insights of Altman, Evans, and Peñaloza on the relationship of markets to gay identity with the historical evidence offered by John D'Emilio, Lillian Faderman, George Chauncey, and others allows the sketching out of the development of the modern "gay market." The gay market has not suddenly burst on the scene; rather, the long-existing gay marketplace has developed gradually, becoming much more visible in an economic climate of heightened competition and insecurity. The developments influencing its increasing visibility include the growing corporate segmentation of consumer markets, the emergence of a "professional homosexual" sector, the development of women's economic power, and a national political environment of vocal debate over the issue of civil rights for lesbian, gay, and bisexual people.

George Chauncey's account of the early development of New York City's gay male world from the late nineteenth century through the Depression reveals the influence of market competition and legal forces in shaping gay men's lives and their commercial institutions. Chauncey argues that this early phase of gay male visibility in New York was characterized by the relative integration of gay men in larger social venues. New York's size and its social and economic complexity also allowed—encouraged, even—the creation of commercial spaces for gay men's social activities, some of which were more integrated than others. In some ways, the development of commercial gay or gay-tolerant spaces uncovered by Chauncey reflected an early form of "niche marketing." Attracting gay male customers was a profitable strategy for what we would now consider small business owners (who were generally heterosexual) of rooming houses, restaurants, public baths, bars, and large community balls. Not only were gay men a source of customers, but in some cases they attracted heterosexual customers interested in the spectacle of gay men socializing or appearing in drag.

Chauncey notes a sharp shift in state regulation of social settings through the first half of the century that influenced the size and number of gay-tolerant commercial institutions. Starting with World War I and continuing through the 1920s, private social purity societies monitored what they considered to be a reprehensible situation in the bars and public baths catering to gay men. The efforts to raid and close those establishments were not, apparently, initiated by the local police in this period but were prompted by the private societies. In response to a perceived subversion of legal authority in New York City during the Prohibition era, though, the state began its own stringent regulation of conduct in bars following the repeal of Prohibition. The new State Liquor Authority (SLA) was authorized to issue liquor licenses and was expected to revoke the licenses of establishments that served homosexuals and other groups considered disreputable, such as prostitutes and gamblers. The SLA used its authority to target gay bars systematically, and gay bars opening in New York from the 1930s through the 1960s had to resort to police payoffs and protection from organized crime to avoid the common fate of license revocation. Many regular bar owners would not risk their licenses by tolerating visibly gay customers, pushing gay men into more exclusively gay social settings (Chauncey 1994, 358). In other words, the segregation that now exists between heterosexual and gay commercial social venues has its roots in this period.

As the modern U.S. gay and lesbian identity developed, this next wave of commercial institutions assumed an important role. Historians John D'Emilio and Lillian Faderman as well as journalist Randy Shilts point out the importance of bars as a relatively safe space for socializing and meeting potential partners. For both gay men and lesbians, bringing their homosexuality into a public place meant that "the bars were seedbeds for a collective consciousness that might one day flower politically" (D'Emilio 1984, 33). In a sense, gay bars were products targeted directly at gay people, since heterosexuals, presumably, would have a much lower relative demand for buying a drink in the company of homosexuals. Of course, men's greater economic power and fewer social constraints in public life in general and bar life in particular are reasons why gay men's bars far outnumbered bars catering to lesbians, and bars were mixed in cities where lesbians could not economically support their own bars (D'Emilio 1984, 98). The gender differences in this first stage of the gay market or "closet economy," as Jeffrey Escoffier calls this era, arose from the different economic and social position of women in U.S. society and have been reproduced in one form or another throughout the subsequent development of the gay market (Escoffier 1997).

Until the 1960s, the expansion of these public sites of gay consumption and identity formation was limited by police harassment, practices of extortion, laws against homosexual sodomy, and pressure from liquor control boards. Customers risked arrest during frequent police raids, preventing growth in demand of the bars' customer base and curtailing further investment by capitalists. Bar owners had added costs in police payoffs or in legal fees—either their own or those incurred on behalf of their clients. D'Emilio reports that the owner of the Black Cat, a San Francisco bar with a largely gay male clientele, fought attempts to revoke his liquor license, a fight that cost the owner over $38,000 in legal fees in the 1950s (D'Emilio 1984, 187). The Tavern Guild, a group of gay bar owners in San Francisco, paid for legal help for those arrested in or near gay bars (189).

Gay men and lesbians began to fight back against police repression in the 1950s, organizing local efforts to persuade the police to cease its raids of bars and harassment of gay people. Although harassment continued to be a problem in various cities for quite a while, in New York and San Francisco, at least, public pressure reduced it to a low enough level in the mid-1960s to encourage a flourishing of gay bars, which increased in number from fewer than twenty in San Francisco in 1963 to fifty-seven only five years later (D'Emilio 1984, 203). There was a similar response to a declining number of raids and liquor license revocations in New York (208). Gay Chicago entrepreneur Chuck Renslow attributed the rapid growth in that city's bar population to Illinois becoming the first state to drop its sodomy prohibition in 1961 (Shilts 1976, 37).

The development and distribution of other products designed for gay people, such as newspapers, magazines, books, and pornography—all contributions to the development of collective gay and lesbian identities—were also hindered by repressive government regulation and antigay attitudes. In the first half of the century, references to homosexuality, even without any overtly sexual content, were enough to deem books or magazines about gay life objectionable (D'Emilio 1984, 131). The FBI harassed and investigated magazine staffs. The Postal Service delayed mailings. Finally, U.S. Supreme Court decisions in the 1950s and 1960s lowered the legal barriers to producing and purchasing sexually explicit materials. A key decision in 1958 reversed a lower court ruling that *ONE* magazine, published by the Los Angeles–based homophile group ONE, Inc., was obscene and subject to seizure by postal authorities (D'Emilio 1984, 134, 115). D'Emilio concludes that this loosening of regulation contributed to the rapid increase in offerings of fiction and nonfiction to gay and lesbian consumers and of pornography to gay men.

But although government pressure eased for the emerging gay press, business pressures did not. Rodger Streitmatter (1995) reports that the earliest gay and lesbian publications, *ONE, The Mattachine Review,* and *The Ladder,* regularly teetered on the edge of financial collapse. Newsstand reluctance to carry gay publications limited sales, so these publications relied on bar sales, membership dues, and out-of-pocket contributions (often by the staff) to publish. Businesses were afraid to advertise for fear of being identified with homosexuality, even when their customers were gay or lesbian (Streitmatter 1995, 29). *ONE*'s very first ad in 1954 for men's pajamas and underwear generated controversy because of its "suggestive" nature, although fifteen years later this ad would have seemed quite tame. *The Ladder,* a magazine for lesbians, surveyed its readers in 1958 and, like much more recent readership surveys, found their readers' income to be triple that of the average female worker. Despite a readership that should have been attractive to advertisers seeking high-income women, *The Ladder* was never able to attract sufficient advertisers, and closed in 1972 (Streitmatter 1995, 152). By the end of the 1950s, the total circulation of all three magazines was only 6,700 (28).

Thus even during the early development of a gay political and social consciousness in the United States, government regulation directly influenced the market's response to profit-making opportunities in the lesbian and gay communities by increasing risk and costs and—in the case of the gay press—indirectly, by making potential advertisers nervous. From a more theoretical perspective, David Evans argues that the state has the power to limit access by sexual minorities to markets, providing the opportunity to later increase access through

> the legalization of previously illegal and thus non-consuming sexual status groups, for example, most spectacularly, male homosexuals, thus "releasing" considerable consumer power and enabling the development of considerable specific minority commodity markets. (Evans 1993, 51)

In practice, this state power is probably overstated by Evans. Presumably he did not mean that lesbians and gay men were literally nonconsuming, since like heterosexuals, homosexuals spent their incomes on life's necessities. At least some goods and services existed specifically for gay men and lesbians in the commercialized gay culture found prior to the loosening of state limitations on gay life.

An example of the state-influenced dynamic suggested by Evans might be the early stages of opening up a commercial space for gays and lesbians in the United States. Only Illinois had repealed its sodomy law outlawing same-sex sexual acts before the 1970s, however, suggesting that the economic space carved out in the 1960s in the United States did not result from a legalization of gay sexuality per se. Instead, the key policy factors in the United States were effective political pressure on police departments and, apparently, a judicial willingness to sever the equation between being homosexual and the committing of "immoral acts," an equation that had allowed police raids and bar closings under existing liquor laws (see *One Eleven Wines & Liquors, Inc. v. Division of Alcoholic Beverage Control* in Rubenstein [1993], 203).

The economic space created for gays and lesbians widened considerably in the late 1960s and 1970s. Not only the did the post-Stonewall surge of gay political organizing preserve and extend commercial space for bars and the gay press, but other events of the 1960s helped to create the conditions for the growth of gay markets. Economic growth plus an increasingly "sexualized society," in the words of D'Emilio and Freedman (1988, 326), provided the backdrop for what Escoffier calls the "liberation economy" (Esoffier 1997, 123).

In this stage of lesbian and gay economic history, gender divergence was pronounced, a pattern ignored by most writers commenting on the development of the "gay" economy (Hyman 1995). Lesbian feminists became the most visible subgroup of lesbians. Influenced by the emerging women's movement, lesbians created new economic and cultural institutions run by and for women, often collectively. Streitmatter counts roughly fifty lesbian publications in 1975 with a total circulation of about 50,000 (the largest publication had a circulation of 9,000), and many of these publications were run by collectives (Streitmatter 1995, 158). Many did not last long, either as publications or as collectives, and financing continued to be a problem for publications with few advertisers other than lesbian-owned bookstores and businesses. Other projects included books, bookstores, record companies, presses, music festivals, food co-ops, health clinics, and child care centers, and lesbians "dreamt grandiosely about multiplying their institutions all over the country so that their values would eventually predominate" (Faderman 1991, 219). Lillian Faderman notes that

> The creation of economic institutions that would lead to financial in-
> dependence was considered particularly crucial to the blueprint for a
> lesbian-feminist community. Such independence was necessary so
> that lesbian-feminists would not have to fear that they would lose
> their livelihood because they "came out." (Faderman 1991, 219)

Consumption of these new products was only half the point. Lesbian production of these products and services was obviously equally important,
given lesbian feminists' concern with financial independence and a more
democratic organization of production.

In contrast, consumerism flourished for gay men. The liberation economy involved an increasing "commodification" of sex in the context of
bathhouses and bars, as well as in growing markets for sexual products
such as sex toys. By 1976, the 2,500 gay bars and 150 bathhouses employed in the United States a workforce of roughly 15,000 people and generated over $118 million per year in revenues (Shilts 1976, 37). Gay en-
trepreneurs created bathhouse dynasties. Jack Campbell's served over a
quarter million members in thirty-six clubs in the United States and Canada
by 1976 (Stone 1976, 41). These businesses appeared to be highly profitable, with profit margins estimated as much as 40 percent for discos and
30-35 percent for the baths (Shilts 1976, 37-38). Dennis Altman argues
that the commodification of gay male sex was a logical outgrowth of consumer capitalism and its emphasis on immediate gratification: "going to
the baths to have sex represents an integration of sexuality into consumerism in a way that encounters in parks or on the streets do not" (Altman 1982, 82).

For David Evans, the development was more complex, involving legal
advances that created a space that "has subsequently largely become one
through which self-preoccupied individuals pass, commodified and de-
politicized." (Evans 1993, 90) The repeal of sodomy laws in twenty-one
states from 1970 to 1980[1] may have facilitated the liberation consumer
boom for gay men, even if sodomy repeal did not start the boom. The risks
that worried bar owners in the 1970s were less likely to be legal and more
likely to be related to a fickle customer base and competition from other
gay bars (Shilts 1976, 37). But in addition to competition, bath owners
still faced police raids in the 1970s that increased investors' risk and often

resulted in legal fees for the bathhouse and for customers. These legal problems and ongoing social stigma limited bathhouse investors' access to bank credit (Shilts 1976, 38).

Newspapers, magazines, and bookstores catering to gay men also developed, but Evans claims that many of those publications were closely related to the commercialization of sex:

> Although social and counseling aspects of the movement were to grow considerably in the 1970s, the bulk of gay interest was in the dissemination of information about subcultural venues of various kinds, and the prerequisites of the specific homosexual lifestyles for which they catered. (Evans 1993, 101)

Although some of the gay male publications were concerned with political issues, many became cultural magazines appealing to more affluent gay men in big cities. In fact, the origins of the current marketing wave were evident in the early days of this phase of the gay economy.

The first known survey of the gay market was research conducted for *The Advocate* in 1968 (Lukenbill 1995, 54). In 1981, a large ad in the *New York Times* touted the high incomes and consumer loyalty of *Advocate* readers ("Gay Buying Power Is Serious Business," 26 May 1981). National magazines catering mainly to gay men, like *The Advocate* and *After Dark,* carried ads for major companies such as RCA Records, MGM, Columbia Pictures, Carnegie Hall, Avon Books, and liquor companies. Budget Rent-a-Car urged *Advocate* readers to "Pick up a hot number in San Francisco—Datsun 280ZX, Camaro Z28, Mazda RX-7" (*The Advocate,* 26 July 1979). Howard Buford points out that liquor and cigarette companies, in particular, were risking little by advertising in gay publications, since those products were already "morally suspect" by antigay conservatives (Buford 2000, 27). Even more important for the financial health of gay publications were ads for bars, bathhouses, and sexual contacts (Anderson 1979, 19). These ads fostered the growth of publications, and gay publications returned the favor by promoting advertisers in their editorial content (Streitmatter 1995, 193). The three hundred gay publications in business in 1975 had a total circulation of 200,000. In 1976, *The Advocate*'s circulation of 60,000 surpassed the total for all lesbian publications, and by 1979 *The Advocate* was a profitable operation (Streitmatter 1995, 188).

The divergence between the economic development of lesbians and gay men raises important issues. For both gay men and lesbians, the products of the liberation economy were parallel to those offered to heterosexuals but were tailored to the needs of lesbians or gay men. And in some cases, gay men's products appeared similar in form to lesbians' products, such as books or newspapers. The similarity ends there, though. In gay men's emphasis on consumption of products related to sex, we see the preconditions of the more recent gay marketing moment: a consumer ethos (or at least habits) related to sexual orientation, relatively apolitical venues in which products could be peddled, and a taste for new products. In the lesbian-feminist emphasis on the means (nonhierarchical, democratic production) as well as the ends (consumption of products), we see something rather different. Why did this gender difference emerge?

The answer appears to be partly economic and partly political. In the 1970s, middle-class gay white men were increasingly free to spend their money on whatever they wanted to buy, whether that was admission to the baths or the latest gay "clone" outfit. But in the 1970s lesbians still had to worry about *earning* money in a labor market that reserved well-paying jobs for men, and creating a significant market for new products required visible and sizable economic resources that lesbians as a group were unlikely to have.

The economic space created for lesbians in the 1970s came not from being freed from the fear of bar raids but from the gains of the women's movement. Increased legal protection against sex discrimination from the Equal Pay Act of 1963 and the Civil Rights Act of 1964 were essential preconditions for lesbians' economic advances, but the wage gap did not show clear evidence of decline until the 1970's (Blau 1998). In 1971, the median annual income of a woman working full-time was $18,558, 59 percent of the median for men (Council of Economic Advisors 1994). The gap has been gradually closing, and in 1998 women earned 74 percent of men's income, which might help to explain increasing interest in the lesbian market.

For political reasons, lesbian feminists did not pursue the kind of commodified sexual world of gay men. Streitmatter's comparison of lesbian and gay male publications finds a big gender split in interpretation of the role of sexual freedom: "Many men wanted the movement to endorse orgies and promiscuity; many women preferred only that the movement sanction same-sex relationships" (Streitmatter 1995, 140). And while lesbians shared gay men's suspicion of monogamy, it was bad "not because it inhibited wild sexual exploration, but rather because it smacked too much of patriarchal capitalism and imperialism" (Faderman 1991, 233). Faderman points out the disagreement that many lesbian-feminists had with gay men's "dominant-submissive modes of sexual relating and their separation of sex from emotional involvement" (211). Over time, lesbian sexuality developed a more public and commercial component, though. In the wake of the so-called "Sex Wars" of the 1980s—when some lesbians challenged the cultural feminist denouncement of pornography, sadomasochistic sex, and butch/femme roles (Faderman 1995, 253)—new products such as lesbian sex magazines (such as *On Our Backs),* lesbian porn videos, lesbian phone sex, lesbian-produced sex toys, and even an occasional lesbian sex club began to appear. The future growth of these new markets for lesbian sex is difficult to predict, but they seem unlikely to reach the size of gay men's sex institutions, even with additional marketing of some products to heterosexual women.

Of greater economic (and political, personal, and cultural) significance in the 1980s, of course, was the HIV/AIDS epidemic, which brought lesbians and gay men into political alliances and began a new economic phase for the still rapidly growing lesbian and gay economy. The human cost of the epidemic cannot be adequately calculated in dollars. The mobilization of lesbian and gay money, time, and love to fight the epidemic and the initial public indifference that exacerbated it, though, has had a lasting economic impact on the lesbian and gay communities.

Perhaps the two most general effects are the joining of lesbians and gay men in the fight against AIDS and the heightened visibility of lesbian, gay, and bisexual people in the United States. A right-wing backlash against gay visibility and gay political success in the late 1970s had begun a gender reunification of the gay political movement. Even though AIDS was at first seen as mainly a gay men's issue, lesbians flocked to the cause (Schwartz 1993; Schneider 1992; Vaid 1995). Vaid and others describe how both the deaths of over 200,000 gay or bisexual men from AIDS since 1981 and the media campaigns directed at the public and policymakers dramatically increased gay visibility (Vaid 1995, 81).

Internally, the need to provide health care and other services to people living with AIDS and the need to fight policy battles required a massive mobilization of gay dollars and labor. Numerous institutions were created to fight the epidemic's battles with volunteers as well as paid staff. National lesbian and gay organizations added staff to address this new issue, too.

Along the way, several things happened. First, the creation of paid staff positions meant that more and more people could make a living working within the gay community in institutions run by and for gay people (Schwartz 1993). Second, the ongoing and daunting fundraising and volunteer needs for AIDS-related causes led to the development of many strategies for wooing donors and volunteers, many of whom would not have given time or money to an explicitly gay cause (Vaid 1995, 77; Kayal

1993). Organizations learned how to find gay donors and how to keep track of them.

Politically, one important part of the response to public homophobia and concern surrounding the epidemic was the "desexualization" of gay men. As government officials tried to close bathhouses and to change gay men's sexual practices, gay leaders sought a way to preserve some sense of the sexual freedom won by gay men while responding to the epidemic.

> The mainstream gay and AIDS movements devised a complex re-
> sponse: distancing itself from the sexual liberation ethic of the seven-
> ties, while at the same time developing new ways to talk about sexual
> practices and transmission (media ads, safer sex workshops, videos,
> posters, and countless other campaigns). (Vaid 1995, 85)

Economically, Evans notes, gay male leisure and the gay economy was desexualized, with declining numbers of bathhouses, escort agencies, and backrooms (Evans 1993, 107; see also Vandervelden, Freiberg, and Walter 1987). Gay male leisure products appeared to shift toward "gym member-ships, vitamins and health care, home entertainment (CD players, videos, home computers, etc.), food, fashion, and travel" (Evans 1993, 105), prod-ucts often produced by more mainstream companies. Sexual commodities had not disappeared entirely, but they had shifted toward those involving safer sex, such as phone sex, and less obvious sexual content, such as tours organized around erotic interests (Vandervelden et al. 1987). The other key sector of the gay economy—the press—continued to grow, as circulation of all gay and lesbian publications roughly doubled over the 1980s to top one million (Streitmatter 1995).

Other products marketed during this period were specifically targeted at HIV-infected people and people with AIDS, especially health care–related products and services. For instance, Burroughs Wellcome spent $25 mil-lion on advertising to convince people to use AZT, targeting ads in gay publications and in gay neighborhoods (Lukenbill 1995, 9). A new prod-uct was invented called "viatical settlements," in which companies buy life insurance policies—at a discount, of course—from people with AIDS whose doctors will certify them as terminally ill. In the 28 May 1996, issue of *The Advocate*, fifteen different companies advertised such offers.

With what Escoffier calls the "AIDS economy," a stage of gay economic history that is obviously not over yet, the setting for queer conspicuous consumption was complete. First, at least partly as a result of the AIDS epi-demic, gay people and the gay market had become visible to the rest of America, including corporate America, in an unprecedented way. The gay and lesbian social movement helped to create an identity that marketers could identify (Peñaloza 1996). Enhanced visibility from political victories in adding sexual orientation to nondiscrimination laws in many cities and a handful of states may have also helped draw many gay men and lesbians out of the closet at work, as chapter 3 implies. And, of course, the conservative backlash against gay people's efforts to win equal rights has kept gay people on the front pages of U.S. newspapers.

Second, some lesbian and gay media were ready to wean themselves from their dependence on sexually oriented advertising revenue that turned off mainstream potential advertisers. Before 1990, Grant Lukenbill points out, all gay magazines accepted such ads, which accounted for half of the billings of Rivendell Marketing, one marketing firm specializing in gay media (Lukenbill 1995, 163). Now, some magazines like *Out* accept no such ads, and others like *The Advocate* have placed them in a separate publication.

Third, openly gay people like Sean Strub, Lukenbill, Buford, Stephanie Blackwood, and others developed expertise in finding and appealing to the gay market. These "professional homosexuals" provided a crucial connection between the gay community and corporate marketers. Both human capital and marketing technologies are important here. Some marketers worry about the identifiability and accessibility of the gay market (Fugate 1993), but Peñaloza has pointed out that at least some gay consumers are willing to identify themselves to surveyors and marketers, and new marketing techniques have made gay consumers much more accessible. Strub revolutionized gay organizations' fundraising through direct mail campaigns, and his company has amassed a mailing list of over three quarters of a million people who have purchased from or donated to some gay-related business or cause (Metamorphics Media 1999). Strub noted that in the 1980s few lists of the gay market were available, but by 1995 over fifty were available, with more added every week:

> Now marketers can choose from many lists of subscribers, merchandise buyers, opportunity seekers, donors, cardpacks, package inserts, ride-a-long programs and more. Maintenance of these lists and targeting of these alternative media vehicles have improved substantially, enabling more sophisticated segmentation and greater deliverability. (Strub 1995)

More recently, the development of the Internet has added a powerful way to reach gay consumers in a relatively private medium.

Finally, a relatively mild recession in the early 1990s might have also enhanced the attractiveness of the gay market (Strub 1995), as companies searched for new sources of revenue in a slack sales period. Companies had created the teenager market in the 1950s, the women's and black market in the 1970s, and the Latino market in the 1980s (Peñaloza, 1996). The selling of the "gay market" was ready to hit the big time. Companies began to market their very mainstream products—liquor, clothing, cars—to lesbian and gay men.

"Gay Market Muscle" or Gay Market Hustle?

A lot of effort goes into selling the "gay market" in the most recent phase of the gay consumer economy. Lukenbill counts over twenty-five marketing, advertising, and public relations firms specializing in selling to lesbians and gay men in the mid-1990s (Lukenbill 1995, 170). Before they can offer services, though, these firms must convince companies that the gay market is worth the investment. The theoretical and empirical basis for selling the gay market is worth examining closely.

The idea behind the "gay market" is that companies can somehow distinguish between different groups of consumers that have different demands for products and services (Dickson and Ginter 1987). Marketers call this differentiation between groups "market segmentation," which has been the basis for marketing strategies for decades. A related concept is "product differentiation" when consumers perceive differences in important characteristics between brands of a similar product, as when one variety of toothpaste is perceived to taste better than another. These two characteristics of a market allow for a variety of marketing *strategies* for a company: trying to convince consumers that the company's product is really different from its competitors' (for example, toothpaste X tastes better than Y); trying to change the relationship between product qualities and the consumer's demand for a product (for example, promoting the idea that plaque-fighting ability is an important toothpaste quality); or trying to create a segment of consumers by changing a group's perceptions of the importance of a particular product characteristic (for example, convincing young single people that toothpaste Y is better at freshening breath). Companies might use strategies based on either segmentation or product differentiation to gain a sales and profit advantage in a market.

Identifying market segments has become a big business for market research firms. Segments are sometimes identified along demographic lines, such as age, gender, race, or ethnicity (Assael 1981). Other "psychographic" lines used to segment markets require analyzing consumers' lifestyles (i.e., their activities, interests, and opinions) or their personalities (more deeply rooted behavioral patterns). As a result of the search for the most profitable marketing strategies, we see marketing and ad campaigns aimed at women, teenagers, yuppies, and Latinos, for instance.

To illustrate how market segmentation could be important to a company's efforts to increase sales, leave aside the issue of advertising for the moment and consider how demand for, say, a bottle of a particular upscale brand of liquor called *Ecohol* might vary between groups. The standard economic story behind differences in product demand is that consumers' tastes for a particular product (or its particular attributes) might vary or consumers' incomes might vary. If tastes and incomes are similar within definable groups, then we might be able to distinguish groups' demand rather than looking at individuals' demand for the liquor. In other words, at a given price, groups with certain strong preferences or lots of income will demand more bottles of *Ecohol* than those with weak preferences or less income.

Maybe attending college encourages people to learn to prefer liquor of high quality. If *Ecohol* is known for its high quality relative to other brands, then college graduates might have a stronger preference for *Ecohol,* even if it costs a bit more than other brands. Liquor is not an essential item like food, clothing, or shelter and is likely to be bought with discretionary income leftover after buying essentials. Therefore, people with higher incomes are also likely to demand more *Ecohol* than would people with lower incomes. Finally, since college graduates tend to earn more than others in the United States and have a stronger preference for high-quality liquor, they would seem to be an ideal group to target in a marketing campaign for *Ecohol.*

Other factors like family structure might also matter in identifying groups. Discretionary income—the money leftover after paying for basic life expenses—depends on the number of people supported by a household income. A family with an income of $30,000 and no kids will have more to spend on liquor than a family with $30,000 and two kids, since kids can be expensive. Many marketers consider the family to be the biggest influence on consumer behavior (Michman 1991).

Obviously, we aren't born with a taste for *Ecohol,* or perhaps for any liquor. Economists are not particularly good at explaining how or why individuals develop certain tastes. Social, cultural, and maybe even biological considerations are likely to be important. Also, put advertising back into the picture. Advertising is both designed to influence people's tastes (changing their demand curves) and to match people who have certain tastes with a product meeting those requirements (a product differentiation strategy). If college graduates are status conscious, then an ad campaign emphasizing quality and exclusivity (another product differentiation strategy) might make *Ecohol* seem particularly attractive to college graduates.

Should we target the gay market in our efforts to sell *Ecohol?* According to some marketing companies, the answer is clearly "yes" if we want to maximize our profits. The strategy would make sense under certain conditions: If gay people have a different demand curve for *Ecohol* than do other consumer groups; or if gay people prefer certain characteristics of liquor that *Ecohol* possesses; or if gay people are more easily convinced to value a particular characteristic of *Ecohol;* or even if only an affluent and amenable subgroup of gay people can be identified, then we might, in fact, want to target the gay market—if that is feasible.

Some marketing firms publicize the results of surveys summarized in table 9 that show the average gay man's or lesbian's household has a much higher income than the typical U.S. household. Even marketers who do not think gays earn more than heterosexuals argue that gay people will have more discretionary income since they have fewer children to pay for (Strub 1995). Plus, some gay people go to bars a lot, perhaps suggesting a relatively strong preference for liquor. Others suggest that gay people might be especially brand-loyal if we market *Ecohol* in the right way (Lukenbill 1995). Before shifting marketing dollars and effort to target gays and lesbians, though, it would be prudent for a company to consider carefully these underlying claims by marketers who have a vested interest in selling ad space in gay magazines or other marketing services.

It is certainly possible that lesbian and gay people could have very different demand curves than heterosexuals. That is, the relationship between product characteristics, including price, and the quantity desired at a particular price might vary according to sexual orientation. We might see differences between gays and heterosexuals for several reasons: different incomes, different household structures, or different product tastes.

Income and Household Structure. The income issue and the claim about the affluence of the gay market have been analyzed above. Chapter 2 describes how some marketing surveys have enhanced the myth of gay affluence. As that chapter notes, the findings of affluence are not applicable to gay people in general since the methods used were likely to seek out and attract high-income people, resulting in a biased sample. The Simmons Market Research Bureau survey, for instance, sought out gay men and lesbians by placing surveys in gay newspapers and magazines. Overlooked Opinions surveyed lesbians and gay men from various sources, including those attending the 1993 March on Washington, who are likely

Table 9 Gay Income Data from Nonrandom Samples

Survey	Year	L/G/B Household Income	U.S. Household Income
(1) Overlooked Opinions	1991	42,689 (gay men) 36,072 (lesbians)	30,126
(2) Overlooked Opinions	1991	51,325 (gay men) 45,927 (lesbians)	36,520
(3) Simmons Marketing Research Bureau	1988	55,430	32,144

Note: "U.S. Household Income" from each source.

Sources: (1) Cronin (1993); (2) Courier News, 1 Dec. 1991; (3) Rigdon (1991); M. Gravois (1991, personal communication).

to have higher incomes to afford the travel and accommodations expenses involved in attending the march. To put it simply, if a survey targets the high-income end of the gay population, any sample of that subgroup will show the high average incomes seen in table 9.

As with the comparison of gay and straight people's *individual* incomes in chapter 2, comparisons of household incomes and structures used in marketing efforts may also be misleading. The overall picture of gay household income turns out to be quite different in tables 10 and 11. As shown in chapter 2, individual gay men tend to earn *less* on average than individual heterosexual men. Individual lesbians appear to earn somewhat more than heterosexual women, perhaps because of more job experience and a greater commitment to the labor force, but lesbians still earn less than either gay men or heterosexual men. Variation in household income primarily stems from differences in the gender composition of households. In the 1990 Census data, households with two male earners earn more on average than do married couples or lesbian couples simply because men typically earn 25–30 percent more than women do. Households with two women earn less than either two men or a male-female couple. And even the male couples' advantage disappears in more detailed comparisons, however (Klawitter and Flatt 1998). Both the Yankelovich Monitor and voter exit polls, which lump together different household structures, find lower incomes for gay and lesbian households or families.

Overall, the more reliable household income figures suggest that gay households are *not* more affluent than heterosexual households. The total income comparison is less important from the perspective of some markets than is discretionary income. Having fewer dependents would mean gay people have more money to spend on themselves. Marketers pushing the DINK stereotype show a clear awareness of some aspects of gay family

Table 10 Average Incomes in Random Samples

General Social Survey		Individual Earnings (dollars)
L/G/B	Male	25,278
	Female	21,248
Heterosexual	Male	28,642
	Female	19,514

1990 Census of Population		Incomes of Couples
L/G/B	Male	58,366
	Female	45,166
Heterosexual (married)		47,193

Yankelovich MONITOR		Incomes of Households
L/G	Male	37,400
	Female	34,800
Heterosexual	Male	39,300
	Female	

Note: For couples and households, figures represent all household income; for individuals, figures represent earnings.

Sources: General Social Survey (1989–96): Black et al. (1998); 1990 Census: Klawitter and Flatt (1998); Yankelovich: Lukenbill (1995).

life—forming committed and economically interdependent couples—while downplaying other aspects, such as raising children:

> But, gay people don't make more than their non-gay peers. However, gays and lesbians are far less likely to have children or a non-employed spouse, but are many more times likely to be living in a $100,000/year dual income household and their discretionary income is higher. (Strub 1995)

> Two lifestyle facts in particular account for much of the difference in the community's patterns of consumption: higher discretionary income and more disposable income. (Buford 2000, 26)

> The gay and lesbian market is an untapped goldmine. Because gays are highly educated and usually have no dependents, they have high levels of disposable income. (Kahan and Mulryan 1995, 41)

At first glance, this seems obvious: same-sex couples will have a harder time adopting or conceiving a child than will heterosexual couples, even if their desire to raise children is equal. But as chapter 6 will show, once again, the typical gay market survey of newspaper readers or some other

Table 11 Income Data from Voter Exit Polls (percentage)

| | 1992 | | | | 1996 | |
Family income	Gay Men	All Men	Lesbians	All Women	Gay Men and Lesbians	Heterosexual Men and Women
Less than $15,000	18	12	26	16	20	12
$15,000–30,000	26	23	26	25	31	24
$30,000–50,000	28	30	29	29	24	27
$50,000–75,000	16	20	12	19	12	20
More than $75,000	12	14	6	11		
$75,000–99,999					6	6
Over $100,000					6	8

Sources: Cronin (1993); Bailey (1998).

selected group of gay people draws a misleading image of how many gay men and lesbians are involved in raising children. Three studies show that lesbians are quite likely to be parents and to have children in their households, with two of the three studies finding that lesbians are just as likely as heterosexual women to be living with children or parenting. Gay men are much less likely to be raising children than are heterosexual men, though.

On their face, these findings have important implications for the DINK stereotype. Many lesbian or gay couples do not conform to the stereotype. Gay male couples are much more likely to match the DINK model, with two incomes and fewer dependents. Lesbians' households might also be more likely to have two incomes than married heterosexual couples, but the lesbians' two incomes are likely to be lower, and lesbians are missing the "NK" half of the stereotype.

Evidence on gay incomes and household structures, then, requires adding other important social factors into the discussion of the gay demand for products, such as gender differences. If marketers are searching for consumers with high incomes who might have a high demand for upscale products, their most promising targets would be gay men. Women's lower incomes would certainly explain advertisers' disproportionate attention to gay men, with explicit overtures to lesbians being a fairly recent phenomenon (Miller 1995). The National Gay Newspaper Guild's ad touting "Gay Market Muscle," for instance, shows a well-dressed, young, white man flexing a biceps muscle under his suit coat. According to the Simmons Market Research Bureau survey cited in the ad, 90 percent of the Guild papers' readers were male (Lukenbill 1995, 66), suggesting that advertisers in those newspapers are seeking the gay male market, and only incidentally the lesbian market. One marketer described marketing that targeted lesbians as "the ultimate taboo"! (Andrew Isen, quoted in Miller 1995).

An even narrower focus on gay *white* men would constitute an efficient strategy given the persistent racial disparities in income, disparities that are likely to be reproduced among gay men.[2] In 1998, the annual income of black men working full-time was 74 percent of white men's income (Council of Economic Advisors 2000). Black women working full-time and year-round received only 64 percent of white men's earnings. Amy Gluckman and Betsy Reed (1997) point out the dearth of images of people of color in ads directed at the gay market. They also mention that surveys of the gay market sometimes fail to ask gay people about whether they read African American newspapers or use services located in predominantly black neighborhoods. The "gay market" clearly means the white gay market.

This discussion demonstrates that, whether deliberately or accidentally, marketers have used lessons learned in their efforts to target the "women's market" or the "African American market" when targeting the gay market. Within broad market segments, further segmentation is likely to be necessary, identifying subsegments like Hispanic women, working women, homemakers, and mothers, in the case of the women's market (Leeming and Tripp 1994), or distinguishing between subsegments of the African American market such as so-called "strivers" (more assimilationist African Americans) and "non strivers" (more black-identified African Americans) (Michman 1991). In the case of the gay market, advertisers appear to recognize that only by targeting the white gay male part of the overall "gay market" can the promise of a high-income group be fulfilled. Coupled white gay men best fit the picture of the dream market.

Differences in Product Tastes and Brand Loyalty. So far, the best evidence on the gay market suggests that lesbians would have less and gay men sometimes more discretionary income than heterosexuals. Even with an average discretionary income, the gay and lesbian markets might still be particularly attractive to companies if gay consumers either have a stronger preference for certain products or certain product characteristics than do heterosexuals or are more brand-loyal and responsive to marketing efforts.

The first question is whether gays and lesbians have distinct consumption patterns that might suggest different consumer preferences. Overlooked Opinions and Simmons Market Research Bureau surveys include questions about product demand as well as demographic information. For instance, the Simmons study for the National Gay Newspaper Guild found distinctive buying patterns for readers of the Guild papers compared with those of the average person in a Simmons study (Rivendell Marketing Co. n.d.):

> 9.1 times more likely to use their Platinum American Express Card . . .
> 10.0 times more likely to purchase thirteen or more compact discs per year . . .
> 3.3 times as likely to own three or more video tape players . . .
> 6.6 times more likely to drink domestic champagne . . .
> 3.5 times more likely to have made a foreign trip in the past three years . . .

This pattern is similar to the reports gathered by Peñaloza in her analysis of the gay marketing phenomenon. Gays are said to spend more on luxury and premium products, such as travel, vacations, phone services, books, recorded music, alcoholic beverages, theater, clothing catalogs, and greeting cards (Peñaloza 1996, 18).

The data on consumption patterns share the same problem with bias as the income figures from those surveys, though. The National Gay Newspaper Guild survey might present good data about readers of newspapers, but there is no reason to think that *all* gay consumers share that consumption pattern. In fact, the different consumption patterns might simply reflect the higher incomes of those readers.

To date, no representative sample has asked detailed questions about gay buying habits that would allow consumption comparisons between gays and heterosexuals who have similar incomes. A recent survey of gay and lesbian Internet users by Greenfield Online and Spare Parts shows some similarities in brand preferences. For instance, consumers rate Tylenol and Advil as first and second, as does the general population (Wilke 1998). Gay consumers rated ABC as the top TV network. But surveys on the Web are new territory for researchers, basically constituting a new form of sampling by convenience or snowball methods, so those results cannot be applied to all gay men and lesbians.

Lukenbill infers potential differences in product preferences from gay respondents' answers to attitude questions on the Yankelovich Monitor, but the connection between attitudes and actual consumption is obviously speculative. He interprets the statistically significant differences in certain kinds of attitude-related questions as highlighting opportunities for companies making certain products. For instance, Lukenbill interprets the higher proportion of gay than heterosexual agreement with statements about the "need for self-understanding," a "commitment to maximizing health and energy," and a "commitment to maximizing physical appearance" (Lukenbill 1995, 101) as a distinguishing "focus on individuality" (134) that has consumption consequences. Although in many cases the gay attitude indicators are significantly different from heterosexual attitudes, often both groups share strong "attitudes." In response to a question about "the need to reduce stress in my life," for example, 85 percent of the gay/lesbian sample and 78 percent of the heterosexual sample agreed (103). These relatively small differences in attitudes might or might not translate into different buying habits. Lukenbill argues that companies can exploit these differences, perhaps because those attitudes strengthen gays' preferences for the kinds of goods and services that might meet those needs. His suggestions focus on the particular opportunities for food and drink, health and fitness, entertainment, clothing, travel, and books and magazines, a list remarkably similar to the one inferred from the non-random marketing surveys. In the end, his argument is not based on direct evidence of gay male or lesbian consumption patterns, but some connection between attitudes and buying habits is plausible.

Similarly, evidence on gay consumers' brand loyalty is suggestive, if not ideal. Some surveys find that gay consumers respond more to ads in the gay press or other marketing efforts. The National Gay Newspaper Guild survey found that 92 percent of readers "are likely to purchase a product or service advertised in our publications," but no studies exist that measure whether actual purchasing *behavior* changes along with intentions. A survey of 1994 Gay Games IV attendees in New York revealed a relatively high degree of corporate sponsor recognition. And half said they would be much more likely to buy a sponsor's product, with another 34 percent being somewhat more likely to do so. Interestingly, some respondents (apparently about 2–3 percent) identified Absolut vodka, which has heavily advertised in the gay market for over fifteen years, as a sponsor, even though Absolut *was not* a sponsor of the Gay Games. The survey's authors conclude that

> [Absolut] has built so strong a franchise among gays and lesbians that the brand is automatically acknowledged as a sponsor or presence at major events, even when it's not really there. (Kahan and Mulryan 1995)

Of course, this was not a random sample of gay consumers, nor necessarily a random sample of Gay Games attendees. In another example, public relations specialist Bob Witeck reports that gay travelers' preference for American Airlines has been consistent over five years of survey data.[3] Evidence from specific ad campaigns such as these and others suggests that the hypothesis of advertising effectiveness and brand loyalty from gay consumers might be real.

Lukenbill offers no firm data on gay consumers' loyalty but argues that companies can develop a relationship with gay and lesbian consumers that will promote brand loyalty. One precondition to wooing the gay market, in his opinion, is implementing progressive employment policies related to gay, lesbian, and bisexual employees, including nondiscrimination policies, diversity training, domestic partner benefits, employee groups, and philanthropy.[4] Lukenbill warns that gay consumers are highly aware of the practices of companies seeking the gay dollar, although there is virtually no evidence on this hypothesis. He offers a few examples, including the Coors beer boycott in the 1970s and 1980s, which resulted from alleged objectionable employment practices such as union busting and lie detector tests that targeted gay employees. But that boycott was begun by union activists and required a great deal of concerted organizing effort within the gay community to convince gay people to act on what were seen as egregiously unfair employment practices (Shilts 1982).

It is not clear that gay consumers would have an equally positive response to gay-positive employment policies, nor is it obvious that the typical reader of *OUT* magazine or *The Advocate* would know much about the employment policies of the many advertisers. And although advertisers could use personnel policies as a marketing tool, they rarely do so now. Some recent survey evidence supports Lukenbill's belief in a strong social awareness among gay consumers, though. In a 1999 survey of gay men and lesbians by Greenfield Online, 77 percent of those surveyed say that they shifted to a brand produced by a company with a gay-positive stance, and 87 percent report shifting brands because of a company's negative stance (Business Wire 1999). Most gay travelers surveyed report considering companies' donations and other support for gay issues in their transportation choices.[5] The effectiveness of this targeted consumer power to promote changes in employment practices is considered more fully in chapter 9.

Corporate expressions and actions might be more relevant when they concern the consumer himself or herself. Expanding the *total* product purchased by a consumer to include the social context of the purchase opens up other possible differences in gay consumer preferences. The social context, including the setting for a purchase (retail, mail order, etc.) and the expectations of the sales personnel or service providers and of other customers, might be influential in decisions. Certainly buying a shot of Absolut in a gay bar takes place in a very different social context than buying a bottle of Absolut from a typical neighborhood liquor store.

Two recent studies suggest that gay men and lesbians may face a hostile or unwelcoming purchasing environment. One study compared the reactions of sales personnel to opposite-sex couples and same-sex couples, who indicated their sexual orientation by holding hands (Walters and Curran 1996). In various retail establishments in one southeastern U.S. shopping mall, salespeople took three times longer to approach same-sex couples than opposite-sex couples. The same-sex couples were also subjected to staring, laughing, pointing, and other rude treatment. The second study sent letters to hotels and bed and breakfasts requesting weekend reservations for either a same-sex couple or an opposite-sex couple (Jones 1996). The establishments granted significantly fewer reservations to same-sex couples. The authors of both studies conclude that the discriminatory behavior observed was the result of antigay prejudice.

Gay consumers could avoid confrontations with hostile businesses, either by shopping alone with no visible markers of sexual orientation (such as a gay-themed T-shirt) or by avoiding the sort of public displays of affection common among heterosexuals. An alternative strategy would be to avoid businesses known to be intolerant or hostile. That strategy implies that businesses wooing the gay market might be more successful if they offer a tolerant social context along with the actual product. A decade ago, this might have meant buying from an openly gay provider. Lesbian businessperson Jeanne Cordova observed in 1987, "Whenever there is the possibility of personal contact—whenever you may have to reveal to your provider your lifestyle—that is when the gay consumer wants to deal with a gay provider" (quoted in Vandervelden et al. 1987, 45).

Now many of the mainstream corporations targeting the gay community are following the lead of gay-owned companies by offering products that allow lesbians and gay men to be out in the marketplace. Car dealerships advertise in gay newspapers to attract gay couples buying cars together. American Express financial advisors' "dual client financial planning" services recognize the particular needs of same-sex couples and also assure gay clients that they can and should be open about their families' financial needs. In this way, companies are appealing to gay and lesbian people based on the *additional* conditions they need as gay consumers: a tolerant social context for buying a product.

To sum up, publicly available evidence of differences between gays and heterosexuals in consumption patterns and brand loyalty is currently less than perfect but suggests possible differences. Similarly, the connection between businesses' employment practices related to gay employees and consumers' product choices has not been clearly established, other than in a few well-organized boycotts. However, a clear connection between gay consumers and businesses emerges when considering antigay discrimination in the marketplace resulting from the homophobic attitudes of salespeople and business owners. In that context, businesses might find that a strategy of product differentiation aimed at satisfying gay peoples' unique product needs would be successful even if gay and heterosexual consumers had very similar product preferences overall.

Hype or Hope? A careful look at the assumptions underlying the gay consumer craze suggests that any community-wide muscle is as yet undefined. According to the best available data, the typical gay consumer does not have the extraordinarily high incomes claimed by some marketers. Lesbians couples' dual earnings are generally reduced because of ongoing labor market discrimination against women, and lesbians often have children to raise and spend money on. Somewhat higher individual incomes for lesbians might make them more attractive than heterosexual women for some purposes, though. Similarly, gay and lesbian people of color will have lower average incomes than the marketing ideal. White gay men come closest to the DINK marketing ideal in having fewer children and, therefore, perhaps more discretionary income. Some anecdotal evidence suggests that marketing to the gay community can develop brand loyalty, regardless of whether gays are naturally grateful for the attention. Perhaps companies' interest in the gay market comes from proprietary survey data confirming the brand loyalty of gay consumers. Otherwise, the attractiveness of this market appears to be tied to identifying the usual source of marketing success for leisure products: consumers who have the right education, race, sex, and household structure to accumulate buying power for the kind of products that rely on high levels of discretionary income.

Does this mean that companies have been duped into marketing in the gay community because of the efforts of those promoting the gay market based on what could be seen as either cynical hype or wishful thinking? Probably not. Companies are not likely to pursue truly unprofitable marketing strategies for long, for one thing. And many of the marketing efforts are practical and quite ethical in their use of statistics. For instance, the National Gay Newspaper Guild campaign encourages companies to advertise to reach affluent gay and lesbian *readers* of Guild papers, an appropriate use of readership surveys (National Gay Newspaper Guild, 1996).

Unfortunately, some gay marketers are more defensive and even secretive about their use of statistics, carelessly promoting an unsupportable stereotype about the entire population of lesbians and gay men. For instance, Lukenbill reports that Overlooked Opinions (now defunct) would not discuss in detail the derivation of its claim that the gay market is worth $514 billion, other than to say they used the Kinsey estimate of the gay and lesbian population plus other data (Lukenbill 1995, 65–67). It is hard to understand the need for secrecy given Overlooked Opinions's frequent appearance in the business press. Multiplying the typical 10 percent incidence rate attributed to Kinsey (one rarely used by social scientists anymore) by the U.S. adult population figure gives a gay population of roughly seventeen million. That suggests that Overlooked Opinions assumed that the typical gay man or lesbian earns roughly $30,000 per year (or more, if they use after-tax income), a figure close to that derived from some nonrandom surveys of the gay market but far larger than the better surveys discussed above. However they derived the $514 billion figure, it appears to be a gross exaggeration of the size of the gay market—perhaps a good reason to keep the derivation secret.

Implications of Queer Conspicuous Consumption

> The basis on which good repute in any highly organized industrial community ultimately rests is pecuniary strength; and the means of showing pecuniary strength, and so of gaining or retaining a good name, are leisure and a conspicuous consumption of goods.
> Thorstein Veblen, *The Theory of the Leisure Class*

Compared with older stereotypes of lesbians and gay men—as child molesters, mentally ill, and narcissistic—the myths of affluence and conspicuous consumption underlying the gay marketing craze seem relatively benign. In fact, one might take early twentieth-century economist Thorstein Veblen to heart and argue that an image of affluence connotes responsibility and economic ability, surely positive images to present to a mainstream audience that is grappling with its opinions about lesbian and gay Americans.

But even as Americans purchase and use enormous quantities of goods and services, they often express ambivalence about the proper meaning of that consumption. The discomfort with a consumer-oriented culture, as Michael Schudson has pointed out, arises from a variety of spiritual and political traditions. Some worry that consumption of goods has become more important than spiritual or civic pursuits; others abhor the extravagance and wastefulness of consumer culture (Schudson 1986). Cornel West blames consumerism's pursuit of pleasure for at least part of "the profound sense of psychological depression, personal worthlessness, and social despair so widespread in black America" (West 1993, 13). Steven Kates's interviews of gay men in Toronto found evidence that gay community consumerism was a source of alienation for many gay men (Kates 1998, 142). From more economic and scientific perspectives come questions about whether the Earth's ecosystem can sustain current levels of consumption growth and current conditions of global inequality in consumption patterns (Daly 1995).

Evaluating the value of gay consumer visibility, then, requires placing this visibility within its economic and political context. Simply questioning whether "queer conspicuous consumption" is unambiguously positive does *not* mean that it would be better to return to the days of invisibility or to the time when gratuitously homophobic images of gay people were dominant and widely accepted. Without thoughtful questioning of the image, though, gay and lesbian America leaves itself passive, allowing others to define what it means to be gay in today's economy. As many observers have noted, consumer markets are about choice, and choice implies the possibilities for resistance to objectionable portrayals or uses of gay themes (Evans 1993, 47; Clark 1993, 198). Being an informed consumer goes beyond looking at the price of a product to ask about its total cost in social and political terms as well as the financial.

Positive images of lesbians and gay men in the media and marketing campaigns are generally considered to be a good thing for gay people, affirming and legitimizing lesbians and gay men across the country. But what exactly does being "positive" entail? As Gluckman and Reed point out, the images are almost universally of white people and are disproportionately male. In other words, they represent only a fraction of the entire gay and lesbian population. From a marketing standpoint, that makes sense, given that gay men have higher incomes and fewer children, as discussed earlier. Politically, though, these portrayals might drive gay people of color and white gay people or lesbians and gay men farther apart—the split is already there—weakening future political organizing on important gay issues (Vaid 1995; Faderman 1991). Further, Vaid and Clark have both pointed out that marketing efforts necessarily appeal to individuals' tastes and desires, pulling them out of their community and political contexts, although consumption of some goods occurs in public and in the company of other gay people, as in a restaurant or on a cruise.

And economic images will be noticed externally, too, with potentially damaging effects. Peñaloza has noted that "By addressing gays and lesbians as consumers, then, marketers and advertisers constitute them in important ways (i.e., render them identifiable and intelligible)" (Peñaloza 1996, 24). In the current marketing wave, heterosexuals are mostly seeing white gay men who have high incomes and time to play. Antigay literature in the Colorado Amendment 2 campaign revealed the dangers of the marketing strategy, inviting voters to view the "facts" on gay people's economic position: "Are homosexuals a disadvantaged minority? You decide!" A table below that headline compares (the biased) gay income figures from marketing surveys to the much lower incomes of African Americans. Everyone from Concerned Women for America to U.S. Supreme Court Justice Antonin Scalia (in his dissenting opinion in *Romer v. Evans*) has referred to marketing survey data to bolster claims that gays seeking protection from discrimination are actually seeking "special rights."

The potency of this image of affluence in hampering gay people's quest for protection from discrimination is likely tied to the larger state of the economy. For decades in the United States, income inequality fell. The rich might have been getting richer, but so were the poor. Although the earnings gaps between blacks and whites and between college-educated and high school–educated workers fell in the 1970s, income inequality within all of those groups quietly began to rise. In other words, for example, rich white people's incomes moved farther up relative to poor white people's incomes. Economists have not completely identified the reasons for this increasing inequality, but the pattern is now indisputable and has been exacerbated by widening gaps between groups: the black-white wage gap has grown recently, as has the gap between better-educated and less-educated American workers (Gottschalk 1997). (Only the gender gap shows some clear progress toward equality.) In this environment, exaggerating the incomes of *all* lesbians and gay men to sell ad space could come at a high cost to the community if the exaggeration aggravates the insecurity and inequality that others already experience.

What about the potential for leveraging market clout into changes in employment practices? Lukenbill warns potential advertisers that their policies affecting gay employees will be scrutinized by gay consumers. But as mentioned above, information about those policies is not always easy to come by. Whether or not gay consumers will vote with their dollars remains to be seen. Competition takes place on many levels. A company observing a drop in sales to gay consumers might not know if that drop is related to a price that is too high, problems with quality, availability of competing products, or lack of domestic partner benefits. Without a political movement to organize consumers, as discussed in chapter 9, any message sent by gay dollars is likely to get lost in the noise.

Turning that around, though, some lesbian and gay employee groups have tried to persuade their employers to offer domestic partner benefits by pointing to the gay market as a reward. Lukenbill describes the example of AT&T's collaboration with LEAGUE, its lesbian and gay employee group, to market long-distance service to the gay community (Lukenbill 1995, 129). He could not get any information from AT&T about the success of the marketing campaign for the company. It took several more years of effort by gay employees and LEAGUE to convince AT&T to offer domestic partnership benefits in 1999.

One apparently unambiguous benefit comes from the financial support provided by advertisers for lesbian and gay media and events. Without that advertising income, gay newspapers and magazines could not publish. However, some observers worry that while circulation of the eleven national gay magazines is over 350,000 and ad revenues rose 16 percent in 1995, topping the $12 million mark (Hanania 1995), those magazines have lost something important:

> Slick, upbeat, glossy gay magazines have arrived over the last few years, pitching the "gay lifestyle." These aren't like the old gay magazines—edgy, alternative publications that focused primarily on political rights. In the new gay glossies, such concerns are lost amid fashion spreads, hair-care products, and Club Med packages. (Harris 1995)

Magazines maintaining a political edge risk offending advertisers. *The Advocate* temporarily lost its American Airlines ads after reporting on an American memo to a flight crew leaving Washington, D.C., after the 1993 March on Washington for gay and lesbian rights. The crew was told to change blankets and pillow cases after the plane landed, apparently out of fear of AIDS transmission from gay passengers (Hanania 1995). American Airlines later apologized for the incident and has since become a supporter of equal rights by granting employees domestic partner benefits and sponsoring gay organizations. Time will tell whether the search for advertising dollars will increasingly depoliticize gay publications.

A similar concern holds for gay events and organizations accepting corporate contributions. This source has become a more important part of fundraising in the 1990s. For instance, Gay Games III, held in Vancouver, Canada, in 1990, had only one corporate sponsor, Molson, who contributed $5,000. Gay Games IV in New York in 1994 raised almost $1 million in corporate sponsorships ("Tanqueray Spends Big on AIDS Ride," 1995). Some activists express concerns that corporate money will turn gay organizations away from more radical political goals or from issues that make corporate underwriters uncomfortable. As yet, no direct examples of this sort of occurrence exist, probably because of the vigilance of gay political organizations.

Ideally, the attractiveness of the gay market could increase choices for gay consumers as companies compete for gay dollars. That is the way markets are supposed to work, anyway. But market competition is not always waged on fair or equal terms, and it is likely to pose a threat to some of the key economic and cultural institutions that have supported and even created a lesbian and gay identity.

Lesbians have already seen this dynamic in action. Lesbian feminists' success in publishing attracted competition from mainstream publishers that led to the closing of some lesbian publishers in the 1970s (Faderman 1991, 225). Although part of the problem for lesbian publishers stemmed from their lack of management expertise and business experience, the big publishers had the money and distribution networks to lure authors away. As a result of this competition and the skimming off of the most marketable books by lesbians, Faderman noted a sharp drop-off in the number of lesbian novels published in the late 1970s compared with the mid-1970s.

More recently, lesbian and/or gay bookstores around the country have faced declining sales from competition with large chain bookstores that offer big discounts and a good selection of gay-related titles (Johnson 1996). In some gay publications, multipage advertisements for mainstream chains like Borders and Barnes & Noble can be found back-to-back with smaller ads for gay-owned bookstores like A Different Light Bookstore (e.g., *OUT*, June 1996 issue). Some of the larger gay bookstores offer 15,000 titles or more (Lukenbill 1995, 168), exceeding the offerings of the chain bookstores. But while gay bookstores might have the competitive advantage in terms of choice, the large chains appear to have an advantage in terms of discounts from publishers (Johnson 1996), an advantage deemed unfair by the American Booksellers Association, which has challenged some publisher pricing practices in court. If competition drives gay bookstores out of business, as it appears in Cincinnati, for instance (Johnson 1996), consumer choice will be diminished rather than improved, and the number of loyal advertisers in gay publications will fall, too. The potential loss of the cultural capital that built the lesbian and gay identity and political movement is a reminder that markets and competition destroy as well as create.

Although market dynamics and the power of competition appear to move inevitably toward mainstream companies' takeover of both profitable products and the public image defining gay people, the current gay marketing moment might not last forever in its current state. For instance, the development of a more powerful antigay backlash could dampen companies' desire to market openly and directly to the gay community. More research on the economic and spending profiles of lesbian and gay consumers might reduce the attractiveness of the market overall, shifting attention to marketing outlets that focus only on the high-income end of the market. On the demand side of the market, consumers can vote with their dollars, and products not meeting gay consumer needs or requirements—including, potentially, the content and images in ads as well as companies' employment practices—will not survive the test of competition.

At the very least, if marketing to the gay community becomes more commonplace, the current high profile of the gay market is likely to fade into the background, taking its place among other market niches. Perhaps someday television viewers will nonchalantly watch commercials with lesbian mothers touting the virtues of some laundry detergent or gay couples extolling the virtues of gourmet family-sized frozen dinners, representing both a new visibility of gay family life and its larger ties to the consumer marketplace.

A Family Resemblance

When Ninia Baehr's mother introduced Ninia to Genora Dancel, a co-worker, she probably did not expect the two women to make national headlines or to spark a political movement. But when Genora and Ninia fell in love and decided it was time to tie the knot, they had to sue the State of Hawaii for the right to marry. News of success in the early stages of the lawsuit swept the country in the mid-1990s and generated a heated public debate over the desirability of marriages by same-sex couples. Thirty states weighed in to say that they would not recognize same-sex marriages from other states, and the U.S. Congress passed the Defense of Marriage Act to reserve the status of marriage in federal law for male-female couples only.

As the attention to marriage suggests, in the 1990s family concerns surged to the top of the list of hotly debated political issues related to lesbian and gay Americans. Choices to raise children or to enter a committed relationship with another adult constitute fundamental aspects of being human, but the thought of gay people making similar choices rarely entered the minds of heterosexual Americans until recently. Anthropologist Kath Weston notes that gay identity has long been portrayed as a rejection of family, since gay relationships are thought to be unstable, without children, and alienating of "true" kin (Weston, 1992, 22). In today's economic context, we still see this implicit rejection of gay people as family members in the representation of gay and lesbian people as the ultimate "DINKs"—double income no kids—and in the myth of the hedonistic gay consumer.

Embedded within the emerging public discussions of gay family issues are several big questions about how gay people live: Do gay people form social structures that we would recognize as "family"? What kinds of family structures emerge in the lesbian and gay communities? What role, if any, does raising children play in these families? What influences the family behavior of gay people? Do lesbian, gay, and bisexual people and their families face different decisions and problems from heterosexuals' families? Because the government regulates the legal form and meaning of relationships between adults and between parents and children, the social reality of diversity in relationships and family structures invites political debate, raising questions about the normative ramifications of gay peoples' family lives. How should policies related to gay families be structured? Do gay people need or deserve access to the same protective institutions and rules offered to heterosexual families? Would legal recognition of gay families be harmful to heterosexual families? While this chapter considers the *impact* of current laws and policies on gay family behavior, specific questions about *changing* policy are deferred to the next two chapters.

Given the nature of these questions, one might wonder in what sense family phenomena and policy questions are related to economics. John D'Emilio links the economic history of the family in the United States to the development of the gay community, especially gay men (D'Emilio 1983). As an earlier discussion in chapter 1 outlined, D'Emilio argues that the increased importance of wage labor during industrialization in the United States and the corresponding reduction in importance of a family-centered agricultural economy loosened the family's hold on individuals. With participation in a household economy becoming less important, individuals could "organize a personal life around their erotic/emotional attraction to their own sex," leading the way to the development of a lesbian and gay identity (D'Emilio 1983, 104). As D'Emilio points out, these same forces of capitalism loosened the economic ties among heterosexual families, as well, requiring an ideological shift toward seeing the family as producing "not only goods but emotional satisfaction and happiness." But as dramatic twentieth-century increases in rates of unmarried cohabitation and divorce would suggest (Casper, Cohen, and Simmons 1999; Monthly Vital Statistics Report 1995), the ideological underpinnings have proven insufficient for maintaining the traditional nuclear family model of lifelong marriage between a male wage earner and a female homemaker.

This perspective suggests that both the creation of a gay identity and the evolution of the heterosexual family are rooted in the broad and insistent pressures of capitalism, but this argument also contributes to setting "gay people" and "families" apart as distinct subcultures. In a more recent analysis, D'Emilio (n.d.) relates the rise of gay family issues and awareness to both political and economic change. Two major political factors are the Christian Right's emphasis on reviving the nuclear heterosexual family and the increasing participation of lesbians, gay people of color, and small-town gay people—for whom family issues and relationships have always been important—in the gay political movement. The AIDS epidemic also highlighted the difficulties inherent in legally unrecognized family relationships, as men were denied access to their dying lovers' hospital rooms or to shared property. Broader economic change reshaped families through "the collapse of community systems of support for families in a time of economic stagnation" (D'Emilio n.d., 8), leaving nuclear families to fend for themselves in replacing women's child-care labor in the home as they entered the workforce.

D'Emilio's argument connects economic pressures to the evolution of the family at a broad historical level. At a more individual and contemporary level, however, economics might seem to be less important than love or biological and cultural factors for understanding the formation and development of both gay and heterosexual families. But even at the individual level, economic factors and reasoning often come into play in family-related decisions, whether made in heterosexual or gay families:

- Should we wait until I find a job before getting married or moving in together?
- Can we afford to have another child?
- Will only one of us be primarily responsible for taking care of our children? If so, which one of us should take on these responsibilities?
- How will I provide for myself if my marriage or relationship ends?
- Should my spouse or partner accept a transfer to a better job in a different city?

Thinking about these questions from the standpoint of economics does not mean that biological or cultural factors are irrelevant or unimportant, but that their influence is intertwined with economic forces. Anthropologists tell us that families have different forms and meanings across different cultures (Collier, Rosaldo, and Yanagisako 1992). Even though each human being has genetic contributions from one male and one female human being, the meanings of the relationships between genetic parents and their offspring and the organization of reproduction and other family tasks vary considerably. Obviously, "culture" and "economy" cannot be neatly separated, since cultural influences are embedded in an economic context. Thus to simply say that a mother's decision to be the primary caregiver for children is either biological or cultural ignores the extent to which her decision might be shaped by her employment and earning possibilities, for instance.

Economists who study families use economic analysis in a number of ways to try to understand *why* and *how* families act as they do. Mainstream economists like Gary Becker think of a family as acting much like a small factory, with one altruistic individual acting as a CEO to make choices among different market goods, allocating time and money to produce goods and services—such as children, prestige, esteem, health, and pleasure—that determine the well-being of family members (Becker 1991). In Becker's world, opportunities in the labor market and in home production will influence how a family divides up labor in the home and market and how many children a couple will choose, for example. So some influences on family behavior are obviously financial, like labor market opportunities, while others reflect economic reasoning, such as the need to figure out the most efficient division of labor among family members.

Other economists have focused on different influences on family decision-making. Some have picked apart the decision-making process more closely, viewing family members' interests as potentially in conflict, reflected in bargaining over the family's use of time and money (Lundberg and Pollak 1996). Nancy Folbre (1994) and others have begun to sketch out the influences of "structures of constraint," such as political rules, cultural norms, and economic assets, in the context of family behavior. Individuals may pursue their own self-interest in family matters, but they also have interests as members of collective groups based on their age, nationality, race, gender, or sexual identities, for instance, that will also shape their behavior as family members. In Folbre's approach, cultural gender norms or legal institutions such as marriage will greatly constrain or guide family members' behavior in economic matters. Structures of constraint will also help to define family members' bargaining power and most efficient economic roles, so the bargaining approach to family behavior can be subsumed by the structures of constraint model.

This chapter explores what we know about lesbian, gay, and bisexual people's families and organizes that information in a way that sheds light on the underlying influences on *why* those families do what they do. Sorting through the influences of efficiency, bargaining power, and structures of constraint—such as gender norms and legal institutions—allows us to identify which economic factors are the most useful for understanding gay and heterosexual families. Comparisons of different kinds of family structures point toward structures of constraint as the most helpful way to think about families.

Do Gay and Lesbian People Have Families?

Discussions of gay family issues often gloss over the obvious: lesbian, gay, and bisexual people have families of origin, and they remain active participants in those families of origin in many cases. Weston reports that families of origin remain central concerns for many of the lesbians and gay men in the San Francisco Bay Area whom she interviewed. The question of maintaining those ties would arise after her gay respondents chose to reveal their sexual orientation to parents, siblings, and other relatives, whose reactions varied along a continuum of complete acceptance to to-tal rejection and disowning (Weston 1991).

The nature of involvement in activities within families of origin can vary enormously, obviously. Anthropologists, sociologists, and historians have identified important and socially recognized family roles in various cul-tures and points in time for people whom today we might identify as gay. For instance, the berdache, or "two-spirit," found in many Native Ameri-can cultures by various observers over the last few centuries (and even to-day), offered important advantages to a family. The berdache, typically a bio-logical male who also took on some female gender roles such as dress, behavior, and social roles, had an androgynous character with spiritual sig-nificance (Williams 1986, 2). The berdache's erotic life could also be char-acterized as nonmasculine, involving sexual relations with men and some-times even marriage to a man. Families highly valued berdaches, who were thought to have a particular talent for educating children and who some-times even adopted older children (Williams 1986, 55). Although a ber-dache might have done some work typical of men, he also took on at least some of women's home production roles and was often expected to per-form the most difficult female jobs (Williams 1986, 59). Anthropologist Walter Williams notes that the berdache's high level of productivity in women's jobs was, not surprisingly, in part due to a freedom from child-care responsibilities. Overall, the berdache was known for high levels of spiritual, intellectual, and artistic skills, which tended to produce material prosperity that benefited the entire family.

John Boswell's study of religious ceremonies uniting two people of the same sex suggests that family-type bonds with economic implications were possible and perhaps common in premodern Europe (Boswell 1994). These ceremonies were not absolutely identical in form or function to opposite-sex marriage ceremonies, but Boswell argued that the visual sym-bolism was strikingly similar between opposite-sex marriages and same-sex unions, and the legal effect of those unions appeared to involve changes in inheritance rights and social and legal obligations of family members. For instance, Boswell describes the union between the Byzantine emperor Basil I and John. John's mother gave the couple extravagant gifts, and af-ter Basil and John both died, John's mother made Basil's son her heir, sug-gesting that others also recognized the ties between the two men (Boswell 1994, 234–40).

From the standpoint of modern evolutionary theory, the potential ad-vantage of having a homosexual family member is also evident, according to E. O. Wilson (1978). Going beyond a simple view of the evolutionary imperative to procreate, the basic issue is the survival of offspring until they are old enough to reproduce. A homosexual and childless uncle or aunt (or other close blood relative) who contributes to the upbringing of his or her nieces and nephews will improve their chances of survival to adulthood. As demonstrated in the case of the berdache, the homosexual family member can be a tremendous economic asset to the family.

Even in modern times, lesbians and gay men often assume very traditional roles as wives, husbands, and parents in the context of legal heterosexual marriage. Probably most of these relationships precede awareness of being gay or lesbian, or they might constitute acts of psychological denial of homosexuality to oneself or to the world. But those relationships may coexist with internal awareness and even with social acknowledgement of sexuality in some cases. For instance, the Reverend Mel White, once a ghostwriter for Jerry Falwell and Pat Robertson, was married to a woman for twenty-four years, producing two children, despite a struggle to accept his homosexuality that began in his youth (White 1994). He and his supportive and loving wife struggled together to overcome the impact of his homosexuality on their marriage after he came out to her. Ultimately, though, White's homosexuality prevented both his *and* his wife's happiness within the marriage, leading to a divorce and his involvement in a subsequent long-term relationship with a man. In other marriages, a husband's or wife's homosexuality might not necessarily end the relationship, but the nature of the marriage surely diverges from the companionate ideal of emotional and physical spousal intimacy.

The human cost of pushing lesbians and gay men into heterosexual marriages suggests that such "family" relationships for lesbians and gay men are not the goal of gays and lesbians seeking family, nor are they the kind of relationship imagined in discussions of gay family issues. Hence to say, "Of course gays and lesbians have the right to marry—as long as they marry someone of the opposite sex"—as some critics of the gay political movement have argued—(probably deliberately) misses the point. Modern gay, lesbian, and bisexual people in the United States are talking about family relationships on their own terms.

Those terms vary from person to person. In some cases, the gay relationship looks much like a heterosexual marriage: two people committed to an emotionally close and materially interdependent life together. They may even choose to celebrate such unions with ceremonies consciously similar to a heterosexual wedding (Sherman 1992; Lewin 1998) and might seek more public or even legal recognition of those relationships in the

U.S. cities that allow registration of such partnerships. Others may reject those formalities but might live lives that are quite similar in form and function. These unions sometimes produce children through adoption, alternative insemination, or surrogacy, or incorporate children from previous relationships into the family.

Other gay people might see themselves as part of very different kinds of family structures. Much like studies by other sociologists and anthropologists like Judith Stacey or Carol Stack of mainly heterosexual family structures, Weston's study of gay and lesbian kinship reveals a model of family structure different from the traditional couple model. Weston finds kinship structures in the San Francisco area in the late 1980s that transcend households and romantic relationships:

> In the Bay Area, families we choose resembled networks in the sense that they could cross household lines, and both were based on ties that radiated outward from individuals like spokes on a wheel. However, gay families differed from networks to the extent that they quite consciously incorporated symbolic demonstrations of love, shared history, material or emotional assistance, and other signs of enduring solidarity. Although many gay families included friends, not just any friend would do. (Weston 1991, 109)

This conceptualization of gay family structures involves an idea of kinship that is rather different from the nuclear family standard. Regardless of the structure, whether a couple with or without children or a larger "family we choose," gay people have created relationships that are recognizably different from simple nonerotic friendship, recognizably similar to legally and culturally sanctioned relationships, and recognizably salient structures in the lives of lesbian, gay, and bisexual people.

Either out of ignorance of these examples or from an ideological desire to discourage their existence, most economists have paid little attention to these gay-related family connections in their modern models. Fortunately, sociologists, psychologists, and anthropologists have been quicker to study gay families. Their work, plus the recent economic studies introduced in previous chapters, allow a closer look at the economics of gay families, revealing along the way some of the shortcomings of economic models that were constructed by looking only at heterosexual families. The sliver of economists' attention to gay families consists largely of stereotypes and ignores the impact of legal institutions and gender norms on the economic decisions of gay households and families (see Becker 1991), factors that also influence heterosexual family decision-making but are often ignored by mainstream economists. And these shortcomings are not be-nign. The way we characterize and explain families matters a great deal in a policy context, whether those families are composed primarily of het-erosexual, lesbian, gay, or bisexual people.

The Theoretical Family

If we start with what families do and what functions they serve, econo-mists appear to have starting points that should include room for explic-itly incorporating lesbian and gay families. Folbre describes the family as the "primary site for the care, training, and maintenance of people—the day-to-day as well as long run reproduction of the labor force" (Folbre 1994, 96–97). In addition to cooking, cleaning, and child care, family members' "caring labor" duties include various forms of nurturance and often sexual intimacy among adults. These functions imply other time-consuming but important activities taking place in families, such as talking, listening, visiting, gift-giving, and meal-sharing (Folbre 1994, 97). Becker argues that the *main* purpose of families is "the production and rearing of children" (Becker 1991, 135), but he also recognizes much broader family functions related to producing the family's material and emotional well-being. Many of the "commodities" produced by families are not available in the marketplace, according to Becker, and they "include children, pres-tige and esteem, health, altruism, envy and pleasures of the senses" (24). Love and caring distinguish family interactions from those of unrelated people (9). Judging from the similarities in the underlying foundation of Becker's and Folbre's notion of the family, their approaches must differ along other lines.

As the discussion above suggests, economists use stylized approxima-tions or "models" of the family to try to explain how and why families ful-fill two of the commonly observed functions: the allocation of time by fam-ily members and the reproduction of the labor force, including both fertility and child rearing. The allocation of time basically involves deciding who does what and includes the dividing up of tasks within the household as well as family members' decisions about whether to work in the paid la-bor market. Economists also use these models of family behavior to predict the impact of various changes in public policy, such as income tax rates, welfare reform, or child-care subsidies.

If, as is apparent, lesbian couples and gay male couples come together for the same reasons modern heterosexual couples marry—to express love and commitment, to share life's ups and downs, to build a larger fam-ily out of individuals—then perhaps it makes sense to use the couple-based models of family economics for same-sex couples. Viewing the family through different theoretical lenses—models based on traditional economics and based on a feminist economic approach—demonstrates how gay families can be thought of in very different ways. Some economists have argued (although rarely in print) that we can simply apply models based on efficiency to lesbian family households and gay male family households, and it should work in the same way, producing reasonable and accurate predictions about how gay couples divide up household labor (see discussion in Badgett 1995a). Other economists and social scientists might argue that economic behavior and outcomes will differ for gay couples for a variety of cultural and legal reasons. Those researchers, and especially feminist economists, would expand the explanatory factors to include a broader set of influences that ultimately affect *all* families' economic behavior, not just lesbians' and gay men's families. Others, like Weston, would reject a reliance on superficial similarity with heterosexual couples and would insist that we broaden our notion of family to include the extended kinship structures she observed among lesbian and gay people. The discussion below begins with an analysis of same-sex couples but eventually returns to Weston's empirically based vision of alternative family structures.

A Tale of Three (Hypothetical) Families and Their Division of Labor

One way to assess the relevance of the various economic approaches to understanding families would be to apply them to opposite-sex couples, for whom the models were primarily designed, and to same-sex couples, whose behavior might be understood with those models—or might not. To illustrate these models, consider the experiences of six members of the (obviously fictional) University of Economia's class of 1995. Sara and Art met at a football game their junior year, fell in love, got married the day after graduation, and bought a house on Elm Street using cash given to them as wedding gifts for their down payment. Gail and Frieda met in a women's studies class their junior year, fell in love, and rented the house next to Sara and Art. Barry and Frank met at a dance sponsored by the Les-Bi-Gay Student Union, fell in love, and rented the house on the other side of Sara and Art's house.

Imagine that all six were lucky in love *and* in the job market, landing good full-time jobs with benefits in their chosen fields. Art and Frieda, both engineering majors, went to work for a computer company for an annual salary of $52,000. Sara got a job using her accounting degree at a small company paying $33,500 per year. Gail and Frank were both English majors but managed to land entry-level clerical jobs at a local magazine at $25,000. And Barry's experience working in a restaurant to pay for college got him a job managing a local upscale restaurant for $32,000. Finally, just to add a few more relevant personal details, assume that Frieda, Gail, and Barry were all brought up by fastidious parents who taught them many housecleaning and maintenance skills as well as an appreciation for a tidy home.

These examples provide a way to explore some of the questions about sexual orientation and families, an exploration that will help in analyzing and comparing the more general explanations for family behavior offered by economists. Are the two same-sex couples forming families that look like the married couple's family in an economic sense? Why do the couples form a family? How do the couples divide up the household work? And how do they decide whether and when (and perhaps how) to have children?

Economic theories of the family have something to say about each of those questions. Our local (also fictional) experts, Professor E. Ficient, a mainstream economist who believes that efficiency is a powerful force in family life, and Professor Fem N. Ist, a feminist economist whose family theories focus on gender roles, bargaining power, and social institutions, will weigh in on how our families operate.

Moving In Together and Forming Families

Let's first imagine Professor E. Ficient's reactions to a peek in the windows of these Elm Street homes. He nods approvingly at Sara and Art, whose decision to marry fits nicely into the professor's view of why families exist. "The other two couples are not what economists like Gary Becker had in mind in writing about the family," our Professor Ficient might say, "But I'm willing to keep an open mind to see if they are acting efficiently by moving in together."

From his perspective, the family is a little factory for producing certain kinds of goods or services, either directly producing them in the home, such as meals or child care or children, or by working in the wage labor market and buying products with earned income (Becker 1991). The family's goal is to maximize the size of the "pie" of goods and services for the family, without worrying too much about who gets what size slice. (Becker assumes that an altruistic head of the household who cares about each member's well-being will dole out the family's output appropriately.) Families like Art and Sara's can produce more together than individuals could separately because family life allows household members to special-ize in tasks for which they are particularly well-suited. This specialization is basically the same phenomenon seen in factories, for instance, where rather than a single worker building an entire product from scratch, a worker does one task and passes the incomplete product on to the next worker for another step in the production process, and so on. Just as this method allows workers who specialize to become particularly adept at their jobs and to make the process as efficient as possible, specialization in the household also allows members to develop and refine skills that will make them even more productive in their chosen family roles.

Another reason why families can use resources more efficiently than single people has to do with a different aspect of the production process. Groups of people who live together and share household tasks, such as meal preparation, child care, or cleaning duties, can take advantage of what economists call "economies of scale." Economies of scale occur when one person can provide goods or services for several people more cheaply in terms of time and money than the individuals can for them-selves separately (see Nelson [1988] for evidence). For instance, it might take Gail an hour and Frieda an hour for each to cook dinner for them-selves individually, but Gail could prepare a meal for them both in an hour and a half. Gail spends a half hour more cooking, but Frieda spends an hour less, saving the couple one half-hour. Even if they trade off cooking responsibilities, they will both have more time available for other activities. Moving in together makes taking advantage of economies of scale easier.

Yet another view on the economic purpose of families comes from Rob-ert Pollak (1985), who argues that family structures serve other important economic purposes by reducing what economists call "transaction costs" involved in creating all sorts of agreements between individuals. The "pre-existing, ongoing, significant personal relationships" (585) present in fam-ilies give the family some advantages in fulfilling social insurance functions in case of old age, divorce, economic hardship, or illness, for example, and in making family farms and businesses more efficient under certain cir-cumstances.[1] This rationale also suggests that forming families promotes efficiency in some sense, and these functions might well be part of the decision-making process of the three couples.

Professor Fem N. Ist's initial impression of our three families would most likely recognize their similarities. "In terms of their choices to live to-gether at this point in their lives, it's hard to tell them apart since each couple takes on caring and maintenance responsibilities," she might note.

"While it's true that they might have some potential for increased efficiency, we will see that efficiency won't be the only guiding principle in their family lives." At least in terms of economic potential, then, economic theories could easily accommodate same-sex couples forming families.

The Household Division of Labor

Points of departure between the theories become clearer when considering how the couples divide up the work done by families. At Sara and Art's house, Sara takes most of the responsibility for laundry, cooking, cleaning, and household financial management. Art is in charge of car maintenance, yard care, household repairs, and some of the grocery shopping, but the total number of hours he spends working at home are roughly half of Sara's.[2] If asked, Sara would say that she does more around the house than Art because his job keeps him at the office until seven o'clock or later many nights, plus he has signed up for a night course to get a master's degree.

Professor E. Ficient thinks they must have taken one of his economics courses at the University of Economia—their division of labor makes perfect sense to him. In a two-adult household, the most efficient division of labor will often be complete specialization, in which one person does all of the household-related jobs, like cooking, cleaning, and child care, while the other works in the wage labor market.[3] Obviously, one important issue is deciding who does which set of tasks. With the goal of maximizing production in mind, the answer requires a purely technical comparison of which configuration produces more for the household, given each person's abilities and options. Being well-suited to a task might mean having certain skills as a result of biology (say for breast-feeding), formal training, or socialization (a kind of informal training). External market conditions will also be important in determining the value of household members' services in terms of wage income, since an hour spent working in the home is an hour's wages lost.

Art and Sara both have jobs outside the home, but although they do not now specialize in the way that might be most efficient in productive terms, they're clearly moving in that direction. Art, whose earnings are higher, is investing more than Sara in his "human capital," that is, in on-the-job training and in education that will increase his earnings prospects. Sara, whose mother taught her how to run a household well, spends more time than Art on the nonmarket side of providing for the family, partly because she is better than Art at housework, partly because she would gain less than Art from spending more hours in the work force, and perhaps partly because she values the results of housework—a clean home—more than Art. Or, to be more technical about it, Art has a "comparative advantage" in market work, while Sara's comparative advantage is in domestic work. To do more housework, Art would give up more in terms of time that could be spent improving his earnings (or future earnings) than Sara would. Sara and Art appear to Professor Ficient to be a model young childless couple.

Peeking in on the neighbors, the good professor would observe somewhat different patterns. Gail and Frieda made a list of household chores when they moved in together, and they now trade individual responsibilities every month, but together they spend less time doing housework than the neighbors do. It takes Frieda a little longer to clean the toilet, cook dinner, or go shopping than it does Gail, and sometimes Frieda drags a bit more after one of her long days at the office (she and Art often commiserate over their demanding job responsibilities), but she manages to fulfill her home duties. While their house is neat, they are willing to accept some dust to make extra time for hobbies and volunteer work.

Frank and Barry took a little longer to work out a division of labor in the home. At first they tried to split the chores evenly. But Barry's long nights and early mornings at the restaurant often left him with no time or energy for housework, even though he was the more efficient housekeeper. Frank willingly picked up the slack, but Barry's housekeeping standards were higher than Frank's, so after a tense month of bickering, they agreed to hire a housecleaner every other week to make up for Barry's lack of time, paid for out of their pool of money for household expenses.

Professor Ficient shakes his head over these arrangements. "In general, I believe that same-sex households will be less efficient than opposite-sex households.[4] Their labor market opportunities will be similar, and they are likely to bring the same kind of housework skills to the relationship, both of which will decrease the advantages of specialization," he argues. "But it's also possible for these couples to allocate their time more efficiently than they do now, given that they have different preferences and productivity levels for housework. Gail and Frieda are being irrational by dividing up housework equally. Gail can do more in less time than Frieda, and Frieda's career prospects might be hurt if she's spending too much energy on housework." Barry and Frank's arrangement makes more sense to Professor Ficient, since the men were able to replace Barry's home labor with someone who was paid less per hour than either Barry or Frank. Their division of labor is greater than that of the lesbian couple.

Professor Fem N. Ist, looking over Professor E. Ficient's shoulder, would see different possible motivations for the families' division of labor. While relative efficiency and different wage employment situations might have played a role in how the couples allocated home responsibilities, she acknowledges, other factors also shape the couples' decisions that mainstream economics often ignores. Even when individuals are making purposeful economic choices, their behavior is constrained by "assets, rules, norms, and preferences that delimit what people want and how they can go about getting what they want" (Folbre 1994, 54). The actual allocation of household members' time might not be much affected by efficiency concerns, which could influence our judgments about the viability and desirability of different household arrangements.

To label Sara and Art's behavior "rational" and Gail and Frieda's "irrational," in other words, is insufficient to explain the couples' choices and the differences between the couples. In particular, the couples' decisions might primarily reflect the influence of strong gender roles, which are supported by centuries of male control over economic assets, cultural norms about appropriate work for men and women, laws and policies inhibiting women's equal participation in the labor market, and even personal preferences shaped by experiences and social expectations. Perhaps Sara does the cooking, cleaning, et cetera, because those jobs are "women's work" that she was taught from an early age, and she was raised to appreciate the value of a clean home. Art might not really notice how clean the bathroom is, but he might also be embarrassed to be seen wearing rubber gloves and cleaning it since men are supposed to cut the grass and empty the trash— acceptable jobs that he is not embarrassed to do in front of his neighbors. If gender roles are very important in explaining heterosexual couples' division of labor, then we would predict that same-sex couples will divide household responsibilities more evenly.[5] Plus, same-sex partners will have more equal bargaining power, in general, since their experiences, social positions, and economic prospects will tend to be more equal than otherwise similar opposite-sex couples.[6]

Existing studies of how couples divide household duties and wage labor suggest that the sketches of the three couples here come close to representing average differences between kinds of couples. Not surprisingly, the biggest body of research focuses on heterosexual married couples, where large-scale surveys of individuals' and families' economic decisions have made it possible to analyze a representative group of heterosexual people. Unfortunately, researchers have had to collect data on lesbian and gay households in a less desirable way, relying on samples of gay people who are not randomly chosen and, therefore, might not be representative of lesbians, gay men, or bisexual people[7] as a whole. But while none of the studies on same-sex couples was conducted in a way that allows generalization, they provide tentative descriptions of several dimensions of the division of labor in gay couples and households.

Studies on Housework. Many studies document a big difference in the amount of housework done by men and women in married couples, providing an important point of comparison for same-sex couples. For instance, a study by Joni Hersch (1991) shows that married women did roughly twice as much housework as married men, with married women's relative effort increasing when she marries and when the couple has children. Even after taking into account many factors, including time spent in wage employment, the impact of wages, and the impact of children's ages, Hersch finds that married women do more housework than unmarried women, while married men and unmarried men work the same amount in the home.

Scott J. South and Glenna Spitze (1994) find that, on average, women always do more housework than men, but the gender gap is higher in married couples than in unmarried cohabiting (opposite-sex) couples or any other living situation. When women live with men, either cohabiting or in marriage, they increase their time spent doing "female-typed" tasks— meal preparation and clean up, housecleaning, laundry, and shopping— with married women increasing their hours more than cohabiting women. Men's average housework time varies little between being never married, cohabiting, or married, but the amount of time spent in female-typed activities is lowest for married men and next to lowest for cohabiting men. South and Spitze argue that these patterns suggest that housework is a way to "display gender" in the context of a male-female union (344), a conclusion consistent with the ideas of economists like Folbre. (The difference between married and unmarried couples suggests a possible direct impact of marriage as an institution, which will be discussed below.)

Several studies using nonrandom samples of lesbian, gay, and/or heterosexual couples found similar patterns for opposite-sex couples but very different patterns for same-sex couples. Blumstein and Schwartz's large-scale study conducted in the late 1970s explicitly compares heterosexual married couples, unmarried heterosexual couples, lesbian couples, and gay male couples to provide a comparison between married and unmarried couples and between opposite-sex and same-sex couples, with further gender comparisons possible by comparing lesbian couples with gay male couples (Blumstein and Schwartz 1983, 144–51).[8] They find that married women in their sample do the most housework and do considerably more than their husbands. Cohabiting women perform less housework than married women but more than their partners. Lesbians and gay men spend far fewer hours on housework than heterosexuals, and lesbians spend slightly less time on housework than do the gay men in the study. In all couple types, time spent in work outside the home reduces the time spent on housework.

Lawrence A. Kurdek's (1993) study of gay, lesbian, and heterosexual couples (all without children) compares more detailed measures of the allocation of housework. Lesbian couples have the most equal sharing of household responsibilities, followed by gay men, whose patterns are closer to but somewhat more equal than patterns of married couples. Wives do the most housework in married couples, while the mechanism for allocating housework in same-sex couples is less clear, with some (inconsistent) findings that higher incomes reduce the amount of housework done (137). Kurdek also finds similar patterns in a review of many studies of the household division of labor in same-sex couples (Kurdek 1995, 248–49).

Overall, the studies of housework suggest that some influences on the division of labor are similar for same-sex and opposite-sex couples, as higher labor market hours reduce housework time. The more striking contrast, though, is that same-sex couples tend to divide labor more evenly than do either married or unmarried opposite-sex couples. It is important to note that this conclusion is a relative one: while lesbian couples and gay male couples do not always divide housework equally, the division of labor is *more* egalitarian than seen in opposite-sex couples.

Studies on Participation in the Wage Labor Market. The other key decision couples must make regarding their production of family-related goods and services involves earning money income in the labor market to supplement the work done in the home and to purchase other "inputs" into that process. In our three families on Elm Street, all six people decided to work full-time when they graduated from college, even though they were in committed relationships that might have allowed more flexibility for one partner to work less than full-time, or even to work producing goods and services in the home full-time. (Although Barry, Art, and Frieda work somewhat longer hours than their partners, the difference is fairly small.) Why would both partners devote forty or more hours per week to the labor market at this point?

Obviously, some aspects of the six different decisions were in place long before these hypothetical individuals had met their future mates. Going to college is, in many ways, an investment in one's earning capacity. By the time our six friends had graduated, they might have wanted to work to gain some return on their investment, to continue to improve their career prospects through formal and on-the-job training, to explore some personal interest, or just to pay back college loans. And earnings tend to increase the most rapidly early in one's career (Murphy and Welch 1990), so forsaking the job market for home and hearth at that stage can severely reduce one's future earnings capacity.

In comparison, the advantages of complete specialization for a couple and the particular individual thinking about working in the home might not be great at this (so far) childless stage of these families' lives. Later we will see what happens to the couples' allocation of time when children are present. At this point complete specialization would mean that one partner, the one with the brighter earning prospects, could be completely freed from housework responsibilities to facilitate further career investment while the partner at home could pursue efforts to increase his or her domestic productivity. Professor E. Ficient suggests investing in knowledge about raising children, cooking, or home decorating for those investing in home production skills.

Professor Fem N. Ist reminds us of those pesky complementarities, though, the "goods" such as physical and emotional intimacy that require some time from both partners to make an ongoing partnership desirable, preventing complete specialization. She also warns that the partner giving up a paying career is risking future economic hardship if the relationship ends.[9] Another big consideration would be how much of what the family wants can actually be produced in the home, especially if the families include no children. Economist Clair Brown argues that over the course of the twentieth century, market goods became more important for providing certain important family "products," such as prestige, which hastened women's entry into the paid labor force (Brown 1985).[10] In short, having a partner working full-time in the home might not increase the couples' status and standard of living very much at this stage of their lives.

The most direct evidence on the degree of specialization between home and market among different family configurations comes from Marieka Klawitter's analysis of data from the 1990 U.S. Census (Klawitter 1995). In 1990, the Census forms allowed individuals to report that they were the "unmarried partner" of the householder (the household reference person), making comparisons possible between married couples, cohabiting opposite-sex couples, and same-sex couples.[11] Specialization implies that partners will not have the same full-time commitment to the labor force, and one person will work more weeks per year and hours per week than the other partner. In 59 percent of male same-sex couples and

51 percent of female same-sex couples, *both* partners worked between forty-one and fifty-two weeks in 1989, while only 37 percent of married couples had similar full-year (or almost full-year) work patterns. Comparing hours worked per week tells a similar story: in 71 percent of male couples, 59 percent of female couples, but only 41 percent of married couples did *both* partners work more than thirty hours per week. (For a point of reference, all three of our Elm Street couples would be counted in those measures as working the same hours and weeks.) Or we could look at how many couples have one person working no hours in paid labor and one working more: roughly 14 percent of married couples fell into this category, while only 6 percent of male couples and 8 percent of female couples could be so classified. Each of these angles of looking at the Census data suggest that married couples are much more likely to specialize than are same-sex couples.[12]

Blumstein and Schwartz's findings from the late 1970s and early 1980s reflect a similar pattern even though they are not based on a random sample of couples. The most striking evidence of specialization again comes only for the married couples: 86 percent of married men but only 38 percent of married women work full-time (Blumstein and Schwartz 1983, 596). One quarter of married women were engaged in full-time housework. In contrast, 63 percent of cohabiting heterosexual women and 69 percent of lesbians worked full-time, with only a small number working at home full-time. Virtually no men in their sample were doing housework full-time.

Overall, all the evidence points in the same direction: in general, lesbian couples and gay male couples specialize much less than married couples, whether looking at how housework is divided or examining individuals' allocation of time between home and the labor market. Of course, this is not to say that *all* married couples completely specialize or that *no* same-sex couples specialize. (In 1998, 48 percent of married women with children under eighteen worked full-time, compared with 90 percent of married men, and both spouses worked in 64 percent of those families.[13]) But adding the greater propensity for both same-sex partners to work to the evidence that same-sex couples divide housework more evenly points to a difference in family decisions. An economist convinced that family decisions are guided by efficiency could explain some specialization in heterosexual households as the result of economic rationality, but we do not see the same patterns in same-sex couples, in which tastes and productivity differences should still guide partners toward rational specialization. Understanding the differences by couple type points toward the kind of factors that feminist economists use to explain family behavior, particularly gender roles, cultural norms, legal institutions, or bargaining power.

Having Children

Procreation defines one central purpose of marriage and families. Let's fast-forward five years to see how our three couples on Elm Street fit into this mold. Sara and Art have experienced the biggest change. Baby Lauren was born ten months ago, bringing new challenges and responsibilities into the family. After much discussion, the proud parents decided that Art would continue to work full-time to support the family while Sara would take on primary responsibility for caring for Lauren, putting her own career on hold for several years. Gail and Frieda, observing their neighbors' happiness as parents, have started to discuss the possibility of adding children to their family, as well. In the meantime, they baby-sit for Lauren from time to time to give Sara and Art a night out. Frank and Barry "ooh" and "ahh" over Lauren, but neither has yet confessed to the other his secret wish that they, too, could raise a child.

According to Professor E. Ficient, again looking in on our families, Sara and Art have chosen to have a child in the same way that they choose any other expenditure of time and money—in other words, children are basically consumption goods like VCRs or cars. Given the strength of their preferences for children compared with other possible ways of spending time and money, Art and Sara will decide how many children to have based on how much a child costs in terms of the time and money available to the couple and how much the child contributes to the family. (The value of time can be measured in terms of the earnings Sara will give up to take care of a child, for instance.) Sara and Art have not decided whether they will have more children, but they are closely observing Lauren's impact on their budget, including future college expenses and the effect of child rearing on Sara's future earnings capacity. (While Lauren might make some future economic contribution to the family through a job or housework, Sara and Art have not consciously factored that into their plans.) Along the same lines, the family's decision to have Sara stay home reflects excellent economic reasoning, since her ability to breast-feed and Art's higher income make strict specialization a good idea.

As for the childlessness of our same-sex couples, Professor Ficient says, "Why, of course, homosexual unions do not result in children!" [14]

In stunned silence, Gail and Frieda look at each other and wonder which century the professor has been living in. Noticing their silence, he blushes and stammers, "Well, come on! It's obvious, isn't it? Do I have to give you a biology lesson, too?"

A year later, the professor has his answer. Frieda has just given birth to Stanley, whose biological father had contributed sperm to a local sperm bank. Of course, Stanley was not conceived in an act of sexual "union" between Frieda and Gail, but his entry into the world was greeted by two loving parents. His conception was a little more planned, a little more complicated, and a bit more expensive than that of Lauren. After much thought, the two women decided that Frieda should bear their child since her employer's benefit package gave her paid parental leave. And since her income was much higher than Gail's, Frieda could return to work and be the primary earner while Gail stayed home with Stanley. That way Stanley would be covered under Frieda's employer's health care policy, since Gail's employer's policy would not have covered a baby who was not legally related to her.

In the face of such evidence, Professor E. Ficient would no doubt be impressed with Gail and Frieda's parental abilities and the similarity between their family and that of Sara and Art. Current reproductive technologies—particularly donor insemination—make it relatively simple for two women to add a child compared with two men, but the traditional economist could not likely help but mention that the added cost to same-sex couples would make same-sex couples much less likely to be raising children. Frank and Barry are a case in point, having made no moves toward adopting or otherwise acquiring children to raise. Or perhaps the professor would argue that same-sex couples would not want to have children as much as heterosexuals do, an assumption that is closely linked to the myth of the hedonistic, irresponsible gay person who would rather buy a new car than make some financial sacrifice to bear and raise a child.

Obviously, other economists might look at children differently. Instead of thinking about the Elm Street children as if they were consumer goods, Professor Fem N. Ist would argue that a better economic metaphor for children is a "public good,"[15] as when the larger society receives some of the benefits of a child in the form of economic productivity and provision of goods and services for retirees. Thus, members of society have an economic interest in the well-being of children and in the decisions made by parents. Individually, couples like Art and Sara or Frieda and Gail make purposeful choices related to childbearing in which costs of child rearing and availability of reproductive technologies will matter, but they do not take into account the impact of their choices on other members of society. The larger institutional context shapes the distribution of those costs (which will not necessarily be equal between two parents), a context that includes laws about parental responsibility and access to reproductive technologies, for instance, as well as cultural norms that support socially and economically desirable population levels.

Sara and Art's decision to have Lauren (and maybe other children in the future) was shaped by the influences on their respective preferences for children (Sara was more anxious than Art to expand their family), by laws that place economic responsibility for offspring on both of them as legal (and in this case, biological) parents, by cultural understandings that women will be available for provision of child rearing services, and by knowledge of the declining obligations of their children to care for Art and Sara in old age. Gail and Frieda face a different set of constraints than that of their neighbors: both are women, changing the role of gender norms and necessitating access to particular reproductive technologies, and only Frieda, as the birth mother and legally recognized parent, will have legal responsibility for Stanley's upbringing and legal rights to determine how he will be raised. Barry and Frank face a much more difficult issue in terms of available reproductive technologies—they must either adopt or, if the laws of their state allow it, contract with a surrogate mother who would carry the biological child of one of the men. Given the differences in constraints, we can reasonably predict that lesbians and gay men would be less likely to be raising children than would heterosexual parents, much like a prediction based on more traditional rational choice analysis.[16]

Surprisingly, recent evidence calls into question the implications of both the traditional and feminist perspectives, that is, that same-sex couples will have fewer children. Estimating how many gay men and lesbians have children is a difficult job, similar to estimating incomes, for instance. Without a representative sample, reliable conclusions are unlikely. Four good surveys discussed in an earlier chapter, the Voter Research and Surveys (VRS), Yankelovich Monitor, General Social Survey/National Health and Social Life Survey (GSS/NHSLS), and 1990 Census provide some insight into the number of children in lesbians' and gay men's households and are summarized in table 12.

The first two surveys find that the proportion of lesbian households with children is roughly equal to the proportion of children in heterosexual women's households (Badgett 1995a; Lukenbill 1995). In the VRS, 31 percent of lesbians and 37 percent of heterosexual women have children under eighteen in their households. In the Yankelovich Monitor, 67 percent of lesbians and 72 percent of heterosexual women are parents;

Table 12 Percentage of Lesbians and Gay Men with Children

	Lesbians	Heterosexual Women	Gay Men	Heterosexual Men
Yankelovich				
Children in household	32	36	15	28
Parents	67	72	27	60
Voter Exit Poll				
Children in household	31	37	22.5	32.5
GSS/NHSLS				
Children in household	28		14%	

	Lesbian Couples	Married Couples	Gay Male Couples
1990 Census	20	57	5

Note: In the Yankelovich and Voter Exit Poll, the differences between lesbians and hetero-sexual women are not statistically significant; the differences between gay men and hetero-sexual men are statistically significant.

Sources: Yankelovich: Lukenbill 1995; voter exit poll: Badgett 1995a; GSS/NHSLS: Black et al. 2000; 1990 Census: Klawitter and Flatt 1996.

32 percent of lesbians and 36 percent of heterosexual women have chil-dren under eighteen in the household (Lukenbill 1995, 97). For women, the figures imply equal child responsibilities, since the differences in both surveys are not statistically significant. That is, the small differences are likely to be the accidental result of the particular samples of women surveyed.

The picture is very different for gay men, though, who are only about half as likely to be raising children as heterosexual men. Only 22.5 per-cent of the gay men in the VRS have children under eighteen in the house-hold, while 32.5 percent of heterosexual men do; and 15 percent of gay men in the Yankelovich Monitor report children while 28 percent of het-erosexual men do. The Yankelovich data also showed that 27 percent of gay men are parents compared with 60 percent of heterosexual men. The differences between gay and heterosexual men are statistically significant.

Other data sources find somewhat lower levels of parenthood for both lesbians and gay men. Black et al. (2000) report that 28 percent of lesbians and 14 percent of gay men in the GSS/NHSLS have children in their households. Using the 1990 Census data, Klawitter and Flatt (1998) find fewer same-sex households with children, regardless of the couples' sex: 20 percent of female couples and 5 percent of male couples report chil-dren, compared with 57 percent of married couples. This difference in the Census data could reflect the exclusion of single lesbians and gay men or a biased reporting pattern for couples. For instance, same-sex couples with children might have been more fearful that disclosing their relationship on a government-sponsored survey that includes respondents' names and addresses could result in custody challenges.

The wording of the question about children in these surveys is also important in interpreting these findings. None of the surveys allow for distinctions between the respondent's biological or adopted children, that is, children for whom the respondent has legal responsibility, and the biological or adopted children of another household member. In other words, the respondent's level of child-raising responsibility is uncertain, and we cannot distinguish between a legal parent, a coparent, or a roommate with no lasting attachment to the child. Further, we do not know whether the child is the product (in its various meanings) of a heterosexual relationship or of a homosexual relationship, so this tells us little about how big the so-called "lesbian baby boom" really is. Given the constraints on deliberately choosing to bear and raise a child in a lesbian or gay family, and given the fairly recent development of the lesbian baby boom, it seems plausible that the majority of those children came from heterosexual relationships. And finally, except for the Yankelovich findings, we know nothing about children residing outside the respondent's household. This last issue is especially important since lesbians and gay men who have children from prior heterosexual marriages face difficulties getting and maintaining custody of such children (Harvard Law Review 1990, 120–21). However, they may continue to bear considerable financial responsibility for these children.

The ongoing saga of our three families suggests that even in their most familiar form (couples), lesbian and gay families may differ greatly from heterosexual families in terms of economic outcomes. And existing survey evidence supports the patterns sketched out by the families. Lesbian couples and gay male couples appear to specialize in tasks far less than do heterosexual couples, both in dividing up housework and in dividing up responsibility for earning income in the wage labor market. The presence of children certainly adds to the amount and kind of work performed in the home, and gay men's families, in particular, appear to differ in this aspect, too. While some evidence suggests that children are as likely to be present in lesbians' homes as in heterosexual women's homes, those children may be the products of previous heterosexual relationships, suggesting that gay male and lesbian couples are, in fact, less likely than heterosexual couples to bring new children into the family.

Looking for explanations

Our imaginary responses from the representative traditional and feminist economists pose differing explanations for variations in economic behavior between same-sex and opposite-sex couples. A focus on efficiency suggests that variations based in preferences and biology are at the root of the couples' different childbearing decisions. In the decisions related to the allocation of time in and outside the home, Professor E. Ficient observed some rational behavior in the couples' actions that took advantage of individual differences in productivity and market opportunity (generally related to gender) and some seemingly inefficient actions in Gail and Frieda's insistence that each woman do an equal amount of housework (which was also Barry and Frank's original goal, approximated only by hiring a substitute for Barry's labor in the home). Professor Fem N. Ist acknowledges the influence of preferences, biology, and efficiency in the couples' actions, but a feminist analysis of why the families made their particular decisions incorporates a broader set of influences, including family law, gender norms, technological access, and economic assets. These constraints on behavior could explain why the same-sex couples acted differently from the heterosexual couples, as well as why all three couples acted as they did.

While sorting out the contribution of these many possible decision-making methods and constraints is a long-term project that will require significant new data collection on lesbian and gay families, we can get a good sense of how important gender roles, legal institutions, and bargaining power might be in shaping family decisions since they often push couples' economic behavior in different directions than would differences in preferences and biology. And if those additional factors are important, then we should conclude that the model of efficiency-calculating behavior by families is less useful for understanding the effect of changes in the economy and policy, for instance, than a more feminist model.

Gender Roles. In trying to account for the differences in patterns of division of labor and fertility across couple types, the importance of gender roles in assigning family-related work looms large. But since gender roles and economic efficiency would both push heterosexual couples toward specialization, it is usually difficult to determine which is the better explanation. Blumstein and Schwartz (1983) consider their study a kind of natural experiment for learning about the influence of gender roles:

> By contrasting homosexual couples with both types of heterosexual couples, we can see how relationships function when there are no

> male/female differences to contend with. By comparing gay men to
> lesbians, we explore differences in male and female contributions to
> relationships. (14)

Their findings and the findings of other researchers discussed above show
that male-female couples, whether married or not, appear to use gender
to assign tasks, with women performing particular female-coded tasks and
men working more hours for wages. The gender-based assignment of
housework holds true even when women also engage in work outside the
home.

Same-sex couples have no such obvious gender differences by which to
assign tasks, and they display much less specialization either within the
household or between household and the labor market. In place of the division of labor through rules of thumb tied to gender roles, some lesbian
and gay couples appear to have developed alternative norms to guide and
support a more equal sharing of earning and household responsibilities
within couples. Blumstein and Schwartz (1983) find that 77 percent of gay
men, 75 percent of lesbians, but only 39 percent of wives and 31 percent
of husbands believed that both partners in a couple should work for pay.
In in-depth interviews, Blumstein and Schwartz also probe more deeply
into the reasons behind the survey answers. Same-sex couples expressed
a belief "that fairness dictates that both partners earn a living" (Blumstein
and Schwartz 1983, 127).

Some observers, such as Colleen Lamos (1995), object to this research
strategy that degenders same-sex couples, however. Lamos asserts that lesbians commonly take on butch-femme roles, which involve adopting characteristics considered masculine or feminine and which may influence the
household's division of labor.[17] No surveys exist to give us the proportion
of lesbians and lesbian couples that identify with these specifically lesbian gender roles, but other survey evidence suggests that lesbians' and
gay men's degree of femininity or masculinity does not influence the tasks
performed. Blumstein and Schwartz (1983) ask questions measuring identification with "masculine" qualities (being outgoing, aggressive, and force-
ful [556]) and "feminine" qualities (being compassionate, tender, and understanding [563]). Kurdek collects similar information from his survey
participants. But neither Blumstein and Schwartz nor Kurdek find any
correlation between masculinity or femininity and who performed more
housework in same-sex couples.[18]

Historians of butch-femme culture provide further evidence that such
roles played relatively little part in the household division of labor, even
when gendered roles appeared to be relatively fixed and more important

158   CHAPTER SIX

for individuals. Elizabeth Lapovsky Kennedy and Madeline D. Davis (1993) found evidence of varying divisions of labor between butches and femmes in Buffalo, New York, in the 1940s and 1950s, with some division along gender lines, but in a very different way from heterosexual couples: "Butch-fem roles . . . symbolically and ideologically associated the butch with the public world, the world of the streets and bars, and the fem with the home" (287). Beyond that symbolic position, however, Kennedy and Davis found no "culturally validated norms" pushing butches to provide for the couple, nor for femmes to take sole responsibility for housework.

> Either because butch and fem both wanted to work or wanted the au-
> tonomy that comes with supporting themselves, or because one
> woman's salary was rarely enough to support a couple, or because
> couples rarely raised children, the butch's role was not primarily that
> of breadwinner. (288)

Participation in the paid work force for both partners appeared to influence the more fluid division of housework compared with that observed in the typical heterosexual home of the time. Overall, couples "had to negotiate their own solutions based on upbringing, temperament, role identity, and work conditions" (292)—gendered roles alone were not sufficient to determine who did what in the home. A more recent exploration of this issue by Weston also reveals considerable diversity in how lesbian gender roles influence the household division of labor and how other factors, such as income, class, and race, complicate a neat association of gender with household roles (Weston 1996).

Gender norms may also play a role in fertility since children impose a commitment of time and resources on parents, who must then decide how to allocate their own time to provide for a child's material and emotional needs. Child care is typically considered a "woman's job," which some see as a natural biological outcome (see Becker 1991, 37). Since women's obvious biological advantage in child rearing is limited to the early months of a baby's life, however, biology can bear little responsibility for assigning birth mothers primary child-care duties throughout childhood. Modern technology has made breast-feeding less essential for children's survival and health, since breast milk can be pumped or formula substituted, which would allow fathers or non-birth mothers to be primary caregivers for infants. Pregnancy has proven to be as compatible with paid work as it is with caring for other children in the home. Since efficiency provides little guide, gender norms might facilitate heterosexual couples' childbearing since gender norms clearly assign responsibility to the partner who is already expected to do housework (the wife).

Same-sex couples must figure out their own division of child-care responsibilities, and they do so in ways that might have nothing to do with
biology, guided instead by economic opportunities (i.e., wages) and other
institutions, as when Frieda went back to work after giving birth to Stanley.[19] However, some evidence from lesbian couples who bear children
through alternative insemination suggests that biology does matter in dividing up child-care responsibilities, particularly when children are infants.
Charlotte Patterson discusses a variety of studies that she and others have
conducted in the United States and Europe that reveal that lesbian couples
divide up care taking much more equally than heterosexual couples, as
gender norm explanations would argue (Patterson 1998). Nonbiological
lesbian mothers spend more time with children than do heterosexual fathers. On average, though, biological mothers spend more time on child
care than do nonbiological mothers. That pattern might reflect considerations of efficiency, but it could also reflect some cultural norm related to the
responsibilities of "motherhood" or perhaps even to some differences in
preferences rooted in a physiological, legal, or cultural attachment to biological children.

Economist Victor Fuchs asserts that women have a stronger demand
for children than do men (Fuchs 1989), although it seems plausible that
any difference could be the result of strong gender norms and socialization. Such gender variation could explain women's primary role in child
care, and it might also explain the difference in parenthood rates between lesbians and gay men observed in the three surveys discussed
above. Some might argue instead—based on anecdotal evidence or convenience samples, since no reliable and representative studies exist—that
lesbians come out later than gay men or are more likely to go through a
significant heterosexual relationship first, which could explain the difference in children observed in table 1. But it seems equally plausible that
the causation could be the other way around: lesbians (or future lesbians)
marry men in order to have children because women have a stronger demand for children.

This level of speculation, though, would not be necessary to explain the
differences between lesbians and gay men, since differences in available
reproductive technologies and the legal institutions supporting those
technologies (discussed below) differ dramatically for gay men and lesbians. Furthermore, if this gender difference in preferences truly exists,
we would actually expect lesbian couples to be *more likely* than heterosexual couples to have children! The fact that they do not could have
several possible explanations: the gender difference does not exist, most

heterosexual couples have an asset advantage (i.e., a ready supply of sperm), or other barriers exist to lesbian couples' choices. The first possibility is plausible, the second is obvious, and the third is also undeniable, as the discussion of institutions below will make clear. While a comparison of families by sexual orientation does not allow us to completely reject the possibility that men and women differ in their desire to have children, we also cannot reject other possible explanations of the patterns observed.

Importance of Policy and Legal Institutions. Closely related to the gender role hypothesis is the possibility that legal and economic institutions, such as marriage, influence couples' decisions, shaping both the preferences and actions of individuals in a couple and changing the conditions for decision-making. Legal marriage is particularly important here. Marriage encourages specialization and financial pooling in a number of ways, both directly through its contractual nature and indirectly by changing married individuals' social status in relation to third parties' actions. (chapter 7 presents other aspects related to these policies.)

The contractual aspect of marriage involves an exchange of promises to deliver certain spousal services over a lifetime, promises that promote the pooling of time and financial resources by the couple and are perhaps most important in a practical sense only if a couple divorces (see Cohen 1987). In economic theory, if not in practical legal outcomes, those promises should protect a woman (or a man) who gives up opportunities to develop skills useful in other kinds of production, such as in a particular occupation, in order to focus on and develop skills to improve productivity in one particular area, such as home production. Without such promises, specialization would be too risky for someone who might later in life have to take on both home production responsibilities *and* a wage-paying job in the labor market. If a marriage ends, institutions like alimony, property division, and child support can at least partly compensate someone who has given up opportunities in other economically necessary roles. But since in practice alimony payments may not be permanent or adequate, husbands and, especially, wives who do not expect their marriages to last a lifetime may be less likely to specialize to begin with. Nevertheless, the legal institution of marriage at least provides a framework for dividing up assets and responsibilities equitably if a marriage ends.

Third parties often recognize someone's marital status in rules about compensation or taxes, for instance, and those practices further strengthen married couples' incentives to specialize. The employment benefits practices discussed in chapter 4 are perhaps the best example of this effect.

The historical evidence reviewed in chapter 4 suggests that, in fact, current benefits practices grew in part out of an ideological belief that such gender-related specialization was the most appropriate form of organizing family life. When employers provide health care benefits for the spouses and children of employees, they facilitate a family's ability to have a spouse engaged in full-time home production. If Sara wanted to go back to school full-time or to stay home with Lauren, Art's employer-provided insurance would extend protection to his wife. If Frieda wanted to return to school full-time or to stay home with Stanley, she would lose her health insurance, since Gail's company only provides coverage for legal spouses. Relative to opposite-sex couples, then, the net benefits of specializing for same-sex couples could be much lower.

Certain government policies also promote specialization. For example, Old-Age and Survivors Insurance, or Social Security, includes a spousal benefit for retired, fully insured workers if the spouse does not qualify for a larger benefit based on his or her own work record (Committee on Ways and Means 1994). As a result, depending on how you want to measure it, a married insured worker with a nonworking spouse receives either a much larger rate of return on payments into the Social Security system or a much lower Social Security tax rate (Boskin et al. 1987; Feldstein and Samwick 1992). The federal income tax code also rewards couples with one partner working only in the home. Compared with unmarried couples, two-carner married couples (where the earnings are similar) pay a "marriage penalty" compared with the total taxes they would pay if unmarried, while one-earner couples receive a "marriage bonus" compared with the total taxes the earner would pay if unmarried.[20] This tax effect can be large, as the marriage penalty averaged $1,244 per family in 1994 and the marriage bonus averaged $1,399 (Feenberg and Rosen 1995).[21]

Since both the contractual and status effects of marriage encourage or facilitate greater specialization, the inability to marry would reduce the likelihood that couples would specialize or pool their time and money resources, even if specialization would improve the household's economic well-being. Since same-sex couples cannot marry, individuals are put in a position of great risk if they specialize and pool resources completely. Some substitutes for legal marriage include contractual agreements between partners about mutual support and property division, for instance, but those substitutes are imperfect since they can be quite expensive, they must be updated, they cannot influence third parties' practices, and they are sometimes ruled unenforceable in court (for more on this, see chapter 7). Lesbian or gay workers' employers rarely extend spousal benefits to domestic partners, as discussed in chapter 4, and gay couples receive no tax advantages from specialization. All of these institutional factors, both legal and economic, would be expected to reduce specialization between home and market production by gay couples relative to that of heterosexual couples.

Some might argue that specialization is itself either undesirable for ethical and cultural reasons or increasingly impractical in the current economy, as families have increasingly relied on income from a second earner to improve their standard of living (Mishel and Bernstein 1993). The point here is not to celebrate or encourage a pattern of lifelong specialization, but to suggest that the *terms of choice,* or structures of constraint, among desired household arrangements are unequal. A lesbian who wants to work in the home either does so under unequal terms or decides that she and her partner cannot afford to do so given possible career risks or health insurance considerations, for instance. This difference in available options hinders same-sex couples' ability to choose household arrangements that improve their well-being, another institutional disadvantage for gay families. The influence of these different constraints and incentives is apparent in the higher labor force participation of lesbians compared with that of heterosexual women.

If the institution of marriage influences economic behavior and family status, one obvious thought experiment is to ask how access to marriage for same-sex couples would change their behavior and the behavior of opposite-sex couples. As the above analysis suggests, many same-sex couples will be likely to marry and might change the way they divide up household responsibilities, depending on how important marriage is in encouraging and supporting specialization. Conservative commentators voice concern about opposite-sex couples in the marriage debate, worrying that same-sex marriage would somehow damage heterosexual families by undermining marriage. Those critics never outline the explicit process by which this damage would occur, but two obvious changes would cover the possibilities. Either opposite-sex couples would choose to form families without getting married, or someone who would have married a person of the opposite sex would instead choose to marry someone of the same sex.

An upsurge in heterosexual unmarried cohabitation is hard to imagine since the institution of marriage—its legal requirements and status related to third parties—would not fundamentally change by expanding the number of people allowed to marry. The incentives for marrying remain in place, leaving opposite-sex couples in the same decision-making context that they are in now. Ironically, allowing same-sex couples to marry might actually increase the number of opposite-sex couples marrying, since some of those couples might now be consciously boycotting an exclusionary legal institution.

The second possibility—that someone would choose a same-sex partner instead of an opposite-sex partner—is difficult to evaluate. Available evidence suggests that sexual orientation is a fundamental human characteristic that is very difficult or perhaps even impossible to change (Haldeman 1999), suggesting that a heterosexual person is unlikely to choose a same-sex life partner for a sexually and emotionally intimate marriage relationship. However, a bisexual person who prefers to be in a legally and socially recognized relationship might, in fact, be more likely to marry a same-sex partner. In this case the number of marriages would not decrease, and any shift away from opposite-sex marriages is likely to be small, given evidence of the small number of people claiming a bisexual identity (see, for example, Laumann et al. 1994). If, as some have conjectured (e.g., Matthaei 1998) or worried, all people have inherent bisexual possibilities, then the shift in marriage could be larger over time. While that possibility seems unlikely, in either case the well-being of the people changing their marriage choices reflects an improvement in their happiness and in the ability of the couple to provide for themselves in economic terms, including the intangible "services" that involve emotional caring and commitment. From this perspective, the likely outcomes suggest a strengthening, not a diminishing, of the salience of marriage in the lives of all individuals, regardless of sexual orientation.

The Institution of Parenthood. Fertility is also likely to be shaped by family law, which varies from state to state. Since the law determines who is considered a parent in allocating legal parental rights and obligations, the legal institution of parenthood seems likely to influence lesbian, gay, and bisexual people's decisions about becoming a parent.

Legal responsibility could affect economic behavior since the law determines which people *must* assume responsibility for a child, and those same individuals have the legal right to participate in and to influence the child's upbringing. Being a legally recognized parent affects the costs and benefits of children, both through the law's determination of the minimum number of adults among whom the cost will be spread and through enforcing which adults will receive the psychological (and possibly monetary) benefits of a child by participating in child rearing. By altering the factors involved in decision-making—even in a rational decision based on efficiency considerations—the law will influence the number of children a couple will choose.

These legal influences could also alter the amount of time and money invested in children, if parents' investment in children is based on an assumption of long-term contact with those children in order to receive the psychological (or perhaps even financial) "returns" from the investment. Even an altruistic person assuming some responsibility for raising a child might be less inclined, for instance, to contribute to a savings account for a child's college education if the adult is unlikely to be closely involved with the child on a regular basis for more than a few years. Frieda had to consider the possibility that she would end up bearing *all* parental obligations (and rights) as a legal parent if Gail were to leave the family. And Gail had to consider the fact that she might have *no* legal parental rights (nor obligations), even as a functional parent, and that Frieda could arbitrarily refuse access to Stanley if she so chose.[22]

This legal uncertainty is likely to reduce the willingness of gay men and lesbians to produce and raise children. But, in the language of mainstream economics, this difference in willingness does not necessarily reflect an entirely different "demand curve" for children for gay men and lesbians; more likely it reflects the much higher expected price of children for gay people, both financially (since sperm banks, surrogacy agreements, and lawyers can be expensive, and one parent will be vulnerable to bearing all financial responsibility) and emotionally (because of the uncertainty of the allocation of costs and benefits). Under the same legal conditions faced by prospective heterosexual parents, gay people would probably have more children than they currently do. Given the complexity of the legal issues involved and the risks taken by gay parents, it seems amazing that as many lesbians and gay men are raising children as the survey evidence suggests.

The perseverance of lesbian and gay parents in the context of legal hurdles to parenthood suggests that another conservative objection to same-sex marriage is unwarranted. Jean Bethke Elshtain, for instance, argues that same-sex couples should be excluded from marriage (but not, in her view, from legally recognized domestic partnerships) because marriage "is and always has been about the possibility of generativity" (Elshtain 1991, 59). That gay and lesbian people share Elshtain's concern with "intergenerationality" is obvious from the extraordinary challenges and risks that gay people have assumed in order to raise another generation of human beings. Regardless of the "true" social and economic purpose of marriage—the happiness and well-being of individual adults or the production of new human beings—empirical studies and economic analysis show that lesbian and gay people fit the bill.

It is obvious that gay men's and lesbians' legal difficulties in parenthood and their lack of access to legally recognized relationships are closely interconnected economically as well as politically, and both will affect the well-being of children and their parents. Even if nonrecognized parents do not reduce their commitment of time and financial resources to the children they are raising, children will suffer if their parents split up and one ceases or is barred from participation in child rearing. Less directly, discouraging gay people from having children and not legally recognizing gay relationships are both likely to reduce the stability of existing relationships. Becker views children as an investment in "marital-specific capital" that will tend to keep parents together, so that discouraging gay parenting contributes to making relationship instability a self-fulfilling prophecy. Legal inequality in family law thus not only diminishes the economic status of lesbian and gay families, but inequality creates a feedback loop that supports the myth that gay people differ from heterosexual people in their attachment to family life and future generations.

Far from the hedonistic, individualistic, adult-centered gay people imagined in the economic myths about lesbians and gay men, many gay people form caring, interdependent family relationships with other adults and contribute to future generations by participating in child rearing. Possible differences in economic behavior are not "bad" in the sense that they reflect gay people's pathological choices, but they might be both individually and socially undesirable to the extent that they are shaped by laws and policies that place gay and lesbian people in an unequal and disadvantaged position. Without the support provided by legal recognition of gay relationships between adults and between adults and their children, lesbians, gay men, and their children are even more vulnerable than they are simply as two women or as two men facing lower incomes from sex and sexual orientation discrimination in the workplace. The next two chapters consider the best ways to redress this inequality.

From a broader theoretical perspective on the family, the awareness that gender norms and legal institutions and rules influence economic decisions in same-sex couples suggests a similar set of influences for opposite-sex couples, influences that ordinarily fade into the background for economists analyzing family decision-making. Imagine that Sara woke up one morning to find that, overnight, she had been transformed into a man, complete with a male body and male socialization, and that the legal tie with Art had been dissolved. Sara and Art would have to recalculate the costs and benefits of their time and resource allocation possibilities, suddenly conscious of the influence of (possibly altered) personal preferences, labor market opportunities, and social expectations. Bargaining power within their relationship and the division of labor would likely shift since gendered solutions to their decisions are no longer available. In terms of parenting, the grounds on which bargaining might take place have shifted dramatically, and though they cannot return Lauren to nonexistence, discussions about her care and any future children will take place in a legal context assigning one parent to a position that is simultaneously legally privileged and economically vulnerable. At that point, the influence of gender and institutions on Sara and Art's family is clear. Short of such experiments, comparisons between heterosexual people's families and gay people's families can serve the same analytical purpose.

The Gay Family as Postmodern Poster Child

This discussion demonstrates that economic logic, both broadly and narrowly defined, can be fruitfully applied to questions about the economic behavior of lesbian and gay couples. The same kinds of economic influences—efficiency, gender, legal rules, and bargaining power—appear to define the context for decision-making in all families, not just those centered on a heterosexual couple. In addition to influencing what families do, these forces also determine what families look like. Aside from the question of how many children are produced in a given family, we could shift away from the focus on couples to ask what determines the number of adults engaged in a common effort devoted to social reproduction of human beings. Clearly the law was set up to encourage the formation of couples by providing material and social incentives to marry, and the larger culture indoctrinates individuals with the belief that nature and biology require such paired matings.

Observers who analyze social issues from a leftist political perspective have worried about the new attention focused on gay couples and gay family issues. These queer family theorists argue that "family" is a socially constructed institution, purposefully designed to segregate and isolate lesbian, gay, and bisexual people outside the boundaries of social acceptability (see Robson 1994). Finding examples of how marriage or appeals to the family are used to marginalize homosexuality and/or gay people is easy. Certainly, contemporary conservative political activists and policy analysts have skillfully used such issues as parental rights, home schooling, and sex education to frame the family as a bastion of moral safety amidst a sea of perverts and other immoral influences.

Within this larger historical and cultural context, legal theorist Ruthann Robson argues, lesbians' seeking or even demanding to be included under the rubric of "family" is a dangerous strategy. Robson reasons that because "family is a cognitive category enforced by law" (Robson 1994, 978), pursuing recognition of same-sex couples in either a formal way (as defined in law) or in a functional way (fulfilling the same functions as formal relationships) will subject lesbian relationships to further state regulation and would exclude the very kinds of relationships, such as nonmonogamous relationships, that could transform the way families work.[23]

If we think about family broadly as an economic and social technology for producing both new and renewed human beings out of the combined time, talents, and resources of individuals, however, using "family" as a concept does not deny the value of having and promoting many kinds of family structures. As noted above in this chapter, simply expanding the image of families to include same-sex couples and their children overlooks the multiplicity of family structures present in the lesbian, gay, and bisexual communities. Weston's notion of "families we choose" shows considerable variability in structure. Similarly, Peter Nardi (1992) has noted, "For gay people, friends often provide the role of maintaining physical and emotional well-being, especially when difficulties arise when soliciting social support from their families and other kin" (110).

Families we choose cut across household lines. Gay families might include a lesbian couple and a gay male couple raising children together. Some are not based on couples at all, with groups of friends, ex-lovers, and even biological kin forming families and providing each other with material, emotional, and social support.

These kinship structures seem to come closer to a "queer" notion of family and represent the kinds of structures that Robson fears will disappear. Indeed, Weston suggests that gays' and lesbians' pursuit of access to traditional relationships with other adults and with children might reorient gay family formation into nuclear forms that exclude friends and individuals outside the household (Weston 1991, 209). But at the same time, her research also appears to find that couples are already the primary *economic* unit. Weston notes that members of families we choose provide some material support in terms of time and money to other family members, but in general a large degree of self-sufficiency is expected: "Individuals distributed their own earnings and resources; where pooling occurred, it usually involved an agreement with a lover or a limited common fund with housemates" (Weston 1991, 114). She finds that partners sometimes provided significant short-term financial support for each other, such as to allow for full-time education or child rearing, suggesting that *couples* within larger family structures are the most economically interdependent units. Nevertheless, Weston's families exhibit a degree of interdependence with people outside of a couple that is not usually associated with hetero-sexual married couples.

The pressure on families we choose to conform to the nuclear family mold will depend on other forces, too. In particular, the collective gay fam-ily structures may actually be held in place by some of the same eco-nomic pressures that heterosexual families face. For instance, Judith Stacey (1992) finds that the notion of "family" among working-class het-erosexual people in Silicon Valley has expanded beyond the nuclear fam-ily to include ex-spouses, adult children, and neighbors from other house-holds. She argues that these developments stem from the decline of the welfare state, increased economic insecurity, and the need for multiple earner families. Access to state- or market-provided substitutes for pos-sible family-provided support will influence the composition and func-tions of a family. Rayna Rapp (1992) suggests that middle-class families have access to nonfamilial economic institutions in times of need, though, such as those offering credit or insurance, lessening reliance on kin (64), so perhaps middle-class gay and lesbian families would not feel the same pressure to expand or to remain larger than couples.

Other economic forces will also shape the family forms that emerge. On one hand, the economic incentives for forming larger family structures like families we choose is clear. If two adults can take advantage of econo-mies of scale and of efficient specialization to increase their standard of liv-ing, then households with more than two adults should be even better off. Adults might not even need to live in the same household to take advan-tage of some of the economies of scale, since meal preparation, child care, and other services can take place in rotating households, for instance. Pooling resources of more adults enhances the social insurance aspects of family life. Given the potential economic advantages (and, for some, the freedom from conventional expectations), we would expect such family forms to attract a large number of gay people, since gay people's access to legally sanctioned couple-type families is restricted.

On the other hand, economists have been skeptical about the ability of larger families to develop and continue for various reasons. Economist Gary Becker argues that larger households are less likely because of the relative ease of shirking one's duties in a big household and because of the desire for privacy (Becker 1991, 48–53). In a somewhat different sense, the com-plexity of the social and economic situation in the United States also makes it unlikely that large, stable family units would form, even if indi-viduals were not socialized to prefer forming couples and were not eco-nomically and legally rewarded for doing so (as they obviously are).

To see the difficulties, consider what would happen if, instead of maintaining three different households and trying to manage modern economic life separately, Barry, Frieda, Frank, Art, Gail, and Sara thought about pooling at least some of their time and money. They could collectively raise Stanley and Lauren, cook and enjoy meals together, pick each other up at the airport, wait at home for repair people, shop for groceries, maintain their houses, or even produce more children—imagine Barry as the sperm donor for a baby carried by Gail. The larger unit would be rooted not just in economic opportunism, but in love, friendship, trust, and common values developed over many years.

This kind of family relationship would be difficult to form and maintain for two reasons. First, entering family arrangements with more than one person is difficult. A commitment to mutual support, pooling of resources, and emotional support for an indefinite period of time is a big promise and requires enormous trust and communication. Judging from the cultural angst expressed by participants around marriage, even a twosome finds this commitment intimidating. Imagine, then, the difficulties of arranging a commitment between more than two people. If Barry is in an emotionally caring and materially supportive relationship with Frank, they may decide that they would like to combine households or otherwise pool resources and join their lives together in a deep and permanent way (at least in intention). Barry may also have a similar depth of relationship with Sara, and the two of them might want to form a larger household and share aspects of their everyday lives and futures. But a household of three can only form in this situation if Frank and Sara want such a relationship with each other. Then the three of them must come up with a mutually agreeable configuration of work, location, and emotional connection to structure that relationship. Sara's relationship and household with Art would make a deal even more difficult to arrange. The more people involved, the more complicated the interactions and the more likely a pairwise failure to agree on an initial family arrangement will be.

Second, larger families mean more complicated negotiations when situations change. If Barry loses his job and can only find a new one in a distant city, or even if he is offered his dream job in a city a thousand miles away, figuring out what the family will do will be a difficult task. As his partner in a couple, Frank might decide to go along with Barry as long as they agree to return to their home city in five years, for instance. But Sara or Art might not be willing to go regardless of the reciprocal gesture offered. The process of seeking compromise and reciprocity in the larger household configuration might be far more difficult than negotiations between two people. Other situations that could generate the need for renegotiation are easy to imagine: decisions about whether and when to have children, housing choices, or job changes, not to mention the complications that arise related to sexual intimacy.

Of course these higher negotiation and formation costs for larger adult family configurations would be at least partly offset by the greater benefits accruing to larger family units, such as having more resources to pool and gaining greater economies of scale. And for some potential families, getting pairwise agreements from all possible combinations might not be difficult. Thus even with cultural pressure to form couples, we would expect to see some of these larger family units, but probably far fewer than couples. More likely, if it is possible to get some of the benefits of pooling time and money without incurring the potential negotiating difficulties likely when developing a long-term, deeply interdependent commitment, then other forms of institutions to share resources and economies of scale are likely to develop. Such arrangements might vary in the depth of mutual obligation and commitment from the relatively low level of commitment of a neighborhood babysitting pool to actually sharing responsibility for child rearing with close friends who are also neighbors.

This analysis suggests that concern about the survival and further development of larger families we choose among gay and lesbian people is probably well founded. But the threat comes only partly from the possibility that increasing cultural and legal recognition of same-sex couples will marginalize or devalue more complex family structures. Despite some economic incentives to form larger families, the complexities of the modern economy are also likely to undermine the viability of intensive relationships beyond the couple. Chapters 7 and 8 focus on public policies that address the inequities identified in this book related to workplace treatment of gay and lesbian people and related to family policy. The discussion of family structures suggests that one important question for policy analysis is whether and how family-related policies should support a variety of family forms.

SEVEN

Reducing Inequities, Part 1:
Public Policy and the Workplace

Lesbian and gay people are actively integrated into the economic life of the United States, even when they are not visible in all economic contexts, as previous chapters demonstrate. Contrary to the rosy picture painted by economic myth, we have seen that this involvement takes place in an environment in which gay people face political and legal disadvantages. Their current position in the workplace, family, and consumer marketplace is the product of the interplay of market forces, public policies (past and present), cultural norms, and collective action. The vulnerability of gay people to workplace discrimination and the lack of legal recognition of gay family structures, in particular, constrain the economic decisions and influence the economic outcomes of gay individuals and their families. Both active efforts to disadvantage lesbians and gay men in the workplace (such as past bans on gay people in federal employment) and in families (such as denying lesbians custody of their children) as well as the more recent see-no-evil approach of governments in some situations (as in the failure to outlaw job discrimination or to recognize gay families) constitute government policies that diminish the economic well-being of gay people.

Gay and lesbian people and their allies have collectively challenged discriminating institutions. Formal and informal efforts to change negative attitudes toward gay people take place in workplaces, churches, schools, and the media. In legislatures and courtrooms across the country, political activists, allied policymakers, and lawyers push for changes in the legal structure that shapes the economic experiences and contributions of gay people. This chapter and the next focus on the outcomes of those efforts—the needed public policies—not the strategic issues involved in the process of change. Chapter 9 looks more closely at the use of economic power, interests, and identities to assert the gay community's needs collectively in the business world.

Sociocultural, economic, and political disadvantages are linked, of course. The law is often said to set an example for citizens, legislating a standard of behavior that might lead to changes in attitudes. Indeed, this role of the law appears to be the major concern for opponents of any legislation that would ameliorate the disadvantaged position of gay people, including even the change of laws regulating private, consensual sexual behavior, or the so-called "sodomy laws," laws which are rarely enforced (see, for example, Finnis 1995, 33–39). Today sodomy laws are less likely to be used to punish illegal sexual activity and more likely to be used as justifications for denying a lesbian mother custody of her children, indicating the continuing symbolic importance of those laws in expressing moral disapproval.

Aside from the symbolic nature of the law, laws and policies have much practical importance. Throughout this book, the role of policy in influencing the economic position of gay people is clear. The failure to prohibit employment discrimination means that some gay men and lesbians will experience discrimination and others will be vulnerable without hope of legal recourse to reverse its harmful effects. The exclusion of gay families from the realm of family policy further burdens already disadvantaged adults and children. The practical impact of policies related to homosexuality is also evident from the role of the law in shaping the commercialization of gay communities, as outlined in chapter 5. Antisodomy laws, antigay liquor laws, and laws *requiring* employment discrimination long restricted the visibility and connectedness of lesbian and gay people.

Given the historical importance of those older laws, the first logical policy questions ask whether explicit statutory disadvantages should be removed. Many of those laws and policies, vestiges of an earlier and more virulent fear and dislike of gay people, no longer exist. Today, eighteen states still maintain laws against certain sexual practices, most often collected under the umbrella term "sodomy laws," and five of those states prohibit only practices between people of the same sex (van der Meide 2000). Remarkably, there is little disagreement among scholars about the desirability of such laws—virtually no one supports them. Even theologians and others who adamantly oppose other progay laws can find little reason to maintain laws against private, noncommercial sexual acts between consenting adults (see Finnis 1995, 14; Posner 1992).

Because of the scholarly consensus about sodomy laws (but not because those laws are irrelevant), this chapter and the next focus on a different set of policies that are among the primary sources of ongoing economic inequality. In this chapter, I analyze civil rights laws prohibiting employment discrimination, and in the following chapter I take on laws that regulate family relationships in the United States. Since the existing debate on these topics uses only the narrowest of economic principles—

if any at all—my goals are both to broaden our understanding of what is at stake in economic terms in these debates and to influence decisions on these policy questions. Thus the rest of the book departs from the spirit of chapters 1–6, which asked questions such as, "*What* is the economic status of lesbians, gay men, and their families?" and "*Why* did these outcomes occur?" In this second part, I address a more difficult question, "What *should* we do?" To answer that question, I appeal to both traditional and feminist principles of what good public policies do, applying four basic policy principles to different policies that address gay people's workplace and family inequality.

The State of the Debate

Thinking about public policies raises numerous questions about strategies for change, about what constitutes a desirable society, and about the proper role of government in shaping that society. Differing political and economic ideologies promote differing levels of government involvement and differing social visions, and those differences are evident in debates about policies related to lesbian, gay, and bisexual people, even among gay people themselves. Although some people seem to think that lesbian and gay people speak with one political voice, in reality lesbian and gay people with quite different opinions often disagree about fundamental practical and strategic matters. The hypothetical comments that follow present some of the range of opinion.

"I just want to be treated equally and have the same rights as everybody else." The most visible ideological position in the gay political movement seeks legal equality and economic equality of opportunity, or what we might call a reformist or "liberal" agenda. Granting gay people the right to marry a same-sex partner, allowing gay people to adopt children, or forbidding employment discrimination against lesbian, gay, and bisexual workers all contribute to making gay people equal in legal status to heterosexual people. A more conservative variant of this liberal political strategy would look to the government to remove only its own impediments to equality, such as the ban on marriage or military service, but would leave private sector businesses to makes their own decisions and policies with respect to employment discrimination or domestic partner benefits, for instance. Andrew Sullivan (Sullivan 1995), former editor of *The New Republic,* Paul Varnell (Varnell 1999), and Richard E. Sincere, Jr. (Sincere 1999) have developed this more conservative approach. Both variations of the reformist or liberal positions leave aside the existing economic differences *within* the lesbian and gay communities and pursue legal equality

for gay people with the generally implicit aim of achieving economic equality with others of the same race, gender, and economic class status.

"I believe that gay people should have the right to get married, but I don't think that should be our political priority. Instead of putting our money and time into that issue, we should be attacking the underlying problems of a lousy health care system and tying benefits to marriage." Those gay people advocating a more radical perspective often object to liberal political efforts to promote equality and acceptance, arguing that such an approach takes the heterosexual world and its values and institutions as given. Building a movement for domestic partner benefits, according to this view, accepts the current system that ties health insurance to employment and to a narrow vision of the meaning of family. Rather than accept that structure, these activists would argue that a more appropriate strategy would be to challenge the objectionable systems directly, building coalitions with other disadvantaged groups and changing heterosexist institutions. And by pursuing this broader strategy to achieve similar ends, gay people can avoid the exclusionary nature of gay identity politics, which focus too much on gay, white, middle-class, and male concerns, and a rigidification of sexual identity categories that reproduce a hierarchical relationship between heterosexuality and homosexuality (see Lisa Duggan [1995], Ruthann Robson [1994], Michael Warner [1993], or Steven Seidman [1993] for discussions of these concerns).

These differences in political perspective *among* gay, lesbian, and bisexual people sometimes result from differences in broader social and political visions and sometimes from differences in judgments about the effectiveness of particular political strategies. In presenting the positions in this stark form, a policy-oriented version of the old assimilationist versus sexual liberationist debate, they appear to be polar opposites. In practice, though, as lesbian activist and thinker Urvashi Vaid has observed, often activists' opinions and lives incorporate elements of both perspectives (Vaid 1995, 205).

Neither position fully addresses the economic position of lesbians and gay men. Formal legal equality between gay people and heterosexual people simply places gay people in the same often precarious position of otherwise similarly situated heterosexuals. For example, laws that require employers to provide the same health insurance to domestic partners of employees that is provided to spouses of employees will not matter to a lesbian or gay man whose employer provides *no* health insurance to its employees. Without formal legal equality, however, even policies that provide broader access to health care or adequate income might exclude or disadvantage gay people. Using the same example of health insurance, proposed public policies that require employers to offer health insurance to employees and their families will leave out gay people's families unless employers treat gay families equally. Discrimination in health care services in the context of a national health care plan would further reduce the well-being of gay people. An economic analysis broader than those implicit in these simple arguments can incorporate both sets of concerns.

A similar lack of completeness characterizes the following various (hypothetical) positions of opponents of lesbian and gay equality:

"God tells us to love the sinner but hate the sin. Homosexuals should be left alone but not granted the same legal privileges currently reserved for heterosexuals." Of course, other less gay-positive political positions exist as well, which advocate against legal acceptance of gay people. The far right holds that any semblance of tolerance or any failure to disadvantage gay people by the government (whether it is state, federal, or local) threatens the values and institutions at the root of American society. Variations of this position admit that in some realms the government has no good place, such as in sodomy laws that in principle police the bedrooms of consenting adults (Finnis 1995), while in others it is the government's role to police the moral order. Allowing same-sex couples to marry or forbidding antigay discrimination by private employers would make homosexuality less onerous and, therefore, these arguments imply, harder to resist.

"Gay people can't help the way they are, and they have a right to exist in our society just like everybody else. What happens in gay people's bedrooms is not my concern." A more libertarian perspective argues that gay people pose no threat to heterosexuals or competition with heterosexuality since being gay is primarily an unchangeable characteristic. This is the underlying assumption of legal scholar and federal court of appeals judge Richard Posner's argument for removing antigay sodomy laws, for instance (Posner 1992). Treating gay people equally does not hurt heterosexual society and cannot encourage heterosexuals to become gay. Given this assumption, respect for privacy and a tradition of equality demand fair treatment in most, if not all, realms of government policy.

One interesting exception to this general libertarianesque principle, however, concerns the right to marry. Many politicians who advocate laws requiring equal treatment of gay people in the workplace, such as President Bill Clinton, have opposed marriages by same-sex couples. Many argue that some privileges—namely, those cultural, social, and economic privileges that go along with marriage—should be reserved for heterosexual couples. For Posner, as an example, allowing gay people to marry is problematic because "marriage is a status rich in entitlements" that were designed primarily to meet the needs of heterosexual couples with children (Posner 1992, 313).

These political viewpoints also omit crucial economic perspectives that illuminate important effects and goals of policy, however. Considering gay, lesbian, and bisexual people's inequality in the workplace and in family situations within an economic framework provides one way of addressing uncertainty about how far the government should go in accommodating the needs of gay and lesbian people. The goal of this chapter is not to supplant policy analysis based on more philosophical concerns or on political principles but to supplement those other kinds of analysis. The assumption here is that being more informed about the economic consequences of particular policies is better than being less informed. For those opposed to full legal equality for gay people, leaving out an economic analysis of policies means ignoring the possibility that the United States or a given state would be pursuing policies that are economically harmful to all. Gay people advocating the abolition of marriage rather than the legalization of marriage for same-sex couples would face a similar tradeoff. And policymakers, in whose hands much authority for making these decisions resides, are certainly likely to be concerned with such tradeoffs, given their responsibility for collecting, managing, and spending the public's tax money. Because economic considerations are important, adding them into the debate could affect the outcome.

Constructing Different Policy Principles

Economists are often asked to analyze and comment on public policy, especially policies related to labor markets, product markets, and even to the family. Beneath each specific issue lurks a general question: What should the state's role be in the economy? Mainstream economists would argue that this question involves both big-picture "macroeconomic" concerns, such as the government's role in preventing or ameliorating recessions, as well as the more "microeconomic" or individual-focused kind of policy, such as tax policies or policies setting up antipoverty programs. Traditional economic analysts have used a simple principle to guide economic policy prescriptions: individuals' self-interested choices about consumer goods and services and firms' equally self-interested choices that maximize profits result in a highly efficient "invisible hand" that allocates our economic resources of time and money to their most efficient or highest valued uses. In most cases, those economists argue that the invisible hand will correct problems such as shortages or surpluses of important items and services, suggesting that markets should generally be free from redistributive government intervention. Government tinkering usually just makes things worse, in this view.

But sometimes the actions of individual consumers or producers do not result in the most efficient use of resources, as when we get too much of things we do not like, such as pollution, or not enough of things that we want and need, such as national parks or education. In those situations, many mainstream economists conclude, the government can step in and change the decision-making context to nudge economic outcomes toward a more desirable allocation of resources. Market forces and an occasional government intervention will maximize the size of the economic "pie" to divvy up. Sometimes, though, equity concerns also emerge if the pie is divided too unequally given people's contributions to the pie. The traditional economic model typically leaves out the important role of collective action, norms, and past public policy in shaping economic outcomes, however.

In a broader view along the lines of the one sketched out in this book, the existing economic situation of gay people and their families would not be seen as an efficient and desirable outcome of individual market transactions that would be undone by state action to address inequality. Instead, economic outcomes emerge from a complex process involving market transactions and self-interested behavior to some extent, but they also reflect the influence of existing social norms, current and past collective action, and explicit state actions. Changing outcomes through policy does not have to work solely through changing monetary incentives for individuals' behavior from this perspective, since change can occur by the state's facilitating or discouraging collective action or by modifying or codifying certain social norms. In particular, changing outcomes through policy does not mean creating new inefficiencies when the state itself has contributed directly to creating inequality, as it has with respect to gay people.

The argument here is not that efficiency is a bad goal for policy but that it should not be the only goal. Other goals are also important for the state to pursue when deciding how and whether to be involved in the economy. The policy issues discussed in the remainder of this chapter promote my own feminist economic vision of the needs of women, men, and children in our society, regardless of their sexual orientation, and of the appropriate role of the government in directly and indirectly meeting those needs. In other words, this policy approach addresses the specific needs of lesbian, gay, and bisexual people under the current policy regime, but places those needs in a larger context that recognizes issues for all people and acknowledges the holes in existing policies. This approach draws together principles developed in the growing literature by feminist economists who are carving out an alternative vision of how the economy works and how it *should* operate (see Folbre 1994; Ferber and Nelson 1993).

Other social scientists have appealed to different principles about how to define appropriate policies in related contexts. For instance, David Kirp, Mark Yudof, and Marlene Strong Franks (1986) argue that policies addressing gender-related concerns in the family and workplace should promote opportunity and autonomy, ensure the capacity to exercise choice, provide information about individuals' options, and tolerate a wide range of choices in those spheres by men and women (Kirp et al. 1986, 132–36). Choice and the capacity to exercise choice fit within certain economic traditions, obviously, and are similar in spirit to my feminist policy principles. But the criteria outlined and used here appeal more directly to a concern about economic outcomes (whereas Kirp et al. focus more on processes that determine outcomes rather than the outcomes themselves) and to the specific debates about policy both within and outside the gay community that were sketched above. In doing so, I can address some of the concerns of both opponents and proponents of gay equality with respect to the particular policies discussed, such as same-sex marriages.

Once we have a set of policy goals or principles, various ways of meeting those goals, or policy options, can be compared and evaluated systematically using a method developed by policy analysts (see Bardach 1996). This method asks how well each policy option meets a set of desirable characteristics and requires balancing conflicting goals when options meet some criteria and not others or when some options are not clearly preferable according to all criteria. Neither the application of the four principles set out below nor the principles themselves are limited to policies related to gay and lesbian people, although the focus here is obviously on policies specific to gay people.

The first principle is a focus on policies that facilitate provisioning, that is, ensuring that people's basic needs are met.[1] For most individuals participating in the U.S. economy, these basic needs do not constitute the only economic choices available, but access to the vast array of consumer products that are not necessary to sustain human life is of secondary importance in this analysis. Basic needs would certainly include culturally and biologically appropriate standards for food, shelter, and clothing as well as necessary health care.

Various rationales for this policy goal have been offered by noneconomists. As noted above, Kirp et al. (1986) argue that promoting liberty requires the capacity to exercise choices and that the government can enhance capacity by creating a safety net to satisfy "the basic social and economic wants of persons" (133). Michael Walzer (1983) suggests that the social contract "is an agreement to redistribute the resources of the members in accordance with some shared understanding of their needs" (82). Even in the context of a belief in self-sufficiency, Richard Mohr (1988) argues for a safety net: "each person is primarily responsible for meeting his own basic needs and . . . the government becomes an active provider only when all else fails" (151). The actual design of a complete set of policies that ensure provisioning but do not significantly undermine individual effort would be a complex project worthy of many more books.

For the purposes of this book, however, the main concern is whether various policies related to gay men and lesbians contribute to meeting this goal. Although the popular image of gay people that has been promoted by the myths dissected in this book is of freewheeling consumers of the latest in computer, travel, fashion, and other more discretionary goods, that image hides the underlying reality for all gay people. Provisioning cannot be taken for granted in a world where the loss of a job or the structure of our health care system threaten access to meeting basic needs. Policies related to provisioning would ensure access to existing public benefits and to the private means to provide for needs, both for gay, lesbian, and bisexual people, for heterosexual people, and for children.

The second feminist policy principle recognizes the necessity of reproduction and values the social and economic labor used to raise children and to care for sick people and elderly people. The "caring" aspect of this labor means that the services provided in a market or in large-scale public provision are not exactly interchangeable with family members' caring labor: "With the general category of emotional needs there is at least one that cannot be adequately met by labor supplied only for money. Love cannot be bought" (Folbre 1995, 75). Nancy Folbre defines caring labor based on its motivations, where caring labor is "labor undertaken out of affection or a sense of responsibility for other people, with no expectation of immediate pecuniary reward" (75). Since labor undertaken based on this motivation might provide benefits to the person cared for beyond whatever specific services are rendered (in other words, caring labor might involve what economists call "externalities"), Folbre argues that it may be undervalued by the market economy and, therefore, is in danger of either extinction or an unfair automatic assignment to women. Because of its importance in coordinating social reproduction, caring labor should be a concern in the rethinking of public policies.

Although most of the costs and many of the benefits of having children accrue to legal parents, children are also "public goods" in the sense that they represent (at the very least) a future workforce, future neighbors,

future artists, future parents, and future voters whose lives will influence
the quality of life for many people other than their legal parents (Folbre
1994). This context suggests that all members of society have a responsibility for engaging in reproductive work in some way, whether through
paying taxes for public schools or by raising children. Lesbian and gay
people should, therefore, be encouraged to participate directly in the raising of future generations as parents and at other levels of involvement with
children, as well as indirectly through taxes that fund schools and other
child-related programs.[2]

A third core principle suggests that public policy should promote justice. Policies determining access to jobs and distributing public resources
should be fair. This principle, with its roots in philosophy rather than economics, requires some further understanding of what would be just. Should
sexual orientation guide such allocations? Or, more specifically, is it fair
to use heterosexuality to favor certain people in workplace and family
policy?

One strong answer—a resounding no—can be inferred from the United
States Constitution's promise of equal protection under the law, a promise related to a moral judgment considered to be one of the roots of de-
mocracy in the United States—that all people are created equal.[3] A more
subtle basis for the same answer derives from Michael Walzer's conception of "complex equality" in which fair distributive principles will vary
according to the particular "sphere of justice." A shared social understanding should determine the principles of just distribution within each
sphere. Those principles would prevail over the influence of characteristics not thought to be properly relevant in that sphere, such as using family relationships to get a job or financial wealth to buy a marriage partner
(Walzer 1983).

More specifically, Walzer argues that in the realm of work the distribution of jobs should be determined by the qualifications of applicants. Defining relevant qualifications involves having "some notion of what doing
[the job] well means, what skills it requires, what attitudes and values are
appropriate, and so on" (145), a standard that excludes any personal characteristics that have no impact on performance such as sexual orientation,
presumably. The distribution of love, parental attention, and mutual aid
occurs through families, so the social processes that lead to the formation
of families also assume great importance. Walzer argues that in modern life
the overarching principle for the formation of families is free choice between consenting adults, again a principle that would apply just as well to
same-sex as to opposite-sex couples.[4]

In a Walzerian view of justice in the realm of work and the family, in other words, heterosexuality should not give someone a favored position, even if heterosexuality were a preferred characteristic of members of the society in some other sphere (perhaps in the sphere of religion, for example). The analysis in this chapter incorporates this third policy principle: using sexual orientation to distribute economic resources in either the private sector or the public sector should not be condoned, any more than race or gender are now allowed to be used to exclude women and people of color from jobs or from full legal equality in forming and maintaining families.

A closely related point is that policies creating equality for lesbian and gay people should facilitate (or at least not block) social progress toward equality based on gender and race. In the context of the specific policies considered here, this principle is applied primarily with respect to gender equality since gender and sexual orientation interact in important ways, as discussed in previous chapters. Some research shows that people holding negative attitudes toward lesbians and gay men also tend to have conservative attitudes about gender roles (Herek 1991, 65). Furthermore, as previous chapters showed, the economic position of lesbians has historically been connected to the economic position of women in general, and lesbians' position has improved as women have been treated more equally in the paid labor markets. For lesbians to gain equality in a meaningful economic sense, a fuller gay policy agenda would address women's issues, too.

Finally, the fourth policy principle appeals to the efficiency-enhancing aspect of some gay-related policies and promotes policies that use resources wisely, as in a more mainstream economic analysis. The difference between my appeal to efficiency and a more mainstream approach is, first, that efficiency is not the only goal or even the most important goal of economic policy, and second, markets will not always lead to efficient outcomes.

The importance of using economic resources wisely is evident from the fact that gay men's and lesbians' challenges to family definitions and to other policies have opened up these issues out of practical concerns. Definitions of family relationships, in particular, exist to serve certain economic and social functions, functions that would continue to exist in some form even without current legal definitions. For instance, the inheritance rights, property division rules, hospital visitation rights, and other aspects of being legally married both designate another adult as a truly significant other to third parties and provide a legal framework for sharing an economic life together. These functions, now fulfilled by legal marriage, might be met in several different ways through various policy strategies. The efficiency principle suggests that one way of choosing from among the strategies is to pick the one that is most cost-effective, where total costs also include hidden social costs.

Public policy can reduce inefficient treatment of gay people in other ways, too. For example, the absence of broad public policies to remove or discourage discrimination means that gay workers must use time and energy to maintain the secrecy of the closet, in some cases, or to organize and urge their employers to adopt nondiscrimination policies and domestic partner recognition. Addressing these issues one company at a time is a slow and costly process that could be speeded up significantly by policymakers, while relying on the competitive process to weed out discriminatory employers means waiting a long time—if that process works at all. Encouraging respect for diversity could conceivably have positive effects in many circumstances, as companies and society draw more effectively on the perspectives and talents of a wider range of people.

Setting out these four policy principles as distinct and seemingly independent disguises the fact that they may interact in practical applications. As an example, encouraging gay people's involvement in reproductive and caring labor could also help to transform the gendered nature of work with young, old, and sick people, promoting more equal sharing of that work between men and women. Traditionally, the caring labor that goes into child rearing and care for the sick and disabled has been the province of women. Gay men have demonstrated that men also have the capacity to provide care as they have responded to the AIDS epidemic with enormous compassion and commitment of time and other economic resources in caring for their sick friends and partners.[5] Or consider the interactions created by policies that encourage efficiency in achieving practical aims. The creation of "domestic partnership" as an option for both same-sex and opposite-sex couples represents a major innovation in family policy that is not a simple mimicking of heterosexual marriage, but provides options for couples to create relationships outside of an institution that ascribes powerful social roles to married men and women. Thus even an apparently reformist policy might have far-reaching implications for establishing equality between men and women, as well as between gay people and heterosexual people.

In the previous chapters, I identified a wide range of policies that shape gay people's economic position. A complete analysis of these policies using the four principles would fill another book, however. Rather than attempt a complete accounting of the changes in policies necessary to meet those guidelines, the following discussion raises a set of the most hotly debated workplace- and family-oriented policy issues for gay people that were identified in previous chapters and sketches out how the policies that have been proposed do or do not meet the criteria laid out above. The next section considers first nondiscrimination policies, along with a brief analysis of the desirability of some form of affirmative action for gay employees, and then takes up policies promoting domestic partner benefits. Chapter 8 addresses family issues within the same framework, considering first the most desirable policy approach for dealing with adult family relationships and then focusing on definitions of parenthood.

Employment Antidiscrimination Laws

One of the most active issues in legislatures and gay activism concerns the position of gay people in the workplace. The primary discussion has focused on civil rights laws that would prohibit discrimination based on sexual orientation, with some consideration of extending employee spousal benefits to domestic partners and a bit of debate about the reach of such laws with respect to affirmative action. The primary appeal of these laws is the fairness principle: access to jobs and benefits should not be based on one's sexual orientation. Because employment is the key to income for most individuals, the treatment of gay people in the workplace also clearly raises issues of access to the means of provisioning.[6] When Cheryl Summerville lost her job as a cook at a Cracker Barrel restaurant because she was a lesbian, she also lost an income that supported her son and paid the mortgage on the house they lived in. Furthermore, most people with health insurance get it through their own employer or a family member's employer, so employment benefits are a key element of provisioning, as well.

Just as antidiscrimination policies require fairness and facilitate provisioning, they also clearly appeal to some of the other policy principles. For instance, nondiscrimination laws open up access to jobs that involve work with children, such as being child-care workers or teachers. Banning gay people from those jobs has often been upheld by courts,[7] suggesting that an explicit law is necessary to prevent such discriminatory treatment and to allow gay people to participate in the raising of the next generation. In addition, if nondiscrimination laws allow gay people to be more open in the workplace, perhaps the cultural assignment of appropriate jobs for men and women will break down in response to the visibility of a group of people often thought to violate gender norms by definition. In other words, a seemingly simple policy that promotes equality of opportunity and treatment in the workplace for gay people could have broader effects that open up possibilities for heterosexual men and women, as well.

Another goal of the feminist policy criteria is to promote efficiency, which is also the mainstream standard for government involvement in economic transactions. Economists have long debated the need for antidiscrimination laws, looking first at the demonstrated need for such policies. In the case of sexual orientation discrimination, the evidence assembled in chapter 2 from statistical studies, from reports by lesbian and gay people, and from employer attitudes makes a strong case that discrimination against gay people exists. This kind of discrimination practiced against lesbian, gay, and bisexual people involves an inefficient utilization of our economy's most important resource—human labor. Discrimination also has a harmful feedback effect on worker productivity by increasing the potential cost to workers of coming out. The evidence in chapter 3 showed that fear of discrimination pushes gay workers into time-consuming and work-detracting efforts to hide their sexual orientation. From this perspective, nondiscrimination laws can increase efficiency by reducing discrimination and increasing disclosure.

The efficiency story gets more complicated when we question the impact of gay workers' coming out on the well-being and productivity of their heterosexual coworkers. If some heterosexual people strongly prefer gay colleagues to remain in the closet, as surveys suggest for a minority of people, then more disclosure will make prejudiced people worse off. To some extent, time and education might alleviate their temporary distress caused by a fairer policy. Even if it does not, the usual practice with respect to civil rights policies in the United States has been to discount this reduction in well-being for those who prefer to discriminate. As Judge Richard Posner points out, allowing this potential distress (Posner calls it "revulsion") to guide policy might lead to further assaults on the rights of those with any unpopular beliefs or behavior, no matter how innocuous those beliefs and behavior might be (Posner 1992, 202).

A more problematic possibility is that heterosexual workers will react in a way that reduces productivity. Chapter 3 suggests that discrimination arises out of employers' fear of disruption and loss of control if heterosexual coworkers react badly to openly gay workers. From this perspective, a nondiscrimination law could be a source of inefficiency if it leads to more disclosure by gay and lesbian workers. But the discussion above also noted that employers can manage new situations of this kind in a way that would reduce or eliminate any short-term backlash.[8] Even a short downturn in productivity resulting from the minority of prejudiced coworkers might also be outweighed over time by the gains from using gay workers' skills and talents more efficiently.

When the source of discrimination is related to employers' own prejudices, though, the question shifts: If discrimination against gay people is inefficient, wouldn't employers have an incentive to end it without requiring government intervention? In Gary Becker's model, discriminators are placing their firms at a competitive disadvantage. By not hiring gay and heterosexual workers based on their productivity, discriminators increase their monetary costs of production and reduce their profits. If other employers exist who do not share the same distaste for gay workers, they can snap up gay workers at a bargain price, since discrimination means that gay workers are paid less. According to this theory, if nondiscriminators are competing with discriminators in the marketplace, the nondiscriminators should have higher profits and should eventually grow large enough to drive their discriminating competitors out of business. The wages of gay people will rise accordingly as they are seen as equivalent to heterosexual workers.[9] This vision of the operation of markets implies that government policies are unnecessary. The inefficiency of discrimination limits its survivability if enough employers do not discriminate.

Should we count on the competitive process to dissolve antigay workplace discrimination rather than resort to an explicit legal prohibition of such discrimination? Even if the source of discrimination is employers' irrational distaste for hiring gay workers, the prospects for a market resolution are not good. First, Becker's original model was designed to explain discrimination against African Americans, but it is clear that unequal treatment of black people is still common despite the even higher cost of discrimination imposed by potential legal penalties.[10] Second, the expectation that competition will completely eliminate discrimination rests on some important conditions that are not likely to exist, such as companies using identical production techniques and engaging in such intense competition with each other that they must seek out all possible ways of reducing costs simply to survive. Finally, even if the market would work in the end, waiting around for this to take place means incurring years, decades, or perhaps even centuries of economic inefficiency. As economist John Donohue has pointed out, a law prohibiting discrimination can improve efficiency over time by speeding up the end of discrimination, even if market forces would eventually eliminate it (Donohue 1986). This discussion suggests that, even according to the classical standards of economic analysis, a government can improve society's use of human resources by prohibiting certain kinds of actions by individual employers.

Economists generally overlook the internal political context of employers' decisions, although that context has important implications for a different efficiency argument for a law against antigay employment discrimination. This argument concerns the inner workings of corporations and some of the economic issues involved in collective action. In an effort to standardize treatment of employees, corporations have guidelines like nondiscrimination policies to guide managers. But corporations do not generally spontaneously change their policies without some internal or external pressure. On issues related to lesbian and gay people, employers do not seem to be very knowledgeable, according to consultants and others who work with corporations, so someone must educate them.[11]

While in a larger social sense this education time is probably well spent if it changes attitudes as well as behavior, the reliance on individual employees' initiative in these situations is inefficient. The process of convincing an employer that nondiscrimination is in her or his best economic interest occurs only at some cost to the individuals lobbying for the policy change. At the very least, those who take on the cause of promoting nondiscriminatory policies give up their time, which sometimes could include work time, as well as risk their jobs if the bosses turn out to be prejudiced against gay people. These costs of promoting the change by taking on the risky proposition of educating the boss are likely to fall to a small number of gay people. But most of the benefits of any policy change are going to be spread among many individuals, and any single individual gains only a small part of the total benefits. As a result, many individuals will shy away from such duty, reducing the amount of education and inhibiting the spread of private sector policies protecting gay people from discrimination.

Pulled together, these arguments suggest that a broad public policy prohibiting employment discrimination based on sexual orientation enhances economic efficiency and the total output of the economy in several ways. Employers are encouraged to use productivity instead of prejudice in making hiring, promotion, and salary decisions. Customers are on notice that companies can no longer cater to negative attitudes toward gay people. And gay employees can focus on their jobs without fear of discrimination and without expending valuable time and energy hiding their sexual orientation.

As critics of *all* civil rights laws complain, nondiscrimination laws limit employers' freedom to do as they please. Concerns about inequity and efficiency have overridden the principle of employers' absolute freedom in many contexts, such as in prohibiting lying in business deals or failing to fulfill contracts (see Mohr [1988], for a more complete analysis along these lines). Similar concerns have driven a national commitment to limit employers' discretion to discriminate when that discretion is costly in terms of economic and social harm. Applying the same standards to sexual orientation discrimination that federal and state governments have applied to discrimination based on race, sex, religion, and disability leads to a similar conclusion: a federal nondiscrimination policy serves the country's economic interest.

Extensions of Affirmative Action

Given those parallels in economic and policy analysis, it is not surprising that gay activists are following in the tradition of older civil rights struggles opposed to discrimination against African Americans, Jews, and women, among others (see Burstein [1985] for a history of such laws). Both the goals—a law banning discrimination and an enforcement process that is driven by filing complaints—and a political strategy that appeals to the harm from discrimination draw on analogies between the situations of gay and lesbian people and of other already protected groups. The parallels raise the question of how far to take the traditional civil rights model, especially with respect to affirmative action.

Laws forbidding race and sex discrimination have been enhanced by affirmative action requirements for federal (and usually state and local) government contractors. Affirmative action has been the subject of enormous debate since the 1970s, but the use of this tool is sometimes explicitly ruled out in legislation related to sexual orientation. For instance, the proposed Employment Nondiscrimination Act explicitly states, "A covered entity shall not adopt or implement a quota on the basis of sexual orientation." [12] But some individual employers, such as colleges like Northeastern University and Antioch College, some nonprofit organizations, and some law firms, have added gays and lesbians to the groups covered by affirmative action, making this an important practical issue at the private and public level. Should gay people be included in affirmative action programs?

The first step in considering this issue is to define affirmative action, a term used in many different ways. One interpretation of affirmative action focuses on ensuring equal opportunity in the *process* involved in making employment decisions and would promote such practices as training programs and extra recruitment efforts (e.g., Reynolds 1986). A second way of defining affirmative action is as a set of results-oriented employment practices. The kind of affirmative action plan required of companies doing business with the federal government, for instance, starts with a "utilization analysis." The employer compares the race and gender composition of its workforce with the race and gender composition of the relevant labor market, which might be based on occupation and location. If a company's workforce has a lower percentage of women or people of color than is found in its relevant labor pool, then the employer must closely examine its hiring procedures and must try to increase the representation of the underutilized groups by choosing from several race- and sex-conscious practices, including targeted recruiting efforts, redesigned selection procedures, and hiring goals with timetables (OFCCP 1980).

Analyzing the need for or desirability of affirmative action for gay people is less an exercise in applying the feminist policy principles and is more one of thinking through the practical issues and outcomes. First, the fact that many gay and lesbian workers hide their sexual orientation to some extent means that utilization analysis would be difficult, if not impossible. Utilization analysis requires two kinds of reliable and detailed data, neither of which is available: the proportion of gay and lesbian workers in local workforces and different occupations and the proportion of gay and lesbian workers in an individual employer's workforce. This means that employers have no way of knowing how many gay workers they "should" hire in a particular job from the perspective of results-oriented affirmative action, even if they know how many gay people already work at a given location.

Second, setting goals and timetables for hiring gay workers is likely to mainly benefit white gay men, thus conflicting with other affirmative action goals related to the employment of women and people of color. White gay men, who are more likely to be out even without affirmative action as an incentive, as mentioned in chapter 3, have the greatest incentive and opportunity for using sexual orientation affirmative action. Gay people who are women or are black or Latino gay men, for instance, are already covered by affirmative action, so they would have relatively little incentive to disclose their sexual orientation to a prospective employer.

Finally and most important, goals and timetables are designed to remedy situations in which some groups appear to have been systematically excluded from certain jobs. The data in chapters 2 and 3 suggest that gay employees are likely to be found in many different kinds of jobs, although they might not be out to their employers. From this perspective, the problem is not exclusion but invisibility, a problem that results-oriented affirmative action is unlikely to address. (It is possible that exclusion could become a

problem if gay workers become more visible, however. If that were to occur, some reconsideration of affirmative action would be in order.)

Altogether, these problems suggest that results-oriented affirmative action is not the best policy instrument for ensuring equality in the workplace for gay people at this time. A faster and more appropriate way to increase the visible representation of gay people in an employer's workforce
is to implement policies that encourage workers to come out. Chapter 3
suggests that explicit nondiscrimination policies reduce workers' fears of
discrimination and result in greater disclosure. Domestic partner policies
also encourage disclosure, both directly by providing a financial incentive
for an employee to declare and document the existence of a same-sex partner, and indirectly by demonstrating the employer's commitment to fair
treatment. Open recruitment of gay employees through ads in gay publications or at gay employee group job fairs also demonstrates an employer's intentions. Inclusion of gay issues in workplace diversity training
could have a similar effect. This general approach, which one might term
"actions of affirmation" in this context, fits into the process-oriented version of affirmative action and promotes the goals of results-oriented affirmative action. This approach also avoids possible outcomes that trigger
fervent opposition to results-oriented affirmative action: since no preference is given to gay applicants, no hint of unfairness should trouble heterosexual employees, and no policy-induced stigma should be attached to
a gay employee.

Compensation Equity through Domestic Partner Benefits

Much of the analysis of nondiscrimination laws is relevant for thinking
about domestic partner benefits, as well. Providing these benefits is usually
treated as an employment issue, although broader legal recognition of domestic partnerships is sometimes proposed as an alternative to marriage-
based benefits, a perspective taken up in the following chapter. In this section, the focus is on policies that would facilitate or even require equal
treatment of gay and lesbian employees' domestic partners and heterosexual employees' spouses. In that sense, partner benefits are a form of
nondiscrimination policy that recognizes that a gay employee with a partner is similarly situated to a heterosexual employee with a spouse in both
a practical and emotional sense.[13]

Applying the feminist policy principles of promoting fairness, provisioning, caring labor, and efficiency shows that domestic partner policies
fit easily into that policy framework. As chapter 4 discussed, a primary reason for increasing activism around partner benefits by gay employees

concerns the unfairness of employer policies that fail to recognize the practical and moral equivalence of gay employees' same-sex partners with heterosexual employees' legal spouses. As such, the traditional policies effectively reduce compensation to gay employees with partners when compared with similarly situated heterosexual employees who are legally married. Although providing additional benefits to married employees appears to be a neutral policy with respect to sexual orientation, the fact that same-sex couples cannot legally marry means that gay people with partners are clearly disadvantaged because of their sexual orientation.

The concept of provisioning is also served since in the United States, for better or worse, access to many of the most important nonwage means of providing for life's necessities comes through employment. Implementing universal health care coverage and more generous social security benefits would certainly be more complete policies for provisioning. But until that happens, health care coverage as well as adequate retirement income will continue to be tied to having a job with an employer who includes those benefits in a compensation package, as chapter 4 also discussed.

These benefits also promote certain aspects of caring labor, such as facilitating care for children and for older people. Companies that offer benefits to spouses generally cover children of employees, too, and benefits like pension plans help to provide for retired employees and their spouses. By allowing time off to care for sick family members, family-related leave policies are designed to ameliorate some of the work-family conflict that employees often experience. Including domestic partners under the definition of family member would further address work-family conflict and would make it easier for gay and lesbian employees to meet their responsibilities for care. Some people argue that the real source of unfairness in employment benefits packages needing change is paying employees with families more than single nonparent employees. This perspective overlooks single employees' long-term social and economic interest in the well-being of other people's children.

Furthermore, challenges by gay and lesbian people to employers' narrow definition of family can expand the options for family roles available to all men and women. Domestic partner benefits aid heterosexual families by opening up the possibility that employers will also include unmarried opposite-sex partners of employees or other dependents, such as a niece or elderly parent. Although pursuing coverage of gay employees' domestic partners does not *require* recognizing and including these other kinds of employee connections, the activism of gay employees is often the direct catalyst for expanding the group covered in employers' definitions of family. Years of activism by gay employees of the University of California system finally resulted in the inclusion of same-sex domestic partners in benefits plans, for instance. At the same time, the U.C. Board of Regents allowed employees to name any financially dependent relative who lives with the employee for health insurance coverage. Similarly, some employers, such as the State of Vermont, have chosen to include opposite-sex domestic partners (they initially included only same-sex partners) after employees with unmarried heterosexual partners complained about discrimination against them (Badgett 1994). This expansion of the relationships recognized as family may help to free men and women from the more restrictive gender roles that might be implied by "husband" or "wife."

Policies promoting the spread of domestic partner benefits can promote efficiency in the same way that antidiscrimination laws do, even though the prospect of efficiency gains has probably not been the driving force behind widespread recognition of partners by employers. Chapter 4 argued that employers might have an incentive to offer partner benefits even if not required to do so, since companies offering them could gain a recruiting or retention advantage that improves their profitability, or their employees might work harder in return for believing that they have been treated fairly. These forces are not likely to be powerful enough to push *all* firms to voluntarily adopt such policies, and chapter 4 set out the other conditions that have promoted the spread of domestic partner policies. In particular, the concentration of partner benefits in certain industries that demand relatively scarce, highly skilled labor, such as lawyers, professors, or software engineers, implies that competitive pressures alone will influence only some employers.

Obviously, requiring companies to give equal benefits to partners would reduce the competitive advantage incentive, since all firms offering spousal benefits would have to offer partner benefits. But as with employment nondiscrimination laws, laws promoting domestic partner benefits would reduce the need for employee anxiety and effort expended in collectively organizing to lobby their employers, increasing the potential productivity of all gay and lesbian workers.[14] Also, to the extent that family-related policies reduce all workers' anxiety about work-family conflict and raise productivity, gay and lesbian employees' anxieties will lessen and efficiency will increase.

More likely, employers will complain about partner benefits boosting employment costs without a corresponding increase in employee productivity. One major concern of employers is that labor costs will rise dramatically, mainly from increasing health care costs. As the data in chapter 4 demonstrate, employers have little to fear with regard to the possibility that workers will sign up their sick friends and partners. The possible cost increases only occur from the fact that employers' health plans will be covering more people than before. Those numbers have proven to be small, typically boosting coverage and costs by less than 1 percent when only same-sex partners are included.

If inclusion of partners were universal, however, the increase for employers could be actually be *smaller* than that. This seemingly paradoxical result stems from analyzing the *net* effect on all employers. Say Tina and Susan are domestic partners, and Tina's employer provides health coverage to spouses. If all employers with spousal coverage decide to cover partners as well, then Tina could add Susan to Tina's employer plan. But if Susan's employer also provided health benefits, then the net change in the number of people covered by *all* employers is zero, since Tina's employer gains a person and Susan's loses one. If Susan had been uninsured, though, the net change is one new person covered by an employer. In other words, the only new people added with domestic partner coverage are those who were previously uninsured by employers.

This example suggests that the crucial variable in assessing total costs to employers will be how many uninsured people have domestic partners with employer coverage for spouses. In 1997, 32 million adults were uninsured. Estimating the number of those uninsured who have same-sex partners who are employed and receive health insurance is not easy, since data on gay people are sparse. But an estimate can be constructed with some reasonable assumptions. Suppose that 5 percent of the U.S. adult population is gay or lesbian and that 50 percent of those workers have a domestic partner.[15] Then we would expect to find approximately 809,275 uninsured domestic partners. Since only 53 percent of people had health insurance through their own employer in 1997, only 53 percent of those uninsured people would likely benefit from their partner's coverage, so roughly 429,000 partners would now get insurance through an employer.[16] Dividing that by the number of employees with health insurance (76.6 million) suggests that employers would experience an average net increased enrollment of 0.6 percent from covering same-sex domestic partners.

The size of this increase is sensitive to the assumption of the proportion of gay people and how many have partners, but the exercise shows that the number is not likely to be large. Even if 10 percent of the workforce was gay or lesbian, the net increase in enrollment would be around 1.1 percent. New enrollment would be lower if some employees chose not to sign their partners up for fear of disclosing their sexual orientation or if the employee cost share for coverage was too high. New enrollment would be higher, though, if the proportion of people with partners were higher.

Given the argument that the costs of offering such benefits are likely to be small and offset to some extent by efficiency gains for some or all employers, the next question is how to use policy to promote the spread of domestic partner benefits. First and foremost, laws that prohibit discrimination based on sexual orientation should specify that compensation plans providing benefits for employees' legal spouses but not for same-sex partners are illegal forms of discrimination. Currently, existing state nondiscrimination laws are silent on that specific topic, although legislation sometimes excludes benefits as a category of employer compensation that is subject to the nondiscrimination requirement. Without specific exclusion, however, the prohibition of nondiscrimination has largely been interpreted as *excluding* benefits defined by marriage, as chapter 4 discusses. While the exclusion of benefits from the jurisdiction of nondiscrimination laws might serve an important political purpose by diluting legislation and incrementally improving protections for gay workers, they do little to change actual institutions that actively discriminate against gay people. So far, two California cities, Davis and Sacramento, are the only ones requiring private employers to treat domestic partners equally with spouses, but only with respect to family-related and personal leave policies (van der Meide 2000, 17).

A second policy lever used to date only by the cities of San Francisco, Seattle, and Los Angeles is for governments to require that businesses and organizations that sell goods and services to the city government offer equal benefits to domestic partners and married employees.[17] (City contractors that do not offer spousal benefits are not required to offer domestic partner benefits.) This policy constitutes a "carrot" to reward employers who do not discriminate rather than a "stick" (like a ban of discriminatory benefit plans) that punishes recalcitrant employers. This kind of policy might also provide enormous leverage, since many contractors are likely to have plants or sites outside of the particular local jurisdiction, and some of those employees might receive such benefits, as well.

As employers themselves, policymakers in governments can also set precedents and "best practice" examples for private sector employers by implementing partner benefits for their own employees. When states demonstrate to private employers that domestic partner coverage is neither administratively onerous nor prohibitively expensive, other employers might be more willing to change their policies voluntarily. Also, to the extent that private sector companies are competing for some of the same workers as governments, the competitive pressure to extend coverage to domestic partners increases when governments act as employers. Some limits to the "best practice" approach exist, however. As chapter 4 describes, state courts ruled that the city of Boston went beyond its state-given powers in providing partner benefits.

A fourth policy approach, which complements the possibilities above, would adjust other policies that sometimes block provision of partner benefits and make domestic partner policies less attractive to employers. In particular, the state commissions that regulate insurance companies have often thrown up barriers unforeseen by gay activists. In several cases, innovative employers have bumped up against insurance regulators who claimed that state insurance laws actually prohibited employers from covering domestic partners. The Insurance Commission in Georgia adamantly refused to allow insurance companies to offer domestic partner benefits until a Fulton County judge ordered the commission to lift the ban in 1999 (*City of Atlanta v. Oxendine*).

Federal tax laws also prevent employers from giving gay and lesbian employees fully equal benefits. One of the ways that federal tax policy encourages employers to provide health care benefits is to exclude the employer's contribution from employees' taxable income. In other words, if an employer pays an employee $1,000 in wages, the employee must pay state and federal income taxes on that $1,000. But if an employer spends $1,000 on health insurance for an employee and his or her spouse, the employee does *not* pay income taxes on that $1,000, increasing the value of the benefit. The Internal Revenue Service has interpreted existing tax laws to mean that employers' payments for domestic partner coverage constitute taxable income for the employee. In practice, this means that an employee in the 28 percent tax bracket would pay $280 more in federal taxes for a benefit worth $1,000, as well as additional state taxes. Unfortunately, the federal Defense of Marriage Act of 1996 forbids the federal government from recognizing same-sex marriages in income taxation, making a change to tax policies difficult.

These policies related to domestic partner benefits are not mutually exclusive. Rather, they constitute a whole package of actions that state, local, or federal governments could and should take to encourage employers to offer domestic partner benefits, even if policymakers stop short of *requiring* employers to do so. Endorsing domestic partner benefits is not equivalent to endorsing our nation's health care policy but is instead a means of pushing institutional equality for gay and lesbian people. Along the way, partner benefits also meet the other feminist policy criteria. This is not to say that some other policy, such as universal health care coverage provided by a centrally financed authority, would not *better* serve the policy principles outlined earlier, but that policy strategy would not directly address the need for institutional equality for gay people in the other kinds of benefits provided by employers.

A more powerful strategy for achieving equal treatment with respect to employment benefits would require a major shift in family policy to give same-sex relationships equal legal treatment compared with heterosexual relationships. Such a strategy addresses but goes well beyond employment-related concerns, allowing an automatic integration of two people's lives in many different contexts. This larger topic is taken up in the next chapter.

Reducing Inequities, Part 2: Family Policies

The questions related to family policy addressed in this chapter ask to what extent and in what way should the government be involved in the construction of lesbian, gay, and bisexual people's families? This question has two dimensions that will be treated in turn: first, the relationships between adults, and second, the legal relationship between parents and children, considered in the second section of the chapter. In general, I will use the principles from chapter 7 to analyze different possible policy options.

From the perspective of gay people themselves, whether the state should be involved in defining adult relationships is not obvious. Some legal and social analysts argue that using heterosexual marriage as a model for gay couples, or even any form of state definition of relationships between adults, undermines the radical potential of gay people to create and promote alternative visions of family (in particular, see Robson 1994; Ettelbrick 1989). For these analysts, giving in to traditional definitions of "family" means giving up the unique contributions of gay people in creating alternative configurations of close emotional and economic ties between adults. However, other gay and lesbian people continue to pursue the right to legally marry, a pursuit that they justify with the abstract notion of full legal equality as well as by the more practical concerns of same-sex couples.

From the perspective of the heterosexual mainstream, the answer is a bit clearer with regard to gay adults. Recent surveys suggest that while some people in the United States are willing to recognize the legitimacy of ties among same-sex couples for certain purposes, such as for inheritance rights or perhaps even employment benefits, few agree that same-sex couples should be granted the right to legally marry. For instance, in 1997 only 35 percent of a national sample supported "legally sanctioned gay marriages," but 62 percent of people in the same survey supported equal inheritance rights and 57 percent supported equal social security benefits for "gay spouses" (Yang 1997, 14–15). Marriage is said to be reserved for male-female couples because (1) marriage is and always has been defined as the relationship between a "husband" and a "wife," making same-sex marriages impossible; (2) the purpose of marriage is procreation, which is impossible for same-sex couples; or (3) expanding access would somehow devalue marriage and would discourage heterosexual couples from marrying.

The discussion in this chapter does not address all of these concerns about state involvement directly (some were addressed in chapter 6), but frames them in a different way that might also be persuasive to some critics of the policies suggested here. A helpful way to think through different policy approaches and the debates related to government involvement in gay family issues first requires understanding the range of possibilities that have been suggested, which include legal marriage, domestic partnership, the status quo of supposedly "unregulated" relationships, "making the family less necessary," or the Scandinavian "marriage lite." In some cases, the characteristics of a particular option are not well developed, while in other cases the characteristics are misunderstood or are incompletely understood by those engaged in the debate over the best policy approach. Once the options are clearer, analyzing them in light of the feminist policy principles will be easier.

Legal Marriage. This legal relationship between two adults is the most clearly defined and the most familiar to people in the United States. Marriage is, however, a complex and changing social construct, often involving religious elements and deep cultural meaning outside of its legal and economic implications. The permanent legal characteristics of marriage are impossible to pin down, since both the state's definition and the social functions served by marriage have varied greatly across time and cultures (Hunter 1995b; Glendon 1989). Many students of the history of marriage point out that what was once a clearly sexist and racist institution in the United States—one that prevented women from owning property and was denied to slaves and later to interracial couples, for instance—has been radically revised into a relationship characterized by formal gender and racial equality. The remaining exception to explicit gender neutrality concerns the requirement that only opposite-sex couples are eligible to marry (see, e.g., Hunter 1995, 111; Glendon 1989, 94). The historical flexibility of marriage law (both in the United States and in other countries) leads law professor Nan Hunter to conclude that many of those opposed to legalizing marriages of same-sex couples, including both the heterosexuals who are antigay and the gay people who are antimarriage, are making the same historical mistake in making claims about some essential quality of the legal relationship known as "marriage."

More formally, marriage is contractual, and the contract is a standard one. Two people agree to particular rights and obligations with respect to the other, including mutual support and an equitable division of the couple's property if the relationship ends. The contract also involves the state, which enforces and has an interest in the marriage. In practice, though, such obligations are commonly subject to direct state regulation only in case of a family crisis, such as death, separation, divorce, or insolvency, as Mary Ann Glendon notes (Glendon 1989, 110). For an opposite-sex couple, entering into this relationship is a simple matter, constrained usually only by laws related to the age, blood relationship, and marital status of the two individuals. William Eskridge points out that it is harder to obtain a driver's license than a marriage license: "The state is sending more of a normative signal about the particular applicant(s) when it issues a driver's license (this character can see, drive, and usually guess the rules of the road) than when it issues a marriage license (these people have filled out the form correctly)" (Eskridge 1996, 107).

Being married is also a status that qualifies a couple for certain advantages and disadvantages with respect to the government and other third parties. Other laws recognize marital status in giving a spouse rights of inheritance, the right to sue third parties for injuring or killing a spouse, the right to make decisions for an incapacitated spouse, the right to receive social security spousal and survivor benefits, the right to preferential treatment according to immigration law, and the right not to testify against a spouse, among others.[1] Third parties, such as employers and other businesses (most notably insurers), sometimes treat spouses more favorably with respect to employment benefits or family discounts. It is important to note that these rights, even those granted by state and federal governments, are incidental to the actual marriage and can be revised or revoked. As noted in chapter 4 on domestic partner benefits, employers offer benefits to spouses of employees only by custom—they are not required to do so. Being married also results in some disadvantages, such as possible tax increases for two-earner couples (see Alm, Badgett, and Whittington [2000], for a discussion of the so-called marriage penalty) and loss of eligibility for certain means-tested government benefits programs.

Unregulated Relationships. Certainly, one policy option for dealing with gay adult relationships would be to continue the status quo, which has provided enormous freedom to gay people to structure their family relationships. Those relationships appear to typically center on couples, some of whom choose to publicly and formally proclaim their commitment to one another in ceremonies (see, for example, Sherman 1992;

Lewin 1998). Others have pointed out that close friendships take on characteristics of family members (e.g., Nardi 1992), including the emotional, social, and even economic support that is typical of family members, as seen in the networks of people that Kath Weston calls "families we choose." Heterosexual couples have a similar opportunity to form such family relationships outside of marriage.

But the unregulated quality of these family relationships does not necessarily remove them from the reach of the law. In many cases couples or members of larger kinship groups might choose to replicate certain features that are automatic for married couples, such as writing wills and relationship agreements or granting powers of attorney to assign someone authority to make decisions in case of incapacitation. The problem for same-sex couples, of course, is that they cannot completely replicate marriage (and some of those documents have been successfully challenged by biological relatives[2]), nor can they create the status that marriage has in the eyes of third parties. Even without written documents or agreements, unmarried couples might be viewed as having some kind of implicit agreement. Courts have ruled on a division of property when a cohabiting (i.e., unmarried) opposite-sex couple breaks up, for instance, generally basing their decisions on explicit and implicit agreements by the members of the couple.[3] In other situations, courts have ruled that unmarried couples, both opposite-sex and same-sex, should be treated as married couples, both in granting benefits (such as the *Braschi v. Stahl* case related to tenant succession in New York City) and in taking away certain benefits where marriage would have eliminated eligibility, such as welfare benefits (Hunter 1995, 115–16). Thus even the lack of a formal relationship does not always eliminate state involvement.

This status quo option is not addressed in detail in this chapter, as it fails to meet some simple tests related to the feminist policy criteria. The current position for gay people treats them quite differently from heterosexuals, violating the fairness criterion and preventing gay people from gaining the social and economic benefits of marriage to be discussed below. And in some sense, unmarried heterosexual partners are in an equivalent legal position, so this option for gay people would not be precluded if gay couples were given access to more formal relationship ties.

Domestic Partnerships. As a social and legal model, domestic partnerships are difficult to define with any precision. On one hand, as discussed in chapters 4 and 7, most of the political action is concentrated in efforts to convince employers to recognize same-sex and sometimes opposite-sex partners of employees as eligible for benefits that those employers grant to employees' spouses. A second and related level of political and policy action has focused on encouraging states and cities to establish registries for domestic partnerships, although such registries are fought for in the hopes that they will someday be connected to the provision of benefits (Chambers 1992, 190). In registering their partnership, two individuals publicly proclaim their exclusive commitment to one another and their economic interdependence. Such registries publicly recognize couples' relationships (see Lewin [1998] for a discussion of the functioning of the registries in San Francisco), and the registries also serve an informational purpose for employers (particularly municipal employers, as in New York and San Francisco, for instance) and other third parties (such as jails or hospitals) who need some mechanism to identify relationships that should be recognized for certain purposes.

Outside of those situations, the meaning of domestic partnership registration is not terribly clear. To register as partners in San Francisco, for instance, a couple must declare that they "are two adults who have chosen to share one another's lives in an intimate and committed relationship of mutual caring, who live together, and who have agreed to be jointly responsible for basic living expenses incurred during the Domestic Partnership" (ordinance quoted in Chambers 1992, 204). Hunter points out that this language suggests a contractual agreement but that registration involves no agreement about ownership of property during the relationship nor the division of property or other obligations should the partnership end (Hunter 1995, 118).

"Marriage Lite." As the debate over legalizing same-sex marriage progresses in the United States and other parts of the world, lawmakers have responded with compromises that grant almost all of the rights and responsibilities of marriage to same-sex couples. In Norway, Sweden, Denmark, Iceland, Hungary, France, and the Netherlands, legislation has allowed same-sex couples to register as partners (or have access to "common–law" marriage status in Hungary) and have almost all of the rights and responsibilities of married couples, with the exception of the right to a church wedding in Scandinavia or the right to adopt children, which is excluded in all of those countries. (The Netherlands is expected to soon allow same-sex couples to legally marry, however.)

In the United States, such efforts to create a compromise relationship would have to be undertaken at the state level, where family policy is rooted. To date, only a few serious efforts have been mounted to create what might be thought of as marriage-minus or partnership-plus policies. Vermont has gone the farthest of any state after a 1999 state Supreme Court ruling in *Baker v. Vermont* that found the denial of the right to marry for same-sex couples was a violation of the state constitution's obligation to provide equal benefits for all citizens. Vermont legislators balked at the simple solution of opening marriage to same-sex couples. Instead, the state legislature created a "civil union" status in 2000 that provides for same-sex couples virtually all of the benefits of marriage that the state of Vermont itself can grant. It is unlikely that other states and the federal government will recognize such a status, however, and the reactions of employers and other third parties are difficult to predict.

No other state has gone as far as Vermont, although some have moved in that direction. In an effort to prevent the legalization of same-sex marriage in 1997, Hawaiian state legislators created a "reciprocal beneficiary" relationship to recognize same-sex relationships (and certain other kinds of relationships between two adults who are not allowed to marry) for purposes of many spousal benefits, including survivorship, health benefits, employment benefits, property rights, and torts (H.B. No. 118, H.D. 1, S.D. 1, "A Bill For An Act Relating To Unmarried Couples"). No requirements of mutual support were included, nor were any changes made to laws related to children. While 435 couples had signed up as of October 1998 (State of Hawaii Auditor 1999), narrow interpretations of the law's impact by the state attorney general and the expiration of certain provisions have limited its usefulness. Lawmakers in California created a domestic partner registry for all same-sex couples and for opposite-sex couples over the age of sixty-two. Registration requires couples to attest that they are "jointly responsible for each other's living expenses" and have a common residence.[4] The bill gives domestic partners hospital visitation rights and allows (but does not require) state and local employers in California to provide domestic partner benefits. Some legislators are also pushing for the use of the new relationship for establishing other rights for partners. In Colorado, a statewide commission appointed by then-governor Roy Romer recommended that a relationship parallel to marriage be created for "committed relationships," with those relationships being granted the same rights and obligations of marriage (Governor's Commission on the Rights and Responsibilities of Same-Sex Relationships 1998).

"Make the Family Less Necessary." A final possibility suggested by feminist critics of marriage is that expanding individuals' range of feasible and desirable family relationships requires the revision of the social structures, laws, and incentives that make marriage the most attractive option for many people. In policy terms, this would mean the stripping away of the material benefits of legal marriage. Instead, benefits that are necessary for

the full health and welfare of human beings would be provided to all individuals, regardless of family status or employment status. So, for example, health care would be universally provided and would not depend on employment or marital status. Adequate retirement income would be guaranteed to all. Child care, housing, and housework assistance would be provided in a more collective manner. Within this policy framework, marriage might remain a choice for individuals but would be one that is not favored with economic incentives provided by the state. Overall, this argument involves no formal alternative to marriage as a legal relationship:

> What is needed is not to build up an alternative to the family—new forms of household that would fulfill all the needs that families are supposed to fulfill today—but to make the family less necessary, by building up all sorts of other ways of meeting people's needs, ways less volatile and inadequate than those based on the assumption that "blood is thicker than water." (Barrett and McIntosh 1982, 411)

Combination Platter. The options described here are not mutually exclusive, of course. Some argue that families should have a range of options for recognizing and structuring their relationships, since particular couples or family groupings might prefer more regulation and standardization than others. Lesbian-feminist critics of marriage worry that allowing same-sex couples to marry would divert the energy and attention of activists currently pressing for the creation of alternatives, such as domestic partnership (e.g., Ettelbrick 1989). This possible objection to pursuing a "menu" of relationship definitions is a prediction about the motives of those involved in domestic partnership efforts, though, not a normative objection to the concept of providing a range of choices.

Given the possible policy approaches to configuring and recognizing gay men's and lesbians' families, the next step involves assessing whether and how well those options fulfill the feminist policy criteria. As developed in chapter 7, some of the criteria are oriented toward practical concerns: facilitating provisioning and the meeting of basic needs, valuing and encouraging caring labor, and achieving these goals in an efficient way. Other criteria are more clearly normative, such as promoting justice for gay and lesbian people. The next section develops the argument that some of the family policy options meet those criteria better than others.

Meeting Basic Needs. On the most practical level, a wide range of family forms can promote provisioning, that is, the meeting of basic human needs for food, clothing, and shelter. Sharing resources with one or more other people expands an individual's potential "provisions" in several ways. Family members might have more to contribute in the way of money or other resources. Furthermore, the availability of other people's resources is a form of insurance, since one individual's loss of a job or ability to do housework is less devastating when other family members' contributions are available (Eskridge 1996, 68). In a country like the United States where the savings rate is quite low and unemployment insurance does not replace all lost income, having access to other people's economic resources can mean the difference between unemployment leading to poverty and homelessness and unemployment as a temporary economic misfortune.

As the discussion of the economic benefits of family units in chapter 6 explains, combining more than one individual's resources allows for a more efficient use of time and money. Economies of scale in household production increase the resources available for provisioning within a family. Within this economic context, particular forms of family arrangements and their accompanying legal arrangements seem likely to promote taking advantage of economies of scale more clearly. The promises inherent in marriage and at least some domestic partnerships (and potential "marriage lite" policies) include an obligation of mutual support between two individuals, giving individuals in those relationships a higher degree of security in their claims on their partner's resources. With both an explicit personal commitment and a legal obligation, one spouse cannot refuse to help meet the basic needs of the other, although this appears to be a rare issue among ongoing coresident couples (Glendon 1989). Pooling of resources within marriage is facilitated by laws about the division of property in case of divorce, which removes uncertainty about how contributions will be treated if the couple splits.

Alternatively, one might ask whether it is possible for policy to make this function of families unnecessary, as Barrett and McIntosh argue. Pooling of resources could take place on a much larger level than that of a couple or even larger family structure. In the United States, taxpayers could contribute to a federally financed pot that is used to ensure that each individual's basic needs are met. This would clearly be a more complete way of providing for individuals since support is neither contingent on being part of a couple or family nor depends on other family members' ability to provide a minimum standard of living. In this policy option, provisioning is moved from the realm of the individual to become a collective responsibility.

The provisioning criterion does little to separate out the possible forms of family policy, other than suggesting that the current situation of relatively unregulated relationships might be less than ideal. Applying the other criteria provides a different ranking of the options, however.

Valuing and Encouraging Caring Labor. As with meeting basic needs, most forms of family relationships have the potential for contributing to care for children, sick people, and older people. These are crucial social functions that have been primarily served by families in the United States, and by women in families, in particular.

Certain family structures might promote caring more than others, particularly those characterized by long-term relationships. Relationships that promote a sense of commitment improve the potential for the availability of caring labor as individuals' needs vary over the life cycle. Commitment also enhances the likelihood of reciprocity in exchanging or sharing caring labor. Thus it makes sense for the state to promote long-term relationships both by encouraging public vows of commitment as well as by making exit from relationships somewhat difficult (or at least less than instantaneous), perhaps discouraging the breakup of relationships for relatively trivial or temporary reasons. As William Eskridge points out, marriage also promotes commitment by providing a signal of the level of commitment one can expect from a partner (Eskridge 1996, 71), and even the need for a discussion about the relationship provides information and promotes the communication process.

Marriage, marriage lite, and domestic partnership policies might all, to some extent, promote the formation of relationships that will have the necessary level of commitment and trust that facilitates caring labor. The "unregulated" status quo for gay people and the policy strategy that makes families less necessary do not, however, work in the same way. Market provision or the sort of large-scale social provisioning envisioned by the marriage skeptics ignores the possibility that providing some services in smaller settings—call them "families"—is likely to promote caring labor that is more valuable to the recipients of that care. Nancy Folbre (1995) and others worry that increased market provision of such services could erode the caring nature of such labor, although Julie A. Nelson (1999) argues that under some circumstances performing such tasks for money would not necessarily have such an effect. Here we begin to see some divergence in the desirability of different family policy possibilities with respect to the policy criteria.

Promoting Justice for Gay People. Fairness might be thought of in two ways with regard to family policy. One way to be fair to gay men and lesbians would be to equalize access to the benefits currently gained through marriage, either by eliminating all monetary benefits tied to marriage or by providing those services universally, without regard to marital status. Unpartnered and childless people sometimes complain about receiving lower total compensation for the same work done as married people, a situation resulting from employers' fringe benefits policies. (As the other criteria suggest, however, there may be good social reasons for allowing employers to take into account workers' family responsibilities.) Universal provision of the material benefits tied to marriage would seem to be a more attractive option. Universal health care and guaranteed pensions tied to individuals instead of couples would reduce the need for marriage to some extent and might even be good ideas unto themselves. But neither abolition of marital benefits nor universal provision of certain kinds of benefits will solve the problem of inequality as long as marriage continues to exist as an institution that excludes same-sex couples and as long as same-sex couples want to be married for religious, social, or economic reasons.

The simplest method of promoting fairness is to make access to any legal relationships available to same-sex couples. As the law now stands in every state, same-sex couples cannot marry, so providing any benefits to married couples by definition results in discrimination against gay people. If same-sex couples could marry, any benefits that go to married people would then be distributed without regard to sexual orientation. In some European countries, "marriage lite" is a partnership relationship that is similar to marriage in that it gives registered partners the same taxation, immigration, inheritance, and social security status as married couples (IGLHRC 1998). But Denmark excludes the right to a state church wedding, and all of these quasi marital statuses exclude the right to adopt children and deny gay couples certain other rights related to children. A range of marriage near equivalents have been enacted or proposed as compromises in some states, from civil unions to Hawaii's reciprocal beneficiary law, but in Hawaii and Vermont those relationships were consciously set up to circumvent pressure for marriage and set up a clearly inferior status for those couples.

Aside from the symbolism of continuing second-class status for gay and lesbian people inherent in these marriage alternatives, excluding parental status from the adult relationships (as in the European forms) constitutes a fatal flaw in the ability of registered partnerships to meet the needs of gay people and their families. As the second part of this chapter will argue, gay people should be allowed and encouraged to be parents through the removal of legal obstacles to parenthood. Within the broader family policy context, equal access to marriage and to any other form of state-regulated relationship (such as domestic partnerships) is clearly the fairest policy for gay people.

Promoting Gender Equality. In the debate over marriage within the gay and lesbian communities, one of the key sources of suspicion about marriage is its history as a patriarchal institution oppressive toward women. At times in the United States, marriage resulted in the loss of property and autonomy for women, and men were able to treat wives and children as property, sometimes abusing this control. As mentioned above, though, current marriage law in the United States is gender-neutral, at least formally. Hunter argues that the law's gender neutrality should remove much of the taint of marriage for feminists, and she believes that same-sex marriages would further a feminist agenda related to marriage: "Marriage enforces and reinforces the linkage of gender with power by husband/wife categories that are synonymous with the social power imbalance between men and women. . . .[Same-sex marriage] would create for the first time the possibility of marriage as a relationship between members of the same social status categories" (Hunter 1995, 112).

Formal gender neutrality does not necessarily translate into practical equality, however. Studies of married couples continue to reveal a division of labor that appears to perpetuate traditional gender roles for men and women. Studies by economists and sociologists show that married women continue to bear disproportionate responsibility for housework and child care (see Blau 1998, for recent evidence). Although married women now participate in the paid labor force to roughly the same extent as unmarried women, having children results in at least temporary withdrawal for many women as well as lower wages. This pattern of expecting women to bear primary responsibility for child care persists despite a law that gives both men and women the ability to take unpaid leave when a child is born (the federal Family and Medical Leave Act).

Sorting out the extent to which these patterns reflect the influence of "marriage" rather than the influence of broader social norms about gender is difficult. We cannot randomly assign some heterosexual couples to marry and others to remain unmarried to see if the legal and cultural institution of marriage itself generates the inequality between husbands and wives seen in the data. Even in the most conservative model of the family, Gary Becker sees the roots of women's household responsibilities in biology and, to some extent, in labor market discrimination, not in marriage per se. As discussed in the chapter 6, evidence from nonrandom samples of couples suggests that unmarried opposite-sex couples also have unequal divisions of labor relative to same-sex couples. Same-sex couples, unmarried by definition, tend to divide household labor *more* equally than do married and unmarried opposite-sex couples, suggesting that gender norms rather than marriage are the primary source of an unequal division of household labor.

Some have contended that the example set by same-sex couples' division of labor negotiations, which cannot obviously factor gender into account, and their more equal division of responsibility for housework could further equality among men and women in opposite-sex marriages by reshaping norms about which spouse should do what. The power of this potential influence on norms is difficult to assess, however, and little evidence exists to support the notion that a much bigger practical change in family economic life—the entry of many married women into the labor force—has had much effect on who does what within the household.

A married heterosexual man watching the nice gay male couple next door sharing chores traditionally done by women might or might not change his willingness to clean the bathroom. Instead, he might see further evidence that cleaning the bathroom is only a proper job for women or for men who are like women, in his view. What seems a bit more likely is that a heterosexual married woman watching the nice lesbian couple next door doing heavy yard work or changing the oil in the car will see further evidence of the fact that she could take on jobs done now by her husband. That knowledge of her potential self-sufficiency might give her the will and bargaining power she needs to push her husband to take on more household labor, but there are no guarantees that she will either try or succeed. Another possibility is that the children next door will develop different expectations of their future household responsibilities given access to different models of the division of labor.

The fact that same-sex marriage will not quickly remove all practical vestiges of sexism in marriage, remnants that have proven resistant to decades of feminist exhortation and legislation, is simply not a good reason to reject a change in the law that brings benefits to society and equality for same-sex couples. It is also hard to imagine how the marriages of same-sex couples would signal gay or heterosexual approval of current gender arrangements within many marriages, given the very different arrangements among same-sex couples' households. Furthermore, the other policy options share the same vagueness with respect to the mechanism by which gender roles will be transformed. Those family analysts who favor "making the family less necessary" hope that removing some of the obvious economic incentives to marry will result in changes in social norms and shifts in the social and economic position of women. But that hope requires the assumptions that norms will change relatively quickly and that couples marry mainly in response to those incentives rather than in response to cultural and social pressures. Both assumptions are problematic, however. On the face of it, there is no obvious reason to think that one strategy to influence gender norms would be clearly more effective than the other.

Promoting Efficiency. Even if marriage did not come with benefits provided by the state and third parties, the contractual aspects of marriage would serve important functions for families that make the institution useful and perhaps even desirable. The contractual nature of marriage facilitates a more efficient use of time and money resources for families than would some of the other policy possibilities. One key function of marriage is to give couples what Eskridge calls "off-the-rack rules" for situations that families might not anticipate, as when a relationship ends from the death of one party or by divorce, or when one partner is incapacitated and cannot make decisions for himself or herself (Eskridge 1996, 69).

In theory, couples could create legal documents that fulfill these same functions without marriage now, in the relatively unregulated family policy regime for same-sex couples, but financial and cultural reasons suggest that relatively few couples would do so. Several widely available books offer advice tailored for same-sex couples on writing wills, living-together agreements, and powers of attorney, for instance (see Hertz 1999 or Curry, Clifford, and Leonard 1996), and lawyers often advertise their expertise on these issues in gay newspapers. But in addition to the price of the book, families must often still pay lawyers to complete legally enforceable agreements, and those agreements are still not always respected by families and courts. In more complicated situations, such as in estate planning, the legal costs could mount quickly. Individuals and couples are often unprepared for unpleasant events that are (sometimes incorrectly) thought to be unlikely, even when preparing for the possibility of death or illness involves little legal effort. Marriage provides a "standard contract" for couples who are financially incapable of or are uninterested in making such preparations.

A second function that marriage performs particularly efficiently is to designate the spouse as a truly significant other to a potentially large number of third parties, some of whom the parties to a marriage might not adequately anticipate. Strangers interacting with individuals in a couple might need to know whom to acknowledge when access to an individual is limited, as in prison or hospital visitation, or when the closeness of a relationship is relevant in some other way. Requirements that limit access and necessitate a screening rule define these situations, so alternative policy approaches that would simply eliminate screening criteria are not feasible. Similarly, removing family status as a screening rule for some purposes, such as in the provision of health care benefits, would not reduce its value in these other kinds of situations.

Employers are probably the most important other third party that uses recognized family relationships to make decisions about allocating employment benefits. Again, this need to recognize significant others results from rationing, since employers want to limit the intrusion of outside obligations on their employees' work time. Employers' family leave policies (and the federal Family and Medical Leave Act) limit the relationships seen as legitimate; one can take time off to care for a sick parent, spouse, or child but not a sick neighbor. Expanding those policies to include relationships not previously considered legitimate, such as a same-sex couple, is less costly if the additions are relatively small in number and are qualitatively similar to the relationships already recognized. Employers are not likely to expand dramatically the pool of relationships recognized and might, if required to recognize many more relationships between individuals, actually eliminate or cut back any nonmandatory employee benefit. A parsimonious set of family designations seems appropriate to assign priority to individuals when providing access to a scarce resource—such as employee benefits or time with someone in an intensive care unit—is in question.

Wider recognition of domestic partnerships as an alternative off-the-rack agreement between two individuals would give couples an additional option. As Hunter notes, the typical domestic partner agreement is different from marriage, including provisions for mutual support during the relationship but implying nothing about property accumulated during the relationship and about postrelationship support (Hunter 1995a, 117-18). Individuals in domestic partnerships could then create more tailored agreements but would have the advantage of announcing the existence of their relationship to the state and third parties in one simple step. Of course, under current law only some opposite-sex couples (sometimes) have the option of choice between marriage and domestic partnership in cities and states with domestic partner registries.

Marriage and its cousin, domestic partnership, thus provide a legal, economic, and social framework for individuals who want to intertwine their lives with another person's life. The need for this framework would not disappear even if individuals' material needs were assured by government income support programs. And marriage accomplishes this for a relatively small monetary cost—the price of a marriage license—instead of the time, trouble, and fees involved in developing substitute legal arrangements or in negotiating with third parties. This benefit of marriage accrues directly to the couple. But economists would also consider the reduction in "transaction costs," or the costs of undergoing all the separate transactions that would otherwise be necessary, a benefit to society, as well.

Further, these benefits come at no cost to the third parties involved and might even make their jobs significantly easier. A legal recognition of same-sex couples would eliminate the need for the many separate processes that employers offering domestic partner benefits have set up. Although the costs of setting up a partner designation system might be small to a single employer, requiring many employers to do this inevitably results in overlapping effort that could obviously be taken care of more easily and efficiently by a single government agency. Thus a centralized and public form of recognizing couples is efficient both for the couples themselves and for third parties.

The need for and the benefits of having a simple, easily accessible, "off-the-rack" agreement and designation for individuals suggests that setting up rules and records is a very good task for the state to take on. By facilitating these relatively simple functions of marriage, the government improves the well-being of individuals and families.

If government involvement in structuring and recognizing relationships between two adults enhances economic efficiency and personal welfare, the question about limitations to that form reemerges. Why, then, should the government not allow and facilitate more extensive relationship building among units larger than two adults? The immediate image of the family relationships between more than two adults that some will have formed earlier in this book is likely to be polygamy, a form of family relationship generally disapproved of in the United States. Aside from the fact that serial polygamy has become quite common as individuals marry, divorce, and then remarry (sometimes going through several cycles), this image is *not* what I am imagining here. Instead, adults might form intense and emotionally intimate but nonsexual relationships with other adults who are thought of as family, as Weston observed in her study of gay people's "families we choose."

None of the discussion so far suggests that a couple is the natural, only, or even best unit to promote provisioning, commitment, and caring labor. In the end, I will argue that the state should allow and promote a variety of family formations, allowing individuals to form families that suit their own tastes and needs and the needs of their children. But if most families are likely to take a particular form, then it makes sense for the state to recognize and facilitate such formations, as long as other formations are not precluded. The fact that most non–single-person households involve an adult couple suggests that those are the most common formations, and chapter 6 presented a number of practical reasons, aside from cultural norms, that larger households would be less viable in the United States today.

The state might facilitate the formation of larger families by allowing something similar to marriage but allowing more than two people to enter into those kinds of agreements. But both theory and some evidence suggest that these larger family configurations are likely to be rare, first of all, and they are also likely to vary significantly in the degree of interdependence found between each individual in the family. Creating a standardized set of rules about inheritance rights, mutual support obligations, and property division, just for example, makes little sense if those rules do not meet the needs of family members. An alternative would be the greater use of wills, living-together agreements, and other documents now used by some unmarried couples but adapted to more complex family arrangements. Enforceability of those agreements might require legislative or judicial action to preserve the usefulness of these arrangements, perhaps even allowing those agreements to trump certain aspects of the implied marital contract or domestic partnership.

The relative rarity and likely complexity of larger family units is at the root of the economic basis for my recommendation that the government formally recognize and structure relationships between two but not more than two adults. Some people will object to this apparent privileging of couples via government recognition, arguing that the sole recognition of one form will itself encourage people to end up only in couples, making the alleged flexibility to form larger units an insincere claim. One response to this objection is simply to note that promoting the formation of couples is not a bad thing for the government to do, for all the reasons noted above. Furthermore, if forming more complex family relationships enhances the well-being of individuals, then evidence suggests that marriage does not stand in the way. The families Weston studied included couples within larger family networks. Sociologist Judith Stacey shows that families and kin networks are flexible enough to meet the economic and social needs of their members, even when individuals are married (Stacey 1996). As more complex relationships become more common and more regularized, or as the particular contexts for the creation of useful legal ties between more than two adults becomes apparent, policymakers might wish to revisit this question.

To sum up, the government's regulatory role in recognizing and shaping relationships among adults serves important social and economic interests in promoting the emotional and material well-being of adults and children as well as in promoting those interests in economically efficient ways. Even if the provision of health care benefits and retirement income were completely separate from marriage, some kind of state-defined legal and economic relationship between adults would still be desirable. The preceding analysis suggests that those relationships should be expanded somewhat to allow marriage, domestic partnership, and even more tailored legal arrangements between larger family groupings, regardless of the participants' sexual orientation and the sex of their chosen partners. Through this expansion of access and options, the government would promote welfare and efficiency, as well as equality for gay people, and perhaps over time a more inclusive family policy will contribute to greater gender equality in heterosexual marriages.

My analysis presents a proactive argument for at least two issues that have been hotly contested in numerous legislative settings, that is, the issue of allowing same-sex couples to marry and creating domestic partnerships for couples. Two objections commonly raised to those proposals have economic dimensions that have not yet been addressed. (I address a third issue in the next section: the role of marriage in raising children.)

One concerns the social role of families and kinship in tying individuals together and promoting "mutual obligations and a commitment to the future of the community" (Knight 1994, 11), or a broader sense of social support than the more nuclear-family-oriented sense of commitment discussed earlier. In this view, families also ensure a concern about long-term interests, especially related to (one assumes) a healthy and prosperous world for one's children. From an economic perspective, encouraging social ties is quite important, as social networks often provide economic support, particularly in the form of direct monetary support and including other services, such as child care or information about employment opportunities. If this is the case, though, it makes no sense to exclude a group of people from those networks. Relationships among same-sex couples can also create social ties between families, just as heterosexual marriages do. And the mutual support aspects of the relationships described here promote the same kind of ties that conservative opponents of same-sex marriage such as Robert H. Knight claim to favor.

The second concern speaks more directly to other impacts of allowing same-sex couples to marry. Some policymakers have argued that because "marriage is a status rich in entitlements," as Judge Richard Posner has put it (Posner 1992, 313), governments could face a hefty bill if they allowed same-sex couples to marry or otherwise have the rights of married couples. As this book has described, most of the big-ticket items, health care benefits, and retirement income, are in fact artifacts of our health care and retirement systems and are not necessarily tied to marriage. Chapter 7 demonstrates that the net cost of universal domestic partner recognition for health care benefits would be low. A further close comparison of the costs to governments and the likely benefits to governments of same-sex marriages leads to the conclusion that policymakers' concerns are misplaced.

A recent analysis of federal taxation suggests that allowing same-sex couples to marry would bring in an additional $0.3 billion to $1.3 billion per year because of the "marriage penalty" (Alm, Badgett, and Whittington 2000). These additional tax revenues would offset increased government costs that might result from providing spousal benefits to more couples.

The most complete existing analysis of this issue sums the costs and benefits of same-sex marriage for the state of Vermont (Badgett 1998). More marriages would improve the state's budgetary position because many same-sex couples would be subject to the marriage penalty, causing an increase in taxes, and because fewer families would require income support from the state. An influx of out-of-state couples arriving in Vermont to marry would boost the state's economy, increasing tourist tax revenues and creating most of the benefits to the state. On the other side of the balance sheet, the state's costs might rise because of increased outlays for employee benefits,[5] because more families would be using the state's family courts, and because property transfer taxes might drop (transfers between spouses are not taxed). Because much uncertainty exists about the number of in-state and out-of-state couples that would marry in Vermont, my study uses very conservative methods that would tend to overestimate the costs to the state but would underestimate the benefits to the state budget. Even after setting up the analysis in a way that pushes benefits to the low side and costs to the high side, the analysis suggests that the state government of Vermont would see a boost of between $18.2 million and $25 million in tax revenues over the first five years while only incurring $0.1 million to $2.2 million in additional costs associated with expanding the number of married people. In other words, the state government's net gain is $18.1 million to $22.8 million. Because much of Vermont's windfall would come as a result of increased tourism, later states allowing same-sex marriages would probably not receive the same boost.[6] Even without more tourism, though, other states' costs are unlikely to outweigh the financial benefits of expanding the right to marry.

Costs might also increase over time if same-sex couples adapt to their new marital status by having more children or spending more time out of the labor force. In that scenario, education costs could rise for the additional children, although the educational investment would be at least partly balanced by the child's future economic contributions. Similarly, if one member of same-sex couples spent some time out of the labor force and had to use spousal benefits more often, such as employment benefits or social security benefits, then government expenditures would rise. But those adaptations are unlikely to generate dramatically higher social security expenditures since married couples only get spousal benefits when the spouse is not eligible for higher benefits based on his or her own work record (see Badgett and Goldfoot [1996] for a longer discussion of this point). Only if many same-sex couples adopt the most traditional strict division of labor over a lifetime—an option that even opposite-sex couples rarely use anymore—would social security expenditures significantly increase.

Policies Related to Children

Missing from most of the above discussion about adult relationships is the issue at the heart of conservative political objections to recognizing same-sex couples' relationships: children. For many people, the main purpose of marriage is procreation. Economist Gary Becker's economic ideas about the family assume that families exist to produce and raise their own children (Becker 1991, 135). And in some ways, the law reflects the connection between two adults' opposite-sex marriage and any children that the female partner gives birth to during that marriage. In a 1989 decision, *Michael H. v. Gerald D.,* the U.S. Supreme Court upheld a California law presuming that a baby born in wedlock is the biological child of the husband, even though a genetic comparison might prove otherwise. Both in the law and in popular rhetoric, adult relationships and children are closely connected and help to define the legal relationship created between parents and children by the government. Not surprisingly, since the legal ties between gay adults are inadequately recognized, the legal ties between gay parents and the children they are raising are also often denied or denigrated in situations in which the parent is not the adoptive parent, the birth parent, or a contributor of genetic material.

One reason for the common separation of the debate over adult relationships and parenting relationships is the assumption that lesbian and gay people will only rarely produce children, an assumption belied by the statistics presented in chapter 6. As the discussion of Becker's work makes clear, biological determinism makes the prospect of widespread gay parenting seem unlikely to many economists and other observers. Leaving aside the biological argument, one with little relevance in an age of adoption, surrogacy, donor insemination, and other reproductive technological advances, gay people seem likely to have and want to have children for the same reasons that heterosexual people have: to contribute to a future generation, to increase their own happiness and fulfillment, to ensure companionship and perhaps even economic security in their old age, or to meet the expectations of society. And while some children raised by gay or lesbian parents originated in a heterosexual relationship, increasingly gay men and lesbians are choosing to have children in the context of their gay families.

When someone becomes a legal parent to a child, that person assumes certain rights and responsibilities that will at least partly determine the costs and benefits of parenthood. For example, parents have the following rights with respect to the child: having custody; making medical, educational, and religious decisions; deciding who will have visitation rights; assigning the child's name; and claiming a right to the child's earnings and services. On the other side, parents must provide financial support, care, education, and medical care, and they must control the child (Polikoff 1990, 468 n.28). Parental authority is not absolute, however, as courts have interpreted family law to give children at least some degree of autonomy, particularly with respect to sexuality (Glendon 1989, 97–98).

While, to some extent, all taxpayers contribute to the upbringing of children through educational and welfare expenditures of tax dollars, parents clearly shoulder much more of the economic burden, measured in both time and money. The state's dependence on parents to provide the primary economic means to raise children, with all the complexity and difficulty that such a task entails, means that the influence of parental designations on the costs and benefits of children will affect the likelihood that someone will want to have kids. Someone might be reluctant to take on the financial burdens of parenthood without some assurance of the ongoing relationship with the child that is necessary to exercise the rights and to enjoy the benefits of parenthood.

Gay men and lesbians people face a big disadvantage in having children as gay people since the law usually assumes that children will have exactly two parents, one female and one male. Gay people will generally not fit into that mold, creating uncertainty about the rights and obligations they will have with respect to the children they want to raise. Uncertainty about having parental rights to make decisions for children or having visitation and custody rights is matched by uncertainty about having obligations to provide for children. The legal uncertainties might mean that lesbians and gay men who are willing and able to make the *same* sacrifices as heterosexuals to raise children will not be able to do so because of legal constraints or because the actual tradeoff of costs for benefits faced by potential gay parents is very different. As chapter 6 notes, the "demand curve" for children could be the same for lesbians, gay men, bisexuals, and heterosexuals, but gay people will have fewer children because of the higher price of conceiving, adopting, and raising them.

The crucial questions for the state are whom to recognize or designate as a legal parent, how many parents a child should have, and how the law should view a gay parent's sexual orientation. This last issue arises directly when gay and lesbian parents have produced children while in a heterosexual relationship. In disputes with former spouses in custody and visitation decisions, judges sometimes raise questions of gay parents' legitimacy as able and adequate parents. In those cases, visitation or custody rights for a gay or lesbian parent might be contingent on the absence of the parent's same-sex partner, for instance. Decades of psychological studies have shown that children are not harmed in developmental or social terms by their parents' being gay, lesbian, or bisexual (see Patterson 1995, 1998). This analysis accepts that conclusion from the experts and focuses on the definitional issues that are most closely related to economic decision making and outcomes, particularly for gay people who have children in the context of a gay existence.

Which adults should be called parents, the people with the responsibility for a child's welfare and those with the authority to make important decisions about where and how the child will live? While a range of possible ways to answer this question has been offered, the possibilities can be summarized simply: (1) a child has at most two parents, one male and one female; (2) a child has two parents, who may be of the same sex and could be gay, lesbian, bisexual, or heterosexual; (3) a child can have more than two parents; (4) regardless of the number of parents, even people who are not so designated could have certain parental rights, typically visitation rights.

Translating those principles into policy strategies is a relatively simple step (at least in the theoretical realm of the present discussion). The first option is typically carried out administratively at birth, when two legal parents are named on a birth certificate, or judicially at the time of an adoption. Lesbian and gay parents' relationships to their children are determined either by biology and law, by separate agreement between the legal parent and his or her partner (usually not legally enforceable), or by judges, who typically take up the issue when a family breaks up because of the death of a parent or the end of the adults' relationship. Taking on parental status under the second and third options might mean a formal "second-parent adoption" or a less onerous administrative declaration comparable to placing both parents' names on a birth certificate.

The first option of applying a two-opposite-sex-parent model to all situations, which reflects the current situation in most states, is the most restrictive in designating legal parents and those who are acceptable parental influences. The parents of a child born to a married woman are the woman and her husband, regardless of the actual source of sperm (as in donor insemination). If a married couple divorces, both parents have custody and visitation rights. Children acquired through adoption, donor insemination, and surrogacy are assigned parents in an analogous way. If an unmarried woman (including a lesbian) has a child, the contributor of sperm (if he is known to the mother) may be considered the legal father who is obligated to support the child and has visitation rights, regardless of his relationship with the mother. Generally speaking, exactly one woman and one man can be considered parents, so children who have only one legally recognized parent, say a mother, cannot be legally adopted by another woman unless the child's mother is willing to give up her parental status.

The second approach to defining parents has been developed by gay and lesbian legal advocates when gay or lesbian people have had children outside of heterosexual relationships, as in donor insemination, surrogacy, or adoption. Rather than relying on the traditional or formal definition of parenthood laid out in the first option, the functional definition of parenthood in this second option looks more closely at the actions and intentions of adults, defining as a parent someone who fulfills the traditional duties of a parent in concert with a biological or adoptive parent. This approach is apparent, for example, in what are known as "second-parent adoptions" in which a judge allows someone of the same sex as the biological or original adoptive parent to become an adoptive parent of a child. Lesbian mothers and gay fathers are regularly granted second-parent adoptions in a few states, including Vermont, New York, California, the District of Columbia, and Massachusetts (Eskridge and Hunter 1997, 866–67).

The third policy option simply extends this principle to break out of the biologically based legal model in which children have only two genetic ties. In this view, children could have more than two legal parents, perhaps including a lesbian biological mother, her female partner, a close male friend who is the sperm donor, and the donor's partner, all of whom take an active, committed, and mutually intended role in raising the child. A different configuration might include a biological mother, a gay male biological father, and his male partner. (Courts have sometimes recognized more than two parents for a child. See Ettelbrick 1993, 549 n.180.)

Several ways of deciding who could be considered a parent in the second and third options have been offered by legal scholars, some of whom have developed criteria for judges to use in ruling on visitation and custody decisions. These methods presuppose a court challenge arising from a family breakup or other crisis that requires a judge's determination of who counts as a parent. Nancy Polikoff suggests, "Courts should redefine parenthood to include anyone in a functional parental relationship that a legally recognized parent created with the intent that an additional parent-child relationship exist" (Polikoff 1990, 573). Paula Ettelbrick provides similar but narrower criteria for lesbian parents, emphasizing the partnership of the two parents (presumed to be women in her analysis), the agreement of the biological or adoptive mother, the partner's involvement in the decision to have a child, and the partner's fulfillment of daily care responsibilities (Ettelbrick 1993, 548). Katharine Bartlett would give wider latitude to judges to grant parental status to nonpartners or individuals with whom a biological or adoptive parent did not intend to be parents. Her proposal requires functional parents to meet strict criteria, including physical custody for at least six months (where custody begins with either the consent of a parent or under court order) (Bartlett 1984, 946–47). She places a greater emphasis than Ettelbrick or Polikoff on the mutuality of recognition of a "psychological parent," so that the child must recognize the parent's position, too.

While these redefinitions of legal parenthood have focused on giving judges guidelines for making decisions about children's lives, they do not directly address the needs of parents in intact families. In addition to second-parent adoptions, these criteria could also form the basis for administrative designations of parenthood similar to the procedures used for domestic partnerships. Within two months of a birth, for instance, parents might file an affidavit attesting to their mutual agreement and intention of taking on full parental responsibility for the child. Unlike domestic partnerships, however, these relationships with children should be considered permanent.[7]

The fourth option reflects the opinions of more radical critics of current family policy with regard to gay people. From this perspective, even the functional approach embodied in the second and third options is problematic. The functional definitions rely on an underlying "property model" of parent-child relations in which those designated as parents have all the rights and nonparents have none (see Sears 1994). According to these critics, limiting parental rights to adults meeting the criteria set out by Polikoff and Ettelbrick fails to protect "the relationships which children value" or to ensure "legal recognition of and support for the true diversity of lesbian and gay families" (569).

Instead, Sears argues for moving beyond the parent/stranger dichotomy to recognize other relationships that are important to children, as in laws that extend visitation rights to nonparents who have developed a significant relationship with a child over time. As an example of a policy that promotes this expanded vision of family relationships, he notes an Oregon statute that allows someone to petition for visitation with a child if the adult has "maintained an ongoing personal relationship with substantial continuity for at least one year, through interaction, companionship, interplay, and mutuality" (as quoted in Sears 1994, 576). This approach, which remains rather undeveloped, would seem to favor unpacking the bundle of rights that go along with being a parent, and perhaps with more development this could also involve a similar unpacking of long-term obligations that go with the rights. Since this issue is clearly separable from the other positions on parenthood (it does not presuppose any one of the other three options being in place), I will focus only on the other three. Just as policies that "make families less necessary" do not remove the desirability of marriage, according to the last section, creating a partial-parent status does not eliminate the need for a better policy related to full parents.

In making decisions related to children, family court judges are supposed to apply a basic rule: what is in the best interest of the child? The feminist policy principles could certainly be viewed in that light while situating the child in an economic context. Applying the principles to possible definitions of parenthood suggests that a more expansive definition than current policy would be in the best economic and emotional interests of the child.

Meeting a child's basic needs—the child's share of the family's provisions—largely falls to parents, with some limited backup from the state through various welfare programs and tax policies. On a material level, parents must provide food, shelter, and clothing. On an emotional and developmental level, parents are legally responsible for decisions related to educational, religious, and disciplinary needs. These are legal obligations and, if necessary, are enforceable through the judicial system. While adults with less formal relationships with children—or even less extensive relationships, as promoted by the fourth option—might be willing to provide this sort of material and emotional support, that support cannot be relied upon by either the child or the child's official parent. A child with only one legally obligated parent is likely to be in a disadvantaged position, with a reduced level of resources potentially available and a heightened vulnerability to his or her single parent's shifting economic positions. Children need stability and security, and access to more adults' economic resources will increase a child's economic security. This criterion clearly argues for a more expansive definition of "parent" instead of a narrow one that would lead to children having only one parent to count on, as does current law in most states.[8]

More inclusive parenthood definitions also increase a child's economic security by broadening his or her access to support provided by third parties, particularly to benefits provided by employers or by government programs. For instance, consider the impact of the legal status on our fictional four-year-old Stanley from chapter 6, who is being raised by Frieda, his birth mother, and her partner Gail, who is not a legal parent but is sharing in the material and emotional aspects of raising Stanley. If Gail's employer provides health insurance and other benefits to employees and their spouses and children, neither Frieda nor Stanley would be eligible unless Gail's employer recognizes domestic partners and their children. As a result, Stanley might not have health insurance or access to a plan as good as Gail's. He would not be eligible for educational, insurance, or other benefits provided to employees' children. If Gail and Frieda were to break up, Stanley could not count on support from Gail, nor would he have any right to coverage through her employer, even if the employer provided domestic partner benefits. If Gail were to die, Stanley would not be eligible for the survivor benefits provided by the social security system to the children of deceased wage earners. If Gail were to die as the result of negligence of some third party, Stanley could not be a party to a lawsuit against the third party to compensate him for the loss of Gail's contribution to his standard of living. If Gail were recognized as a legal parent, however, Stanley could count on her economic contribution to his life, even if the larger family structure were disrupted by unforeseen misfortunes.

A more inclusive parenting definition would also promote caring labor. Accepting nonbiological gay and lesbian people as active and legally recognized parents expands the pool of adults who are available and are even required (to some extent) to provide their time to care for children. This status acknowledges both the ability and responsibility of gay people to be involved with raising the next generation. Confirming parental rights might increase an adult's willingness to commit his or her emotional resources and time to a child, since a parent can count on having a long-term relationship with a child. Since being a parent also involves costly obligations, deliberately taking on that status implies a much stronger and long-term commitment, a commitment that is likely to include and promote a greater emotional commitment. Limiting legal parenthood to its traditional definitions would reduce the potential amount of caring labor available to children.

Expanding the definition of parent would also further the principle of just treatment of gay and lesbian people. As has been made clear, the current family-related laws and policies place gay people who want to be fully recognized parents at a disadvantage. The requirement that a lesbian biological mother give up her own parental status before her female partner can legally adopt the child points out the absurd logic of legal inequality. To some people, though, making parenthood a civil rights issue sounds selfish: "Proponents of homosexual adoption often defend their view as an issue of freedom and individual rights, putting their political and social agenda ahead of the possible impact on children. But adopting children is not a right." (Knight and Garcia 1994, 1) Perhaps the rhetoric related to the laws on parenting disproportionately frames the issue in terms of rights, which unfortunately hides the fact that gay people are at the same time seeking the ability to have the same *obligations* of parenthood, not just the rights. Regardless of the prominence of "rights" in the public debate, equality for gay people requires an ability to acquire the same legal statuses available to heterosexual people. And as the discussion above shows, having equal access to legal parenting status benefits children and society at least as much as it would benefit gay and lesbian parents. Equality is hardly a selfish goal in this case.

Even more controversial is the relationship of parenting rights to the issue of gender equity. Some might argue that the two-parent model, even two parents of the same sex, reinforces the idea that two is the "natural" number of parents because of the biological complementarity of male and female contributions to conception, further enshrining traditional notions of men's and women's roles in parenting. Others argue a quite different critical position, claiming that allowing two adults of the same sex to be parents undermines children's development of traditional gender identities. Growing up in a household with only male adults or only female adults means that some children will lack role models of their own sex. The primary concern raised for conservative activists appears to be that the children of lesbians and gay men will grow up to be gay themselves as a result of the lack of appropriate role models (for example, see Knight and Garcia 1994, 4–8).

With respect to the second concern, reason and research suggest that growing up in a household headed by a gay couple is not likely to greatly influence a child's eventual sexual orientation, even if sexual orientation is not (as it now appears to be) a relatively fixed characteristic determined by genetics or by very early developmental influences. First, as many gay people like to point out, growing up in households headed by heterosexual couples appears to do little to discourage or reverse the development of a gay identity. Second, studies of children raised by lesbians and gay men find no evidence that such children are more likely to be gay than those raised by heterosexuals (see review of literature in Patterson 1995).

Even so, the conservatives might just as likely fear that being raised by two adults of the same sex will subvert traditional gender roles, a prospect that feminists and gay radicals might applaud. Again, the research evidence suggests otherwise, however. Most studies of children raised by lesbians show that their gender identities (the child's self identity as female or male) and gender-role behavior (whether behavior is considered masculine or feminine in the larger culture) is indistinguishable from that of children with heterosexual parents (Patterson 1995, 1998). While that news might be disappointing to those who had hoped that children of gay people would represent a gender-bending vanguard, the results are not surprising given that, in practice, children will have a variety of gender role models, both deliberately cultivated by their gay parents and incidentally presented by the larger society.

Perhaps the more important contribution to undermining gender inequity would come for adults. With two or more parents, using simple gender differences to assign "mothers'" tasks and "fathers'" tasks is harder, if not impossible when the parents are all of the same sex. Two men raising a baby will have no mother to rely on to change diapers. Two women raising a child will have no father to send out to be the family's breadwinner. Allowing parents to be of either sex *requires* gay and lesbian parents to resist traditional gender roles. Men become caregivers; women bring home the bacon. As with the gender implications of same-sex marriage discussed above, the modeling effect on heterosexual adults might be limited, but it seems more reasonable to suppose that when gay parents' children are themselves parents the shifts in gender norms related to household responsibilities will be more apparent.

Finally, applying the efficiency criterion to the policy possibilities also argues in favor of a more inclusive definition of parent. The narrow, bio-logically rooted definition of parents in the first option has failed to dis-courage gay people from having children. As a result, perhaps millions of children must make do with only one legal parent, even though in their own minds and lives one or more other "legal strangers" is also actively in-volved in parenting. In those situations, parents have cobbled together a variety of private agreements, some of which are of questionable enforce-ability, that simulate legal parenthood. Some of those agreements allow the unofficial parent to authorize medical care and to make school-related decisions, while others set out agreements about what to do in case of the death of the legal parent or the breakup of the couple. But no private agreement will lead third parties, such as employers or the government, to recognize those relationships without a protracted and, in most states, un-successful effort to convince a family court judge to allow a second-parent adoption.

For basically the same reason used in the analysis of marriage, efficiency concerns warrant the continued packaging of rights and responsibilities into something called "parenthood." With one designation a variety of questions are answered for all others who need to know whom to turn to for important decisions about a child or for material support for that child. This relatively simple (and usually one-time) designation would greatly cut down on paperwork, legal fees, and potential misunderstandings for families.

Taking the analysis as a whole, feminist principles push a conclusion that legal definitions of parents should encompass the possibility that chil-dren will have two parents of the same sex or even more than two parents. In particular, children are better off and are likely to have greater access to material resources and to parents' caring labor when they have more than one parent. A more inclusive definition would promote equality for gay people and their range of family structures, while at the very least not pro-moting narrow gender roles. And finally, changing legal parenthood makes sense from a practical efficiency perspective, providing greater security and understanding for families at a lower cost than the current law allows.

Conclusions

Applying a set of policy guidelines that considers the economic well-being of individuals and families as well as the efficiency of how those needs are met demonstrates that promoting equality for gay and lesbian people also makes good economic sense. Forcing one group of people into a position where their ability to provide for life's necessities is compromised and where their contribution to the economy as a whole is unnecessarily diminished is bad public policy. Maintaining second-class citizenship for gay and lesbian people comes at a cost to us all.

Making civil rights and family policies inclusive of gay, lesbian, and bisexual people serves many important economic, social, and legal purposes. Even were the United States to adopt much more radical proposals related to the provision of health care or to the economic support of adults and children, relationships like "partner," "spouse," and "parent" would still be useful and necessary. More radical visions of policy change do not necessarily eliminate the need for these categories thought to be regressive by some gay activists.

My analysis also suggests, though, that while equality *promotes* economic well-being and is a *necessary condition* for well-being, equality does not *guarantee* economic well-being. My main focus in this chapter has been on the more widely known political debates on how gay people should be treated. But it is also possible that achieving victory in establishing laws against the unequal treatment of gay and lesbian people could result in a hollow equality. Legal parity for gay people and their families simply leaves them on the same shaky economic ground that many heterosexual families find themselves on, suggesting that a more complete policy agenda that would truly achieve the goals set out by the feminist policy principles will require gay people's involvement in other efforts not traditionally seen as "gay issues."

In the preceding chapters, I have sketched out how public policies have influenced the current economic position of gay and lesbian people as workers, family members, and consumers. Changes in policy would alter the context for making economic decisions and would extend access to new resources for gay people and their families. In the same way that past liberalization in the law's treatment of gay people opened up new opportunities, so too would the changes outlined here improve and equalize the economic position of gay and lesbian people.

Thinking Homo/economically:
Economic Strategies for Social Change

Lesbian, gay, and bisexual people have come together to form local, statewide and national organizations to promote some of the public policies
outlined in chapters 7 and 8. Those organizations devote most of their resources to traditional political organizing of grassroots supporters (both
gay and nongay) and to efforts of more experienced lobbyists, all of whom
contact and pressure lawmakers. Newer forms of gay activism have
adopted some of those political goals but have moved beyond the focus
on laws and elected officials to different institutions, deploying economic
power that comes from the different roles that gay people play in a market economy as workers, consumers, and investors.

Boycotts, gay workplace groups, investment "screens," and marketing
have become the tools of the economic activist's trade. Instead of roaming
the halls of state capitols to lobby legislators, gay workplace activists seek
out human resources managers. Rather than flood a governor's office with
calls and letters, investor activists e-mail corporate CEOs. Instead of threatening politicians with votes, consumer activists threaten boycotts to punish homophobic corporations and voters or even promise "gaycotts" to reward progressive employers and communities.

On one level, this movement could be seen as simply defensive, matching conservative efforts to wield economic power with gay clout. Southern Baptists decided to boycott Disney to protest that company's progressive policies toward gay employees and its distribution of objectionable
(from the Baptist point of view) entertainment products. Conservative
Christian groups have established investment mutual funds that will not
invest in companies offering domestic partner benefits (Timothy Plan
1999). Gay people have done more than respond defensively, however, establishing far-reaching efforts to leverage their economic influence.

New activist possibilities have brought with them a host of challenging
strategic and internal issues for the gay community. Are the tactics and
goals of economic activism merely addressing the limited demands and
needs of middle-class gay white gay men and lesbians? Is there a role for

the gay or lesbian secretary or factory worker or part-time cashier in the gay workplace organizations formed by gay managers and professionals? Does a rhetorical appeal to the bottom line—raising profits—fit with the social justice motivation of many activists? Will efforts focused on corporations make any difference in legislative battles? Does working within corporations mean selling out on the larger goals of more radical activists who would prefer to reform or eliminate market capitalism? As these questions suggest, economic strategies generate as much controversy among lesbian, gay, and bisexual individuals and activists as do the political strategies. A crucial task for activists is thinking through the potential long-term usefulness of business- and financial-oriented strategies and some of the controversies surrounding them.

This chapter describes those strategies and analyzes their likely effects within a larger social context. The next section outlines the goals and targets of economic activists, which tend to focus on a specific business instead of the broad range of employers typically targeted by public policy and political activists. The decentralized nature of this kind of activism raises strategic questions about the use of activists' energy and financial backing. The rest of the chapter analyzes the actual deployment of collective economic power to further gay-related issues. Gay activists have successfully organized and exerted consumer power, worker influence, and investor pressure to change corporate policies and practices. Activists have also invested resources of time and money into ongoing nonprofit organizations to organize change efforts and to provide the services and support that are not provided by the government or marketplace. These various forms of activism are not mutually exclusive, of course, and coordinated forms of pressure could have an even greater influence.

Targeting Policies and Internal Controversies

Economic activism only has value for gay people if it sets appropriate goals and uses effective strategies. It is obvious that a single end result, such as the implementation of domestic partner benefits at one company, could change the lives of many gay, lesbian, and bisexual people for the better, but thinking about the means to that end is also important for gay people as a whole. Linking many smaller goals, as in systematic company-by-company lobbying for domestic partner benefits to build toward legislative recognition of gay couples' relationships, is one way to expand the value of a single campaign. The tactics used within companies, for example, might very well affect legislators' willingness to pass progay laws. Company-specific strategies that enlist the support of nongay allies and organizations or of high-ranking officials could pay off later in political coalitions or testimony and lobbying from CEOs. Once a target or goal is chosen, then the usual question is how to best achieve that goal. "Best," in some cases, might mean most quickly or with the least expenditure of political and financial resources or, as the argument below suggests, best could mean the way that maximizes gay influence in the next issue or in related venues.

Choosing specific targets of activism has been relatively easy since inequality for gay people is the rule rather than the exception in the U.S. economy. Most of the focus of economic activists has been more specific than that of legislative activists: getting employers to treat gay employees equally through specific policy changes. Few employers have the range of policies called for by the Equality Project, for instance, which has proposed a very specific set of gay-related policies, or "Equality Principles," that companies should implement:

1. Explicit prohibitions against discrimination based on sexual orientation will be included in the company's written employment policy statement.
2. Discrimination against HIV-positive employees or those with AIDS will be strictly prohibited.
3. Employee groups, regardless of sexual orientation, will be given equal standing with other employee associations.
4. Diversity training will include sexual orientation issues.
5. Spousal benefits will be offered to domestic partners of employees, regardless of sexual orientation, on an equal basis with those granted to married employees.
6. Company advertising policy will bar negative sexual orientation stereotypes and will not discriminate against advertising in publications on the basis of sexual orientation.
7. Companies will not discriminate in the sale of good or services on the basis or sexual orientation.
8. Written nondiscrimination policies on sexual orientation must be disseminated throughout the company. A senior company official will be appointed to monitor compliance corporatewide. (Equality Project 1999)

Those policies pick out specific sources of workplace disadvantage that put gay people in a vulnerable economic position. Other policies could be included in such a list, of course, and sometimes activists' concern is an employer's charitable contributions (either to gay organizations or to antigay organizations) or political endorsements.

Whether or not these political targets and goals are the most appropriate focus of a political movement by gay people is not universally agreed upon among gay and lesbian people, however. Recall the concerns of Ruthann Robson and Michael Warner about too narrowly defining a "gay issue." As the analysis of public policies in the previous chapters notes, part of the objection by some radical gay people to fighting for and devoting resources to limited goals is not simply a disagreement over the proper form that policies should take but is related to political and strategic concerns. One overarching strategic concern in picking goals and targets is that choosing one short run political goal over another means the diversion of time and money into particular organizations and efforts. Choosing the "wrong" goals, or goals that are too limited, means that other concerns will be left out.

The fight to end the military ban on gay and lesbian servicemembers was controversial at least partly for this reason. Millions of dollars went to a cause that many gay people appeared to think was less important than other issues (see discussion in Vaid 1995). Similar concerns have arisen over the pursuit of the right to marry. In fact, for many years same-sex marriage was seen as an unwinnable fight, and national gay organizations shied away from explicit work on that issue. From the perspective of those prioritizing other issues, the money and volunteer effort that goes into achieving one particular political goal is taken away from other worthier or more winnable causes. Even worse, radical activists predict that victory in those battles would not necessarily mean that time and money will then be transferred to the next and perhaps more ambitious and radical goal.

To some extent, this strategic concern is related to different ways of addressing an obvious problem. For instance, many of the forty-four million people without health insurance in the United States are likely to be gay or lesbian. Winning the right for same-sex couples to marry will lead to more but certainly not all gay people getting health insurance through a spouse's employer. A more comprehensive policy that ensures coverage for all would be a universal health care system with a single payer, a goal of some gay activists. The strategic issue is whether those goals are mutually exclusive in practical organizational terms, since a marriage victory will not necessarily lead to a large shift of money and people into the fight for universal health coverage.

This concern is probably well founded, since some of the activists and couples fighting for marriage will not agree with the political sentiment behind a single payer plan. The resources of those activists, then, might not have been truly "lost" during the struggle over marriage. But some activists who would have joined up with the single payer folks might be too tired or too financially drained to move on to another big political campaign after winning the right to marry. This competition scenario is too simplistic and unnecessarily pessimistic, however. A victory in one area might instead provide an energy boost that would carry activists into a new cause, and those enjoying the fruits of their victory, the right to marry in this example, might soon sign up for the single payer cause when they realize that marriage has not solved all of their problems with access to health care.

A second strategic concern places individuals in the context of their fuller set of identities related to race, class, and gender, in particular, and highlights the competing demands on people's time and financial resources available for political activism. Why should a lesbian factory worker insist that her union demand a contract clause forbidding sexual orientation discrimination or granting domestic partner benefits when a more pressing concern is that her employer is threatening to shut the plant down and move production to another country? Why would a gay man working as a janitor for minimum wage and no benefits become part of a gay workplace organization whose main goal is to win domestic partner benefits? A black lesbian worried about being promoted to a job held historically only by white men might find that being a lesbian is the least of her concerns. In the context of more pressing needs, issues related directly to one's sexual orientation might fade into the background for some people. Placed in this context, sexual orientation nondiscrimination policies or other gay-specific policies could be seen as an indulgence relevant mainly to middle-class, white, gay men (and perhaps white lesbians) whose economic position and access to jobs is relatively secure. The active pursuit of those goals might only attract the active support of middle-class gay white people.

While that analysis captures some important concerns about the incomplete nature of a gay-specific policy agenda, the choice of political goals for lesbians and gay men should not mean abandoning gay-specific issues. The argument throughout this book, and in the previous two chapters in particular, is that those policy goals are necessary and desirable on many levels, even if they appear less important or irrelevant at different times in individuals' lives. For Ernest Dillon, being black was not the source of workplace violence and harassment—being perceived as gay was. Someone whose employer treats gay and straight employers equally in most situations might very well never feel the direct bite of sexual orientation discrimination. But the potential impact of gay people's economic vulnerability is always just around the corner, arriving with a homophobic new boss or with a partner's loss of health insurance coverage. We buy auto insurance for financial protection in case of car accidents, even when we don't expect to have them. Nondiscrimination laws can play a similar role. They provide routes to challenge and redress discrimination if it occurs, and such laws might even help to discourage discrimination.

The point here is simply that first, *all* gay and lesbian people are vulnerable to discrimination in our current policy environment, and second, that an individual gay person's choice of political goals does not determine his or her lifetime political involvement, nor does the presence of other pressing issues unrelated to sexual orientation mean that being gay will never matter. Arguing for a goal that appears to be more limited does not in and of itself imply capitulation to a more conservative agenda. People and organizations are capable of working on many political issues throughout their lifetimes. Gay-specific political efforts and campaigns for policies with a broader impact are better thought of as complementary instead of competitive.

But the controversy over goals and the possible connections between them also point out the importance of choosing strategies that build coalitions and allies. Since the direct gay-specific goals themselves may not have widespread support or relevance, those goals might be stepping stones to larger goals. In addition to pursuing change in economic and social structures with built-in inequality for gay people, economic strategies should incorporate more process-oriented goals. As part of a workplace-centered or consumer-oriented campaign, gay economic activists could be following strategies that will build bridges and links to other groups whose efforts can aid and supplement the gains to gay and lesbian people. Such groups might include other civil rights "constituencies," like African American organizations or disability activists as well as environmental, health care, and union activists. In the long run, those links are likely to facilitate victory on gay-specific issues and to enhance the breadth and depth of change that occurs. In terms of economic theory, process-oriented strategies come with positive externalities, or positive side effects. To make the fullest use of activist efforts, the gay communities must internalize these externalities, including them in decision making about how to use activists' resources of time and money.

Thinking about the means as well as the ends intended by activism sheds a different light on the effectiveness of different kinds of economic activism. This might mean choosing from consumer boycott, workplace organizing, and investor activism strategies with the process impact in mind, or constructing particular campaigns that consider process as well as outcomes. While each form of activism offers a route to success in changing corporate practice, each presents different challenges and opportunities with regard to process.

Consumer Activism—Carrot and Stick

Mention the possibility of "using our economic power" to a lesbian or gay man, and they are likely to think of the "gay marketing moment." Thanks to the efforts of marketers and the news media, the predominant economic image of gay America today is that of the mighty gay consumer, the man (or occasionally woman) whom any forward-thinking, profit-maximizing company should be wooing. The means by which this consumer "power" will translate into actual social and legal change for lesbian, gay, and bisexual people is usually left unspecified, however, and the goals are similarly vague.

Three different strategies can be detected through the marketing rhetoric and the few examples of explicit political appeals to consumer power. In some cases activists argue that gay and lesbian people should develop a consumer identity to use gay spending as a carrot to entice companies. In return for the loyalty of the gay market, businesses will equalize their own employment policies or promote positive images of gay people in marketing. In other cases, gay consumer spending can be used as a stick to threaten boycotts of discriminatory companies or even communities that enact homophobic policies or laws. And occasionally gay entrepreneurs will promote a "queer capitalism," arguing that gay people buying from gay-owned companies also serves gay political and economic interests. In the terms of this book's analysis, the value of consumer strategies depends on their effectiveness and on the ability of consumer-oriented strategies to link groups in coalitions and to build alliances that will last beyond a single effort.

Queer Conspicuous Consumption. The use of consumer power as a carrot to achieve gains in gay people's social position requires making gay consumption visible and desirable. As chapter 5 noted, economist Thorstein Veblen argued at the end of the nineteenth century that, in general, visibility of consumption enhances social status. Thanks in part to the efforts of marketers who portray gay people as an attractive and affluent group of consumers, along with the myth of hedonistic, childless gay people with money to spend, gay people have become conspicuous consumers in U.S. society. But is conspicuous consumption—and the attendant development of a consumer identity—a useful strategy for lesbian, gay, and bisexual people?

The first concern with this form of economic activism is that its goals are often poorly defined, if they are defined at all. Gay marketers suggest that their efforts to promote a consumer identity help the gay community because employers will have an incentive to treat its gay workers fairly. But the assumptions behind that model are not obvious. How would a reader know whether the airline buying a full-page advertisement in a gay magazine offers domestic partner benefits or forbids discrimination against gay people? For instance, United Airlines's advertising campaign in gay magazines predated its agreement to provide health care and other benefits to same-sex domestic partners of employees. Few people are likely to have the knowledge to make decisions on that basis.

The responsibilities involved in being an "informed consumer" are not very clear, either, although consumers would have to gather and assimilate enormous amounts of information. Using gay dollars as a carrot implies that gay people should reward companies with purchases. But if a lesbian dislikes Coors beer, should she buy it anyway because Coors offers domestic partner benefits? If a brand X computer is cheaper than computers made by IBM, should a gay organization buy IBM anyway because they have progressive policies related to gay people and support gay organizations? When pressed, some marketers suggest that being an informed gay consumer means that if everything else is at least roughly equal—quality and price, in particular—gay people should buy the product made by the gay-friendly company.

Recently some explicit efforts to gather company data and to educate consumers have been launched. To at least some extent, the explicit goals of groups like the Equality Project include changing consumers' buying habits to support gay-friendly companies. Daniel B. Baker, Sean O'Brien Strub, and Bill Henning (1995) and Grant Lukenbill (1995) have also compiled company policy and practice information that they encourage consumers to use. These efforts have not obviously generated widespread changes in gay consumer spending, nor do they appear to be closely coordinated by any organization, which is likely to diminish the strategy's success. One marketing study of gay people who use the Internet (a relatively affluent and educated segment of the gay population) suggests an increasing consumer consciousness of a limited sort, as 80 percent said they would prefer to buy from a company that advertises to gay people (Greenfield Online 1998). The lack of a clear connection between advertising and corporate policy toward gay people suggests that gay consumers may not be reacting in a politically useful way, though.

Second, as previous chapters have clearly noted, some of the assumptions behind the interest in marketing to gay people are wrong or misleading. On average, gay, lesbian, and bisexual people are not overachieving yuppies with no kids to worry about. The image of the double-income-no-kid high-income gay couple comes from marketing surveys that are biased toward finding high-income people. Other more reliable and representative surveys reviewed above show that either as households or individuals, gay people are not more affluent than their heterosexual counterparts and, in addition, that many gay people are raising children. A subset of gay people, predominantly white gay men, have higher than average personal and household incomes with no responsibility for children, but they are not typical and they constitute no greater proportion of their overall community than do affluent heterosexual people.

Other concerns about conspicuous consumption are more strategic and process-oriented. Several factors suggest that a strategy of conspicuous consumption would be detrimental to building coalitions. After several decades of falling income inequality in the United States, the tide turned in the 1970s and 1980s, and the spread between rich and poor in the United States began to grow again (Gottschalk 1997). Despite long-term economic growth in the United States in the 1990s, high levels of income and wealth inequality persist. In this era of growing inequality, cries of injustice coming from an apparently prosperous group are likely to fall on resentful ears. The right wing has seized on the image of the affluent gay consumer to drive wedges between gay people and potential coalition partners, frequently using comparisons of gay marketers' income data and the much lower incomes of African Americans.

Furthermore, in making product choices based on employment policies, conflicting loyalties are likely to crop up. A product from a nonunion company that has good gay-related policies will not be attractive to a gay union activist or supporter. A product from a company that offers domestic partner benefits but has a history of discrimination against black customers or workers would create a similar conflict for those working for racial justice and equality.

Distinguishing between "friends" and "enemies" is not always an easy task, even when focusing only on clearly gay-related issues. Consider the case of Coors Brewing Co. Although at one time Coors was said to have regularly engaged in clearly antigay and antiunion practices, the company now provides domestic partner health benefits and has a policy against sexual orientation discrimination. Coors has also advertised in gay magazines and has donated money to gay organizations, including $110,000 to the Gay & Lesbian Alliance Against Defamation (GLAAD) (Freiberg 1998). Those characteristics suggest that Coors is one of the good companies deserving of gay business. But Coors customers are also patronizing a company whose profits support the Coors family's Castle Rock Foundation, which funds well-known antigay organizations such as the Heritage Foundation, a think tank that opposed ending the ban on gays in the military (Kilhefner n.d.). As a result, a raging debate continues in the gay community about whether Coors should be considered a friend or foe, as well as whether gay organizations should even accept Coors donations.[1]

Overall, conspicuous consumption is an inadequately defined economic strategy that is difficult to implement and creates potential liabilities for the gay community in return for a very uncertain gain. This is not to say, however, that gay activists should try to stop companies from marketing its products to the gay community. If appealing to a gay niche market leads to the demise of homophobic images in advertising, increases the use of positive gay images in more mainstream marketing, and helps support gay magazines and newspapers, then some community benefit could result. The point here is that the active pursuit and embracing of marketing attention from particular companies is not yet a well-developed *economic or political* strategy to meet the gay community's larger goals.

Wielding the Green "Stick." Gay people do not have to develop a consumption-based identity to wield consumer power, however. Consumption consciousness rather than conspicuous consumption is the key to successful boycotts. The gay community has used consumer boycotts of Coors, Cracker Barrel Old Style Restaurants, United Airlines, and the state of Colorado, for instance, to exert economic pressure to reverse homophobic employment practices and laws.

Unlike the conspicuous consumption strategy, the boycott strategy generally involves carefully chosen targets, although the goals are not always entirely clear. After Cracker Barrel restaurants enacted a policy of firing any known gay or lesbian workers, boycotters picketed the company's restaurants to encourage the corporation to rescind the policy of active discrimination, to rehire the fired workers, and to enact an explicit written policy of nondiscrimination based on sexual orientation (Baker et al. 1995; Tarquinio 1997). Antigay and antiunion actions by the Coors Brewing Company led to a combined Teamsters and gay community boycott of Coors beer (Shilts 1982). United Airlines refused to comply with an ordinance requiring companies that contract with the city of San Francisco to offer spousal benefits to domestic partners as well, and instead United sued the city to challenge the ordinance (*Out & About* 1999). In response to United's leadership in the effort to strike down the San Francisco law, the Human Rights Campaign, a national gay and lesbian organization, and Equal Benefits Advocates, a San Francisco–based organization, mounted a national boycott of United that eventually pushed the company to provide domestic partner benefits. In 1992, Colorado voters amended their state constitution to forbid laws that would *prohibit* discrimination against gay people, prompting a massive effort by gay activists to divert conventions and tourists away from the state. In the Colorado case the goal was mostly retribution rather than an attempt to get a specific institution to change its practices.

In all of these cases, the decision to target a particular company or place stemmed from something more than the everyday inequality present in most companies' benefits policies. The boycott efforts were responses to a demonstration of explicit corporate will to discriminate against gay people.

From a larger strategic angle, boycotts present opportunities for coalitions, making them a potentially valuable tool. Union activists and environmentalists, in particular, have skillfully used consumer action, and many other groups concerned about employment fairness, animal rights, and reproductive rights include consumer action in their arsenals. Coalitions could take the form of mutual support of boycotts directed at different companies or combined forces targeting one company. And those alliances might continue outside the workplace in the electoral arena, as when gay participation in the Coors boycott in the 1970s gained the Teamsters' support for Harvey Milk's election as the first gay supervisor in San Francisco (Shilts 1982).

The potential benefits of boycotts suggest they are a useful tactic, but they, too, come with drawbacks. The effectiveness of boycotts is uncertain, for one thing. The big economic issue is whether a boycott can make a dent in a state's economic activity or in a company's profits or consciousness. The economic effectiveness of a boycott is difficult to measure, since so many other factors influence companies' sales revenues and can hide the impact of even a well-organized boycott (certainly a difficult feat considering the national markets for most products). The Colorado boycott received a great deal of media attention, and the Colorado Tourist Board lost $100 million in canceled conventions and another $20 million in meetings and business relocations that went elsewhere (figures collected in Parsons 1995). But the state's economy continued to grow at roughly the same rate as it had in the five years before the boycott, perhaps in part due to two years of great snowfalls and a papal visit (Parsons 1995). Either the boycotting conventioneers were replaced (perhaps by a Southern Baptist Convention, as the Christian Action Network claimed) or other tourist spending made up the difference.

The primary outcome of a boycott might simply be bad public relations, which companies also prefer to avoid. Sometimes companies under attack have changed policies, as did Coors, but whether those changes were the result of economic pressure or the result of public relations concerns is impossible to say. For one reason or another, whether companies are more concerned about the economic or public relations impact of boycotts, policy changes sometimes follow boycotts (Snyder 1991; Putnam 1993).[2]

With uncertain benefits, the high potential costs of boycotts as well as other strategic drawbacks reduce their attractiveness as the primary tool to achieve changes in workplace policies. First, an effective boycott requires the kind of long-term coordination and communication that is expensive and has been difficult to achieve with gay organizations. Publicly announcing a boycott and mobilizing initial support reduces the confusion that results from rumors of boycotts, but if a company does not capitulate quickly, then over time confusion is likely to return as consumers forget which companies to avoid. Cracker Barrel eventually replaced its policy of discrimination but refused to rehire previously fired employees or to make public its new policy, so the boycott has never really been "officially" lifted—but it is not clear who would act as such an official should Cracker Barrel improve its policies. The Coors boycott continues for many gay activists (Kilhefner 1999). The national boycott of United was called off by the Human Rights Campaign when United announced it would provide domestic partner benefits (HRC 1999a), even though United is still attacking the San Francisco law in court (Arndt 2000). As the globalization of product markets proceeds, contacting and convincing a company's customers to withhold purchases will become more and more difficult.

Second, boycotts often have a built-in accountability problem. The issue of who chooses which companies to boycott and decides when it ends is a difficult one that is rarely discussed. Unlike in workplace activism, where the people who are taking the risks are also the ones who will gain from changes in policies, the consumer activists who target a company or location with a boycott are not always the ones bearing the primary costs or benefits of the boycott. An economically successful boycott is designed to hurt a company's management or shareholders, but that also means that the company's workers will be hurt as well. In the case of the Colorado boycott, the businesses that appeared to be hurt most were those in the cities and towns that had opposed Amendment 2 and had always welcomed lesbian and gay visitors to Colorado, and some of those business were owned by gay people. This dilemma suggests that the targets of boycotts must be chosen carefully.

A related problem is that consumer action might involve difficult choices for activists who have conflicting loyalties or who want to pursue alternative strategies. A lesbian union member who is asked to boycott products made by members of her union who work for a non–gay-friendly company, for example, faces such a predicament. Similarly, a company might have bad policies related to gay people but a good record of promoting people of color. Some gay workplace organizations have discouraged outsiders from putting direct consumer pressure on the group's employer, preferring to work through internal political processes first. To avoid alienating future or current allies and coalition members, consumer activists should explore possible conflicts before pursuing a boycott.

Finally, the fundamental kind of engagement that is encouraged by boycott strategies is inaction, that is, the avoidance of a particular business. When those businesses have many competitors, probably many or even most gay men and lesbians will not be customers of that business and will not be directly engaged in the boycott effort. Furthermore, nonacting/boycotting gay people and their allies will not generally be engaged in education of the company's workers and management. (In many boycotts, of course, people are also encouraged to write letters to the business or to wear buttons indicating support for the boycott if a customer must continue to do business with the company being boycotted. Individuals who take such actions are likely to be a relatively small group compared with the number of gay people who will simply not be buying from the offending business, though.) The removal of human faces and human stories from the day-to-day political process of a boycott is likely to reduce its long-term effectiveness.

Overall, while political risks exist when using boycotts, withholding consumer dollars has the potential for being a powerful tool when companies take outrageous actions and no legal recourse or other means exists to oppose those actions through a union or gay workplace group. Boycotts are costly and difficult to maintain, though, so they are not likely to become a significant tool to fight garden-variety corporate discrimination in benefits, for instance. But under the right circumstances and with the right strategy and commitment of resources, boycotts will occasionally turn out to be powerful forms of economic activism.

Queer Capitalism. Thriving U.S. capitalism plus concentrations of gay people in large urban areas has made a queer economy possible in certain gay enclaves. Should gay people come together as producers and consumers to create a queer capitalism? A completely separate economy is difficult to imagine, but "gay neighborhoods" exist, and gay- and lesbian-owned businesses have been a part of the gay community for decades, such as bookstores, bars, cafés, book publishers, magazines, and newspapers, providing much-needed social and cultural bases for gay lives and organizing. Over the 1990s, however, a new breed of entrepreneurs (both gay and straight) have begun to market products to lesbian, gay, and bisexual people that were already available in their mainstream forms, such as beer, credit cards, and long distance telephone service.

If gay entrepreneurialism is good for at least some gay people, it may seem odd to question it as a option in the menu of several economic strategies for social change. Gay people could vote with their dollars, probably indicating that some but not all such businesses are worthwhile. In a market economy, of course that will happen, but the political implications of accommodating or pursuing a queer capitalist strategy are trickier. The marketplace is dynamic, and successful gay businesses and products will inevitably attract the attention of mainstream capitalists who are always looking for profit-making opportunities.

This happened in both the retail and publishing end of the book business, for example, as the mainstream spilled over into the tributaries nurtured by small gay and lesbian presses and bookstores. For a time in the 1990s, large publishers offered sizable advances for books targeted at gay communities, and big chain bookstores developed large lesbian and gay sections in stores located in or near gay neighborhoods (Mann 1995). This placed some gay publishers and bookstores in a precarious position. The key question is whether gay and lesbian people owe gay-owned businesses any economic loyalty in a positive reversal of consumer action via boycott. Even if competition is fair, would gay people want to protect gay-owned or targeted businesses from cutthroat competitors since gay businesses support gay political activities? Or should gay people just shop at the cheapest bookstore and find the cheapest credit card available and then donate their savings directly to a worthy political organization (perhaps the economically "rational" decision)?

Using the two basic criteria applied above, the choice of goals and the process-oriented value of this form of economic organizing, queer capitalism does not appear to be a useful or complete economic strategy for political and social change. In particular, the political goals are quite fuzzy and are not universally espoused by gay-owned businesses. The early generation of gay and lesbian businesses, bars, cafés, and bookstores that still anchor gay-defined neighborhoods, had some direct and indirect political potential, often intentionally. Those businesses created meeting places that facilitated political organizations and the spread of important ideas, news, and information to gay people, making the further development of gay, lesbian, and bisexual culture and politics possible.

Many of the newer businesses' products are not specific to the gay community, such as beer, long distance services, or retail operations, but some argue that this movement represents progress toward equality and prosperity for gay people. Some gay people are apparently willing to buy an inferior restaurant meal or to put up with poor service at a gay-owned business as a way of supporting "the community" and strengthening their own ties to the gay community (Kates 1998). The larger value of this support in the context of political efforts is not clear, however. At the very least, as this argument goes, gay-owned businesses should be gay-friendly places to work that gay consumers should support. Prosperous business owners, and perhaps prosperous employees, will have more money available to contribute to social and political organizations, further strengthening the community. In some cases, businesses even pledge a portion of profits or sales revenues to gay organizations. Other gay people are more suspicious of the motives of entrepreneurs and see little broader social value to a business whose overriding goal is profits for the owners.

Some notable cases suggest that fulfilling philanthropic promises could generate significant financial support. Tzabaco, a now closed catalog and on-line retailer of clothing and gay-themed products, contributed to several organizations like the National Gay and Lesbian Task Force and GLSEN, the Gay, Lesbian, and Straight Educators' Network. The Rainbow card, an "affinity" Visa credit card, contributes a portion of every purchase made with the card to the Rainbow Endowment, a fund that has given $600,000 in grants to gay organizations in its first four years of operation (Rainbow Card 1999).[3] Some wealthy gay entrepreneurs, such as Tim Gill and Andrew Tobias, have set up funds or foundations to support gay community efforts. No systematic studies of the philanthropic behavior of gay-owned firms has been done, nor does research exist on the employment practices of those companies, but looking through the list of donors to major gay organizations uncovers more mainstream, that is, nongay, corporate supporters than names of gay-owned companies. With some exceptions, queer capitalism appears to have the same main goal as mainstream capitalism, in other words—the pursuit of maximum profits for owners rather than focusing on gay community interests.

The broader process-oriented implications of an explicit strategy of queer capitalism are more damaging. By definition, a separatist economy is not well-suited to coalition building between the gay community and

other people whose support is essential in legislative or other forms of political work. Even worse, an overemphasis on developing a gay economy
could be internally divisive, placing gay people with competing economic
loyalties, such as those based on race, ethnicity, or gender, in a difficult position. Furthermore, access to capital and credit to start a new business
varies significantly by race, wealth, and gender. A queer economy is likely
to reproduce racial, gender, and class inequality within the gay community.

Given that risk, it might seem that the sink or swim approach toward
gay businesses is best suited to meeting the gay community's needs. But at
this point, distinctions between products offered by gay-centered businesses become important, and the difference involves whether markets,
without concerted economic action by gay people, would provide the
kinds of goods and services needed in the quantities desired by gay and
lesbian people. Ideally, markets are supposed to supply the goods and
services that consumers want; otherwise, businesses have a profit-making
opportunity available. If the rate of profit is not high enough, however,
mainstream companies might not shift into a gay market. This dynamic
clearly exists, as when Time canceled plans for a magazine targeted at gays
and lesbians, citing a lower than expected profit potential as the reason
(Carmody 1994). But other publishers of gay magazines and newspapers,
presumably lesbian, gay, or bisexual themselves, have accepted losses as
well as profit rates far lower than the return that Time required from its
investment. In other words, some gay-targeted products and retail establishments (e.g., bars, bookstores, and publications) constitute a basic community infrastructure that might be worth protecting because those businesses provide and preserve something better than what mainstream
nongay-run companies could supply. From this perspective, a limited form
of queer capitalism might serve the community well without risking the
kind of divisiveness resulting from a more vigorous and undifferentiated
movement to support gay entrepreneurs.

Workplace Activism

The increasing attention to gay men's and lesbians' role as workers suggests a very different form of economic activism. Being a worker or employee has long been a source of class identity and politics. For centuries
workers have organized themselves into unions and other kinds of groups
to exert their collective influence on wages and working conditions. Collective action by employees to convince companies to adopt policies like
the Equality Principles described above or other goals is an obvious extension. Even as the degree of unionization in the U.S. economy has fallen

over the last few decades,[4] gay employees have tapped into this source of influence on their employers. In some cases, explicit bargaining over non-discrimination policies or domestic partner benefits has occurred between unions and company management. The first known domestic partner health coverage resulted from contract negotiations between the Village Voice and District 65/UAW in 1982 (Frank and Holcomb 1990, 33). More often, gay, lesbian, and bisexual workers have organized formally or informally in their own groups to lobby and pressure an employer on gay-related issues. When gay and lesbian workers are in a union that bargains over benefits, then the union instead of (or in addition to) the corporation might be the target of a lobbying process to get gay issues on the bargaining agenda.

The goals of these groups bear directly on equality for gay people. Typically, a gay workplace group's general goal is reducing homophobia in the workplace, while more specific goals might focus on adding sexual orientation to a company's nondiscrimination policy and extending spousal benefits to domestic partners. Other common issues are the inclusion of gay topics in diversity training, corporate funding of lesbian and gay organizations, or corporate endorsement and lobbying on legislative issues of concern to gay people.

Unlike unions, gay workplace organizations (GWOs) do not have a formally defined legal relationship with an employer, which means employers are not legally required to meet and bargain with a GWO. This limits the gay group's ability to use its collective economic power to go on strike to pressure its employer, as unions can do. Gay workplace organizations are also unlike unions in that employees might organize for other purposes, such as socializing or providing emotional and moral support in an unwelcoming work environment. For some gay workers, in other words, employment issues might not be the pressing reason for seeking out other gay people.

Instead of acting like a union, these workplace groups tend to mobilize their collective influence using other resources to lobby for change in a process that can resemble grassroots political lobbying. After identifying the key decision-makers, effective gay organizations plot a strategy to get the necessary information to put pressure on those individuals. Activists might solicit support from customers and high-ranking corporate officials. Individual employees often come out to supervisors or coworkers and use those interactions to educate them or to advocate specifically for particular policy changes (Creed and Scully 1999a). Tapping into group members' professional networks and into other workplace groups concerned about discrimination, such as women's groups or groups for people of color, adds to the number of voices pushing for change. For instance, Federal GLOBE, an umbrella group of organizations of gay, lesbian, and bisexual federal employees, advises new affiliates to seek out union cosponsorship in order to achieve agency support (Federal GLOBE 1993, 2).

The direct engagement between gay and lesbian activists and their coworkers creates the process benefits that add to the value of work on a single issue or employer. In many workplaces, discussions about gay issues are likely to occur one-on-one between coworkers. In some places, though, the discussions are more public and observable.

Universities have been the site of enormous gains in the effort to get partner benefits and are good examples of the power of workplace activists to publicly educate heterosexuals about gay and lesbian people's lives (Badgett 1994). In the mid-1990s, activists at the University of Maryland, College Park, worked to get campus-level benefits for partners, including benefits like library cards, access to child-care facilities, and family rates for football tickets. What initially looked to be a quick and successful movement through the campus Senate's approval process, however, was turned into a cumbersome political process by an influential campus conservative.

But this cumbersome process turned to the activists' favor when public hearings brought many lesbians and gay men out to tell the stories of their families, stories that many heterosexual coworkers had never imagined. After listening to the experiences of their lesbian and gay coworkers, many heterosexuals present said that they had learned something important and had, in many cases, changed their initially negative opinions to support the proposal. Some of them became important political allies on campus. The lobbying efforts also took activists to many other organizations on campus, leading to support from campus unions as well as from organizations of African American staff and faculty and other groups. Ultimately, the gay workplace organization won at the local level when the campus Senate voted overwhelmingly to recognize domestic partners. Unfortunately, the university system's governing Board of Regents, a group with virtually no public accountability, has so far refused to allow the campus to act on its own resolution.

Private employers rarely exhibit an open political process, but researchers have discovered that a similar political process occurs privately. In the early 1990s, a group of gay and lesbian employees at Minnesota Mining and Manufacturing Company (3M) who were meeting socially realized that they shared certain workplace concerns, especially concerns about discrimination and about benefits.[5] They began to meet with the director of human resources to educate him about their workplace issues and to push for policy changes. One employee described how he could not take family emergency leave to care for his lover, who had terminal cancer. Other gay and lesbian workers explained their belief that they would lose their jobs if they came out at work. Managers at one 3M plant told the human resource manager that a nondiscrimination policy was "the right thing to do." That argument clicked with the human resources manager, who recommended a corporate policy change and argued for it in a companywide magazine. Over time, other changes have occurred, too: diversity training materials include gay issues, for instance, but the company does not yet offer domestic partner benefits.

Employees at Financial Services Company, a pseudonymous company in the Minneapolis area, began to organize in the early 1990s with the help of supportive heterosexual allies in the company's human resources department (Foldy and Creed 1999). Together they created an informal network of gay, lesbian, and supportive heterosexual people to conduct a grassroots educational process throughout the company. A direct one-on-one educational session between a key lesbian activist and the vice president for human resources proved to be a crucial moment in building support for policy changes. After "two long years of careful behind-the-scenes advocacy, extensive educational programming, extramural work on launching the WPA Executive Forum and cementing the infrastructure of a regional GLBT employee network, and extensive research on other companies' experience with instituting DPBs," the company announced that both same-sex and opposite-sex domestic partners would be eligible for benefits (Foldy and Creed 1999, 8).

In another example, Libby Bishop and David I. Levine find that gay activists at one high-technology company used computer-mediated communication to organize an effective workplace organization across far-flung company locations owned by TekCo (a pseudonym) (Bishop and Levine 1999). TekCo employees began to organize in 1984, and a few years later when they became an official company group, they added an e-mail list and electronic bulletin board to their internal communication methods. The group used e-mail to collect and disseminate information from other companies, to communicate within the group, to educate nongay employees, and to lobby managers for changes in policies. Group members discussed strategies and prioritized issues together over e-mail. Eventually, the company decided to offer spousal benefits to employees' domestic partners.

The case studies highlight certain kinds of actions and conditions that facilitate workplace activism. Actions by brave individuals play a crucial role, such as the lesbian who conquered her fears of being out and agreed to place her name on a companywide announcement that initiated a gay workplace organization (Foldy and Creed 1999, 7). Doug Creed and Maureen Scully find that individuals influence change in different ways, "initiating the process as early champions, taking advantage of opportunistic moments, and playing out the implications of shifts in the macro terrain" as other companies change policies, for instance (Creed and Scully 1999b, 21). While appeals to business values, such as developing a customer base or employee productivity, have an important and perhaps crucial appeal in workplace-related change (Foldy and Creed 1999, 12), other more personal appeals also have power in changing a company's organizational norms and practices (Foldy and Creed 1999). The telling of stories in personal encounters with others in the workplace helps to create empathy (Creed and Scully 1999a, 25) and leads to personal change as individuals question their own norms about gay and lesbian people (Foldy and Creed 1999, 7).

Certain economic conditions are also likely to aid successful workplace activism (also discussed in chapter 4). First, a booming economy and growth in product demand might insulate employers from a harmful political and economic backlash. When the Southern Baptist Church boycotted Disney for its policies of treating gay employees equally (such as offering domestic partner benefits), Disney continued to record higher profits, and its stock price increased dramatically through mid-1998.[6] Second, reduced health care cost pressure might make employers more willing to add domestic partners. Domestic partner benefits grew the most rapidly while health care costs were growing at the slowest pace in many years. Third, low unemployment rates give workers greater bargaining power and make it tougher for companies to replace disgruntled gay workers who leave for companies with better treatment of gay workers. Low unemployment also means that employers have to work harder to recruit new employees, perhaps leading to enhancement of benefits packages. Given those influences, the spread of domestic partner benefits in the 1990s is not surprising, since all of those conditions were present in many places.

Capitalizing on a favorable economic environment, as activists have done in the 1990s, is likely to lead to a continuation of those gains through the kind of labor market pressure outlined in chapter 4. These ties to the larger marketplace present the possibility of expanding the gains at a single workplace to other employers. Groups of gay and lesbian union activists, such as Pride at Work, Boston's GALLAN, the Gay and Lesbian Labor Activist Network, and the Lesbian and Gay Labor Network of New York have provided support and information for union members organizing for domestic partner benefits and other gay supportive policies.

Hollywood Supports, an example of a nonunion coordinating body, was organized by entertainment leaders in 1991 to end discrimination based on HIV status and sexual orientation in the industry (Hollywood Supports 1999). Hollywood Supports helps employees form workplace gay organizations, and many large entertainment companies now have gay workplace groups, including Disney, MCA/Universal, Time-Warner, Fox, MGM, NBC, ABC, and CBS. The organization has used educational seminars and a model policy for domestic partner benefits, which appear to enhance economic pressure on entertainment industry employers. As a result of the organization's efforts, along with gay employees in the industry, almost all of the major studios now offer domestic partner benefits.

As displayed in the Hollywood Supports situation, connecting individual company efforts to market forces suggests that the spread of domestic partner benefits might be hastened by industrywide strategies. No other industrywide gay and lesbian groups exist, but the Pride Collaborative is a national coalition of workplace organizations, and some of the national political organizations have workplace projects that could promote strategizing and collaboration across companies in a single industry. Using the labor market pressure point, especially when key groups of employees are hard to attract and retain, should enhance the ability of gay workplace groups to achieve a domino effect, as one company after the other feels compelled to offer domestic partner benefits. Sometimes, however, companies competing for the same workers are also competing for the same customers. In that case, it might be harder for gay organizations to work together directly, but the separate organizations should still be able to appeal effectively to their employers, using both the labor market argument and, perhaps, the competition for the gay market niche as economic pressure points. Gay political organizations could serve as centers of industrywide strategizing that can avoid the tricky concerns about product market competition issues. This cross-fertilization occurred in the Minneapolis area, as the Minnesota Workplace Alliance provided training and information for activists in many companies (Creed and Scully 1999b, 17).

In this discussion of the power and promise of gay workplace organizations, the inevitable question arises as to how important organizing and collective action truly are to achieving movement toward gay equality in the workplace. Sometimes the influence of enlightened key officials or a chance event—as when the CEO is sympathetic because he has a lesbian daughter or when a competitor offers domestic partner benefits—may seem more important than the combined efforts of gay employee groups. But if the efforts of isolated individuals were sufficient to generate the kinds of changes corporations have enacted, then we should have seen changes long ago.

More concretely, consider the progress of a closely related issue: the granting of domestic partner benefits to *opposite*-sex partners of employees. The visibility of cohabiting unmarried couples soared in the 1960s and 1970s, when countercultural and sexual liberation influences made such household arrangements more common and open than they had been. Furthermore, all available evidence on the usage of domestic partner benefits in companies suggests that far more opposite-sex couples need and use such benefits. And yet we did not see the implementation of this needed and valuable benefit until gay and lesbian people began to organize and push their employers to change policies for all unmarried couples. Indeed, as chapter 4 suggests, heterosexual people in unmarried relationships have often gained from the hard work and risks taken by their gay and lesbian coworkers. Apparently, heterosexuals in unmarried relationships had little incentive or ability to organize themselves in the workplace, even though it is possible that people in those unmarried relationships were also stigmatized and penalized in the workplace. Without a collective effort, individual heterosexuals in unmarried couples either lacked the vision or the clout to change their employers' policies. Recent workplace organizing by gay employees and their allies appears to be the crucial catalyst for changes in compensation practices.

Even if workplace gains cannot be directly attributed to an employee group's efforts or if groups are not immediately successful, the collective nature of the effort creates the process-oriented benefits that increase the value of workplace activism by helping to change a homophobic workplace culture. In the University of Maryland story described in this chapter, public education helped to improve the local climate for gay staff, faculty, and students, and other campus gains have been made even though the University still does not provide partner benefits. Many gay employee groups, such as GLEAM at Microsoft, the Lesbian and Gay Employee Association at Levi Strauss & Co., and the Employee Association for Gays and Lesbians have in their mission statements a pledge to educate their coworkers and to work with other employee groups on issues of mutual concern. An ambitious education and lobbying *process* in the workplace can create progress as coalitions are formed, alliances are forged, and attitudes are changed, even if a specific institutional change is not achieved immediately.

Some examples demonstrate the broader power that efforts in a single workplace can have. Newly educated allies can become powerful agents for change in other locations or other companies. After a companywide announcement of a gay pride event sparked an angry antigay backlash from employees in distant offices of one company, the CEO of the company visited protesting offices and met with hundreds of employees to explain the company's rationale behind its diversity policies. After the explanation, the CEO suggested that those who could not live with such policies might need to seek work elsewhere (Foldy and Creed 1999, 8). In another case, a heterosexual executive was moved by educational efforts by gay and lesbian employees within her own company, and she later initiated a luncheon for human resources managers in other companies to strategize about extending domestic partner benefits and other gay-positive policies (Creed and Scully 1999a, 27).

Workplace activism has room for improvement in terms of process-oriented concerns, it should be noted. No systematic research on gay workplace groups has analyzed the composition of these groups, but my own observations at conferences and on other occasions suggest that the membership and leadership of many, if not most, gay workplace organizations comes from the managerial and professional ranks. Whether this is because gay blue-collar or lower level white-collar workers do not find gay issues particularly important or because they have not been recruited into the organizations is not clear. It is also possible that the missing members are part of a growing number of gay and lesbian union activists whose work has focused on their unions. Limiting a group's membership reduces the process value of workplace organizing, however, since different groups of workers will provide links to different possible coalition members. Maximizing the influence of a gay workplace organization and increasing the overall value of workplace organizing will require casting a broader net for members.

Investing for Social Change

The third form of economic activism highlights the investment activity of gay people. In economic terms, investments involve giving up something now for some future return, and investors play an important role in any market economy. For most people, "investing" calls to mind buying stocks, or shares of ownership in a profit-seeking company, and lending money to businesses, either directly through bond purchases or indirectly through bank accounts. This traditional way of thinking about investment provides another economic lever to put pressure on companies, a lever that has been addressed in different ways by gay investors and their allies.

But we could think about investment from a broader social perspective, too, including the contributions of time and money that individuals make to nonprofit organizations providing the services and support that turn a group of people into a community. Organizations that provide or promote mental and physical health services, cultural creativity, political organizing, or educational activities, just to suggest a few things that nonprofits do, enrich current community members and enlarge future possibilities. Gay, lesbian, and bisexual people are just as actively investing in a community as they are in investing for their retirements. This section analyzes how both kinds of investing are used to promote social change.

Targeting Financial Investments. Investor activism is similar to consumer activism. Just as businesses want to attract customers, they also need to be able to attract investors. Most shares of companies that change hands in the nation's stock exchanges go from one individual to another, so no money goes to the company whose shares are bought and sold. Stockholders pressure managers to keep the value of the company's stock high. And when companies need to raise money, either by selling shares of the company or by selling bonds to borrow money, they want to get the highest price possible, so maintaining their attractiveness to potential investors is essential.[7]

As in consumer activism, gay investment dollars can be held out as a carrot to companies. If investors prefer to own shares of companies that treat gay employees fairly, then they will seek out companies with good policies toward gay people and reward those companies by buying their stocks. One socially responsible investment firm argues that firms with gay-positive policies should be attractive to all investors interested in financial returns:

> Productivity and morale suffer in an intolerant or hostile environment. Unaddressed discrimination or abuses can lead to grievances and costly lawsuits in the states and cities that prohibit discrimination on the basis of sexual orientation. Reputations and sales decline if a company is perceived as tolerating bigotry. On the other hand, nondiscriminatory policies are a signal that a company is better positioned to benefit fully from the diversity in the workplace. They sharpen a corporation's edge as it competes for the best talent. (Trillium Asset Management 1999)

As chapters 2 and 3 suggest, the connection between competitiveness and the treatment of gay employees is not always so simple. Regardless of the rationale for investors, whether political or economic, investor concern would give companies an incentive to have gay-friendly policies.

Recently, new options have emerged for people who want to direct their investments in this way. Some mutual funds, or bundles of stocks, target firms thought to be socially responsible because they meet certain criteria, or "screens," which might include having a sexual orientation nondiscrimination policy or domestic partner benefits. Some financial consultants will advise investors in picking individual company stocks from among a group that passes the screens. One mutual fund, the Meyers Pride Value Fund, focuses exclusively on stocks in companies that have at least a nondiscrimination policy that includes sexual orientation. The proportion of money invested in these socially conscious funds is relatively small, though. The total invested in all kinds of socially responsible funds, not just those screening on gay issues, is $1.2 trillion, or just 9 percent of the total dollars under professional management (Sullivan 1999, 14).

While the need to be attractive to investors provides some leverage for gay investment activists, this economic strategy shares some of the problems of consumer activism. The basic premise—that companies will be better investments if they treat gay people well—is difficult to prove. Nevertheless, it is important to note that the Meyers Pride Value Fund was a top performer in its sector in 1999 ("Top-Performing Sector Funds" 1999). Even a clear correlation between a company's gay-positive policies and economic success could be the result of reverse causation: companies that are very successful can afford gay-friendly policies. Furthermore, convincing enough investors to target their investments in this way would be a difficult task. Many people own stock through retirement plans or mutual funds, but that places investments in specific companies in the hands of third parties. Usually those third parties have a "fiduciary responsibility," or legal obligation to invest in companies with good financial returns, regardless of whether the companies' actions are socially responsible.

A potentially more powerful weapon than investor demand exists for investor activists, though. Stockholders are owners of a company and, at least in theory, can help shape the company's policies. The Pride Value Fund managers and Trillium Asset Management analysts work directly with companies in their portfolios to encourage change in polices related to gay people or, if necessary to put another form of pressure on the company's management. Shareholders are allowed to place resolutions related to a company's policies before all of the company's shareholders. Gay investor activists can use their economic power to place resolutions that would add sexual orientation to a company's nondiscrimination policy, for example. Rather than face an embarrassing or divisive vote, sometimes companies will make changes before a resolution is voted on.

Some barriers make formal resolutions difficult to place. The Securities and Exchange Commission limits which issues shareholders can require companies to place on the proxy ballot that goes to shareholders before a company's annual meeting, and a resolution previously considered must meet a threshold vote before appearing on the ballot in a subsequent year (U.S. SEC 1999). For instance, some people believe that the SEC would rule that decisions about domestic partner benefits fall under the category of "ordinary business," which is excluded from shareholder resolutions (Freiburg 1998). Placing formal resolutions on social issues is rare, and winning a vote is practically unheard of. In 1997, for instance, only 22 out of the 376 shareholder resolutions filed were approved in shareholder votes, and all 22 concerned matters of corporate governance, not social issues (U.S. SEC 1999).

This particular economic strategy to push for social change is relatively new when compared with consumer boycotts or workplace activism, making an evaluation of its direct effectiveness difficult. Anecdotal evidence suggests that the use of shareholder resolutions in campaigns related to other social issues, such as divestment from South Africa during the apartheid era, environmental destruction related to the Exxon Valdez disaster, and product testing on animals, led to some success through negotiation, even when a vote failed (Mathiasen 1995).

No gay-related shareholder resolutions have passed, even when companies have committed acts that outraged gay activists. When Cracker Barrel fired its known lesbian and gay employees, a general outcry arose, and opposition quickly took shape in a consumer boycott. From the investment side, activists at the Interfaith Center for Corporate Responsibility got a large Cracker Barrel stockholder, the New York City Employees' Retirement System, a major pension fund with over $20.5 billion in total pension funds in 1992, behind a shareholder resolution to implement a sexual orientation nondiscrimination policy. (Gay/Lesbian/Bisexual Corporate Letter 1992, 1) After legal challenges related to putting the resolution on the ballot were resolved, a 1993 resolution to change Cracker Barrel's personnel policy won 15.6 percent of the vote; a similar vote five years later received 16 percent of the vote (Boerner 1998). In the context of shareholder votes, 16 percent is relatively high, but not high enough to force the company to include sexual orientation in its written nondiscrimination policy.

Even though resolutions have not passed, companies' desire to avoid shareholder votes provides another route to success. Johnson & Johnson, Chrysler, American Home Products, and McDonald's added sexual orientation to their corporate nondiscrimination policies to avoid the bad publicity that might have resulted from a shareholder vote (Alpern 1999, and

Alpern personal correspondence). Other companies are more stubborn, though, and General Electric and Exxon Mobil have resisted a similar push from investor activists.

These experiences suggest that even owning part of a company is not sufficient for quickly making change. Like worker and consumer activism, investor activism is simply a tool for putting economic pressure on an employer to change policies, and it has its limits in terms of applicability and in terms of more general process effectiveness. Many, but not all, companies sell shares to the general public, so some companies and all nonprofit employers would be exempt from this kind of pressure. Nor could investor pressure be easily targeted at a political entity's offensive actions, as with the Colorado boycott.

More important for this analysis, investor activism tends to focus on a relatively small number of decision-makers—other stockholders and business managers—sometimes without involving workers or generating a grassroots educational process in a company. For shareholders, this is a backroom strategy, allowing gay and lesbian people to promote a political agenda relatively quietly. Pride Value Fund president Shelly Meyers describes her work with companies as "behind the scenes": "There's no use in our making it public, because that would just be counterproductive. It's the private, one-on-one discussions that really get results" (quoted in Sullivan 1999, 15). Although investors might be successful in promoting change through education with top management, the invisibility of the effort reduces the potential political and social value of their actions.

This process weakness is exacerbated by the fact that most stocks are owned by a relatively small number of people, and wealth inequality is rising (Wolff 1998, 135). In 1995 the richest 10 percent of households owned 88 percent of stocks and mutual funds directly (140). While 41 percent of all households owned stocks in some form, including mutual funds and pension accounts, the richest 10 percent of households held 82 percent of the value of all different forms of stock ownership (139). Clearly the most powerful investor activists will be those at the upper end of the gay income distribution, leading to a greater class bias of this strategy than in the other two kinds of economic strategies. The skewed distribution of wealth in the United States also means that this strategy will involve a disproportionate number of white people. In 1995, the net worth of the average African American household was only 17 percent of the net wealth of the average white household (141). Thus the potential for building broader coalitions with other groups of investors is much less obvious than with other forms of activism.

To some extent this class bias would be lessened by working with unions or other pension funds who have socially active pension fund investment strategies. Pension funds as a whole owned roughly one-third of corporate stock and 40 percent of corporate bonds and were worth over $4 trillion in 1993, suggesting a great deal of potential leverage (Ghilarducci 1994). But the current federal law regulating pensions, ERISA, requires pension fund trustees to invest in the interest of the plan's participants, which has been widely interpreted as limiting the ability of funds to further any goal other than maximizing a risk-adjusted rate of return on investments (Ghilarducci 1994). Even if funds could pursue "economically targeted investments" designed to promote broader community economic goals, it is not clear that employee diversity would be considered a means to the larger end, much less whether gay issues as a whole would be seen as important in socially conscious investment decisions. Without a great deal of gay political involvement in activism motivated by a very dry and indirect goal (freeing pension funds from constraints on investment strategies), pension funds are not likely to be a significant vehicle for achieving equality in the workplace for gay and lesbian people in the near future.

Perhaps because of the relatively limited nature of its applicability and appeal to activists, investor pressure has not been the main tool used by gay and lesbian activists seeking change in individual workplaces, even though it has the potential to complement pressure from consumers and workers.

Investing in a Community. The usual way of thinking about people's economic activities used so far is simple: one either spends money on consumer goods or saves it; one spends time either at work or in consuming the goods and services purchased. But many people in the United States spend their money and time in other ways. In particular, gay, lesbian, and bisexual people often give their money and time to nonprofit organizations run by and for gay men and lesbians. While those donations do not generally result in an immediate or specific payback to the contributor, the organizations provide services or even goods that are valuable to a larger community. Gay, lesbian, and bisexual organizations provide many such goods and services, most of which are specifically designed to meet the cultural, political, intellectual, and social needs of gay people, needs that neither the marketplace nor mainstream nonprofit organizations have been willing to meet. Nonprofits produce plays by gay people, exhibit lesbians' artwork, organize gay political activists, teach courses on gay history, write reports on gay policy issues, represent gay litigants, hold gay-supportive religious services, support openly lesbian candidates, and deliver meals to incapacitated gay people, just to name a few specifics.

Individual gay people appear to target their involvement in these organizations deliberately. A 1998 study of gay, lesbian, bisexual, and transgendered (GLBT) people who were involved with a wide variety of GLBT organizations in three cities, San Francisco, Milwaukee, and Philadelphia, uncovers why those individuals are or were involved with a GLBT organization as a donor or volunteer (see Badgett and Cunningham 1998). The predominant motivations are wanting to help other gay people, contributing to social and political change, building social networks, and supporting good organizational characteristics (such as board diversity and fiscal responsibility). The study also finds that many people get involved with gay organizations as part of the coming out process or as a result of other transformative personal experiences, such as an experience of antigay discrimination or threats.

These activist motives are echoed in the observed patterns of giving. Most strikingly, gay people support political organizations much more heavily than any other kind of organization, including cultural, health (not AIDS-related), or religious organizations. Over one-quarter of volunteer hours and 37 percent of monetary contributions go to gay political campaigns and gay advocacy organizations. This contrasts sharply with the typical U.S. giver, who contributes only about 2 percent of contributions to advocacy groups (Independent Sector 1996).

This kind of economic activism helps to achieve important goals. Targeting dollars toward political uses suggests a clear investment mentality among gay people, since political change does not happen overnight or even with the election of an openly gay candidate. Targeting economic resources toward nonprofit organizations involves a much more direct relationship between effort—contributing time and money—and outcomes than in other kinds of consumer activism (which is also focused on how one spends money). The time and money given to many gay organizations can be quickly turned into a concrete service benefiting a gay man or lesbian. Organizations are not always effective in their efforts, of course. Some portion of every monetary contribution is used to raise more money; management skills are not always adequate. But nothing suggests that gay organizations are any more prone to those problems than are mainstream organizations with a heterosexual-oriented mission.

The clearest problem for nonprofits is the inadequacy of resources contributed by gay people. (Gay organizations get very little money from foundations and corporations [Badgett and Cunningham 1998].) Preliminary data from a study by the Gill Foundation, the foundation supported by gay philanthropist and software developer Tim Gill, found that the total budget of most national, state, and local gay organizational budgets in 1998 was almost $100 million (Freiberg 1999).[8] Twenty-six national organizations received 38 percent of all funding, and 75 percent of the state and local group funding went to organizations in California and New York. While $100 million represents tremendous growth in organizational effort, this total for all gay organizations was less than the $120 million budget of Focus on the Family, an antigay organization. Even if all $100 million went to political groups—which it did not—the inadequacy of that figure when compared with the economic power of gay people's sworn political enemies is obvious.

Available data clearly point to the problem: too few gay people contribute, and those who do contribute do not always give enough. In general terms, the vast majority of the money going to all nonprofits in the United States (86 percent in 1996) comes from individuals. So although foundations and corporations could be more actively involved in funding gay organizations, the underlying problem is that gay people do not give enough to support the number of organizations necessary to meet the political, social, and cultural needs of gay people. The three-city study mentioned earlier found that the gay people surveyed, who were on existing organizational mailing lists and are therefore likely to be among the *most* active donors and volunteers in the GLB community, give less than 1 percent of their incomes to gay organizations.

The $100 million total for all gay organizations suggests that the problem is even bigger, since many gay men and lesbians do not give at all to gay organizations. Suppose gay people make up 5 percent of the U.S. population over the age of eighteen, or roughly ten million people.[9] Then the per person average gift to all gay organizations is $10. In other words, if every gay, lesbian, or bisexual person skipped a couple of movies per year and instead donated $20 to a gay organization, the resources for gay organizations would double. Even that larger contribution would still represent well under 1 percent of the average person's income.

Given the meager resources currently available to nonprofit organizations, it is clear that gay people who want to see a different world need to think ahead. Openly gay financial guru Andrew Tobias talks about giving to political and charitable organizations as if they were investments for gay and straight people alike (Tobias 1997). By investing in community organizations and their "products," gay people change their world in ways that are at least as important as changing workplace practices or accumulating assets for retirement. This book and other research shows that mainstream institutions have not changed for gay people over the last fifty years without an explicit and collective response coordinated by formal organizations, suggesting that large-scale future change will require a shift in gay people's financial commitment to their community.

Process issues also arise in thinking about gay organizations. On the positive side, an indirect process benefit comes from the value of building a shared identity and set of concerns among gay people across organizations. This side benefit even adds to the value of gay organizations that are not engaged in direct political lobbying or in economic activism. On the negative side, lesbians and gay people of color sometimes appear to be alienated by the activities and goals of many gay organizations. As a result, the organizations that define the "gay community" to the larger public are often mainly made up of white gay men and lesbians, an outcome that can inhibit the forming of coalitions among many different organizations. To meet their own needs, organizations specifically for lesbians or for African American lesbians, for instance, have formed in many cities, and LLEGO (The National Latina/o Lesbian, Gay, Bisexual, and Transgender Organization) and the National Black Gay and Lesbian Leadership Forum exist nationally. While the process generating the proliferation of organizations is often a rancorous one, the outcome, that is, continuing organizational development, gives hope that bridges can be built to more mainstream organizations in the civil rights movement and other kinds of groups even as new coalitions will be formed within the gay, lesbian, and bisexual communities.

Finally, although this section has focused on gay people's giving to gay organizations, the three-city study finds that gay people give just as much of their incomes to nongay organizations. This implies a level of involvement and investment by gay people in the broader community that most heterosexual people would not expect. The study suggests that gay people are as much a part of the Red Cross, the PTA, the United Way, and the local hospital as they are involved with the local gay community center. That finding further chips away at the myths of gay hedonism. No one has yet studied the motivations for or outcomes of this broader community involvement, but more gay people coming out in their volunteer work and donations suggests another possible route to social and political change through mainstream nonprofit community organizations.

Putting Strategies Together

The different strategies related to gay people's roles as consumers, workers, and investors are not mutually exclusive. The strategies are often complementary and could be used in concert to maximize the economic pressure on companies to change their policies. Collaborative targeting is necessary to avoid conflicts. In particular, employee groups might prefer to be seen as "team players" who are not pursuing consumer and investor strategies that would embarrass or otherwise damage their employer's business. An implicit tag team approach that involved subtle internal pressure from gay employees and simultaneous blunt external pressure by investors and consumers might be much more effective than isolated efforts.

For individuals making decisions about how to spend their activist time, energy, and money, however, this economic analysis of strategies suggests that the biggest benefit for the buck comes in workplace organizing. All of the strategies can put economic pressure on employers, but workplace organizing usually involves the most within-workplace education, visibility, and potential coalition-building. Workplace activism also creates a larger feedback loop that affects other gay people's visibility and disclosure in the workplace, as chapter 3 suggests that gay workers' coming out decisions are heavily influenced by both employer policies and by the experiences of their openly gay colleagues in the workplace.

Investing economic resources of time and money in support of gay and lesbian nonprofit organizations is another powerful way to create a world that accepts and even nurtures gay and lesbian people. Organizing collectively to provide cultural, social, and political services and coordination requires effort and money, and current levels of funding for gay organizations suggest much room for improvement in giving by gay people. These organizations are often valuable in and of themselves, but they also facilitate a sense of shared interest among gay people and provide resources and coordination for economic and political activism.

Gay people's investment in organizations is also a reminder that economic activism is not the only strategy for social change. More traditional political activism—lobbying legislators, working for candidates, or even engaging in direct action—requires stable and well-funded organizations. Consumer, workplace, and investor activism do not replace activism in the political realm but instead add to the set of potentially powerful tools available for activists.

Prospects for Change

From some perspectives, lesbian, gay, and bisexual people have made enormous progress in achieving equality over the last few decades:

- The Stonewall Inn, the scene of the 1969 riots that pushed the gay rights movement into more assertive political strategies, went from being the target of police harassment in the 1960s to being named a National Historical Landmark in 1999.
- Tammy Baldwin is the first out lesbian (or gay person) to be elected to Congress in her first Congressional race.
- A Massachusetts court recognized the right of a lesbian mother to visit her daughter after a relationship breakup.
- As many as 10 percent of U.S. companies offer equal spousal benefits to gay employees' domestic partners.
- Many cities and eleven states (California, Hawaii, Nevada, Wisconsin, Minnesota, Massachusetts, New Jersey, Vermont, Rhode Island, Connecticut, and New Hampshire) have outlawed sexual orientation discrimination in employment.

Despite those victories, much work remains before gay people can claim equality of opportunity and of economic and political outcomes. One of the main purposes of this book was to demonstrate that gay men's and lesbians' lives are characterized by economic disadvantage. The impact of disadvantage is partly revealed by income figures, which find lower individual incomes for gay men and lower household incomes for lesbian and gay households. Inequality is evident in the emotional distress and economic disruption caused by the lack of recognition for gay family relationships. Losing child custody, being turned away from a partner's hospital room, paying to patch together legal agreements, and living with uncertainty are all visible consequences of gay inequality.

To make matters worse, conservative political activists seek to close off all recognition of gay families and would even like to eliminate the option of legislation that would address inequalities in other areas were the U.S. Supreme Court to relax its vigilance in protecting the rights of minorities.[1]

Active opposition to political efforts for change shows that continued progress toward equality for gay people is not inevitable.

As in the political realm, the evolution of the U.S. economic image of gay and lesbian people is not unambiguously positive. The glossy picture framed by the myths of affluence, protective invisibility, conspicuous consumption, and DINK heaven persists, deliberately painted by marketers and gay rights opponents and supported by the public focus on affluent gay and lesbian celebrities. These myths and stereotypes are slow to fade from the public's memory, despite growing evidence of outright discrimination and of gay people's vulnerability. Spreading the word about gay men's and lesbians' continuing vulnerability to job loss and harassment, their experiences of discrimination in compensation, and their lack of access to economic support available to heterosexuals' families seems unconvincing or even ungrateful in light of recent political and alleged economic successes.

Future political success is likely to depend on a broader public understanding of ongoing inequality, combined with explicit efforts to redress gay people's unequal position. I hope that this book will contribute to that broader public understanding. In terms of explicit effort, this book has argued that both the achievements and the remaining goals of the gay, lesbian, and bisexual political movements depend heavily on the ability of gay people to mobilize their allies and assets to make changes in political and economic institutions. Most obviously, groups of lesbians, gay men, and their allies have worked together to change oppressive laws at least since the 1950s, with the formation of the Mattachine Society and the Daughters of Bilitis (D'Emilio 1984). Moving beyond traditional political organizing by combining political goals with gay people's financial influence is another potentially potent way to reduce the inequalities identified in this book.

Economic activism to address economic inequality is one of many factors that can lead to reducing inequality, but as this book shows, change has been a complex process. Collective action to resist even more oppressive past political and economic structures shaped the current economic position of gay people, but so did many other influences outside of the direct control of lesbians and gay men.

Changes in political ideologies and social norms, quite important factors in shaping civil rights and family law as well as employers' compensation practices, are the product of many influences, some of which are amenable to future influence of gay people and some of which are probably not. For instance, the current struggle to redefine affirmative action in the workplace is a debate about the meaning of civil rights laws and how they will be applied. On one hand, gay people's pursuit of basic civil rights protections could be constructed as part of an effort to maintain the country's current civil rights approach and commitment, affirmative action and all. In that scenario, gay people work in coalition with nongay people who are also concerned about preserving civil rights laws and policies. On the other hand, at least some of the desire on the part of employers who want to maintain affirmative action is the need to cope with increasing workforce diversity. Gay people could do little to influence this factor involving big changes in the nation's labor supply.

Broad market forces are also largely beyond the direct control of gay people. Changes in consumer tastes, increasing global competition, evolving government policies, and unpredictable macroeconomic conditions are important factors that have shaped and will continue to influence political and firm-level responses to gay and lesbian people's call for change. Sometimes in the past these forces have worked in favor of gay people: Low levels of unemployment in the 1990s made plausible the claims that skilled gay people would flock to companies offering domestic partner benefits and would avoid employers without such benefits. Sometimes economic forces have worked against gay people: During the recession in the early 1990s, the myth of affluence helped to fuel antigay rhetoric and referenda in Oregon and Colorado.

The importance of government policies that grant access to restitution for acts of illegal discrimination, to the social insurance and third-party support for families, or to particular business opportunities (such as holding liquor licenses for gay bars), for example, cannot be underestimated in this account of the economic position of gay men and lesbians. Change in this realm is facilitated by the public accountability of politicians and other policymakers and, to some extent, of judges. If gay and lesbian people can enlist decision-makers in their cause, as has occurred in cities and states with antidiscrimination laws and domestic partner benefits, then changes in the law are likely to improve gay people's economic standing.

Putting these pieces together into a larger picture has required going beyond a mainstream economic analysis of social issues, which begins and ends with the role of the individual. This book's economic analysis of gay people's position reflects a broader theoretical perspective incorporating the role of public policies related to the family and workplace, social norms about sexuality and gender, and collective action by like-minded individuals, while also acknowledging the importance of markets and of individual decision-making. Although positive change in gay people's current position is not assured, economic and legal inequality is also not inevitable. In the end, progress toward equality and its speed will likely depend on how lesbians and gay men use their current economic potential. Through action as consumers or producers of goods and services, as investors in a financial or community future, and as political actors in grassroots and electoral politics, lesbians, gay men, and their allies can attack the inequities identified in this book and can contribute to long run equality for people of all sexual orientations.

Chapter One

1. By discrimination, economists mean that a heterosexual worker would be hired over a gay applicant even though the gay applicant is equally (or more) productive.

2. Sociologists define institutions as "social practices that are regularly and continuously repeated, are sanctioned and maintained by social norms, and have a major significance in the social structure" (Abercrombie, Hill, and Turner, 1988, p. 216).

3. For example, a finding of immutability might meet one often used criterion for a judicial standard of review that would make it much more difficult for the government to justify laws singling people out because of their sexual orientation. But see Janet Halley (1989) for a discussion of why such a use is neither desirable nor necessary.

Chapter Two

1. Dan Miller's story is told in James B. Stewart, "Gentleman's Agreement," *New Yorker,* 13 June 1994, 74–82.

2. Cheryl Summerville and Ernest Dillon both told their stories at hearings on the Employment Non-Discrimination Act, Hearing of the Committee on Labor and Human Resources, U.S. Senate, on S. 2238 to prohibit employment discrimination on the basis of sexual orientation, 29 July 1994. Other cases of sexual orientation discrimination are contained in an appendix to the hearing transcript.

3. As quoted in Louis Weisberg, "Gays Ousted at Iowa Health Center," *Windy City Times,* 5 June 1997, 4.

4. Peter Freiberg, "President's Order Protects Workers," *Washington Blade,* 5 June 1998, 29, no. 23, 1.

5. In addition, 30.6 percent considered themselves to be homosexual (33 individuals), 12 percent bisexual (13 individuals), 9.3 percent "something else" (10 individuals), and 1.9 percent "don't know" (2 individuals).

6. In the post-*Bowers v. Hardwick* era, some states have continued to prohibit same-sex sexual acts. As a result, gay civil rights lawyers and activists sometimes try to distinguish between categorizing people by their *status* as lesbian, gay, bisexual, or heterosexual as opposed to engaging in what may be illegal *acts.*

7. In general, economists prefer to use age minus years of education (also

subtracting off five years for preschool time), a closer measure of a worker's potential experience. The coding of the NHSLS data do not permit such a calculation, however.

8. In my 1995 study, lesbians earned less than heterosexual women in the detailed comparison, but that difference was not statistically significant. In other words, that income difference might simply reflect the chance that the particular sample of lesbians and heterosexual women are economically uncharacteristic of women as a whole. The importance of that caveat is evident in the updated findings, in which lesbians earned slightly more, but again that difference is statistically insignificant. The overall conclusion from both studies is the same: we cannot say confidently that lesbians earn either more or less than comparable heterosexual women.

9. The main goal of their study was to see whether living in an area covered by a law barring discrimination based on sexual orientation reduced the earnings gap between men in same-sex couples and opposite-sex couples. They found no observable effect of such laws.

10. These two studies differ from mine in categorizing people as gay/bisexual based on the sex of their sex partners over the last year or over the past five years. While the idea that recent sexual activity is a better indicator of identity seems plausible, anecdotal accounts in the gay media suggest that self-identified lesbians sometimes have sex with men, and self-identified gay men sometimes have sex with women. It is also not obvious to me that more recent behavior is the best indicator for purposes of studying current labor market status, which captures the influence of a lifetime of choices and treatment. The fact that the patterns are generally consistent (and their different findings for lesbians fall into the range implied by my findings here) is important for establishing the "robustness" of these income differences, though.

11. In the simplest version of Becker's employee discrimination model, the profit maximizing employer strategy is to hire only members of one group, resulting in complete workplace segregation but equal average wages for each group. A more realistic version, incorporating groups of complementary workers, results in lower wages for one group (Becker, 1971, 59–60).

12. The U.S. Supreme Court struck down the amendment in 1996 in *Romer v. Evans.*

13. But see Audrey Light and Manuela Urita (1992) for evidence that employers can no longer infer higher turnover rates for young women compared with young men simply based on sex.

14. The report was written by Michael McDaniel for the Defense Department's Defense Personnel Security Research and Education Center (PERSEREC) but apparently was never submitted to the Pentagon.

Chapter Three

1. The question did not specify in which specific circumstances disclosure would be objectionable or if it would be more or less objectionable in the workplace.

2. This body of work reflects different theoretical approaches. See Doeringer and Piore (1971) or Edwards (1979).

3. But see Badgett (1997a) for an argument that their general conclusion is not adequately supported by their methodology and data.

4. Mainstream economic models describe individuals' preferences and choices as "rational" as long as four simple criteria are met: (1) more income (or disclosure) is always preferred to less income (or disclosure), holding all else equal; (2) preferences are consistent; (3) each combination of items (such as an amount of income and a level of disclosure) can be compared with all other combinations of those items; and (4) the more of one item an individual has, the less additional an amount of that item will add to the individual's satisfaction.

5. Approximate circulation data are from a telephone conversation with Jeffrey Escoffier, publisher of *Out/Look,* 25 February 1994.

6. Incorporating this feedback effect requires more sophisticated econometric techniques that should be explored in future research with more complete data, including data from heterosexuals.

7. Even when the motive might be politically oriented toward a policy change that will have effects on other people, the motive to come out is based on a potential—not actual—change in policy and could be largely related to a self-interest in the outcome, as someone with a partner might have when coming out to advocate for domestic partner benefits.

8. Some productivity effects are "internalized" in gay workers' decisions when the gay worker himself or herself bears the impact of lower productivity in the form of lower wages or less frequent promotions. "External" effects are those imposed on other parties.

9. The job competition model also implies conflict and lower productivity, but the analysis following this paragraph would also apply.

Chapter Four

1. There are exceptions to this generalization, of course, particularly with respect to the impact of private pensions and social security benefits on the retirement and labor force participation of workers. But those studies tend to focus on the impact of pensions as deferred income rather than on the social features of the policies.

2. See Foster (1998) for differences in benefits for part-time and full-time workers. Hersch and White-Means (1993) show that women and black men are less likely than white men to receive health and pension benefits.

3. Some exceptions exist. Moral concerns related to norms of fairness sometimes pop up in economists' models of why employers might pay some workers more than others and more than people doing similar jobs in other companies. In this case, employees might compare their wages to those of others and will decide on how much effort to give on the job in response to the perceived fairness of their wages (Akerlof and Yellen 1990). But employers and managers are reacting to their employees' norms, not acting on their own norms.

4. 482 N.W.2d 121 (Wisc. App. 1992), reprinted in Rubenstein (1997).

5. Grievance of B. M., S. S., C. M. and J. R., VLRB Docket No. 92-32.

6. *University of Alaska v. Tumeo,* 933 P.2d 1147. In the meantime, however, the state legislature changed the benefits law to make spousal benefits legal under the nondiscrimination law (Eskridge and Hunter 1999, 214).

7. For instance, the proposed federal Employment Nondiscrimination Act of 1994 specifically excluded the provision of benefits and disparate impact analysis, which might have otherwise allowed a finding of discrimination if practices disproportionately disadvantaged gay employees as compared with heterosexual employees. Under current marriage law, spousal benefits would clearly have an disparate impact on gay workers.

8. That case was *Gay Teachers Assoc. v. Board of Education of N.Y.,* 585 N.Y.S. 2d. 1016 (App. Div. 1992). See Stipulation of Settlement and Discontinuance, Oct. 29, 1993.

9. One negative decision, *Air Transport Association of America v. City and County of San Francisco,* 922 F. Supp. 1149 (N.D. Ca. 1998), held that the city was effectively (and illegally) regulating benefits controlled by a federal law, the Employee Retirement Income Security Act (ERISA), when applied to airlines.

10. The databases included Hoover's, Standard & Poor's, IAC, and DCA.

11. This does not include over two thousand more employees that adopted domestic partner benefits as a result of the San Francisco Equal Benefits Law.

Chapter Five

1. Alaska, California, Colorado, Connecticut, Delaware, Hawaii, Indiana, Iowa, Maine, Nebraska, New Hampshire, New Jersey, New Mexico, North Dakota, Ohio, Oregon, South Dakota, Vermont, Washington, West Virginia, and Wyoming (Hunter 1995).

2. Unfortunately, the sample sizes of the better data sets are too small to examine racial differences in income among gay men and lesbians.

3. Bob Witeck, personal communication, 28 May 2000.

4. Some of Kates's (1998) gay male respondents reported that they considered the gay-friendliness of company policies when making buying decisions.

5. Witeck, personal communication, 28 May 2000.

Chapter Six

1. In terms of family farms and businesses, Pollak argues that by creating long-term incentives, by monitoring work effort, and by promoting altruism and family loyalty, personal relationships reduce individual selfish behavior that would undermine the economic viability of the family enterprise (Pollak 1985, 585-86).

2. Data suggest that women continue to do far more housework than men, and the amount tends to increase when women marry. See Blau (1998) for a discussion and presentation of recent data.

3. The degree of specialization might be tempered somewhat since some products require the involvement of *both* members of a couple (presumed to be one man and one woman), such as "sexual enjoyment, the production of children, and possibly other commodities" (Becker 1991, 39) Becker noted that the need to

spend at least some time together producing these complementary "goods" does not typically outweigh the general gains from specialization, though.

4. "Households with only men or only women are less efficient because they are unable to profit from the sexual difference in comparative advantage"; and "Complementarity [in sexual enjoyment and the production of children] implies that households with men and women are more efficient than households with only one sex" (Becker 1991, 39).

5. This argument is developed in Blumstein and Schwartz (1983) and Badgett (1995a).

6. Of course, forms of inequality other than gender could influence an individual's relative bargaining position. Having a privileged race, income, or age position, for instance, could alter one partner's bargaining position relative to the other's. This might explain why Frank, earning 62 percent of Barry's earnings, does more housework. But those factors can also work within heterosexual couples, perhaps balancing out the gender effect in some cases.

7. Bisexual people are likely to be included on both sides and might be miscategorized in both cases: bisexuals in opposite-sex relationships will be mislabeled as heterosexual, while those in same-sex relationships will be mislabeled as gay or lesbian. Following bisexuals across relationships and couple types while collecting data on household division of labor would provide for an interesting longitudinal study. Such data would provide further insight on the role of gender (and other social factors) and institutional factors in determining division of labor, where at least one partner's skills and preferences are held constant.

8. Many of their respondents were from New York, San Francisco, and Seattle, and the couples were disproportionately white and well educated (548). But they made efforts to gather a large sample through various means and ended up with usable questionnaires from 4,314 heterosexual couples (roughly 15 percent were unmarried), 969 gay male couples, and 788 lesbian couples (547), providing the most comprehensive survey in this area to date.

9. For similar points, see Folbre (1994, 23) or Bergmann (1986, 204).

10. Other reasons offered for women's rapid rise in labor force participation include the increase in wages available to women, either because increasing demand for labor could not be met by men or through the breaking down of discriminatory barriers to higher wage jobs.

11. This allows identification of men who have male partners and women who have female partners, whom we might reasonably presume to be lesbian, gay, or bisexual. Unfortunately, the Census form did not ask unpartnered lesbian or gay people any identifying questions, and suspicions of a serious undercount seem reasonable given that very few people indicated a same-sex partner (only 0.16 percent of all households). The Current Population Survey now asks a comparable question, and in 1998 found same-sex unmarried partner couples in 1.6 percent households, ten times the proportion found in the Census. (U.S. Bureau of the Census 1999b)

12. Looking more generally at the number of couples that have roughly the same (given Klawitter's categories) numbers of weeks and hours rather than focusing on cases in which both are working full-time and full-year gives the same pattern. In 53 percent of married couples, 56 percent of unmarried opposite-sex

couples, 67 percent of male couples, and 64 percent of female couples, both partners work the same number of weeks (none, 1–40, or 42–52). In 55 percent of married couples, 65 percent of unmarried opposite-sex couples, 76 percent of male couples, and 69 percent of female couples, both partners worked the same number of hours (none, 1–30, 31 and over).

13. These figures are for married men and women with a spouse present. The BLS did not report whether the spouses were working full-time or part-time in reporting on the percentage of families with both spouses working (U.S. Department of Labor BLS 1999b).

14. See, for example, Becker's comment on same-sex couples' procreative abilities: "Homosexual unions do not result in children" (Becker 1991, 330).

15. See Folbre for an example of this argument (Folbre 1994, 254).

16. In her book, Folbre does not discuss fertility among gays and lesbians, but she does consider the impact of social pressure to have children (what she calls "coercive pro-natalism") on gays' and lesbians' political position (92).

17. She appears to undermine her argument, though, by also asserting that "these roles may alternate or be flexibly adopted" (Lamos 1995, 60), in which case something other than lesbian gender must motivate the couple to switch roles, such as, perhaps, the desire to share the household duties that correspond to each role.

18. See Blumstein and Schwartz (1983, 148); Kurdek (1993, 137). Kurdek actually found two statistically significant correlation measures (partial correlations) that indicated that both lesbians who have a more masculine orientation *and* lesbians with a more feminine orientation do more housework. But because that was only true for one set of lesbians and not for their partners, he concluded that gender role orientation did not affect household labor allocation for lesbian couples (136).

19. Writer Phyllis Burke described a similar decision made with her partner after the birth of their son (Burke 1993, 31).

20. The marriage bonus occurs because the positive income is averaged with the zero income, allowing the couple to pay taxes at a lower marginal tax rate. The marriage penalty occurs primarily because people with similar earnings are pushed into a higher tax bracket than if they were single.

21. Other tax advantages for married couples include tax exemption for employer-provided health benefits (while those for domestic partners are taxed), ability to declare a nonearning spouse a dependent, tax-free transfers to a spouse upon death, and exemptions from certain other taxes, such as property transfer taxes. While these advantages might make marriage more attractive, they would not (except perhaps for the first) clearly increase the value of specialization.

22. With a few exceptions, judges have held that same-sex partners who are not legal parents do not have visitation or custody rights to children they may have raised for years (Rubenstein 1997, 915).

23. Robson frames her critique in terms of "family," but her discussion of specific examples of family structures and laws include only couples, and she does not consider the implications of using family to describe the kinship structures observed by Weston. Paula Ettelbrick (1989) has critiqued marriage more explicitly using this same concern about the marginalization of alternative family forms.

Chapter Seven

1. Julie A. Nelson argues that the proper subject for economists to study is provisioning (Nelson 1993).

2. This policy principle also raises other issues not considered here, such as allowing gay people to participate in other youth-oriented programs such as scouting or Big Brothers/Sisters.

3. The Supreme Court has ruled that this constitutional principle may be overruled by some rational or compelling state need (see Eskridge and Hunter [1997] for a discussion of the application of the equal protection clause to gay issues).

4. In his only comment on the subject, Walzer suggests that allowing same-sex marriages would be "redistributive" and would create "a new arrangement of commitments, obligations, responsibilities, and alliances" (Walzer 1983, 228). Presumably redistribution occurs because family memberships (and the resulting distributions of love, etc.) will change, not because something is taken from some families and given to others.

5. See Philip Kayal's work on volunteers for the Gay Men's Health Crisis (Kayal 1993, esp. 120 , 129–47).

6. Concern about housing discrimination raises similar issues, since access to shelter is an element of provisioning. Many civil rights laws (both proposed and enacted) prohibit discrimination based on sexual orientation in the rental or sale of housing.

7. See the discussion by Editors of Harvard Law Review (1990), pp. 85–93.

8. Chapter 3 also mentions that in Becker's coworker discrimination model, employers would react by segregating gay and heterosexual employees but otherwise paying them the same wage, an outcome that seems improbable in this situation given the relatively small number of gay people in the population.

9. To be more precise, Becker shows that in this model the level of discrimination should fall to that of the employer who has the least distaste for the group, assuming that firms have similar ways of producing their products. If that least-discriminating employer does not discriminate at all, then discrimination would disappear completely over time (Becker 1971, 45).

10. Studies that send black applicants and white applicants with the same qualifications out to apply for the same jobs find that black applicants receive less favorable treatment and fewer job offers than the white applicants (Turner, Fix, and Struyk 1991).

11. For discussions of ways that workplace activists and consultants approach employers, see Liz Winfeld and Susan Spielman (19995) or Brian McNaught (1993).

12. H.R. 2355, "To prohibit employment discrimination on the basis of sexual orientation," U.S. House of Representatives, 106th Congress, Section 8(a), June 24, 1999.

13. Obviously the legal obligations involved and the legal requirements for ending the relationship are different for marriage and most domestic partnerships. But since neither the historical record nor modern employment practices suggests an obvious link between a voluntarily offered benefit of employment and the elements of an ever evolving legal definition of marriage, the differences in legal obligations seem unimportant in this limited employment-related context. In other

words, the fact that married couples have certain legal obligations that gay couples do not (and cannot) have does not mean that employers would be justified in treating them differently. For instance, employers treat employees with employed or wealthy spouses the same way they treat employees with economically dependent spouses, even though the employee with the economically dependent spouse might be seen as more worthy or needy than the employee with the wealthy spouse.

14. The adoption of partner benefits is a one-time decision that firms make and is, therefore, unlike the ongoing wage negotiation of unions that is also resource-intensive but would not be easy or desirable to eliminate.

15. The assumption that 5 percent of the workforce is gay and that half of gay people have partners falls within the range of estimates of those values. See a discussion of such values in Alm, Badgett, and Whittington, 2000.

16. The calculation is 32,371,000 (uninsured adults) $\times$ .05 (proportion of gay people) $\times$ .5 (gays with partners) $\times$ .53 (workers with own employer-provided coverage) = 428,916. U.S. statistics are from Bennefield (1998).

17. The effort to enact equal benefits ordinances parallels the "living wage" movement strategy for raising the wages of employees of city contractors.

Chapter Eight

1. See Eskridge (1996), 66–70.

2. As noted in Rubenstein (1997), 762.

3. See the discussion of *Marvin v. Marvin* in Eskridge and Hunter (1997), 783–84.

4. California Assembly Bill No. 26, chapter 588, approved by Governor October 2, 1999.

5. Because Vermont already provided health care benefits to state employees, no additional costs would be expected if same-sex couples could marry.

6. The state's creation of civil unions is unlikely to have the same tourism effect since that status is probably not transferable to other states.

7. Of course, the usual exceptions to permanence of parental status would exist, as in cases of abandonment or abuse.

8. This analysis clearly implies that limiting parenthood to one adult or denying a lesbian or gay parent the right to live with their same-sex partner, as judges sometimes do in custody and visitation decisions for children from heterosexual relationships (Eskridge and Hunter 1997, 114), impedes parents' ability to meet children's basic needs.

Chapter Nine

1. The National Gay and Lesbian Task Force's annual Creating Change conference for activists has held several panels taking up the issue of accepting donations from Coors and other corporate sponsors.

2. A study of several well-organized national consumer boycotts in response to price increases finds that a boycott might lead to a very short term but not a long term reduction in price (Friedman, 1995).

3. See the Rainbow Card Web site, <www.rainbowcard.org>) (accessed 13 July 1999).

4. In 1998, only 13.9 percent of U.S. workers were union members (U.S. Department of Labor BLS 1999c).

5. This example comes from Woods (1993), 223–26.

6. Since 1998, Disney's profit and stock price record have been less favorable. Stock analysts and the company attribute losses in 1999 to poor performances in its consumer products division and home video business (*Los Angeles Times* 1999). Revenues at theme parks were strong, however. The financial health of the theme parks plus the timing of Disney's troubles (well after the 1997 boycott announcement) both imply that the boycott was not responsible for Disney's short-run woes.

7. The fact that a growing number executives receive stock options as a form of compensation adds to management's desire to see a high stock price.

8. The $100 million includes $7 million from national organizations covered by a *Washington Blade* survey but not by the Gill Foundation study (Freiberg 1999). Gill Foundation officials also note that their survey left out some organizations.

9. The U.S. Census Bureau (1999) estimates that the population of people over eighteen was 201,667,000 as of 1 January 1999, so 5 percent is approximately ten million.

Chapter Ten

1. The U.S. Supreme Court's ruling in *Romer v. Evans* suggests that attempts to prevent passage of sexual orientation antidiscrimination laws will run into constitutional difficulties, but a law similar to Colorado's Amendment 2 was passed in Cincinnati, Ohio, and was allowed to stand by the Supreme Court's refusal to hear challenges to that law.

REFERENCES

Abercrombie, Nicholas, Stephen Hill, and Bryan S. Turner. 1988. *The Penguin Dictionary of Sociology.* Third edition. London: Penguin Books.

Adam, Barry. 1981. "Stigma and Employability: Discrimination by Sex and Sexual Orientation in the Ontario Legal Profession." *Canadian Review of Sociology and Anthropology* 18: 216–21.

Aigner, Dennis J., and Glen G. Cain. 1997. "Statistical Theories of Discrimination in the Labor Market." *Industrial and Labor Relations Review* (April): 175–87.

Akerlof, George A., and Janet L. Yellen. 1990. "The Fair Wage–Effort Hypothesis and Unemployment." *Quarterly Journal of Economics* 105: 255–83.

Alm, James, M. V. Lee Badgett, and Leslie A. Whittington. 2000. "Wedding Bell Blues: The Income Tax Consequences of Legalizing Same-Sex Marriage." *National Tax Journal* 53 (June): 201–14.

Almaguer, Thomas. 1991. "Chicano Men: A Cartography of Homosexual Identity and Behavior." *differences: A Journal of Feminist Cultural Studies* 3: 75–100.

Alpern, Shelley. 1999. "McDonalds Adopts Nondiscrimination Policy; Similar Proposals Go to Ballot at GE, Exxon." *Investing for A Better World.* <http://www.trilliuminvest.com/pages/social/social_frame.html>. Accessed 14 July 1999.

Altman, Dennis. 1982. *The Homosexualization of America.* New York: St. Martin's Press.

Anderson, Scott. 1979. "The Gay Press Proliferates—And So Do Its Problems." *Advocate,* 13 December.

Arndt, Michael. 2000. "United Tries for Gay-Friendly Skies." *Business Week Online.* <http://www.businessweek.com/bwdaily/dnflash/bnfarch.htm>. Accessed 24 May.

Assael, Henry. 1981. *Consumer Behavior and Marketing Action.* Boston: Kent Publishing Co.

Badgett, M. V. Lee. 1994. "Equal Pay for Equal Families." *Academe* 80, 3 (May): 26–30.

———. 1995a. "Gender, Sexuality and Sexual Orientation: All in the Feminist Family?" *Feminist Economics* 1 (1): 121–39.

———.1995b. "The Wage Effects of Sexual Orientation Discrimination." *Industrial Labor Relations Review* 49 (4): 726–38.

———. 1996a. "Choices and Chances: Is Coming Out at Work a Rational Choice?"

In *Queer Studies.* Edited by Brett Beemyn and Mickey Eliason. New York: New York University Press.

———. 1996b. "Employment and Sexual Orientation: Disclosure and Discrimination in the Workplace." *Journal of Gay and Lesbian Social Services* 4: 29–52.

———. 1997a. "A Queer Marketplace: Books on Lesbians and Gay Consumers, Workers, and Investors." *Feminist Studies* 23: 607–32.

———. 1997b. "Beyond Biased Samples: Challenging the Myths on the Economic Status of Lesbians and Gay Men." *Homo Economic: Capitalism, Community, and Gay Life.* Edited by Amy Gluckman and Betsy Reed. New York: Routledge.

———. 1997c. "Vulnerability in the Workplace: Evidence of Anti-Gay Discrimination." *Angles: The Policy Journal of the Institute for Gay and Lesbian Strategic Studies* 2 (1): 1–4.

———. 1998. "The Fiscal Impact on the State of Vermont of Allowing Same-Sex Couples to Marry." Institute for Gay and Lesbian Strategic Studies, Technical Rep. 98-1.

Badgett, Lee, Colleen Donnelly, and Jennifer Kibbe. 1992. *Pervasive Patterns of Discrimination against Lesbians and Gay Men: Evidence from Surveys across the United States.* Washington, D.C.: National Gay and Lesbian Task Force Policy Institute.

Badgett, M. V. Lee, and Nancy Cunningham. 1998. *Creating Communities: Giving and Volunteering by Gay, Lesbian, Bisexual, and Transgender People.* New York: Working Group on Funding Lesbian and Gay Issues and Institute for Gay & Lesbian Strategic Studies.

Badgett, M. V. Lee, and Josh Goldfoot. 1996. "For Richer, for Poorer: The Freedom to Marry Debate." *Angles: The Policy Journal of the Institute for Gay and Lesbian Strategic Studies*: 1–4.

Bailey, Robert. 1998. *Out and Voting: The Gay, Lesbian, and Bisexual Vote in Congressional House Elections, 1990–1996.* Washington, D.C.: Policy Institute of National Gay and Lesbian Task Force.

Baker, Daniel B., Sean O'Brien Strub, and Bill Henning. 1995. *Cracking the Corporate Closet.* New York: Harper Business.

Bardach, Eugene. 1996. *The Eight-Step Path of Policy Analysis: A Handbook for Practice.* Berkeley: Berkeley Academic Press.

Bartlett, Katharine T. 1984. "Rethinking Parenthood as an Exclusive Status: The Need for Legal Alternatives When the Premise of the Nuclear Family Has Failed." *Virginia Law Review* 70: 879–963.

Barrett, Michele, and Mary McIntosh. 1982. *The Anti-social Family.* London: NLB.

Becker, Gary S. 1971. *The Economics of Discrimination.* Chicago and London: University of Chicago Press.

———. 1991. *Treatise on the Family.* Cambridge, Mass.: Harvard University Press.

Beckett, Jamie, and Gavin Power. 1995. "The Grocery Strike." *San Francisco Chronicle,* 11 April.

Bennefield, Robert L. 1998. *Health Insurance Coverage: 1997.* Current Population Reports, P60-202. Washington, D.C.: U. S. Department of Commerce Census Bureau.

Bergmann, Barbara. 1986. *The Economic Emergence of Women.* New York: Basic Books.

Bishop, Libby, and David I. Levine. 1999. "Computer-mediated Communication as Employee Voice: A Case Study." *Industrial and Labor Relations Review* 52: 213–33.

Black, Dan, Gary Gates, Seth Sanders, and Lowell Taylor. 2000. "Demographics of the Gay and Lesbian Population in the United States: Evidence from Available Systematic Data Sources." *Demography* 37: 139–54.

Black, Dan A., Hoda R. Makar, Seth G. Sanders, and Lowell Taylor. 1998. "The Effects of Sexual Orientation on Earnings." Department of Economics, Carnegie Mellon University. Photocopy.

Blandford, John M. 2000. "The Nexus of Sexual Orientation and Gender in the Determination of Earnings." Department of Economics, University of Chicago. Photocopy.

Blanton, Kimberly. 1993. "To Insure, or Not to Insure: Big Insurance Companies Balk at the Coverage of Unmarried Partners." *Boston Globe,* 13 October, 39.

Blau, Francine D. 1998. "Trends in the Well-Being of American Women, 1970–1995." *Journal of Economic Literature* 36: 112–65.

Blumrosen, Alfred W. 1993. *Modern Law: The Law Transmission System and Equal Employment Opportunity.* Madison: University of Wisconsin Press.

Blumstein, Philip, and Pepper Schwartz. 1983. *American Couples.* New York: William Morrow & Co.

Boerner, Heather. 1998. "Stockholders Reject Ban on Bias." *Washington Blade,* 11 December, 14.

Boskin, Michael J., et al. 1987. "Social Security: A Financial Appraisal across and within Generations." *National Tax Journal* 40: 19–34.

Boswell, John. 1980. *Christianity, Social Tolerance, and Homosexuality.* Chicago and London: University of Chicago Press.

———. 1994. *Same-sex Unions in Premodern Europe.* New York: Villard Books.

Brandes, Stuart D. 1976. *American Welfare Capitalism, 1880–1940.* Chicago and London: University of Chicago Press.

Brause, Jay K. 1989. "Closed Doors: Sexual Orientation Bias in the Anchorage Housing and Employment Markets." In *Identity Reports: Sexual Orientation Bias in Alaska.* Edited by Melissa S. Green and Jay K. Brause. Anchorage: Identity Incorporated.

Brewis, Joanna, and Christopher Grey. 1994. "Re-Eroticizing the Organization: An Exegesis and Critique." *Gender, Work and Organization* 1: 67–82.

Brinkley, Mark A. 1994. "Employer Costs for Employee Compensation to Include Information on Part-Time and Full-Time Workers." *Compensation and Working Conditions* 46: 1–11.

Broadus, Joseph. 1994. Testimony. Employment Non-Discrimination Act of 1994: Hearing of the Committee on Labor and Human Resources, United States Senate, One Hundred Third Congress, second session, on S. 2238 to prohibit employment discrimination on the basis of sexual orientation, 29 July. Washington: U.S. Government Printing Office.

Brody, David. 1968. "The Rise and Decline of Welfare Capitalism." In *Change and Continuity in Twentieth Century America: The 1920s.* Edited by John Braeman, Robert H. Bremner, and David Brody. Columbus: Ohio State University Press.

Brown, Clair. 1985. "An Institutional Model of Wives' Work Decisions." *Industrial Relations* 24: 182–204.

Brown, Laura. 1999. "Court Overturns Ban on DP Benefits." *Southern Voice,* 1 September, 22.

Buford, Howard. 2000. "Understanding Gay Consumers." *Gay & Lesbian Review* (spring): 26–28.

Burke, Phyllis. 1993. *Family Values: Two Moms and Their Son.* New York: Random House.

Burstein, Paul. 1985. *Discrimination, Jobs, and Politics: The Struggle for Equal Employment Opportunity in the United States since the New Deal.* Chicago and London: University of Chicago Press.

Business Wire. 1999. "Lesbians and Gays Purposely Direct Spending toward Progressive Companies, Online Study Finds." 17 June.

Campanello, Russ. 1991. "Spousal Equivalent Benefits Announcement." Human resources internal memo, 3 September. Lotus Development Corporation, Cambridge, Mass.

Carmody, D. 1994. "Time Inc. Shelves a Gay Magazine." *New York Times,* 6 June.

Carnegie Mellon's Association of Lesbian, Gay and Bisexual Employees. 1996. Press release. 10 January.

Carroll, Vincent. 1992. "Coloradans on the Gay Amendment." *Wall Street Journal,* 15 December.

Casper, Lynne M., Philip N. Cohen, and Tavia Simmons. 1999. "How Does POSSLQ Measure Up? Historical Estimates of Cohabitation." Population Division Working Paper, no. 36, U.S. Bureau of the Census. <http://www.census.gov/population/www/documentation/twps0036/twps0036.html>.

Chambers, David. 1992. "Tales of Two Cities: AIDS and the Legal Recognition of Domestic Partnerships in San Francisco and New York." *Law & Sexuality* 2: 181–208.

Chauncey, George. 1994. *Gay New York: Gender, Urban Culture, and the Making of the Gay Male World, 1890–1940.* New York: Basic Books.

Clark, Danae. 1993. "Commodity Lesbianism." In *Lesbian and Gay Studies Reader.* New York: Routledge.

Cohen, Lloyd. 1987. "Marriage, Divorce, and Quasirents; Or, 'I Gave Him the Best Years of My Life.'" *Journal of Legal Studies* 16: 267–303.

Collier, Jane, Michelle Z. Rosaldo, and Sylvia Yanagisako. 1992. "Is There a family? New Anthropological Views." In *Rethinking the Family: Some Feminist Questions.* Edited by Barrie Thorne and Marilyn Yalom. Boston: Northeastern University Press.

Committee on the Status of Lesbians and Gays in the Profession. 1995. "Report on the Status of Lesbians and Gays in the Political Science Profession." *PS: Political Science and Politic* 28: 561–74.

Committee on Ways and Means, U.S. House of Representatives, 103d Congress, 2d Session. 1994. *Overview of Entitlement Programs: 1994 Green Book.* Washington D.C.: U.S. Government Printing Office.

Cooper, Phillip, and Barbara Schone. 1997. "More Offers, Fewer Takers for Employment-based Health Insurance: 1987 and 1996." *Health Affairs* 16 (Nov./Dec.): 142–49.

Council of Economic Advisors. 2000. *Economic Report of the President.* February. Washington, D.C.: Government Printing Office.

Creed, W. E. Douglas, and Maureen Scully. 1999a. "Songs of Ourselves: Employees' Deployment of Social Identity in Workplace Encounters." Boston College. Unpublished.

———. 1999b. "Switchpersons on the Tracks of History: Situated Agency and Contested Legitimacy in the Diffusion of Domestic Partner Benefits." Boston College. Unpublished.

Creed, W. E. Douglas, Maureen Scully, and John R. Austin. 1999. "Ready to Wear? The Tailoring of Legitimating Accounts." Boston College. Unpublished.

Cronin, A. 1993. "Two Viewfinders, Two Pictures of Gay America." *New York Times,* 27 June.

Croft, Jay. 1999. "Atlanta Suit Seeks Extended Benefits." *Atlanta Journal-Constitution,* 16 March.

Courier-News. 1991. "Companies Aim for Gay Market." 1 December.

Curry, Hayden, Denis Clifford, and Robin Leonard. 1996. *A Legal Guide for Lesbian and Gay Couples.* Berkeley: Nolo Press.

D'Emilio, John. N.d. "Here to Stay: A Working Paper on Lesbian and Gay Issues." Washington, D.C.: Policy Institute of the National Gay and Lesbian Task Force.

——— . 1992. *Making Trouble: Essays on Gay History, Politics, and the University.* New York: Routledge.

——— 1983. "Capitalism and Gay Identity." In *Powers of Desire: The Politics of Sexuality,* 100–13. Edited by Ann Snitow, Christine Stansell, and Sharon Thompson. New York: Monthly Review Press.

———1984. *Sexual Politics, Sexual Communities: The Making of a Homosexual Minority in the United States, 1940–1970.* Chicago and London: University of Chicago Press.

D'Emilio, John, and Estelle B. Freedman. 1988. *Intimate Matters: A History of Sexuality in America.* New York: Harper & Row.

Daly, Herman. 1995. "Consumption and the Environment." *Philosophy and Public Policy* 15: 4–9.

Darity, William, Jr., and Rhonda M. Williams. 1985. "Peddlers Forever? Culture, Competition, and Discrimination." *American Economic Review* 75: 256–61.

Dickson, Peter R., and James L. Ginter. 1987. "Market Segmentation, Product Differentiation, and Marketing Strategy." *Journal of Marketing* 51 (2): 1–10.

Doeringer, Peter, and Michael Piore. 1971. *Internal Labor Markets and Manpower Adjustment.* New York: D.C. Heath and Company.

Donohue, John J., III. 1986. "Is Title VII Efficient?" *University of Pennsylvania Law Review* 134: 1411–31.

Duggan, Lisa. 1995. "Queering the State." In *Sex Wars: Sexual Dissent and Political Culture,* 179–93. Edited by Lisa Duggan and Nan D. Hunter. New York: Routledge.

Dyer, Kate, editor. 1990. *Gays in Uniform: The Pentagon's Secret Reports.* Boston: Alyson Publications, Inc.

Edwards, Richard. 1979. *Contested Terrain.* New York: Basic Books.

Elshtain, Jean Bethke. 1991. "Against Gay Marriage." In *Same-Sex Marriage: Pro and Con.* Edited by Andrew Sullivan. New York: Vintage Books.

Equality Project. 1999. <www.equalityproject.org>.

Escoffier, Jeffrey. 1997. "The Political Economy of the Closet: Notes toward an Economic History of Gay and Lesbian Life before Stonewall." In *Homo Economics: Capitalism, Community, and Lesbian and Gay Life.* New York: Routledge.

Eskridge, William N., Jr. 1996. *The Case for Same-Sex Marriage.* New York: Free Press.

Eskridge, William N., Jr., and Nan D. Hunter. 1997. *Sexuality, Gender, and the Law.* 1999 Supplement. New York: Foundation Press.

Ettelbrick, Paula L. 1989. "Since When Is Marriage a Path to Liberation?" *OUT/LOOK National Gay and Lesbian Quarterly* 6: 14-17.

———. 1993. "Who Is a Parent? The Need to Develop a Lesbian-Conscious Family Law." *New York Law School Journal of Human Rights* 10: 513-53.

Evans, David T. 1993. *Sexual Citizenship: The Material Construction of Sexualities.* New York: Routledge.

Faderman, Lillian. 1991. *Odd Girls and Twilight Lovers: A History of Lesbian Life in Twentieth-Century America.* New York: Columbia University Press.

Federal GLOBE. 1993. "'First Steps' Guidelines in Establishing Agency Gay, Lesbian, Bisexual Associations." Washington, D.C.: Federal GLOBE.

Feenberg, D. R., and H. S. Rosen. 1995. "Recent Developments in the Marriage Tax." *National Tax Journal* 48: 91-101.

Feldstein, Martin, and Andrew Samwick. 1992. "Social Security Rules and Marginal Tax Rates." *National Tax Journal* 45: 1-22.

Feenberg, D., and H. Rosen. 1995. "Recent Developments in the Marriage Tax." *National Tax Journal* 48: 91-101.

Ferber, Marianne A., and Julie A. Nelson. 1993. "The Social Construction of Economics and the Social Construction of Gender." In *Beyond Economic Man: Feminist Theory and Economics,* 1-22. Edited by Marianne A. Ferber and Julie A. Nelson. Chicago and London: University of Chicago Press.

Fields, Suzanne. 2000. "The Gaying of America." *Washington Times,* 23 March.

Finder, Alan. 1993 "Orders by Dinkins to Broaden Rights of 'Domestic Partners.'" *New York Times,* 8 January.

Finnis, John. 1995. "Law, Morality, and 'Sexual Orientation.'" *Notre Dame Journal of Law, Ethics, and Public Policy* 9: 11-39.

Folbre, Nancy. 1994. *Who Pays for the Kids? Gender and the Structures of Constraint.* London: Routledge.

———. 1995. "'Holding Hands at Midnight': The Paradox of Caring Labor." *Feminist Economics* 1: 73-92.

Foldy, Erica Gabrielle, and W. E. Douglas Creed. 1999. "Action Learning, Fragmentation and the Interaction of Single-, Double- and Triple-Loop Change: A Case of Gay and Lesbian Workplace Advocacy." *Journal of Applied Behavioral Science* 35 (June): 207-28.

Foster, Ann C. 1994. "Employee Benefits in the United States, 1991-92." *Compensation and Working Conditions.* Washington D.C.: U.S. Department of Labor Bureau of Labor Statistics.

———. 1998. "Employee Benefits in the United States, 1994-95." *Compensation and Working Conditions* 3 (spring): 56-62.

Foulkes, Fred K. 1980. *Personnel Policies in Large Nonunion Companies.* Englewood Cliffs, N.J.: Prentice-Hall, Inc.

Frank, Miriam, and Desma Holcomb. 1990. *Pride at Work: Organizing for Lesbian and Gay Rights in Unions.* New York: Lesbian and Gay Labor Network of New York.

Freiburg, Peter. 1998. "Shareholders Can Vote on Job Policy." *Washington Blade,* 29 May.

———. 1998. "President's Order Protects Workers." *Washington Blade,* 5 June.

———. 1999. "Gay Budgets Near $100 Million." *Washington Blade,* 19 July.

Friedman, Monroe. 1995. "American Consumer Boycotts in Response to Rising Food Prices: Housewives' Protests at the Grassroots Level." *Journal of Consumer Policy* 18: 55-72.

Friskopp, Annette, and Sharon Silverstein. 1995. *Straight Jobs/Gay Lives.* New York: Scribner.

Fuchs, Victor R. 1989. "Women's Quest for Economic Equality." *Journal of Economic Perspectives* 3: 25-41.

Fugate, Douglas L. 1993. "Evaluating the U.S. Male Homosexual and Lesbian Population as a Viable Target Market Segment." *Journal of Consumer Marketing* 10: 46-57.

Gay/Lesbian/Bisexual Corporate Letter. 1992. "Cracker Barrel Seeks SEC Dismissal of First Gay Rights Shareholder Action." (Sept.-Oct.): 1.

———. 1995. "Mergers and Acquisitions." (summer): 7.

Ghilarducci, Teresa. 1994. "U.S. Pension Investment Policy and Perfect Capital Market Theory." *Challenge* 37: 4-11.

Glendon, Mary Ann. 1989. *The Transformation of Family Law.* Chicago and London: University of Chicago Press.

Gluckman, Amy, and Betsy Reed. 1997. "The Gay Marketing Moment." In *Homo Economics: Capitalism, Community, and Lesbian and Gay Life.* Edited by Amy Gluckman and Betsy Reed. New York: Routledge.

Goffman, Erving. 1963. *Stigma: Notes on the Management of Spoiled Identity.* Englewood Cliffs, N.J.: Prentice Hall.

Gordon, David M., Richard Edwards, and Michael Reich. 1982. *Segmented Work, Divided Workers.* Cambridge: Cambridge University Press.

Gossett, Charles W. 1994. "Domestic Partnership Benefits: Public Sector Patterns." *Review of Public Personnel Administration* 14: 64-84.

———. 1999. "Dillon's Rule and Gay Rights: State Control Over Local Efforts to Protect the Rights of Lesbians and Gay Men." In *Gays and Lesbians in the Democratic Process.* Edited by Ellen D. B. Riggle and Barry L. Tadlock. New York: Columbia University Press.

Gottlieb, Rhonda. 1984. "The Political Economy of Sexuality." *Review of Radical Political Economics* 16: 143-66.

Gottschalk, Peter. 1997. "Inequality, Income Growth, and Mobility: The Basic Facts." *Journal of Economic Perspectives* 11: 21-40.

Governor's Commission on the Rights and Responsibilities of Same-Sex Relationships. 1998. "Report, Findings and Recommendations." State of Colorado, 1 July.

Greenfield Online. 1998. "As America Ponders Death of Gay College Student, New Internet Study Offers Insights about Gay Community Beliefs and Habits." 15 October.

Greenough, William C., and Francis P. King. 1976. *Pension Plans and Public Policy.* New York: Columbia University Press.

Grossman, Glenn M. 1992. "U.S. Workers Receive a Wide Range of Employee Benefits." *Monthly Labor Review* (Sept.): 36–39.

Gruson, Lindsey. 1993. "Meeting Gay Bias Face to Face in Class." *New York Times,* 17 October, B1.

Haldeman, Douglas C. 1999. "The Pseudo-science of Sexual Orientation Conversion Therapy." *Angles: The Policy Journal of the Institute for Gay and Lesbian Strategic Studies* 4: 1–4.

Hall, Marny. 1989. "Private Experiences in the Public Domain: Lesbians in Organizations." In *The Sexuality of Organization,* 125–138. Thousand Oaks, Calif.: Sage Publications.

Halley, Janet E. 1989. "The Politics of the Closet: Legal Articulation of Sexual Orientation Identity." *UCLA Law Review* 36: 915–76.

Hamer, Dean, and Simon LeVay. 1994. "Debate: Is Homosexuality Biologically Influenced?" *Scientific American* (May): 43–55.

Hammonds, Keith H. 1991. "Lotus Opens a Door for Gay Partners." *Business Week,* 4 November.

Hanania, Joseph. 1995. "Closet No Longer." *Los Angeles Times,* 29 October.

Harvard Law Review. 1990. "Sexual Orientation and the Law." Cambridge, Mass.: Harvard University Press.

Harris, Daniel. 1995. "Out of the Closet, and into Never-never Land. *Harper's* (Dec.): 52–54.

Hartmann, Heidi I. 1981. "The Family as the Locus of Gender, Class and Political Struggle: The Example of Housework." *Signs: Journal of Women and Culture in Society* 6: 366–94.

Hawaii, State of. Office of the Auditor. 1999. "Overview: Study of the Fiscal Impact of Providing Certain Benefits to Reciprocal Beneficiaries." Report no. 99-17.

Hellinger, Fred J. 1998. "Cost and Financing of Care for Persons with HIV Disease: An Overview." *Health Care Financing Review* 19: 5–18

———.1993. "The Lifetime Cost of Treating a Person with HIV." *The Journal of the American Medical Association* 270: 474–78.

Heredia, Christopher. 2000. "Vallejo's All the Rage." *San Francisco Chronicle,* 14 January.

Herek, Gregory M. 1991. "Stigma, Prejudice and Violence against Lesbians and Gay Men." In *Homosexuality: Research Implications for Public Policy.* Edited by John C. Gonsiorek and James Weinrich. Newbury Park, Calif.: Sage Publications.

Herek, Gregory M., and John P. Capitanio. 1996. "'Some of My Best Friends': Intergroup Contact, Concealable Stigma, and Heterosexuals' Attitudes toward Gay Men and Lesbians." *Personality and Social Psychology Bulletin* 22: 412–24.

Herek, Gregory M., and E. K. Glunt. 1993. "Interpersonal Contact and Heterosexuals' Attitudes toward Gay Men: Results from a National Survey." *Journal of Sex Research* 30: 239–44.

Hersch, Joni. 1991. "Male-Female Differences in Hourly Wages: The Role of Human Capital, Working Conditions, and Housework." *Industrial & Labor Relations Review* 44: 746–59.

Hersch, Joni, and Shelley White-Means. 1993. "Employer-Sponsored Health and Pension Benefits and the Gender/Race Wage Gap." *Social Science Quarterly* 74: 851–66.

Hertz, Frederick. 1998. *Legal Affairs: Essential Advice for Same-Sex Couples.* New York: Henry Holt and Co., Inc.

Hewitt Associates. 1991. "Domestic Partners and Employee Benefits, 1991." Research paper. Lincolnshire, Ill.

————. 1994. "Domestic Partners and Employee Benefits, 1994." Research paper. Lincolnshire, Ill.

Hill, Herbert. 1984. "Race and Ethnicity in Organized Labor: The Historical Sources of Resistance to Affirmative Action." *Journal of Intergroup Relations* 12 (4): 5–50.

Hoffman, Mark. 1992. "Company Policies Regarding Spousal Equivalents." Internal memo. Sybase Inc., Emeryville, Calif.

Hollywood Supports. 1999. "Entertainment Industry Project Counters Workplace Fears/Discrimination." <http://hsupports.org/hsupports/mission.html>. Accessed 3 November 2000.

Hostetler, Dennis, and Joan E. Pynes. 1995. "Domestic Partnership Benefits: Dispelling the Myths." *Review of Public Personnel Administration* 15: 41–59.

Human Rights Campaign. 1999a. "HRC Lauds United Airlines' Historic Decision to Become the First Major U.S. Airline to Offer Domestic Partner Benefits." Press release, August 2.

————.1999b. "States, Cities and Counties that Prohibit Discrimination based on Sexual Orientation in Private Employment as of August 5, 1999." <http://www.hrc.org/worknet>.

————. 2000. *The State of the Workplace.* Washington, D.C.: Human Rights Campaign Foundation.

Hunter, Nan. 1995a. "Life after Hardwick." In *Sex Wars: Sexual Dissent and Political Culture.* Edited by Lisa Duggan and Nan D. Hunter. New York: Routledge.

————. 1995b. "Marriage, Law and Gender: A Feminist Inquiry." In *Sex Wars: Sexual Dissent and Political Culture.* Edited by Lisa Duggan and Nan D. Hunter. New York: Routledge.

Hymen, Prue. 1995. "Lesbian Economics—How Lesbian Feminist Perspectives Might Improve Feminist Economics: 'Their' Economy and 'Our' Economy." In *Women's Studies Association Conference Papers.* Wellington: Women's Studies Association of New Zealand.

International Gay and Lesbian Human Rights Commission (IGLHRC). 1998. "Registered Partnership, Domestic Partnership, and Marriage." Fact Sheet.

International Society of Certified Employee Benefit Specialists (ISCEBS). 1995. "Census of Certified Employee Benefit Specialists: Domestic Partner Benefits." Brookfield, Wisc.

Iannuzzo, Catherine, and Alexandra Pinck. 1991. "Benefits for the Domestic Partners of Gay and Lesbian Employees at Lotus Development Corporation." Simmons College Graduate School of Management, unpublished manuscript, November 1991.

Independent Sector. 1996. *Giving and Volunteering in the United States.* Washington, D.C.: Independent Sector.

Jacoby, Sanford M. 1985. *Employing Bureaucracy: Managers, Unions and the Transformation of Work in American Industry, 1900–1945.* New York: Columbia University Press.

Jefferson, David J. 1992. "MCA to Extend Health Insurance to Gay Couples." *Wall Street Journal*, 18 May.

Johnson, David K. 1994–95. "Homosexual Citizens: Washington's Gay Community Confronts the Civil Service." *Washington History* 6: 44–63, 93–96.

Jones, David A. 1996. "Discrimination against Same-Sex Couples in Hotel Reservation Policies." In *Gays, Lesbians, and Consumer Behavior: Theory, Practice, and Research Issues in Marketing*. Edited by Daniel L. Wardlow. Binghamton, N.Y.: Haworth Press.

Journal of Taxation. 1992. "Health Benefits for Employee's Domestic Partner Not Taxed." (Nov.): 316.

Juhn, Chinhui, Kevin M. Murphy, and Brooks Pierce. 1991. "Accounting for the Slowdown in Black-White Wage Convergence." In *Workers and Their Wages: Changing Patterns in the United States*. Edited by Marvin H. Kosters. AEI Studies, no. 520. Washington, D.C.: AEI Press.

———— 1993. "Wage Inequality and the Rise in Returns to Skill." *Journal of Political Economy* 101: 410–42.

Kahan, Hazel, and David Mulryan. 1995. "Out of the Closet." *American Demographics* (May): 41–47.

Kahn, Philippe. 1992. Press release. Borland International, Inc., Scotts Valley, Calif.

"Kaiser Offers Benefits to Employees' Partners." 1994. *San Francisco Chronicle*, 19 March.

Kates, Steven M. 1998. *Twenty Million New Customers! Understanding Gay Men's Consumer Behavior*. Binghamton, N.Y.: Haworth Press, Inc.

Kaufman, Bruce E. 1994. *The Economics of Labor Markets*. Fourth edition. Fort Worth: Dryden Press.

Kayal, Philip M. 1993. *Bearing Witness: Gay Men's Health Crisis and the Politics of AIDS*. Boulder: Westview Press.

Kennedy, E. L., and M. D. Davis. 1993. *Boots of Leather, Slippers of Gold: The History of a Lesbian Community*. New York: Routledge.

Keohane, Nannerl O. 1995. "Comparable Benefits to Be Offered." *Duke Dialogue*, 6 January, 2.

Kessler-Harris, Alice. 1990. *A Woman's Wage: Historical Meanings and Social Consequences*. Louisville: University Press of Kentucky.

Kilhefner, Don. 1999. "Coors Boycott—Now More than Ever: A Call to Gay and Lesbian Conscience." <http://members.macconnect.com/users/c/coorsboycott>. Accessed 5 August 1999.

Kinsey, Alfred C., Wardell B. Pomeroy, and Clyde E. Martin. 1948. *Sexual Behavior in the Human Male*. Philadelphia: W. B. Saunders Company.

Kirp, David L., Mark G. Yudof, and Marlene Strong Franks. 1986. *Gender Justice*. Chicago and London: University of Chicago Press.

Kite, Mary E., and Bernard E. Whitley, Jr. 1996. "Sex Differences in Attitudes toward Homosexual Persons, Behaviors, and Civil Rights: A Meta-analysis." *Personality and Social Psychology Bulletin* 22: 336–53.

Klawitter, Marieka, and Victor Flatt. 1998. "The Effects of State and Local Antidiscrimination Policies for Sexual Discrimination." *Journal of Policy Analysis and Management* 17 (fall): 658–86.

Klawitter, Marieka. 1995. "Did They Find or Create Each Other? Labor Market Linkages between Partners in Same-Sex and Different-Sex Couples." Paper presented at the annual meeting of the Population Association of America, San Francisco, Calif., June 1995.

Knight, Robert H. 1994. "How Domestic Partnerships and 'Gay Marriage' Threaten the Family." *Insight* (July): 1–14.

Knight, Robert, and Daniel S. Garcia. 1994. "Homosexual Adoption: Bad for Children, Bad for Society." *Insight* Family Research Council.

Kurdek, Lawrence. 1993. "The Allocation of Household Labor in Gay, Lesbian, and Heterosexual Married Couples." *Journal of Social Issues* 49: 127–39.

———. 1995. "Lesbian and Gay Couples." in *Lesbian, Gay, and Bisexual Identities over the Lifespan.* Edited by Anthony R. D'Augelli and Charlotte J. Patterson. New York: Oxford University Press.

Lambda Alums. 1996. "Alumni Announce Boycott of Giving to Carnegie Mellon." Press release, Pittsburgh, Penn. 1 January.

Lambda Legal Defense and Education Fund. 1995. "Lambda Legal Defense and Education Fund's Compilation of Employers Extending the Same Employment Benefits to Unmarried Employees with Partners as Those Offered to Married Employees with Spouses." New York: LLDEF.

———. 1999. "*A.A.U.P. v. Rutgers, the State University of New York.*" <http://www.lambdalegal.org/cgi-bin/pages/cases/record?record=13>. Accessed December 8 1999.

Lambert, Wade. 1991. "Gay GIs Told, Serve Now, Face Discharge Later. *Wall Street Journal,* 24 January.

Lamos, Colleen. 1995. "Opening Questions." *Feminist Economics* 1: 59–62.

Laumann, Edward O., John H. Gagnon, Richard T. Michael, and Stuart Michaels. 1994. *The Social Organization of Sexuality: Sexual Practices in the United States.* Chicago and London: University of Chicago Press.

Leeming, E. Janice, and Cynthia F. Tripp. 1994. *Segmenting the Women's Market: Using Niche Marketing to Understand and Meet the Diverse Needs of Today's Most Dynamic Consumer Market.* Chicago: Probus.

Levine, Martin. 1980. "Employment Discrimination against Gay Men." In *Homosexuality in International Perspective.* Edited by Joseph Harry and Man Singh Das. New Dehli: Vikas.

Levine, Martin, and Robin Leonard. 1984. "Discrimination against Lesbians in the Work Force." *Signs: Journal of Women and Culture in Society* 9 (4): 700–10.

Lewin, Ellen. 1998. *Recognizing Ourselves: Ceremonies of Lesbian and Gay Commitment.* New York: Columbia University Press.

Light, Audrey, and Manuelita Ureta. 1992. "Panel Estimates of Male and Female Job Turnover Behavior: Can Female Nonquitters Be Identified?" *Journal of Labor Economics* 10: 156–81.

Los Angeles County Bar Association Committee on Sexual Orientation Bias. 1994. "Report." June. Los Angeles: L.A. County Bar Association.

Los Angeles Times. 1999. "Disney Earnings Drop." 5 November.

Lukenbill, Grant. 1995. *Untold Millions: Positioning Your Business for the Gay and Lesbian Consumer Revolution.* New York: Harper Collins.

Lundberg, Shelly, and Robert A. Pollak. 1996. "Bargaining and Distribution in Marriage." *Journal of Economic Perspectives* 10: 139-58.

MacCoun, Robert J. 1996. "Sexual Orientation and Military Cohesion: A Critical Review of the Evidence." In *Out in Force: Sexual Orientation and the Military,* 157-76. Edited by G. M. Herek, J. B. Jobe, and R. M. Carney. Chicago and London: University of Chicago Press.

Mann, William J. 1995. "The Gay and Lesbian Publishing Boom." *Harvard Gay and Lesbian Review* (spring): 24-27.

Matthaei, Julie. 1995. "The Sexual Division of Labor, Sexuality and Lesbian/Gay Liberation." *Review of Radical Economics* 7 (2): 1-37

———. 1998. "Some Comments on the Role of Lesbianism in Feminist Economic Transformation." *Feminist Economics* 4: 83-88.

Mathiasen, Carolyn. 1995. "Shareholder Proposal Success Stories, 1985-95." *IRRC Social Issues Reporter* (Oct.): 7-14.

May, Martha. 1982. "The Historical Problem of the Family Wage: The Ford Motor Company and the Five Dollar Day." *Feminist Studies* 8: 399-424.

McCracken, Ed. 1992. "Change in Benefits Program." Memo, 31 August. Silicon Graphics, Mountain View, Calif.

McNaught, Brian. 1993. *Gay Issues in the Workplace.* New York: St. Martin's Press.

Metamorphics Media. 1999. List page. <http://www.metamorphics.com/Lists/Default.html>. Accessed 10 December 1999.

Mickens, Ed. 1994. *The 100 Best Companies for Gay Men and Lesbians.* New York: Pocket Books.

Michman, Ronald D. 1991. *Lifestyle Market Segmentation.* New York: Praeger, 1991

Miller, Cyndee. 1995. "'The Ultimate Taboo.'" *Marketing News,* August 14.

Mishel, L., and J. Bernstein. 1993. *The State of Working America, 1992-1993.* Armonk, N.Y.: M. E. Sharpe.

Mohr, Richard. 1988. *Gays/Justice: A Study of Ethics, Society, and Law.* New York: Columbia University Press.

Monthly Vital Statistics Report. 1995. 43: 9.

Moore, David W. 1993. "Public Polarized on Gay Issue." *Gallup Poll Monthly* 331: 30-34.

Moxley, Scott. 2000. "Lou Sheldon's Nightmare." *OC Weekly,* 3 March.

Murphy, Kevin M., and Finish Welch. 1990. "Empirical Age-Earnings Profiles." *Journal of Labor Economics* 8: 202-29.

Nardi, P. M. 1992. "That's What Friends Are for: Friends as Family in the Gay and Lesbian Community." In *Modern Homosexualities.* Edited by K. Plummer. New York: Routledge.

National Lesbian & Gay Journalists Association. 1999. *Directory of News Media Companies/Unions with Domestic Partner Benefits.* Washington, D.C.: NLGJA

Navarro, Mireya. 1995. "Disney's Health Policy for Gay Employees Angers Religious Right in Florida." *New York Times,* 29 November.

Nelson, Julie A. 1988. "Household Economies of Scale in Consumption: Theory and Evidence." *Econometrica* 46: 1301-14.

———. 1993. "The Study of Choice or the Study of Provisioning? Gender and the Definition of Economics." In *Beyond Economic Man: Feminist Theory and Economics*, 23–36. Edited by Marianne A. Ferber and Julie A. Nelson. Chicago and London: University of Chicago Press.

———. 1999. "Of Markets and Martyrs: Is It OK to Pay Well for Care?" *Feminist Economics* (Nov.): 43–59.

Noble, Barbara Presley. 1992. "Benefits for Domestic Partners." *New York Times*, 28 June.

"Office Dating Is Less of an Issue as Rules Are Relaxed in the Tight Labor Market." 2000. *Wall Street Journal*, 8 February.

Out & About Magazine. 1999. "Nasty Turbulence in the Friendly Skies." <www.unitedpride.org/whatwedo/news-990318-guest-4x.html>. Accessed 7 July 1999.

Parsons, Kathryn. 1995. "Strategies to Combat Amendment Two." Women's Studies Program, Yale University. Photocopy.

Patterson, Charlotte. 1995. "Lesbian Mothers, Gay Fathers, and Their Children." In *Lesbian, Gay and Bisexual Identities over the Lifespan: Psychological Perspectives.* New York: Oxford University Press.

——— 1998. "The Family Lives of Children Born to Lesbian Mothers." In *Lesbian, Gay, and Bisexual Families: Psychological Perspectives.* Edited by Charlotte J. Patterson and Anthony R. D'Augelli. New York: Oxford University Press.

Pattullo, E. L. 1992. "Straight Talk about Gays." *Commentary* 94 (Dec.): 21–25.

Peñaloza, Lisa. 1996. "We're Here, We're Queer, and We're Going Shopping! A Critical Perspective on the Accommodation of Gays and Lesbians in the U.S. Marketplace." In *Gays, Lesbians, and Consumer Behavior: Theory, Practice, and Research Issues in Marketing.* Edited by Daniel L. Wardlow. Binghamton, N.Y.: Haworth Press.

Pines, Deborah. 1993. "Lesbian Partner Denied Rights to Pension." *New York Law Journal*, 29 March, 1.

Polikoff, Nancy. 1990. "This Child Does Have Two Mothers." *Georgetown Law Journal* 78: 458–575.

Pollak, Robert A. 1985. "A Transaction Cost Approach to Families and Households." *Journal of Economic Literature* 23: 581–608.

Posner, Richard. 1992. *Sex and Reason.* Cambridge, Mass.: Harvard University Press.

PR Newswire. 1997. "Affluence of Gay Market Confirmed." 3 February.

Putnam, T. 1993. "Boycotts are Bursting Out All Over." *Business and Society Review* 85: 47–51.

Rainbow Card. 1999. <http://www.rainbowcard.com>. Accessed 1999.

RAND. 1993. "Sexual Orientation and U.S. Military Personnel Policy: Operations and Assessment." Prepared for the Office of the Secretary of Defense. Santa Monica, Calif.: RAND.

Rapp, Rayna. 1992. "Family and Class in Contemporary America: Notes toward an Understanding of Ideology." In *Rethinking the Family: Some Feminist Questions.* Edited by Barrie Thorne with Marilyn Yalom. Boston: Northeastern University Press.

Reich, Michael. 1981. *Racial Inequality: A Political-Economic Analysis.* Princeton, N.J.: Princeton University Press.

Reid, John (Andrew Tobias). 1973. *The Best Little Boy in the World.* New York: Ballantine Books.

Reynolds, William B. 1986. "Stotts: Equal Opportunity, not Equal Results." In *The Moral Foundations of Civil Rights.* Edited by Robert K. Fullinwider and Claudia Mills. Totowa, N.J.: Rowman & Littlefield.

Rigdon, J. E. 1991. "Overcoming a Deep-Rooted Reluctance, More Firms Advertise to Gay Community." *Wall Street Journal,* 18 July.

Roberts, Sally. 1995. "Private Benefits, Public Controversy." *Business Insurance* 11 (Dec.): 7.

Robson, Ruthann. 1994. "Resisting the Family: Repositioning Lesbians in Legal Theory." *Signs: Journal of Women and Culture in Society* 19: 975–95.

Rubenstein, William B. 1997. *Cases and Materials on Sexual Orientation and the Law.* St. Paul: West Publishing Co.

San Francisco Human Rights Commission. 1998. "Rules of Procedure for the Nondiscrimination in Contracts: Equal Benefits Provisions of Chapter 12B of the San Francisco Administrative Code." Revised August 13. <http://www.ci.sf.ca.us/sfhumanrights/lgbth/rules.htm>.

Scalia, Antonin. 1996. *Romer v. Evans.* Decision dissent. <http://supct.law.cornell.edu/supct/html/94-1039.ZD.html>.

Schneider, Beth E. 1986. "Coming Out at Work: Bridging the Public/Private Gap." *Work and Occupations* 13: 519–64.

———. 1992. "Coming Out at Work: Bridging the Private/Public Gap." *Work and Occupations,* 13: 463–487.

Schudson, Michael. 1986. *Advertising, the Uneasy Persuasion: Its Dubious Impact on American Society.* New York: Basic Books.

Schwartz, Ruth L. "New Alliances, Strange Bedfellows: Lesbians, Gay Men, and AIDS." In *Sisters, Sexperts, Queers.* Edited by Arlene Stein. New York: Plume. 1993.

Sears, Brad. 1994. "Winning Arguments/Losing Themselves: The (Dys)functional Approach in *Thomas S. v. Robin Y.*" *Harvard Civil Rights-Civil Liberties Review* 29: 559–80.

Seidman, Steven. 1993. "Identity and Politics in a 'Postmodern' Gay Culture: Some Historical and Conceptual Notes." In *Fear of a Queer Planet: Queer Politics and Social Theory.* Edited by Michael Warner. Minneapolis: University of Minnesota Press.

Servicemembers Legal Defense Network. 1999. "Discharge Chart." <www.sldn.org/scripts/sldn.ixe?page=discharge_chart_99>. Accessed 22 January.

Sherman, Suzanne, editor. 1992. *Lesbian and Gay Marriage: Private Commitments, Public Ceremonies.* Philadelphia: Temple University Press.

Sherrill, Kenneth S., Scott Sawyer, and Stanley Segal. "Coming Out and Political Attitudes: The Experiences of Lesbians and Gay Men." Paper presented at the annual meeting of the American Political Science Association, 1991.

Shilts, Randy. 1976. "Gay Bars and Baths Come Out of the Bush Leagues." *Advocate,* June 2.

———. 1982. *The Mayor of Castro Street: The Life and Times of Harvey Milk.* New York: St. Martin's Press.

————. 1993. *Conduct Unbecoming: Lesbians and Gays in the U.S. Military, Vietnam to the Persian Gulf.* New York: St. Martin's Press.

Shulman, Steven. 1991. "Why Is the Black Unemployment Rate Always Twice as High as the White Unemployment Rate?" In *New Approaches to Economic and Social Analyses of Discrimination.* Edited by Richard R. Cornwall and Phanindra V. Wunnava. New York: Praeger.

Simmons Market Research Bureau. 1989. "1989 Study of Media and Markets." Publications: Total Audiences." M-1, vii–viii.

Sincere, Richard E., Jr. 1999. "Pro-Gay Ruling in New Jersey Hurts Gay Rights." *Wall Street Journal,* 11 August.

Smith, James, and Finis R. Welch. 1989. "Black Economic Progress after Myndal." *Journal of Economic Literature* 27 (2): 519–62.

Snyder, A. 1991. "Do Boycotts Work?" *Adweek's Marketing Week* 32: 16.

SocialFunds.com. 1999. "Resolution Status Report." <http://www.socialfunds.com/activism/companies.cfm>. Accessed 14 July 1999.

South, Scott J., and Glenna Spitze. 1994. "Housework in Marital and Nonmarital Households." *American Sociological Review* 59: 327–48.

Spencer's Research Reports on Employee Benefits. 1992. "Design Features of Domestic Partner Benefits." 327 (4–5): 5–8.

Spero, Sterling Denhard, and Abram L. Harris. 1968. *The Black Worker, the Negro and the Labor Movement.* New York: Atheneum.

Stacey, Judith. 1992. "Backward toward the Postmodern Family: Reflections on Gender, Kinship, Class in the Silicon Valley." In *Rethinking the Family: Some feminist Questions.* Edited by B. Thorne and M. Yalom. Boston: Northeastern University Press.

————. 1996. *In the Name of the Family.* Boston: Beacon Press.

Stein, Edward, editor. 1990. *Forms of Desire: Sexual Orientation and the Social Constructionist Controversy.* New York: Garland.

Stewart, James B. 1994. "Gentleman's Agreement." *New Yorker,* 13 (June): 74–82.

Stone, Christopher. 1976. "Florida's Jack Campbell." *Advocate,* 2 June.

Streitmatter, Rodger. 1995. *Unspeakable: The Rise of the Gay and Lesbian Press in America.* Boston: Faber and Faber.

Strub, Sean. 1995. "Gay and Lesbian Lists Continue to Expand." *DM News,* 28 August.

Strub, Sean O'Brien, Daniel B. Baker, and Bill Henning. 1995. *Cracking the Corporate Closet: The 200 Best (and Worst) Companies to Work for, Buy from, and Invest in if You're Gay or Lesbian—and Even if You Aren't.* New York: Harper Business.

Sullivan, Andrew. 1995. *Virtually Normal.* New York: Vintage Books.

Sullivan, Kevin. 1992. New Domestic Partners Policy. Memo, 26 June. Apple Computer, Inc., Cupertino, Calif.

Sullivan, Mark. 1999. "Mixing Principal with Principles." *Washington Blade,* 1 January.

"Tanqueray Spends Big on AIDS Ride." 1995. *Quotient: The Newsletter of Marketing to Gay Men and Lesbians* 6: 1.

Tarquinio, J. Alex. 1997. "King of Grits Alters Menu to Reflect Northern Tastes." *Wall Street Journal,* 9 September, B1.

Thaler-Carter, Ruth E. 1997. "EMA Model Defines Cost-Per-Hire as Part of Staffing Performance." *HR Magazine* (Dec.):
<http//www.shrm.org/hrmagazine/articles/default.asp?page=1297rec.htm>. Accessed 13 February 2001.

Timothy Plan, The. 1999.
<http://www.timothyplan.com/principles&objectives.htm>. Accessed 10 December 1999.

Tobias, Andrew. 1997. *My Vast Fortune.* New York: Harcourt Brace.

"Top-Performing Sector Funds." 1999. *Wall Street Journal,* 4 October.

Trillium Asset Management. 1999. "Sexual Orientation in the Workplace: An Issue for Investors."
<http://www.trilliuminvest.com/pages/social/social_frame.html>
Accessed 14 July 1999.

Turner, Margery Austin, Michael Fix, and Raymond J. Struyk. 1991. *Opportunities Denied, Opportunities Diminished: Racial Discrimination in Hiring.* Urban Institute Report 91-9. Washington, D.C.: Urban Institute Press.

U.S. Bureau of the Census. 1999a. "Health Insurance Historical Table 1."
<http://www.census.gov/hhes/hlthins/historic/hihistt1.html>. Accessed 9 September 1999.

———. 1999b. "Marital Status and Living Arrangements: March 1998 (update)." P20-514.
<www.census.gov/prod/99pubs/p20-514.pdf>.

———. 1999c. "Union Members Summary." USDL Rep. 00-16.
<http://stats.bls.gov/news.release/union2.nws.htm." Accessed 19 July 1999.

U.S. Bureau of the Census, Population Division, Population Estimates Program. 1999a. "Resident Population Estimates of the United States by Age and Sex: April 1, 1990 to May 1, 1999, with Short-Term Projection to June 1, 2000."
<http://www.census.gov/population/estimates/nation/intfile2-1.txt>. Accessed 25 June 2000.

U.S. Department of Labor, Bureau of Labor Statistics. 1996. "1995 Survey of Employer-Provided Training-Employer Results." USDL Rep. 96-515.
<stats.bls.gov/news.release/sept1.nws.htm>. Accessed 13 February 2001.

———.1999a. "Employer Costs for Employee Compensation Summary—March 1999."
<ftp://146.142.4.23/pub/news.release/History/ecec.06241999.news>. Accessed 9 August 1999.

———. 1999b. "Employment Characteristics of Families in 1999." USDL Rep. 00–172.
<http://www.bls.gov/news.release/famee.nr0.htm.> Accessed 30 May 2000.

U.S. Department of Labor, Office of the Chief Economist. 1996. "A Look at Employers' Costs of Providing Health Benefits." <www.dol.gov/dol/_sec/public/media/reports/costs.htm>. Accessed 31 July 2000.

U.S. Department of Labor, Office of Federal Contract Compliance Programs, Equal Employment Opportunity. 1980. "Code of Federal Regulations Pertaining to ESA, Title 41, Chapter 60."
<www.dol.gov/dol/allcfr/ESA/Title41/chapter_60.htm>. Accessed 29 October 2000.

United States Securities and Exchange Commission. 1998. "Final Rule: Amendments to Rules on Shareholder Proposals." 17 CFR part 240. <http://www.sec.gov/rules/final/34-40018.htm>. Accessed 14 July 1999.

Varnell, Paul. 1996. "Once Again, the Basics." *Windy City Times,* 15 February, 15.

Vaid, Urvashi. 1995. *Virtual Equality: The Mainstreaming of Gay and Lesbian Liberation.* New York: Anchor Books.

Van der Meide, Wayne. 2000. "Legislating Equality: A Review of Laws Affecting Gay, Lesbian, Bisexual, and Transgendered People in the United States." Washington, D.C.: Policy Institute of the National Gay and Lesbian Task Force.

Vandervelden, Mark, Peter Freiberg, and Dave Walter. 1987. "The Surprising Health of Gay Business." *Advocate,* 3 March, 43–49.

Veblen, Thorstein. [1899] 1934. *The Theory of the Leisure Class: An Economic Study of Institutions.* New York: Modern Library.

Vernon, Steven G. 1993. *Employee Benefits: Valuation, Analysis, and Strategies.* New York: John Wiley & Sons, Inc.

Waitzman, Norman J., Patrick S. Romano, and Richard M. Scheffler. 1994. "Estimates of the Economic Costs of Birth Defects." *Inquiry* 31: 188–205.

Walker, Martha A. C., and Bruce J. Bergman. 1998. "Analyzing Year-to-Year Changes in Employer Costs for Employee Compensation." *Compensation and Working Conditions* 3 (spring): 17–28.

Walters, Andrew S., and Maria-Cristina Curran. 1996. " 'Excuse Me, Sir? May I Help You and Your Boyfriend?': Salespersons' Differential Treatment of Homosexual and Straight Customers." In *Gays, Lesbians, and Consumer Behavior: Theory, Practice, and Research Issues in Marketing.* Edited by Daniel L. Wardlow. Binghamton, N.Y.: Haworth Press.

Walzer, Michael. 1983. *Spheres of Justice: A Defense of Pluralism and Equality.* New York: Basic Books.

Warden, Sharon. 1993. "Attitudes on Homosexuality." *Washington Post,* 25 April, A18.

Warner, Michael. 1993. Introduction to *Fear of a Queer Planet: Queer Politics and Social Theory.* Edited by Michael Warner. Minneapolis: University of Minnesota Press.

Washington Blade. 1993. "New York City Employees Get Partner Benefits." 5 November.

Weisberg, Louis. 1997. "Gays Ousted at Iowa Health Center." *Windy City Times,* 5 June.

Welch, Finis. 1967. "Labor-Market Discrimination: An Interpretation of Income Differences in the Rural South." *Journal of Political Economy* 75: 225–40.

West, Cornel. 1993. *Race Matters.* Boston: Beacon Press.

Weston, Kath. 1991. *Families We Choose: Lesbians, Gays, Kinship.* New York: Columbia University Press.

———— 1996. *Render Me, Gender Me: Lesbians Talk Sex, Class, Color, Nation, Studmuffins.* New York: Columbia University Press.

White, Mel. 1994. *Stranger at the Gate: To Be Gay and Christian in America.* New York: Plume.

Wilke, Michael. 1998. "Fewer Gays Are Wealthy, Data Say." *Advertising Age,* 19 October.

Williams, Walter L. 1986. *The Spirit and the Flesh: Sexual Diversity in American Indian Culture.* Boston: Beacon.

Wilson, E. O. 1978. *On Human Nature.* Cambridge. Mass.: Harvard University Press.

Winfeld, Liz, and Susan Spielman. 1995. *Straight Talk about Gays in the Workplace.* New York: Amacom.

Wolff, Edward N. 1998. "Recent Trends in the Size Distribution of Household Wealth." *Journal of Economic Perspectives* 12: 131–50.

Woods, James. 1993. *The Corporate Closet: The Professional Lives of Gay Men in America.* New York: Free Press.

Yang, Alan. 1997. "From Rights to Wrongs: Public Opinion on Gay and Lesbian Americans Moves toward Equality." *National Gay and Lesbian Task Force.* Washington, D.C.: NGLTF Policy Institute.

THE
PLASTIC
OCEAN

THE
PLASTIC
OCEAN

JULIE DECKER / ANCHORAGE MUSEUM
BOOTH-CLIBBORN EDITIONS / LONDON

A Cataloguing-in-Publication record for this book
is available from the Publisher.
ISBN 978-1-86154-355-4

Printed and bound in China

Front cover image
NASA/GODDARD SPACE FLIGHT CENTER SCIENTIFIC
VISUALIZATION STUDIO

Back cover image
COURTESY OF NOAA

CONTENTS

Evelyn Rydz, detail from **LOST AND FOUND**
Pencil and colored pencil on drafting film, 18 x 33"
2012

A SCHOOL OF JACK MACKERAL ARE ILLUMINATED
BY THE SUN'S RAYS UNDERWATER
Photograph by Kip Evans

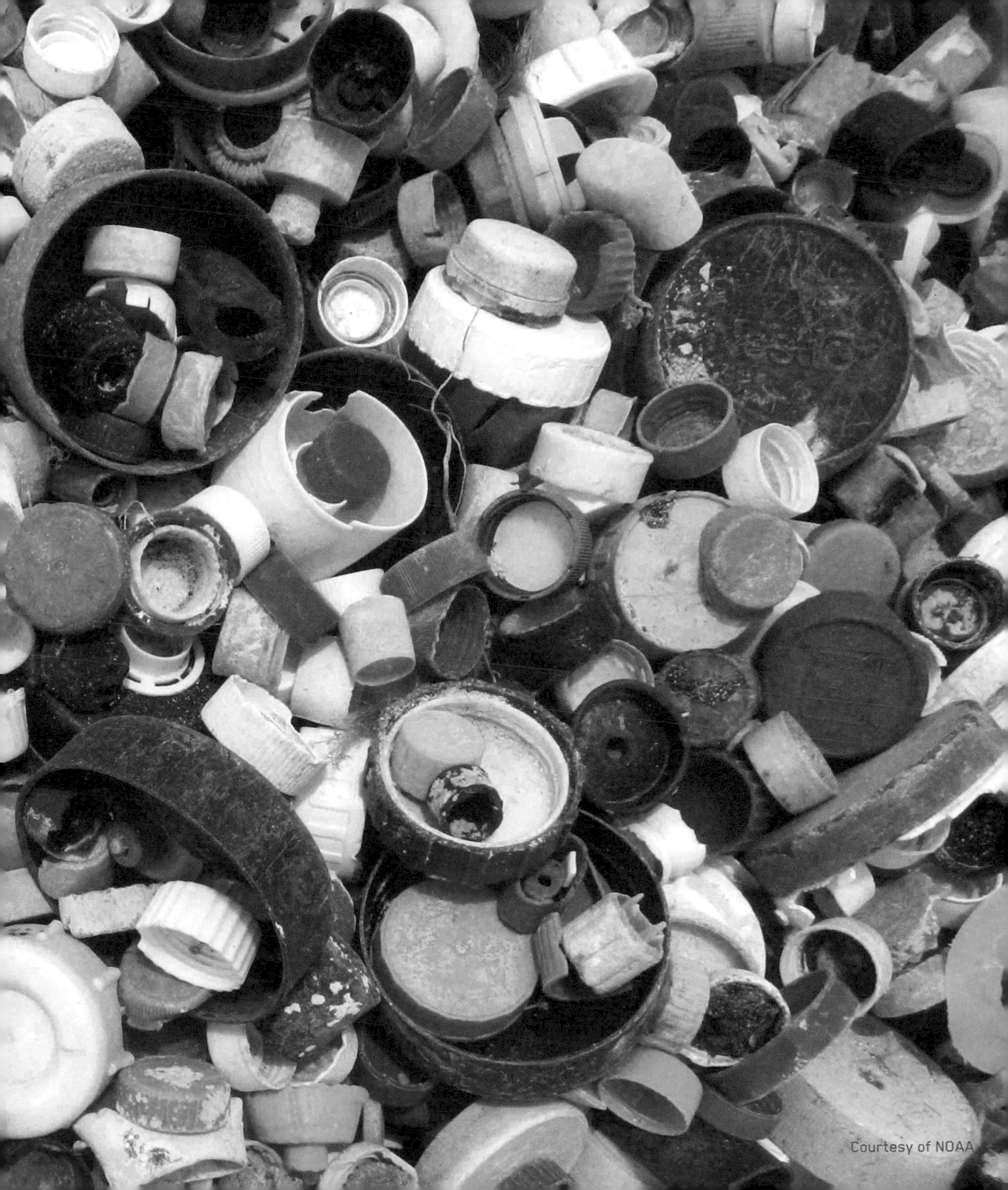

Courtesy of NOAA

Judith Selby and Richard Lang, **SHOVEL BANDS**
digital photograph

GYRE

Preface

Julie Decker

BOTH RISING SEA TEMPERATURES AND ACIDIFICATION are due to become increasingly extreme throughout this century, along with other climate change impacts such as rising sea levels and more frequent and severe storms. Other modern inventions, too, affect the health of our ocean, including fishing methods and large catches, oil and gas extractions, alien species, and pollution.

Most pollution in the ocean originates from industry, agriculture or domestic sources on land—whether dumped directly into the sea or reaching it via rivers and air currents. The release of sewage and wastes into coastal ecosystems has complex impacts, including being transferred up the food chain to impact human health.

One of the most visible types of ocean trash is plastic. It can be seen walking along a beach. Everything from straws to foam carryout containers and bottle caps wash up on shores around the world. Plastic is a modern material, used in many aspects of daily life and therefore a big part of the waste stream. It's not easy to imagine the plastic straw used to sip a soda in a movie theatre becoming an attractive plaything for a marine mammal, but once waterborne, plastic travels.

A gyre is a large-scale circular feature made up of ocean currents that spiral around a central point, clockwise in the Northern Hemisphere and counterclockwise in the Southern Hemisphere. Worldwide, there are five major subtropical oceanic gyres: the North and South Pacific Subtropical Gyres, the North and South Atlantic Subtropical Gyres, and the Indian Ocean Subtropical Gyre. The North Pacific Subtropical Gyre is the one most notable because of its tendency to collect debris. It is made up of four large, clockwise-rotating currents—the North Pacific, California, North Equatorial, and Kuroshio. It is very difficult to measure the exact size of a gyre because it is a fluid system, but the North Pacific Subtropical Gyre is roughly estimated to be 7 to 9 million square miles. Since plastic floats, many of these gyres are colorful testaments to human consumption.

On March 11, 2011, a devastating 9.0 earthquake and tsunami struck Japan. The disaster claimed nearly 16,000 lives, injured 6,000, and destroyed or damaged countless buildings and infrastructure. As a result of the disaster, a portion of the debris that the tsunami washed into the ocean reached U.S. and Canadian shores over the next several years, including Alaska and Hawai'i, some of the most beautiful and seemingly remote beaches in the world.

The world shrinks as we all become connected through our trash, yet somehow we are still severed from the problem we've created. Garbage is impacting the life that depend on the ocean as a source of food and habitat.

The GYRE project started in Alaska. The Anchorage Museum and the Alaska SeaLife Center partnered to bring an international team of artists, scientists and educators to the Alaska coastline in 2013 to observe, document and collect marine debris. Artists from the expedition and from around the world created project-specific artwork from the experience and the materials collected. The exhibition debuted at the Anchorage Museum in 2014, featuring contemporary art from international artists commenting on the trash found on beaches around the globe.

Art and science come together in this project as a way to provide an impactful visual narrative for scientific data and investigation. While scientists might seem more likely to comment on ocean trash, artists, too, are keen observers and tireless researchers, moving from observation and documentation to awareness and activism.

This project looks at human consumption, modern materials, and environmental change and their impacts upon one of the largest, most mysterious and critical components of our planet: the ocean. Through the voices of scientists, artists, writers and others, we explore the ways in which we are all connected— both by trash and by the sea, and through our individual actions.

FROM GIANT GRAY WHALES

TO THE TINIEST CORALS:

EVERYDAY PROBLEM WITH REAL IMPACTS

Nancy Wallace, Director NOAA Marine Debris Program

IN 2010, A 37-FOOT DEAD GRAY WHALE washed up on a rocky beach in West Seattle. While it was not the first whale to die in the Puget Sound that year, the necropsy surprised responders. Plastics, duct tape, rope, fishing line, sweat pants, towels, a juice pack, a sock, a golf ball, a *5 A Day* fruit and vegetable bag, and a host of other foreign items swirled around in its stomach. According to Cascadia Research, a non-profit that helped lead the examination, while there was no clear cause of death, the amount of human debris in the whale's stomach was larger than what they had ever found before.[1] "Most of the gray whales we see have plant material and wood chips in their stomachs," said Jessie Huggins, a stranding coordinator with Cascadia Research. "We hadn't seen that volume of trash before, so it was very surprising."[2]

Gray whales are bottom feeders, which means they eat near the sea floor, filtering tiny prey from water, sediment, and foreign objects through large baleen plates.[3] Unfortunately, the food they filter is not always food; it can be plastic bags, textiles, or any other debris found in industrial, coastal waters. The irony of a whale eating the very non-nutritious plastic remains of a *5 A Day* nutrition campaign should not be lost on anyone.

There is no solid data on how many marine mammals ingest plastic and other debris each year, but the Seattle incident is certainly not isolated. There are anecdotes from all over the globe, covering a range of species. For example, two sperm whales stranded on the Northern California coast in 2008 had large amounts plastic debris and fishing nets in their stomachs—nearly 134 different types of nets between the two. One whale's stomach was ruptured, and the other whale was emaciated. Both likely died from the debris blockage.[4] Just recently, in March 2013, scientists in southern Spain found nearly 38 pounds (17 kg) of plastic sheeting used to make greenhouses protruding from a dead sperm whale's stomach. One responder reportedly said, "there was so much plastic that it finally exploded."[5]

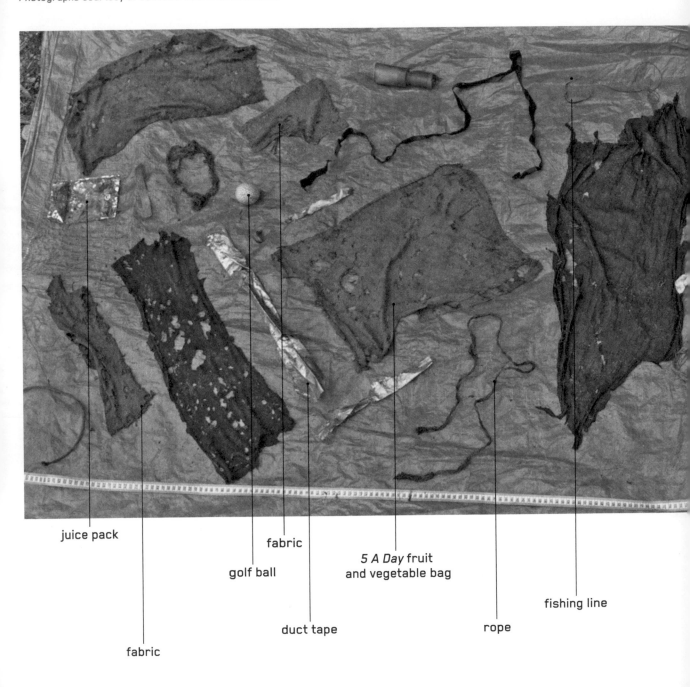

WEST SEATTLE, 2010
A dead gray whale washed up on a rocky beach in West Seattle in 2010.
Photographs courtesy of Cascadia Research Collective

juice pack

fabric

golf ball

fabric

duct tape

5 *A Day* fruit
and vegetable bag

rope

fishing line

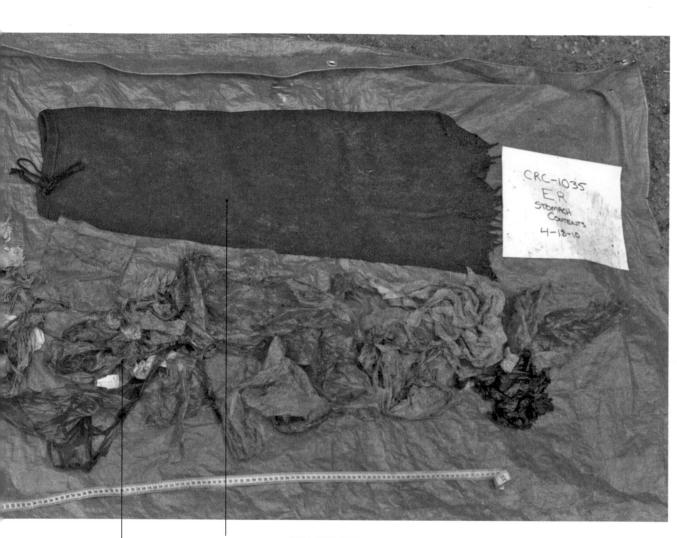

sweat pants

plastic grocery bags

Global Impacts to Natural Resources

Even the most remote areas of the world suffer from the impacts of marine debris. Refuge managers on Midway Atoll in the Northwestern Hawaiian Islands have come across the carcasses of Laysan albatrosses with lighters, bottle caps, and colorful bits of plastic spilling from their skeletons. Where a whale might inhale debris through its large mouth by accident, birds, fish, and other marine mammals can mistake broken-down plastics for prey and eat it. If it becomes stuck in their guts, they may not digest real food properly, which can lead to starvation and death.

We can observe the direct impact of debris ingestion, but what about what we can't see? Some plastics contain chemicals such as flame retardants and BPA *(bisphenol A)*, which may leach out in the ocean under the right circumstances. Plastic materials can also act as a sponge, absorbing persistent organic pollutants like PCBs *(polychlorinated biphenyls)* from the surrounding environment. If a plastic bottle enters the ocean, what happens to the chemicals in it? The bottle could hold on to its chemicals or release them—or both, depending on the environment.[6] If a Laysan albatross chick or marine mammal eats part of the bottle, does it absorb the chemicals into its muscle tissue? Today, there is an ongoing effort around the globe to answer these questions.

Besides ingestion, a major issue that has a profound impact on natural resources, especially around the Pacific Rim, is entanglement. Discarded nets, rope, crab pots, and fishing line will continue fishing, even as they drift through the ocean. They can entangle animals, maim them, or prevent them from hunting food. Surveys of Stellar sea lions in Alaska, whose populations have suffered declines over the past several decades, determined that entanglements were a greater problem than previously recognized. Plastic packing bands and rubber bands were the number one culprit.[7]

Marine debris also impacts habitats. Commercial crab pots and fishing nets sometimes weigh hundreds of pounds and, when they are lost, they can scour precious reefs and sea beds and entrap important target and non-target species for years. What's more, coastal communities spend millions of dollars annually trying to prevent and remove debris from washing up on their shorelines. It not only degrades our coasts' natural beauty, but it threatens the safety of those who work and play there.

Let's Solve the Problem

In 2010, Americans generated 250 million tons of trash—31 million tons of which were plastics.[8] If someone throws a plastic bag in the trash, it's possible that it will end up ingested by a whale, like the one in Seattle. It can stay in the ocean for decades, slowly degrading from salt and sunlight, or it can land on a remote coastline across the world. Everything is interconnected—streets and landfills connect to storm drains, which lead to rivers and estuaries, which empty into the ocean. Once that bag enters the marine environment, it can travel hundreds of miles from its starting point, carried by currents and winds.

So how do we solve this? The marine debris problem, on one hand, is very simple. Humans put debris in the marine environment, which means that we can keep it from happening. Marine debris is a very tangible issue, and it's preventable.

On the other hand, it is a very complex issue, with many factors—including multiple sources and types of debris, different global policies and initiatives—affecting what and where debris accumulates around the world. It is because of this complexity that there is no single solution. Addressing the marine debris problem requires responsibility and action at every level, collaborative efforts from governments, the private sector, and individuals to implement marine debris prevention initiatives and other solutions.[9] And indeed, these initiatives are happening every day across the globe—from organized cleanups by non-profits, to stronger waste management policies by municipalities, to increased awareness and action among the fishing industry. It's these types of initiatives, along with individual decisions that will help reduce the impacts of marine debris.

As individuals, we need to change how we live. While it may seem cliché, *The Three R's*—reduce, reuse, and recycle—are easy and effective ways for people to help prevent waste from entering the marine environment. Of the 31 million tons of plastics we generated in 2010, we recovered only eight percent from recycling.[10] Limit single-use items, join a cleanup, and raise awareness among your peers. Everyone has a contributing hand in the problem, which also means everyone can and must help solve it. We are the main cause of the problem, but also the key to the solution.

1 Cascadia Research Collective. 2010. "Examination of gray whale from west Seattle reveals unusual stomach contents but no definitive cause of death." http://www.cascadiaresearch.org/WSeattle-ER.htm

2 Quote from primary source – taken from phone conversation between author and Ms. Huggins on March 25, 2013.

3 NOAA Fisheries Office of Protected Resources. 2013. "Gray Whale (Eschrichtius robustus)." http://www.nmfs.noaa.gov/pr/species/mammals/cetaceans/graywhale.htm

4 Jacobsen et al. 2010. Fatal ingestion of floating net debris by two sperm whales (Physeter macrocephalus). Marine Pollution Bulletin 60 (2010) 765–767. http://www.marinemammalcenter.org/assets/pdfs/vetsci-stranding/scientific-contributions/2010/sperm-whale-fatal-ingestion.pdf

5 AFP. 2013. Beached whale in Spain dies from ingesting plastic waste. Quote attributed to Renaud de Stephanis from the Donana Biological Station. http://www.google.com/hostednews/afp/article/ALeqM5iBRsN6hi4VT2jPHYU_GiS7NaC4Mg?docId=CNG.c7a205fd-35088508f7ab23370e7d70e6.9e1

6 Teuten et al. 2009. Transport and release of chemicals from plastics to the environment and to wildlife. Phil. Trans. R. Soc. B (2009) 364, 2027–2045. http://rstb.royalsocietypublishing.org/content/364/1526/2027.abstract.

7 Raum-Suryan et al. 2009. Alaska Department of Fish and Game. Lose the loop: Entanglements of Stellar sea lions, Eumetopias jubatus, in marine debris. http://www.adfg.alaska.gov/static/home/about/management/wildlifemanagement/marinemammals/pdfs/entanglement_poster_oct_2009.pdf

8 Environmental Protection Agency. 2010. Municipal Solid Waste Generation, Recycling, and Disposal in the United States: Facts and Figures for 2010. p. 7, http://www.epa.gov/epawaste/nonhaz/municipal/pubs/msw_2010_rev_factsheet.pdf

9 National Oceanic and Atmospheric Administration, United Nations Environment Programme. 2012. The Honolulu Strategy. P 1-2. http://5imdc.files.wordpress.com/2011/03/honolulustrategy.pdf

10 Environmental Protection Agency. 2010. Municipal Solid Waste Generation, Recycling, and Disposal in the United States: Facts and Figures for 2010. p. 7, http://www.epa.gov/epawaste/nonhaz/municipal/pubs/msw_2010_rev_factsheet.pdf

PACKING BANDS ARE THE NUMBER ONE CULPRIT FOR ENTANGLEMENTS IN THE STELLAR SEA LIONS THAT ARE SURVEYED.

NO ISLAND
IS AN ISLAND

Carl Safina

DOWN THE BEACH, A PLUMP YOUNG SEAL tosses around a plastic soap bottle drifted in from the farther side of our small world. A different young seal that came ashore while we were working has a plastic packing strap stuck around its body, just past its flippers. That's potentially lethal, because it could cut through the skin and flesh as the seal grows. We have a pair of pruning shears for just this purpose. This particular seal had previously gotten stuck in a different packing strap. So that's odd. A few days ago we found one with a loop of rope and some gill-net on him, lying snug against a big heap of hawser rope that had drifted onto this shore.

A lot of fishing nets drift great distances before hanging up along beaches. Some fishing gear washes overboard in violent storms. Some is purposely jettisoned because it is easier and cheaper to dump unwanted nets and lines at sea. People have often found seal pups, fish, whales, turtles, and seabirds—alive and dead—tangled in discarded nets.

Human thoughtlessness continually clutters this and just about every other remote coast. Here in the middle of the Pacific, thousands of miles from the nearest continent and hundreds of miles from the nearest inhabited island, the colorful shoreline is a jetsam jubilee, a festival of cast-up trash.

This shoreline is a beach of burden, staggering under a bright array of mostly-plastic rubbish that would look striking on a poster. The strand line is a wide band of bottles, floats, shoes, tires, plastic—everything from boogie boards to booze bottles. If you're on the beach, you're seldom more than a few paces away from something that doesn't belong on beaches.

A quick scan around confronts your eye with plastic beverage bottles, pieces of plastic pipe, empty containers of everything from laundry detergent to talcum powder to chocolate syrup. And various cast-up footwear. Glass bottles abound, too. Here's a bottle saying Coca-Cola in English on one side and in Japanese on the other.

An albatross chick drags its fat belly across the sand and then digs a little divot for itself next to a piece of rusted metal. There are a lot of coconuts on the beach, and some beautiful shells, like this large, gorgeous spiral snail about twice the size of a fist. Little red shapes sometimes turn out to be shell fragments and sometimes plastic bits. Plastic bottle tops are prominent. There's a desiccated mummy of a unicornfish, its spines fixed and formidable, its eye sockets vacant, its mouth frozen in eternal surprise. It lies amid the cowries, clams and barnacles—and trash.

Three adult Laysan albatrosses rest next to what looks like a dark glass fishing-net float on the beach. For some reason, the clear, spherical glass floats—many of which have probably floated around the Pacific for decades—have universal aesthetic appeal. Like most people, I find them quite attractive. But on closer inspection, this sphere turns out to be a bowling ball.

The debris piles up at certain spots. On the south point, a hellacious concentration of trash, plastic fishing floats, and bunched-up fishing net stretch for a quarter mile. The northwest side of the island is a postcard of debris of the central Pacific. It's a monk seal obstacle course, with seal tracks threading their way among buoys and bottles and balls.

The Black-footed albatrosses here densely nest among a psychedelic garden of round plastic fishing net floats, colored to be visible on the sea. It's a surreal sight—big dark birds among big colored bubbles on a white sand beach against the blue ocean—like someone's bad hallucinatory trip. To paraphrase Coleridge: garbage, garbage everywhere, as nobody thought to think. You would not guess that dumping plastics into the ocean has been illegal since the early 1990s.

Some of the debris is bizarre: Flashlights. A fake-grass welcome mat. A plastic wheel from a child's tricycle. A big coffee pot and a scrub brush. Half a kitchen cutting board, well used. Suddenly there are three umbrella handles within three feet of each other, as though several people had been swept to their death together in a torrential rain and washed far out to sea, with only their umbrellas making the voyage all the way here.

Every few steps reveal new types of junk: A golf tee. A small perfume bottle. A plastic folding hairbrush. A toy cowboy. A thread spool. A vacuum tube from an old television set. A syringe. A refrigerator door. Small rubber balls. A human skull—of plastic. A toy truck. Toy soldier. A three-inch plastic dinosaur (Tyrannosaurus rex). A plastic elephant. Plastic cat. Even some of the fish on this beach are plastic ones.

The warm Kuroshio Current streaming past Japan, whose waters eventually pass Hawai'i as the North Pacific Current, is troubled with trash coming from Asia because that's the direction the flow takes it. This trash, conveniently swept from its sources by the grace of moving water, gets inflicted on the ocean's wildlife.

As you'd guess, the middle of the North Pacific isn't the only place with this problem. In the middle of the South Atlantic, to give just one example, at an island appropriately named Inaccessible—uninhabited, seldom visited— bird researchers Peter Ryan and Coleen Moloney documented "exponentially increasing" accumulations of litter, mostly plastic from South America, 2,000 miles distant.

Here on Laysan Island, someone once found a sign saying in Japanese, SAVE OUR OCEANS AND RIVERS—DON'T POLLUTE.

I continue walking. Here's an insulated beverage container from a brand called Kansai Attaché. It reads: "The power of nature to suit the mind of the city dweller." I find myself poetically inspired to answer their empty-headed slogan with a haiku:

City dwellers' trash
Fouling shores of paradise.
More is on the way.

Like many of the beaches I've traveled, this beach also bears multitudes— tens of thousands—of chemical lightsticks. In the world's oceans they're used by the millions to attract swordfish and tuna to baited longlines. Also abundant: fishing-net floats of oblong foamy plastic. They're probably from the super-scale "curtains of death" driftnets of the 1980s and early 1990s, still floating around, still causing problems.

People here say they've seen adult albatrosses regurgitate these floats and pass them to chicks. At six inches long and two inches wide, the floats would occupy a lot of space inside an albatross that should go to food.

These fishing implements hint toward pressures untold and uncontrolled on the Pacific's underwater wildlife. We use these implements to empty the oceans, and then the sea itself casts them up to heap havoc on the remotest shores. From the time this fishing gear is manufactured, everywhere it goes—it's trouble.

Courtesy of NOAA

I'd noticed several hooks hanging in the cooking tent. One of them looked like a halibut hook. One was a shark hook. The crew found them next to bird nests. Two days ago, an albatross chick had a braided plastic cord emerging from its throat. Others have had monofilament line hanging from their mouths. Likely they've swallowed hooks.

I wonder what happens then. A few steps farther is one small albatross chick's carcass with bright bits of plastic sticking through its ribs. You get the feeling the plastic will remain here even after the bones themselves bleach and pulverize into dust and blow away. A little farther along lies another dead albatross chick, its whole rib cage packed with plastic—various shades of blues, pinks, orange, various pieces of bottles, and even the plastic legs of a toy soldier. And a colored cigarette lighter. Lighters are one of the more horrifying—and more common—things you see in these dead chicks. This fresh carcass seethes with maggots, making the bits of colored plastic look woozily alive.

In fact, every decomposed chick carcass seems to have plenty of little colored bits of plastic. You can often tell where chicks died last year because piles of colorful plastic particles that used to fill their stomachs now mark their graves like Technicolor tombstones.

It is unlikely that any living albatross chick on the island is free of plastic. Pacific albatrosses eat greater volumes and more varieties of plastics than any other seabird. Of 109 identifiable plastic items found inside Laysan albatrosses in a formal study, 108 had originated in Japan. Plastic can't be good for the birds, and it must kill a few. Large volumes of plastics might give a false sensation of satiation and suppress their appetites. This may be enough to starve or fatally dehydrate chicks already in poor condition. Birds may absorb toxic chemicals from plastics and other artificial things they swallow.

One coughed-up bolus contains both natural and unnatural items: a couple-dozen squid beaks and several smooth pumice stones light enough to float, plus a couple of plastic bottle caps, and a bit of gill net festooned with fish eggs. Mere eating has turned high-risk for the albatrosses.

On the ground is a lot of pumice that albatrosses have eaten and spit up. We know that in this part of the ocean, fish eggs are sometimes adhered to floating objects. This might be the best clue to why albatrosses eat hard plastic—they probably eat naturally-occurring drifting objects for the attached egg masses and other digestible creatures growing on them.

They've been eating pumice for millennia, and it's likely that they've simply transferred the habit to anything swallowable that floats, like cigarette lighters. The pumice the birds disgorge is rounded and worn smooth. But the plastic can break into sharp shards that can block the esophagus or stomach, or cause internal tears or punctures.

I come suddenly upon a strange opaque black bottle in the sand. Its rounded bottom attenuates into an elegant neck with an unusual cap. It's a genie bottle, certainly. For the world's oceans, the evil debris genie has already been uncorked; mere anarchy loosed upon the world—and it seems there's no putting it back.

A sleek adult Laysan albatross—gliding in low on seven-foot wings—has probably flown thousands of miles to get back here. She settles her dark wings over her snowy back for the first time in days. Her feet have not touched anything solid, nor have her legs supported her weight, for perhaps two weeks. She surveys the scene through lovely, dark, pastel-shadowed eyes, then calls a rusty-gate-hinge "Eh Eh Eh."

A chick immediately comes over, calling. But she knows it's not her chick's own voice, and she continues waddling along, calling and looking. Another chick answers, also hoping to con her into misplacing her precious cargo into its crucial belly.

One by one, five more chicks come begging and calling as the albatross continues walking along. Each chick that rushes forward gets a sharp rebuke from her hooked bill. Except one.

The adult begins directly approaching the last of this line of hungering hopefuls. But she veers away from it at the last moment (perhaps the voice seemed familiar, but the scent was wrong?). Another youngster, much more developed, comes hopping, jumping, and flapping across the road.

She ignores it.

Our adult walks about thirty yards farther. Over there, a chick has just started calling. And to this call, she is responding, calling softly, matter-of-factly, with little excitement or energy. She simply walks directly to the chick.

Parent and youngster meet and greet, the adult acting confident that this is the right child. People often seem incredulous that seabirds can recognize each other among thousands. But give them a little credit. We recognize voices on the telephone. We can recognize each other in cities among millions. And we do so without the sense of smell so well developed in other mammals and in albatrosses.

Considering the life-or-death stakes involved in recognizing your own chick or parent or mate, animals certainly evolved proficiency for recognizing individuals a long, long time ago. We've merely inherited that capability from much earlier ancestors. But, bubble-wrapped within our estrangement from our extended family, we fail to appreciate other animals' competencies. We withhold recognition of their cognitive abilities. Blinded to stark evidence of our relatedness to other living beings, we heap praise on ourselves for supposedly "unique" abilities, whose origins are so plain and so much better accomplished in birds and bees.

The whining chick begins eagerly nibbling the adult's bill with its own clattering mandibles. Its ravenous aggression seems nearly to overwhelm the adult, which at first tries to duck the advances. But the bill-battering builds and this necessary food foreplay works as usual to stimulate her into regurgitating her delivery load. The adult hunches forward, neck stretching. The chick, with sudden frenzied expectation, thrusts its bill up tight to the adult's gaping mouth, forcing her wider and wider open.

The adult abruptly pumps out several thick boluses of food: semi-liquefied squid and purplish fish eggs, which the chick bolts down. Both pause. Then the chick renews its drive for more. The adult arches her neck and is retching, retching. Nothing comes. More retching.

Is something wrong?

Slowly, the tip—just the tip—of a green plastic toothbrush emerges in the bird's throat. The sight is surreal—so out of place, so wrong, that my racing mind is interrogating my eyes over and over: Are you sure that's a toothbrush?

The chick, in a flurry of furious hunger, presses.

With her neck arched, the mother cannot pass the straight toothbrush. She re-swallows it and several times repeats the attempt to bring it up. Each time, she cannot pass it fully out.

It's one thing to find plastic items on the ground and know the birds have carried them, but seeing this bird in distress, this vital mother-child interaction interrupted, is very hard to watch. It's one of the most piercing things I've ever experienced.

The parent albatross re-swallows a final time and, with the toothbrush stuck inside her, wanders away from her chick.

In the world that shaped albatrosses, the ocean could be trusted to provide only food; parents to provide only nourishment. Through the care-bond between parent and offspring passes the continuity of life itself. That the flow of this intimate exchange now includes our chemicals and our trash indicates a world wounded and out of round, its most fundamental relationships disfigured.

The main message from the albatross is this: No matter what coordinates you choose, from waters polar, to solar coral reefs, to the remotest turquoise atoll—no place, no creature remains apart from you and me.

A few albatrosses still fly who were already ranging the vast and open ocean when, holding my mother's hand, I walked to my first day of kindergarten. Many of these birds knew the sea before it became so filled with plastic bottle caps and cigarette lighters; before the strain of driftnets, before boats with multi-mile longlines laced their feeding grounds with hundreds of millions of tantalizing hooks.

To share close quarters among creatures that mastered a world so different— within their lifetime and your own—is to realize how abruptly we've changed even the farthest reaches of the planet. Unlike deforested or urbanized landscapes whose alterations plainly show, the ocean rolls on as always. But once you perceive the message of the albatross, the ocean's deceptively constant surface no longer fools you. Once you see and feel the disparity between what animals learned to expect and what they now get—when you see over and over how traits and habits fine-tuned for survival seem turned against so many living beings—the world seems on fire.

Seeing a parent albatross gagging up a toothbrush brought me a new view. In my mental map, society no longer stops at the borders of continents, or of species. The world is no longer small enough for that. We've woven the albatross into our society. That creates a certain moral obligation. Fortunately, recognizing limits means seeing the opportunity to create a better world.

Less trash, less habitat destruction, less contamination, less atmospheric disturbance, and less overfishing, would mean more life.

We need the birds and the seas more than they need us. Will we understand this well enough to reap all the riches that a little restraint would engender?

Nothing could prepare albatrosses for the changes that have come in the flash of one long lifetime. Our calling cards, in waters and upon the winds, cycle through all living things. In all the far reaches of the wide, wide seas, every single bird, fish, mammal, and turtle carries the trademark of human chemical manufacturing within its cellular tapestry. Antarctic penguins, who'll never suspect that the world contains so many people, carry the imprint of humanity in their flesh; in the Arctic, some polar bears now have the deformity of having both male and female sex organs, the result of hormone-mimicking contaminants acquired in the womb from their mother's food; from us.

But don't pity just them. We have also made ourselves subjects in a new but uncontrolled experiment. No less than a mother albatross delivering cigarette lighters and toothbrushes, a human mother has no ability to avoid the pesticides, food additives, hormones, hormone mimics, antibiotics, PAHS, POPS, and other unsavory alpha-bits spelling trouble and signaling sos to a world newly transformed by modern manufacturing and chemical agriculture.

Like toothbrushes—but invisible—this hazardous soup comes between every mother and child. No nursing woman can avoid pumping a stream of industrial by-products into the pure new life at her breast. No less than in the sea, no less than to the birds and seals and turtles, many of the changes affecting us arrive unrecognized for what they are.

And so the albatross speaks to us of how much the world is changing, and how little difference exists between us—and of what it means to be kin and sibling in the net of time and events that enmesh us all.

Four centuries ago, poet John Donne posited that no person is an island. Four hundred years later, not only is no person an island, no island is an island any longer.

Albatrosses inhabit a few islands. Humans inhabit only one island, a blue and white marble in a fragile bubble, adrift in the great dark sea of the universe.

"No Island Is An Island" is adapted by the author from *Eye of the Albatross* by Carl Safina, published by Henry Holt Co, and winner of the National Academies Communication Award for best book.

PACIFIC ALBATROSSES EAT GREATER VOLUMES AND MORE VARIETIES OF PLASTICS THAN ANY OTHER SEABIRD.

PLASTICS
UNWRAPPED

Ruth Pelz, Burke Museum of Natural History and Culture

WHEN BURKE MUSEUM STAFF GATHERED a few years ago to discuss potential exhibits, one subject leapt to the top of the list: plastics! Of all the suggestions discussed that day, nothing else expressed so vividly the relationships between people and the environment. Nothing else, we suspected, could better embody the museum's vision: inspiring people to value the interconnectedness of all life—and act accordingly.

Our suspicions were confirmed over the following months, as we undertook a journey of discovery with the generous assistance of experts from across the University of Washington, local industries, and the community. With their help, we explored questions we hadn't thought to ask before: What are plastics anyway? What did we do before we had them? What are the impacts of our choices to use them? Can our relationship with plastics be changed?

The answers turned out to be fascinating, nuanced, and often surprising.

Life before plastics

The most startling aspect of plastics' history, we quickly discovered, is that it's so short. Invented just over a century ago, plastics didn't became part of everyday life until the 1950s, after the end of World War II. Unless you're older than a baby boomer, you probably can't remember life without them.

So what did people use before that? How did they carry water, store food, or keep dry in the rain? All human cultures have faced and solved these challenges, often in beautiful and inventive ways. But until very recently, they were limited to materials derived from nature, such as wood, leather, shell, bone, plant fibers, metal, glass, and clay.

The Burke's anthropology collections include many captivating examples of pre-plastic materials. They are all functional and some are breathtaking, but they have clear limitations. Gathering, preparing, and shaping the materials took time and skill, and many objects were fragile, heavy, or rare. It should be remembered that pre-plastic materials had environmental impacts, too. In the 1800s, for example, elephants were hunted to near extinction to make billiard balls from their tusks!

HOW TO MAKE A
WATERPROOF GUT PARKA:

❶ Kill seal or other large sea mammal

❷ Remove and clean the intestines, inside and out

❸ Set out to dry, then cut into strips

❹ Stitch strips together with waterproof seams, using thread made from twisted sinew

TIME REQUIRED: About one month to make an adult parka

❶ Gather new willow branches in spring; strip bark and scrape into evenly sized rods

❷ Soak strips for a day in water, then weave into a jar-shaped basket

❸ Rub with a mash of pounded cactus or juniper leaves to fill spaces

❹ Cover with pitch from the piñon tree *(melted to a thick syrup, poured into interior, and brushed onto the outside (add heated rocks to keep pitch warm while it flows into all openings)*

TIME REQUIRED: 1–2 weeks

HOW TO MAKE A
WOVEN WATER BOTTLE

The promise of "miracle materials"

Given the challenges of pre-plastic materials, people dreamed of better solutions, and countless inventors devoted their lives to the quest. Throughout the 1800s, determined researchers sought ways to improve on natural materials by applying heat, pressure, and a wide range of chemical additives. When successful, they created what we now think of as plastic precursors: materials that were modified from their naturally occurring chemical form but not yet fully synthetic. (Vulcanized rubber is an example. In its natural state, rubber melts in heat and stiffens in the cold. Charles Goodyear discovered a process to make rubber more usable in 1839.)

The first fully synthetic plastic material, Bakelite, was patented in 1909 by its namesake, Leo Baekeland. The plastic age had begun. Innovations continued and, as each new plastic was invented, it was greeted with great excitement. Imagine living without plastic food containers, synthetic fabrics, and other items on the timeline (to the right), and you can begin to understand why.

When World War II began, plastics were still new and rare. The industry shifted its focus to help meet military needs, from life rafts to radar development. Production boomed. At war's end, factories had huge capacity, and switched their production to consumer products.

Until this point, people generally used things until they wore out. The economics of plastic demanded a change, since production costs for 100 items or 10,000 were nearly the same. Advertisements began to promote the convenience of using things once and then throwing them away. By the 1970s, disposability was a way of life.

Plastic science: It's a matter of molecules

Our word "plastic" come from Greek: plastikos, meaning a thing that can be formed or molded. The almost infinite adaptability of plastics comes from their chemical structure: they're made up of polymers—long molecules with repeating units, like links in a chain. These molecular chains can be formed into a huge variety of shapes. There are many possible chemical units ("monomers") and ways they can combine, so thousands of different plastics can be made—each with different properties.

PLASTICS: THE FIRST 100 YEARS

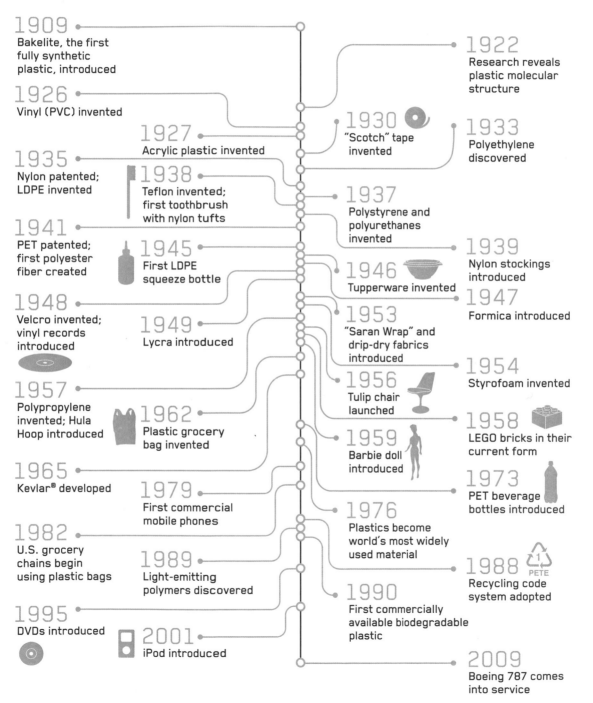

1909
Bakelite, the first fully synthetic plastic, introduced

1922
Research reveals plastic molecular structure

1926
Vinyl (PVC) invented

1927
Acrylic plastic invented

1930
"Scotch" tape invented

1933
Polyethylene discovered

1935
Nylon patented; LDPE invented

1938
Teflon invented; first toothbrush with nylon tufts

1937
Polystyrene and polyurethanes invented

1941
PET patented; first polyester fiber created

1945
First LDPE squeeze bottle

1939
Nylon stockings introduced

1946
Tupperware invented

1947
Formica introduced

1948
Velcro invented; vinyl records introduced

1949
Lycra introduced

1953
"Saran Wrap" and drip-dry fabrics introduced

1954
Styrofoam invented

1956
Tulip chair launched

1957
Polypropylene invented; Hula Hoop introduced

1962
Plastic grocery bag invented

1958
LEGO bricks in their current form

1959
Barbie doll introduced

1965
Kevlar® developed

1979
First commercial mobile phones

1973
PET beverage bottles introduced

1976
Plastics become world's most widely used material

1982
U.S. grocery chains begin using plastic bags

1989
Light-emitting polymers discovered

1988
Recycling code system adopted

1995
DVDs introduced

2001
iPod introduced

1990
First commercially available biodegradable plastic

2009
Boeing 787 comes into service

CRACKING THE CODE

Because all plastics are not chemically the same, you can't just melt them together and make a new bottle out of the mix. The plastics industry came up with a coding system to distinguish the plastics most often used in disposable containers. That's what the symbols on the bottom of the containers mean.

CHEMICAL NAME Polyethylene Terephthalate
NICKNAMES PET, PETE, Polyester
PROPERTIES Clear, tough, impermeable
COMMON USES Beverage bottles, food jars, fabrics
ISSUES/FACTS About 50 billion PET bottles thrown away each year, even though demand for recycled PET is high

CHEMICAL NAME High Density Polyethylene
NICKNAMES HDPE
PROPERTIES Relatively stiff, good chemical resistance, translucent
COMMON USES Bottles for milk, juice, household cleaners; cereal box liners,
ISSUES/FACTS One of the safer plastics

CHEMICAL NAME Polyvinyl Chloride
NICKNAMES PVC, Vinyl
PROPERTIES Stable, inexpensive, versatile; can be rigid or flexible
COMMON USES Plumbing, window frames, IV bags and tubing, meat wrap, shower curtains
ISSUES/FACTS Can release lead, phthalates, and other toxins

CHEMICAL NAME Low Density Polyethylene
NICKNAME LDPE
PROPERTIES Transparent, touch, flexible
COMMON USES Clear wraps and bags, flexible lids and bottles, coatings for cartons and cups, toys
ISSUES/FACTS Like HDPE, a safer plastic.

CHEMICAL NAME Polypropylene
NICKNAME PP
PROPERTIES Strong, resistant to acids and solvents, high melting point
COMMON USES Containers for medicine, condiments, yogurt; fabrics; molded parts for cars and appliances
ISSUES/FACTS One of the safer plastics

CHEMICAL NAME Polystyrene
NICKNAMES PS, Styrofoam
PROPERTIES Versatile, can be rigid or foamed, significant stiffness, good insulation as foam
COMMON USES Cups, plates, cutlery, meat trays, protective packaging, CD cases, building insulation
ISSUES/FACTS Can leach toxins when heated (never use in microwave)

NAME 7 is used for any plastic other than those labeled 1-6
PROPERTIES Variable, depending on type of plastic
ISSUES Plastics labeled 7 may be biodegradable polymers (PLA and others) that can be composted but not recycled; other plastics that are relatively safe but not typically recyclable (ABS, SAN), and polycarbonates (PC) that can leach BPA.

The fossil fuel connection

Traditional plastics are petroleum products; they're made from oil and natural gas. These fossil fuels are formed from plants and animals that lived hundreds of millions of years ago.

You've probably heard of hydrocarbons. These are the simple molecules, composed of carbon and hydrogen, that are the energy sources in fossil fuels and the main building blocks of plastics.[1] Living plants have hydrocarbons too, and new "bioplastics" are made from renewable sources, such as corn.

The chemical bonds in plastic are extremely strong; it takes a lot of energy to break them apart. That's good if you want an object to last a long time, but a serious problem if you don't. Plastic waste is everywhere because it takes a long time to degrade. How long? It depends on the kind of plastic and where it ends up.

In sunlight, most plastics break down into smaller bits over time, but those plastic bits never fully disappear. This process is very different from biodegradation, in which microorganisms digest organic waste, turning it back into water, carbon dioxide, and other basic compounds.

In the ocean, a plastic beverage bottle will likely take about 450 years to degrade[2] (In contrast, a paper towel takes 2–4 weeks; a tin can about 50 years). In a landfill, however, where there's no sunlight or air, the process is slower. Even natural materials break down slowly in landfills; plastics may take a thousand years.

With hundred of millions of tons of plastic produced each year, plastic waste is a global problem.

Engineering makes them better

Think plastics are cheap and simple materials? Think again! Researchers are developing highly-engineered plastics to do things that early inventors never dreamed of. These are some promising new directions:

- **Composite materials.** Composites combine two or more distinct materials to achieve new properties. The carbon composites used to create strong, lightweight parts for airplanes, cars, and sports equipment, are made by embedding thin carbon fibers in plastic resin. The Boeing 787 is the first commercial jetliner made mostly of composite materials. Lighter in weight than conventional planes, it uses less fuel and is quieter.

- **Bioplastics.** Engineers are creating new plastics from plant products such as sugar, starch, or cellulose, instead of fossil fuels. Relatively expensive now, they have promise as renewable and biodegradable replacements for the plastics we know.

- **New properties.** Most plastics are insulators. In fact, the need for electrical insulation was a powerful driver of early plastic discoveries and developments. But scientists have discovered that some plastics can conduct electricity. You might have an example of these new conductive materials in your pocket—plastics that glow in different colors when current is applied are now used in (OLED) cellphone displays.

Plastics and health

Nothing embodies the benefits and drawbacks—the yin and yang—of plastics as clearly as health issues. On the plus side, plastics have made modern medicine possible. From full-body scanners to the tiniest flexible tubing, pacemakers to prosthetics, plastics are essential components of medical devices. Plastics keep us healthier in other ways, too, from fresher foods to safer cars. Consider the following examples and imagine trying to make them with earlier materials, such as wood, metal, and glass.

- **Sterile disposables:** gloves, syringes, packaging

- **Medication delivery:** IV systems, tamper-proof medicine bottles

- **Prosthetics:** dentures, hearing aids, artificial joints and limbs

- **Auto safety:** airbags, child seats, impact-absorbing bumpers

On the other hand, there are many kinds of plastics—with thousands of chemical additives—and some raise real health concerns in the short and long term. Some additives of special concern are phthalates, used to make plastics soft and flexible, and bisphenol A (BPA), used in hard, clear plastics. Research is showing that even small amounts can disrupt hormones and damage health over time. Children, whose endocrine systems are still developing, and pregnant women face the greatest risk.

Additives can leach out when plastics are heated. To limit exposure, avoid heating plastic containers used with food. Unless the label says it's safe, don't microwave plastic food containers, use with hot liquids, or run through the dishwasher.

Medical waste is another problem, a huge one—an estimated 1,800,000 pounds annually. Efforts are under way to reduce it, but the task is complicated, because safe and sterile conditions are hospitals' first priority.

Toward solutions

Plastics are popular for good reasons, but we need to revise how we use (and misuse) them. Solutions depend on everyone: consumers, producers, governments, scientists, and engineers. Fortunately, there are plenty of people in each of these groups who are tackling the task. They're pointing out many ways to reduce our personal plastic footprint, make a difference in the community, and support organizations that are working for change. Here are a few opportunities.

Reduce/Reuse/Refuse: The best way to reduce plastic trash is not to acquire it. Think "Do I really need that?" before you bring more plastic home. Take it one step at a time. You could begin by:

- Saying NO to bottled water. It's hundreds of times more expensive than tap water and no safer. Rely on reusable containers instead. The options include water bottles with built-in filters if you don't like your tap water's taste.

- Reducing plastic packaging. Over 30 million tons of plastic are discarded in the U.S. each year, and much of this is packaging. You can help reduce plastic waste by choosing products with minimal, recyclable, and/or compostable packages and buying in bulk.

- Refusing disposable plastic bags. Bring your own reusable bags when you go shopping.

Recycle: The environmental benefits of recycling are clear—reductions in energy use, carbon emissions, pollution, and landfills. (Plastics take up about 25% of the space in landfills worldwide, and that space is disappearing fast.) A few things to consider:

- The resin codes included with this chapter can help you become an expert, but recycling agencies will tell you to start by paying attention to the shape of the container. If it looks like a beverage, milk, or detergent bottle or is shaped like a yogurt tub, it's probably recyclable. (Different places have different rules, so be sure to check out yours.)

- Compostable plastics are a good option if you live in a city like Seattle with a public compost program —these materials are designed to degrade in commercial compost facilities, not backyards or landfills. Just be sure to dispose of them in the yard-waste bin—NOT recycling or in the trash.

- Recycling has many benefits, but has to make business sense, too, in order to grow. There has to be a source and market for the product, and expenses have to pencil out. Individual actions help (the more recycled products we buy, the more industry will produce), but the real solutions depend on scale: public recycling programs, policies, and laws.

Shop smart: Look for products with minimal packaging, and safe, recycled/reusable materials. For example:

- Choose safer toys and baby products. Look for plastics without BPA and phthalates and non-plastic alternatives. Avoid vinyl (PVC).

- Buy recycled. Making products from recycled plastic requires less energy than producing with new materials, produces fewer greenhouse gases, and reduces landfill. Shoes and clothing made from recycled plastic can be just as high-performance as those made from new materials. Buying recycled goods from developing countries supports artisans and their families and helps reduce plastic waste in their communities.

Lobby for Change: Committed communities have shown that improvements are possible when people join together to change policies and laws. For example:

- Seattle has reduced landfill waste from homes by 70% through curbside recycling and compost programs

- New York—one of ten states that require a deposit on beverage containers—estimates that the "bottle bill" has saved two million barrels of oil and recycled almost four billion containers each year.

- Most developed countries have stronger laws on recycling than the U.S., including "extended producer responsibility" laws that require manufacturers to "take back" their used products in ways that are free, easy, and environmentally sound.[3]

Wrapping up

In just a few decades—a very short piece of human history—plastics have transformed the planet in ways we're just coming to understand. While they've made our lives safer, more convenient, and more colorful, they've also had unwanted side effects on people, wildlife, and environments around the globe.

As a natural history museum, it was the visible impact of plastic waste on world environments that drew us to this topic. When we began our investigation, we were prepared for a precipitous journey into despair. As we proceeded, though, we were inspired again and again by encounters with people committed to change. Researchers, retailers, activists, government workers, engineers, and entrepreneurs—each pushing the effort ahead in their varied areas of expertise, not dramatically, perhaps, but doggedly, one step at a time. These efforts haven't been around as long as plastic but already the incremental steps were adding up. It gave us confidence that we could do the same. At the end of our journey of discovery, we all agreed that it is time to rethink our relationship with plastics—and we can.

---

1 Ironically, because of the carbon, plastics are considered organic chemicals. When chemists use the word "organic" they are talking about substances that are carbon based.

2 Since plastics have only been around a few decades, researchers base their estimates on current, observed rates of decay.

3 Such as the Waste Electrical and Electronic Equipment Directive (WEEE) of the European Union

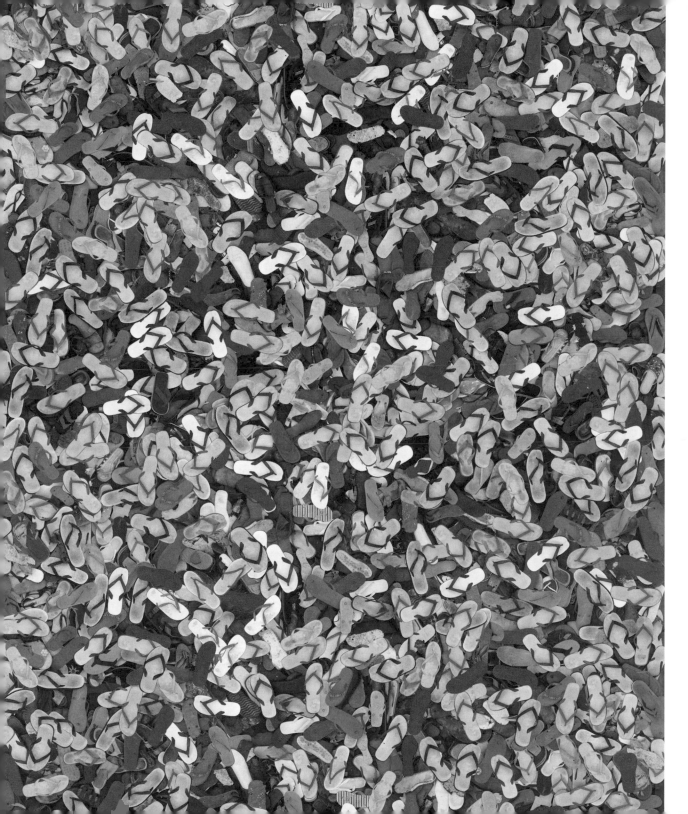

PLASTICS TAKE UP ABOUT 25% OF THE SPACE IN LANDFILLS WORLDWIDE.

ART AND THE ENVIRONMENT

Julie Decker, Anchorage Museum

ARTISTS OF THE LATE 19TH AND EARLY 20TH CENTURY went west in America, portraying the romantic landscape where man was insignificant and passive in the natural environment, a mere observer, dwarfed by the grandeur of Mother Nature and her majestic beauty. Ansel Adams, Thomas Cole, Albert Bierstadt, Frederic Edwin Church and others presented this optimistic, spiritual vision, which became central in American art.

The later part of the 20th century saw new approaches to artists as a voice for the environment. Earth art, or land art—a movement started in the 1960s—drew renewed attention to the natural world and expanded the definition of sculpture. The movement sought to reject the commercialization of art. These artists, too, went west, working in the outdoors, far away from the commercial galleries of the East Coast.

By the 1970s, artists were creating mile-wide designs on and in the landscape. Christo and Jeanne-Claude brought their *Umbrellas* and *Running Fence* to the desert, and Robert Smithson added his *Spiral Jetty* to the Great Salt Lake. Other artists, ambitious with their palette, used stomper-boards to press down wheat and other crops to stamp out designs in farmland, deserts, and other remote regions, creating works to be viewed from foot as well as from above—or, in some cases, not to be viewed much at all. Smithson drew connections between his artwork and ancient Native American forms of Earth Art, which included constructed hills in the form of animals that could be seen from space.

In a nod to environmental change, Smithson's *Spiral Jetty*, created in 1970, was often not visible when water levels were high. The giant coil of black basalt rocks was stark in its contrast to the pink-ish water of the lake. But, since 1999, as drought has lowered the water level, the 1,500-foot earth sculpture has slowly re-emerged and is now completely exposed; the rocks are encrusted with white salt crystals and the surrounding water is shallow. Thousands of people have visited the once-mysterious artwork and have taken off parts of it as souvenirs.

Andy Hughes, from the series DOMINANT WAVE THEORY
Malibu Beach, Los Angeles 2004

While Smithson surely would not rejoice in the environmental degradation that has led to such public participation with his work, provoking discussion was always part of his design. Artists such as Smithson, Michael Heizer, Christo and Jeanne-Claude, and others were interested in the aesthetic value of the art, but also in its social value. Land artists became ecological agents, creating works that facilitated discourse and deliberation and educated the community about its relationship with its environment. Many of the projects spurred community ownership and an emotional connection to the land they impacted.

Christo and Jeanne-Claude's *Running Fence* was 18 feet high and 25 miles long, running east-west through Sonoma and Marin Counties, north of San Francisco. The project included almost two years of public planning to realize construction and the cooperation of 59 ranchers whose private property it crossed. There were dozens of public hearings, three sessions at the Superior Courts of California, and a 450-page Environmental Impact Report. Although the *Running Fence* only existed two and a half weeks once it was constructed, the long build-up prompted much public debate about the land it encountered. Garnering the most attention was a 1,000-yard strip of the fence, which ran over a coastal cliff and into the Pacific Ocean. Christo and Jeanne-Claude had obtained a permit to run the fence through this fragile ecological zone, but a group called the Committee to Stop the Running Fence appealed the permit. As a result, the artists were fined $10,000 in addition to $500 per day the fence ran into the water. The visual effect of the fence appearing to rise out of the water was lauded as its most spectacular and defining feature, by art critics and the public alike, though it was the most hard fought. The result was also the permanent formation of a coastal commission for protection of the coastal area Jeanne-Claude and Christo illegally ran their fence through, part of a bill that was signed by the governor of California shortly after the project. It was a roundabout way for artists to initiate conservation legislation, and the effect was long lasting.

While this earlier land art was done mostly in the deserts of the American west, by the end of the 1970s and the beginning of the 1980s, works moved into a more public sphere. Artists like Robert Morris began engaging county departments and public arts commissions to create works in public spaces such as an abandoned gravel pit.

Christo, THE UMBRELLAS
© Tonya Evat/Sygma/Corbis

Andy Goldsworthy, **INSTALLATION AT ASSE VALLEY**
© Chris Hellier/Corbis

Herbert Bayer used a similar approach and was selected to create his Mill Creek Canyon Earthworks in 1982, which was not just aesthetic but also functional, serving as erosion control—a reservoir during high rain periods, and a 2.5-acre park during dry seasons. In 1982, Joseph Beuys staged his "ecological action" called *7000 Oaks* as part of Documenta. The artist and his assistants highlighted the condition of the local environment by planting 7000 oak trees throughout and around the city of Kassel. Just as the earthworks in the deserts of the west grew out of notions of romantic landscape painting, the growth of public art stimulated artists to pursue the urban landscape as another kind of landscape and also as a platform to engage a larger audience in a discussion of ideas and concepts about the environment.

Christo and Jeanne-Claude described themselves in their promotions as, "the cleanest artists in the world: all is removed, large scale works of art are temporary, the sites are restored to their original condition and most materials are recycled." Being an environmentally-friendly environmental artist is one of the many complications arising out of an increasingly astute artistic and scientific community, as well as a public that now speaks the language.

With environmental art today, a distinction is drawn between environmental artists who do not consider the damage to the environment their artwork may incur, and those who intend to cause no harm to nature. Despite its aesthetic and historical merits, Smithson's *Spiral Jetty* inflicted permanent damage on the landscape. Smithson used a bulldozer to scrape and cut the land, with the spiral itself impinging on the lake. If Smithson created his *Spiral Jetty* today, environmental advocates may not embrace it in the same way as they did in 1969.

Some contemporary environmental artists even set out to create work that involves restoring the immediate landscape to a natural state. British sculptor Richard Long has for several decades made temporary outdoor sculptural work by rearranging natural materials found on the site, such as rocks, mud and branches—therefore having no lingering detrimental effect on the site. Crop artist Stan Herd uses indigenous materials to create his large field works. He plots his designs and then executes them by planting, mowing, and sometimes burning, or plowing the land, inspiring the term "living sculpture." Dutch sculptor Herman de Vries, the Australian sculptor John Davis, and the British sculptor Andy Goldsworthy base their work on leaving the landscape they have worked with unharmed, though sometimes altered.

The recent work of John Grade, a contemporary artist based in Seattle, not only reflects the earthscapes, but also, for a while, becomes part of them. His works combine traditionally-conceived natural products, such as clay, wood, stone, metal, and animal hides, with space-age materials to form structures designed to spend as much as a decade outdoors going back to nature. These sculptures are designed to be exposed and worn by sun and tides, and eaten by bugs and birds. One of Grade's best-known works, *Fold*, is a large wood and resin structure, which is being slowly consumed by termites somewhere underground in Idaho. Later, it will be exhumed for display.

In the years before his death in 1973, Smithson was planning and proposing a number of reclamation projects to mining companies in the United States. He believed that the best sites for earth art were sites that had been disrupted by industry, reckless urbanization, or nature's own devastation. Along these lines, many contemporary artists with their new environmental convictions, blur the lines between art and activism. These artists connect with the land and force viewers to do so as well. At a time of heightened awareness of environmental degradation, many artists are voices for change—whether simply depicting a changing landscape, or urging human action to affect change.

Fascinated by landscapes that have been intentionally and perhaps irrevocably altered by modern human industry, Canadian artist Edward Burtynsky creates works that do not just address environmental destruction across the globe, but also paradoxically reveal the beauty of the resulting topography. His series of photographs titled *The Industrial Sublime* asks viewers to consider the tension between consumerist society's thirst for new products and ongoing sources of energy, and the need for environmental sustainability. Burtynsky, and then the viewer, find both beauty and repulsiveness in these images of consumption, manufacturing, mining, and waste disposal.

Other artists strive for optimism, celebrating nature's power of renewal, such as photographer Stephanie Lembert, whose images of pristine and lush landscapes are, in fact, depictions of reclaimed landfills around New York and Boston. The images are overlaid with text that tells the story of the transformation of these once-degraded places into healthy natural environments. In 1965, artist Alan Sonfist proposed *Time Landscape to New York City*, which became a permanent installation of native trees at La Guardia Place and West Houston Street in Manhattan. The work introduced the key environmentalist idea of bringing nature back into the urban environment.

Others use beauty to call attention to what they see as the ugliness of man's impact on the environment. Subhanker Banerjee's photographs at first glance appear to be stunningly beautiful documentary images of the northern regions of Alaska. But here the sunsets are the result of toxins released into the air, and the footprints of the polar bear represent the footprint of both nature and man onto the northern landscape. At the artist's encouragement, the photographs have been used by environmental groups as illustrations to argue against the opening up of the Arctic National Wildlife Refuge in Alaska to oil drilling. In 2008, some of Banerjee's photographs were shown at the United Nations headquarters in New York. The artist, in this instance, is no longer a passive observer depicting a pristine wilderness. Banerjee, like the romantic artists before him, traveled to remote places unfamiliar to a mass culture, but he, unlike Bierstadt or Cole, suggests that today these wildernesses are anything but untouched.

The latest iteration of environmental art and ecocriticism may be found in museums and galleries on land, but much of this art is about the ocean. Beyond the industrialization of the west and the development of the Arctic, artists and scientists are looking to the sea for evidence of man's continual struggle to advance without destruction.

Both rising sea temperatures and acidification of the ocean from the intake of carbon dioxide are due to become increasingly extreme throughout this century, along with other climate change impacts such as rising sea levels and more frequent and severe storms. Increased human consumption means increased waste, more and more of which finds its way along currents and into the ocean, where it gets tossed about and spun around. As inland trash finds water, local litter can easily become world traveled, floating across borders, changing course in ocean gyres, and breaking down underwater until a micro problem has macro consequences. Artists living along beaches collect trash as non-traditional material and artists even far inland note the scale of the ocean and of the problem, and they create work to explore their own emotional response to the degradation as well as to encourage others to find a reason for action within their visual narrative.

Mark Dion
CONCRETE JUNGLE—THE BIRDS
1992

Taxidermic birds, cardboard
boxes, tires, toy truck, wash
basin, motor oil canister, chair
cushon, rolled carpet, linoleum
flooring, wooden crates, aluminum
cans, newspaper, plastic bags,
containers, cups, bottles, other
assorted rubbish

150 x 420 x 130 cm

Courtesy of the artist and Tanya
Bonakdar Gallery, New York

Artist Mark Dion has long been associated with blurring the boundaries between human action and the natural environment through his work, with intricate installations involving the study of science and nature. Dion challenges the traditional ways in which knowledge is presented through his sculpture, photography, and works on paper. Dion suggests that our ideas about nature have led us to behave in an ecologically suicidal manner. With traditional presentations such as his series, *Cabinet of Curiosities*, Dion displays found objects and ocean trash in encased repositories. In another work, *Trichechus manatus latirostris*, a large manatee skeleton is suspended in a glass case over an assortment of tar-covered, mass produced objects, emphasizing the impact of production on nature. Tar, a central theme in Dion's work, often represents the oppressive effects humans have on organic materials. *Marine Invertebrates* combines ordinary consumer objects with models of aquatic organisms, questioning notions of classification and relationships between the natural and built environment. Installations such as *Sea Life*, a replica of a cart containing nautical-themed books and texts, and *The Documents*, a case of papier-mâché sculptures made to look like Sterling Clark's diaries during his expeditions to Northern China, look at the imperfections of history as presented through popular literature, guide books, and the subjective act of journaling.

Alexis Rockman takes the ecocritical suggestion that the apocalyptic approach may be the most accessible to his large-scale paintings of current and future environmental doom. Rockman's post-apocalyptic natural world is depicted in realistic and surrealistic detail, though his vision is not strictly imaginative. Rockman is keenly interested in natural history and biodiversity. Large-scale murals, such as *Evolution* (1992), a primeval landscape composed of a swamp and a spewing volcano, is populated with prehistoric and mutant creatures, and *Manifest Destiny* (2004) is a depiction of Brooklyn, New York, far in the future, when global warming has reduced it to a toxic wetland. Rockman has trekked to Guyana, Tasmania and Madagascar to research his work. He has consulted scientists and architects, who aid him in suggesting what an environmentally degraded future might look like. Rockman then creates the paintings in his studio, based on his photographs, sometimes manipulated with Photoshop software and images he culls from the Internet. The ocean has long been a subject of his imagined futures. *Biosphere: The Ocean* (1994) depicts a shark with a long, bionic sawfish beak, and *Still Life* (1993) features a pile of fish and marine specimens, evoking reference to the 1935 James Whale horror film *Bride of Frankenstein.*

Artist Chris Jordan has focused a large body of his recent work in photography and film to document the accumulation of plastic debris in the world's oceans, most notably its effect on the Laysan albatrosses of Midway Island, where adult albatrosses mistake pieces of plastic for squid and fish and feed them to their chicks, killing the young. Jordan says he has faith in the human ability to correct a course and hopes that haunting images will cause us to feel and, in turn, act.

Photographer Susan Middleton also spent time photographing the albatrosses at Midway Atoll, as well as exploring the Northwest Hawaiian Islands. On assignment for *National Geographic*, Middleton photographed an albatross chick on Kure Atoll, eventually naming the chick "Shed Bird," before it was discovered dead one morning. Photographs of the necropsy of Shed Bird show an open chest cavity, exposing a stomach that was perforated by plastic and which contained two disposable cigarette lighters, several bottle caps, an aerosol pump top, a piece of a shotgun shell, broken clothespins, toys, and more. In total, Shed Bird was stuffed with 12.2 ounces of plastic and other indigestible material, which led to malnutrition, dehydration, and eventually death.

In 2006, during a trip to South Point, Hawai'i, the southern tip of Hawai'i's big island, artist Pam Longobardi discovered massive debris deposits that had accumulated on the shoreline. Forever changed by this discovery, Longobardi has since focused her artwork on ocean advocacy. That same year she founded the Drifters Project, an environmental intervention project that focuses on plastic in the oceans and the ability of marine debris to travel long distances. In 2008, she began working with community groups to expand the scale and scope of the project to new locales and to create collaborative public art.

Photographer Andy Hughes of the UK depicts beach litter by showing its incongruous beauty. His work focuses on the accumulation of garbage washed up on the shores where he surfs. Images of plastic and glass, like stunning still lives, capture the conflict between the color interjected into nature and the permanence of these remnants of consumption.

Exhibiting in Canada and the United States, Max Liboiron's artistic work is a mix of experimentation, cultural laboratory experiment, and environmental activism, focusing on issues of environmental sustainability and plastic pollution. She uses scavenged trash in both large installations and delicate miniatures. Her work can be seen as a defense of man. Through public interaction with her work, she demonstrates that people can be creative in problem solving and sincere in seeking a common good.

Anne Percoco traveled to Vrindavan, India, in 2008 from the US and was inspired to make inventive use of materials at hand to make a statement about consumerism and the environment. The resulting work, *Indra's Cloud*, was a floating sculpture made of more than a thousand empty water bottles bundled together to resemble a cloud. Percoco had observed an annual retreat of a Shivananda Yoga group and watched foreign students going through water bottles at a surprising rate and the bottles piling up in the hallways. Percoco was struck by the need for the group to use such a vast quantity of mineral water as a result of the environmental devastation of the Yamuna River.

As a result of this experience, Percoco set out to draw attention to the severely polluted condition of the river. As she learned about the Krishna stories, it brought to mind the story of Indra, the "middle-man" of the water, and the disruption that results when human beings forget that they are simply stewards and not the ultimate controllers of nature's water resources. After sewing together more than a thousand bottles, mostly gathered from the foreign yogis, she had them carried in sections to the Yamuna. There she assembled them into the cloud-like float, which she then sailed around the town, talking to residents about the river. Eventually the cloud was dismantled and the bottles were used to grow saplings for trees.

Similarly, Mandy Barker's work aims to engage with and stimulate an emotional response in the viewer by combining a contradiction between initial aesthetic attraction and a subsequent message of awareness. Her recent photographic projects have been focused on the representation of material debris in the sea and more recently on the mass accumulation of plastic in the world's oceans.

Anne Percoco
INDRA'S CLOUD
2009

Plastic bottles, rope, boat
Site-specific project in Vrindavan, India
Sponsored by the Asian Cultural Council and
Friends of Vrindavan

Her two series, *Soup* and *Snow Flurry,* are composed of beautiful images of objects floating against a dark background, like stars in space. Upon close inspection, the objects are thousands of pieces of ocean trash, floating and infinitely expanding into the background.

A lifelong collector, artist Fran Crowe uses the trash that she finds along the English east coast as the material for her artwork. She estimates that she has collected (and recycled) over 100,000 pieces of plastic debris while walking on beaches near her home. She sees her installations as a kind of self-portrait of ourselves: a contemporary— and disturbing—archaeological dig. Her work *Souvenir Packs* is an installation of hundreds of pieces of trash collected from beaches around the world, packaged with irony into "souvenirs."

Elizabeth Leader is surrounded by the impacts of abandonment and pollution in her home in Buffalo, New York. The sights of this post-industrial city inform her artwork. She employs a wide range of materials and techniques to communicate her ideas about people, the environment, and disposal. Leader focuses on individual actions—how the trash that is left out on the curb, or tossed along roads, or dumped into waterways becomes, on a larger scale, brown fields, shuttered factories, desolate neighborhoods and polluted waters. This trail reveals our history and our constantly developing technology. Leader's *Troubled Waters* is a series of large mixed media drawings that grew out of her concern for what we are doing to our waterways and oceans.

Based in Helsinki, Finland, Tuula Närhinen's images are derived from scientific investigation, along with a dry sense of humor. Her works are installations that consist of a series of photographs, drawings or sculptures. She has built cameras that produce images of what she imagines the world looks like to a fly or a bear, developed methods for letting trees trace the shape of wind on their branches, and found techniques for using cold winter air to create patterns on paper and glass. Her topics are landscape, natural phenomena and environmental issues, including marine debris. Her projects *Mermaid Tears* and *Frutti di Mare* consist of c-prints on aluminum and floating sculptures in aquarium-like plastic cases partially filled with water. The floating sculptures are made of plastic waste washed up on the seashore in Helsinki. The photos of the half-submerged creatures

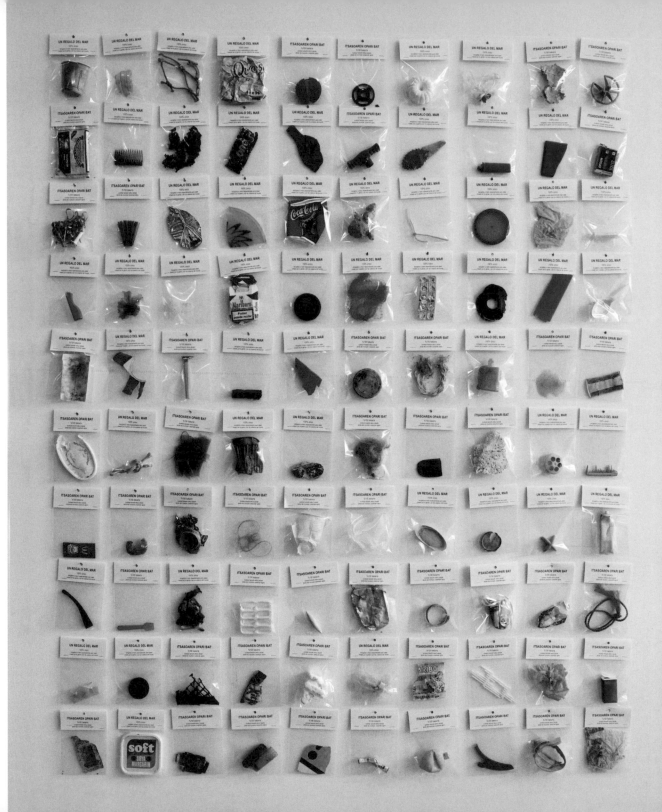

make them look colorful and charming, not unlike the wonders we see floating by behind the glass of the local aquarium. But viewed in their white plastic cases on metal shelves, they look more like organized trash. Among clumps of seaweed or flotsam washed up on the shore, it is common to find 'mermaid tears,' small plastic pellets resembling fish eggs. Plastic resin pellets have widely spread across the world's seas. Some are the raw materials of the plastics industry spilled in transit from processing plants. Others are granules of domestic waste that have fragmented over the years. The mermaid tears remain everywhere and are almost impossible to clean up, and the plastic is then ingested by seabirds and various marine organisms. Närhinen uses these mermaid tears to create jewelry and small sculptures.

Evelyn Rydz creates detailed drawings based on her photographs from various coastlines of lost and discarded objects that have washed ashore. Focused on the narratives these found objects have gathered on their journeys, Rydz explores the history and possible interconnection between these displaced objects. Her recent works use found rope from East Coast shorelines to explore the paths of ocean currents around the globe. She creates large-scale colored pencil drawings and a group of small drawings in series such as *Gulf Piles, Driftlines, 1000 years, Castaways*, and *Drifting Islands*.

John Dahlsen is an Australian contemporary artist exploring environmental issues through photography. He uses found objects, primarily plastic bags, from Australian beaches as subject matter. He discovered marine debris as an art medium when he was collecting driftwood on a remote stretch of the Victorian coastline. He had intended to make furniture. Instead, he stumbled upon vast amounts of plastic ocean debris. The new palette of color and shape was a revelation to him, as was the environmental impact of plastic.

Dianna Cohen is a Los Angeles-based artist and the co-founder of the Plastic Pollution Coalition, a group that addresses plastic pollution. She was inspired to co-found the group by her work as an artist—because her chosen material is the ubiquitous plastic bag. With the Coalition, she hopes to raise awareness of non-degradable plastic in our ocean and everyday strategies to cut down the amount of plastic we use and throw away.

Fran Crowe, **PRESENT FROM MUNDANE**
Mixed media

Even in Alaska, where one assumes to still find nature untouched by man, artists are creating work with ocean trash as material and message. Photographer Tim Remick, graphic artist Karen Larsen, and mixed-media and installation artist Sonya Kelliher-Combs explore Alaska's shores for evidence of pollution, particularly the trash from the 2011 tsunami in Japan that is now washing up on Alaska's shores.

In a time of great environmental change, artists offer visual records and interpretations of how human action and consumption are global, and not just local issues. The artists are looking at their own beaches, as collectors and researchers, to create artwork to convey this contrast between man and nature, to suggest the impact of consumption and the things we discard into our environment, and to reveal their own personal connections to the ocean.

Artists offer public insights that they hope will lead to a greater understanding, broader perspective, and celebration of our natural world. As adept observers, artists are uniquely poised to offer personal insights and shared views of the environment—views that are complex and multi-faceted, rather than the romantic presentations of artists of earlier times. This new environmental art is not passive or detached. It suggests activism, not observation; science, not romanticism; and new knowledge, not conventional wisdom. These artists require multiple perspectives and fields to imagine situations and outcomes that venture beyond the traditional.

Elizabeth Leader, **PLASTIC REEF**
Pencil drawing

TURNING THE TIDE ON MARINE DEBRIS

Nicholas Mallos, Ocean Conservancy

They had harnessed the energies of the sun and fossil fuel, diverted a large part of the fresh water for their own use, acidified the ocean, and changed the atmosphere to a potentially lethal state. 'It's a terribly botched job of engineering,' the visitors might say…

E.O. WILSON, *SOCIAL CONQUEST OF EARTH*

What people have the capacity to choose, they have the ability to change.

MADELEINE ALBRIGHT

Perspectives from "Away"

33o 52' 39.73" N, 146o 39' 49.79" W

Glassy, indigo-blue water as far as the eye can see. Clouds crisp and white against the blue sky, rivaling only the water for the bluest of blues. The sun suggests 3 o'clock, and its intensity and sweltering heat support the claim. This is the North Pacific Gyre, better known to many as the "Great Pacific Garbage Patch," or the floating "island of trash." The reality is that there is no floating island of garbage twice the size of Texas. In fact, sitting atop the mast, 90 feet above the deck of the 152-foot tall ship *Kaisei*, Big Blue could not have appeared more true to her name. From my perspective, the Gyre's waters look as pristine as any I've ever seen; a deep blue penetrating down some 9,840 feet below. But things are not always as they seem, and nowhere does this hold more true than in the Gyre, where, equipped only with the naked eye, the whole truth is not revealed.

Do not let appearances fool you; the marine debris problem in the Gyre is serious. It is not, however, due to a floating island of trash so immense that hotels could be built upon it, vacationers could visit it or surfers could catch an epic break on its coastline. In the Gyre, there are plenty of discernible items afloat (like plastic bottle caps and fishing floats) but as is the case in all the world's gyres, the majority of debris lurks just below the water's surface, silent and inconspicuous to anyone or any creature who happens upon it. Here in the center of the Gyre—some 1,100 miles from the nearest land mass—exorbitant quantities of fragmented plastics float in the upper 3 to 6 feet of the water column.

ATOP THE *KAISEI* MAST
Photograph by Nicholas Mallos, Ocean Conservancy

Scoop your hand just below the water's surface, and it emerges clad in a glove of brightly colored plastic confetti. How did these plastics arrive here? We don't know for sure, but the plastics' journey most certainly commenced on one of the seven continents. All forms of plastics or debris that enter the ocean began on *terra firma*. Many of these plastics started their journey to the Gyre as large, everyday household goods like detergent, shampoo or beverage bottles. Others, like fishing nets and buoys, moved into a stream of commerce at the nearest bait and tackle shop that ultimately resulted in their end of useful life in the Gyre.

From atop the mast of the *Kaisei*, the Pacific's blue waters stretch uninterrupted in all directions to the distant horizon. But beyond that horizon, 1,700 miles southeast, lies Midway Atoll and the final resting place for many of the sub-surface and floating plastics in the North Pacific. I have had the great fortune to visit this amazing place. Midway consists of three small islands that, combined, measure less than 2.5 square miles. Part of the Papahānaumokuākea Marine National Monument, Midway is at the northwestern end of the Hawaiian archipelago, roughly equidistant from Asia and North America.

Midway is truly "out there." The atoll's nearest population center is Honolulu, which is 1,200 miles to the southeast and a five-hour trip by plane. Words alone do not suffice to accurately describe Midway. Having reviewed the literature, perused the photos and watched the films, I thought I was prepared for my 2010 research trip. But I was not. Midway is more than beauty. Lying literally in the middle of nowhere, it is a deeply surreal place, mystical and transformative. The sounds that constantly fill the air are deafening yet spiritual. At night, Bonin petrels, small nocturnal seabirds, flock the skies in the hundreds of thousands, emitting shrieks eerily synonymous with their avian counterparts in Alfred Hitchcock's, "The Birds." During the day, petrel shrills are replaced by the relentless chatter of more than 1 million Laysan and black-footed albatross. Midway is the largest nesting colony for Laysans and the second largest for black-foots. Offshore, the roar of the ocean is equally sonorous with a monster swell that breaks over the atoll's fringing reefs.

Seventy years ago, Japanese and U.S. military forces pummeled these islands with artillery during the Battle of Midway, one of the most important naval battles of the Pacific Campaign of World War II. It remains inconceivable how any living thing—plant or animal—could have survived the pounding these islands endured, but many have. And seven decades later, Midway's robust flora and fauna are living testaments to the resilience of our natural world. But despite decades without troops or thunderous artillery, these islands remain endangered by a far more persistent threat manufactured by humankind: plastics. The Northwestern Hawaiian Islands act like a filter in the North Pacific, ensnaring large amounts of drifting fishing gear and debris on its fringing reefs and sandy shores. Some shorelines around the world serve as an ocean plastics source, meaning debris and other rubbish washes into the marine environment through wave and tidal action. Shores that are receivers of ocean plastics and floating debris act as oceanographic sinks. Midway's central position in the Gyre makes it a sink.

The daily accumulation of large debris on Midway's shores—almost entirely plastics—threatens the monk seals and sea turtles that haul out on its beaches and forage in the atoll's shallow waters. With only 1,200 monk seals remaining in the world, the loss of even a single animal can substantially impact the species. Entanglement in debris and ingestion of plastics are serious concerns for Hawaiian green turtles as well, a subspecies that is genetically distinct from all other green sea turtles found throughout the world.

Each year, approximately 5 tons (nearly 10,000 pounds) of plastics are brought to Midway not by currents or wind, but in the stomachs of birds (Klavitter, 2010). Seabirds, most notably albatross, are not exempt from the risk posed by non-plastic debris, but the plastics threat they face on Midway is extreme. Mothers and fathers forage at sea for weeks in search of fish eggs, squid and other prey in hopes of nourishing their newly hatched chicks that wait anxiously hundreds or even thousands of miles away. All too often, adult albatross return to Midway and regurgitate offerings more reminiscent of a convenience store than that of a natural albatross diet. Plastic bottle caps, cigarette lighters, fishing floats and great quantities of plastic fragments are now part of the albatross diet. Unlike their parents, Laysan chicks do not possess the ability to regurgitate; once consumed, these plastics are often fatal to chicks through a variety of mechanisms including starvation, stomach rupture or asphyxiation.

I witnessed the unintended consequences of plastics on Laysan and black-footed albatross during a two week stay on Midway in 2010, where my colleagues and I completed a preliminary assessment of plastics' impacts on marine wildlife.

TOADFISH AND
MOTOR OIL
Photograph by
Nicholas Mallos,
Ocean Conservancy

GREENS HAULED OUT
ON TURTLE BEACH
Photograph by
Nicholas Mallos,
Ocean Conservancy

LAYSANS OF MIDWAY
Photograph by
Nicholas Mallos,
Ocean Conservancy

A LAYSAN AMONG BUOYS
Photograph by
Nicholas Mallos,
Ocean Conservancy

Trekking around the islands, it was impossible to avoid plastics; colorful shapes of all sizes speckled the ground while other types of plastic protruded from the guts of recently perished albatross chicks. These lifeless forms rested only steps from the nests where their parents had diligently nurtured the newly hatched chicks. It was a stark reminder of the fine line between life and death on Midway Island.

By analyzing the stomach contents of a deceased chick found lying on the old airstrip amid the sprouting grass, I further deconstructed the plastics-albatross relationship. Finding specimens was not difficult. Hundreds of dead chicks were available on that same runway. Each was distinguishable from the other by the colors of the plastics in each bird's gut. The stomach contents of my single albatross included nine plastic bottle caps, two strands of dental floss, one 5-inch orange fishing float, 103 miscellaneous plastic pieces, six pumice stones and 60 squid beaks—the latter two items being the only naturally-occurring components of a Laysan's diet. While this was only a single sample, the total mass of the synthetic stomach contents was roughly 100 grams, about the same as a quarter-pound hamburger.

The magnificent albatross on Midway Island are not just birds. As part of our natural world, they are an object lesson in how we are treating our planet. Albatross, along with the other inhabitants of Midway, are the recipients of the collective impacts of the "out of sight, out of mind" mentality that permeates our global society. While I have been fortunate to visit these animals in this far-off world, one need not travel to Midway or the North Pacific Gyre to witness the persistence and proliferation of marine debris. The ocean plastics crisis is just down the road or over the nearest sand dune. Whether you live in New York City, New South Wales or Papua New Guinea, the trash you find says volumes about who we are.

Insights from Citizen Scientists

In 1986, one woman decided to do something about the appalling amounts of trash on her local Texas beach. Compelled not only to clean up the trash she found, Linda Maraniss also was curious to know which trash items were the most prevalent. From that first beach cleanup, Ocean Conservancy's International Coastal Cleanup© was born. It has since grown into an unparalleled global effort that mobilizes volunteers around a single purpose: to keep trash out of the ocean. Each year, up to 800,000 citizen scientists participate in the Cleanup for the purpose of removing trash and debris from local beaches, rivers, waterways or favorite underwater dive spots. More than 10 million volunteers, representing over 150 countries, have come together over the past quarter century, making the Cleanup the world's largest volunteer effort on behalf of ocean and waterway health. The collective effort has kept more than 164 million pounds of trash and debris from entering the ocean, while documenting each item collected. The data are compiled by Ocean Conservancy and aggregated to create the Ocean Trash Index—an annual item-by-item, location-by-location account of the most persistent forms of trash littering our beaches and ocean.

Each year, the numbers in the index are astounding, but the data only offers a glimpse into the problem. Globally, the magnitude of debris far exceeds what is documented during the Cleanup, because much of the world's coastline remains undocumented. Still, after almost three decades, Cleanup volunteers have itemized over 180 million pieces of debris.

Cleanup volunteers have found all types of trash, including cigarette butts, food wrappers and takeout containers, plastic bags, abandoned fishing gear—even the proverbial kitchen sink. Over the decades of collecting information, items made of plastic have always been at the top of the list. Plastics make up roughly 84 percent of all items collected during the Cleanup; if you include unidentifiable plastic fragments, this percentage soars even higher. Every year, the top 10 most common items found are consistently comprised of the plastic items we use in our everyday lives to eat, drink and recreate (Fig 1). Plastic bags, beverage bottles, bottle caps and lids, and an array of other single-use disposable plastic products are found in greater abundance than other items.

The scale is astonishing. During the 2012 Cleanup, volunteers found enough food packaging for someone to get takeout for breakfast, lunch and dinner every day for 858 years. Do the math starting at the first Cleanup and you can get takeout for the next 15,000 years. The amount of oil required to manufacture the 10 million plastic bags collected over this same period equates to roughly 23,000 gallons of gasoline, enough fuel to drive a car around the Earth three times (75,000 miles).

Trash is not just alien to the ocean; it is dangerous to a range of marine organisms that rely on a healthy marine ecosystem. During the Cleanup alone, volunteers have documented more than 4,400 entangled animals, including a range of sea turtles, sharks, porpoises and seabirds. And don't forget that this is just what was found during a single day's effort *(Fig 2)*. Accounts of physical interactions between plastic debris and invertebrates, fishes, turtles, seabirds and mammals in the scientific literature indicate the magnitude of impact is far greater, with estimates ranging from 267 to 663 species affected (Laist, 1997; CBD, 2012). These scientific studies, combined with anecdotal observations, indicate plastic packaging materials and fishing gear are most responsible for negative impacts to organisms. Most notably, fishing nets and fishing line are most responsible for ingestion-related mortality in marine mammals (Baird and Hooker, 2000; Florida Department of Natural Resources, 1985; Gomercic et al., 2009; Gorzelany, 1998; Jacobsen et al., 2010; Levy et al., 2009), whereas plastic bags, small plastic products (like bottle caps), hard plastic fragments and virgin plastic pellets comprise the majority of ingested plastics found in fish, seabirds and turtles (Balazs, 1985; Carr, 1987; Cawthorn, 1985; Colabuono et al., 2009; Laist, 1987; Lazar, 2011; Ryan, 2008; Stamper et al., 2009).

When plastic items enter the ocean, they do not decompose. They become brittle and break down by mechanical means, fragmenting into smaller and smaller pieces over time, continuing to persist even at the microscopic level (Barnes et al., 2009; Thompson et al., 2004). Plastics are doubly toxic in the marine environment: first, toxic substances added to plastics during production can leach into surrounding environments. Second, toxic substances already present in the water can attach to plastic surfaces. As plastics fragment into smaller pieces, the total surface area of the original plastic debris increases. Plastics concentrate contaminants in greater concentrations than their surrounding environment as surface area increases. Increased fragmentation in the ocean therefore also augments the threat of plastics to marine animals (Teuten et al., 2009; Rochman et al., 2013). In both cases, these processes can put marine animals at risk (Endo et al., 2005; Teuten et al., 2009; Rochman et al., 2013).

(Fig 1)

2012 INTERNATIONAL COASTAL CLEANUP® TOP TEN ITEMS FOUND

The resulting item-by-item, location-by-location Ocean Trash Index that Ocean Conservancy compiles each year provides the only global snapshot of the marine debris littering coasts and waterways around the world.

2,117,931
cigarettes/cigarette filters

1,140,222
food wrappers/containers

1,065,171
plastic beverage bottles

1,019,902
plastic bags

958,898
caps/lids

692,767
cups/plastic silverware

611,048
straws/stirrers

521,730
glass beverage bottles

339,875
beverage cans

298,332
paper bags

Adapted from designs and data created by Ocean Conservancy.

(Fig 2)

THREATS TO WILDLIFE

Graphics depict global stats from 1986-2012
International Coastal Cleanups.

253 mammals
found entangled in rope,
fishing gear, and other debris

188 reptiles
found entangled in crab traps,
fishing nets, or plastic bags

45 amphibians
found entangled in beverage
bottles and debris

1,551 birds
found entangled in fishing
line and nets

995 invertebrates
found entangled in crab traps,
fishing nets, or plastic bags

1,440 fish
found entangled in fishing line,
or plastic bags

17 coral & sponges
found entangled in fishing line,
or other debris

Adapted from designs and data created by Ocean Conservancy.

Shifting Our Ocean Relationship

The International Coastal Cleanup has provided an incomparable snapshot of the most persistent trash items on our world's coastlines, but at present it's addressing the symptoms of marine debris and not the disease itself. In essence, it's a bandage, not a cure. In his 1968 essay, Garret J. Hardin described society's abhorrent pollution problem as a tragedy of the commons in reverse: "Here it is not a question of taking something out of the commons, but of putting something in ..."(Hardin, 1968). Almost 50 years later, the tragedy of the commons remains alive and well in our ocean. The exorbitant input of plastics into our marine environment is perhaps the greatest failure we face as a global society.

One hundred years ago, plastics did not exist. Plastic pollution certainly was not part of our everyday vernacular, and a "sustainable" lifestyle was simply referred to as "living." Reusability and waste reduction were matters of necessity and at times the difference between life and death. Yes, plastics certainly have made our lives easier and in many ways better, but at a time when their production is rampant while their impacts on ocean and human health are not wholly understood, we must slow down and take a moment to examine our course. In our current plastics landscape, out of sight may mean out of mind, but it certainly does not mean out of the ocean.

Plastic pollution is personal. It affects our local economy, our local beaches and our health and food safety. The everyday decisions we make have very real, lasting implications for the well-being of the ocean and ourselves. If we are content to allow our burgeoning ocean plastics crisis to continue unabated, then we must accept the plausible scenario of future generations without a productive, clean and resilient marine ecosystem.

Turning the Tide on Plastics: A Manifesto

Despite the current unremitting global production of plastics, there is still a beacon of hope on the horizon, and its light is getting brighter and brighter. At its core, marine debris is not an ocean problem; it is a people problem. And because people are at the center, this means we can solve it if we have the vision and the temerity to confront the problem head-on.

The ocean and coasts are our greatest public trusts. As a public resource, the ocean does not belong to those with the fastest boats, the biggest nets or the largest market share—it belongs to all of us. Yet, to date, we've repeatedly allowed too much to be taken out of the ocean and have allowed far too much to be put into it. The increasing degradation of the ocean from plastic pollution is perhaps the most tangible example of how society's private choices impact our public resources. Indeed, 500,000 volunteers turn out each September to clean up after the rest of us.

These are our resources and as such, "we the people" should no longer accept that the ocean is the final receptacle for our throwaway society. We need change. It is time for all of us—citizens, private businesses and public officials—to embrace our collective power to stop trash from ever reaching our coasts and waterways. Now is the time for us to embrace a deeper commitment to a healthy ocean and pledge to end the need for the International Coastal Cleanup once and for all. To meet this challenge, we need a holistic approach that tackles the problem at every level of responsibility. To succeed, no single person, entity or law will suffice. Everyone has a role to play.

Action I: Redefine consumers' relationship with convenience—disposable is no longer acceptable.

Change must start with us, the consumers of products that end up in the ocean. It is unfair for us to demand change by the plastics industry, product manufacturers and government while we—the users of these products—do not accept responsibility for our personal consumption habits. Look around: It is virtually impossible to look more than a few feet without finding an item that has a lifespan of less than 30 seconds after the consumer uses it. Single-serve plastic stirrers, coffee creamers, individual plastic-wrapped candies packaged in yet more plastic . . . the list goes on and on. Combine this with items like bottled water and food wrappers and you quickly realize we live in a world dominated by disposable plastics.

Cleanup data show that convenience items are much of what is found on our coasts and in waterways. Much of this is surely left behind by individuals who litter, either intentionally or unintentionally, and despoil the very environment they've come to enjoy. Our global society has been built on a mentality of convenience, which to date has intrinsically been linked to disposability. Intervening here must be the first step in a comprehensive solution, for convenience need not equal waste.

Fifty years ago it did not. Minimalist lifestyles and the need for reusability were the norm prior to the introduction of plastics in the marketplace. In fact, the plastics industry spent millions of dollars in the 1960s to persuade consumers that throwing stuff away was acceptable precisely because a philosophy of conservation and reuse was so ingrained in people's daily lives (Freinkel, 2011).

Single-use plastics have made us speed up our lives, but now it is time to slow back down. As consumers, we must redefine our relationship with convenience so that it again becomes synonymous with durability, not disposability. We can start by re-evaluating our daily behaviors and making choices to use reusable bottles, eliminating our reliance on one-time-use disposable plastics. It should go without saying that everyone should always recycle. These individual, incremental changes may seem insignificant, but taken collectively they can greatly improve ocean health.

Action II: Support business and product innovation through consumers' collective purchasing power.

Regular people like you and me must support businesses that are true innovators. While our individual and collective choices are imperative to reduce plastics' impacts on marine ecosystems, equally important are the signals these choices send to the marketplace. As consumers we must not underestimate the leverage we possess in our collective purchasing power. The purchasing decisions we make control the market; the marketplace does not control us. When we buy items packaged in excess plastic or take an extra bag at the grocery store, these actions reinforce a feedback loop that drives increased plastics production. If we channel our purchasing power to businesses that account for the ocean and the broader environment in their products' lifecycles, we create the opportunity for new businesses to thrive and encourage existing companies to accelerate the innovation process up and down the supply chain.

Action III: Support a transition to a circular economy.

Businesses must recognize both their contribution to the problem of plastic pollution and embrace their power to be an agent for change. With few exceptions, the global manufacturing industry is predicated on an outdated linear business model that converts resources into products that are then sold, used and ultimately destined for disposal. In the future, we need to shift to a "circular economy" where little distinction is made between waste and resources. To do so, we must demand innovative manufacturing processes that approach product production from a closed-loop "cradle-to-cradle" perspective.

If we as a global society move toward a fundamentally different model—one of a circular economy—products will be designed with the expectation that after their useful life, they will be recovered and the materials reused in new and creative ways. Such a shift will rebuild capital of all kinds—financial, manufactured, human, social and natural—and ensure a continuous flow of technological and biological materials through the "value circle" (Ellen Macarthur Foundation, 2013). Through this approach, a product's life cycle can be designed with a restorative mentality, where end-of-life products are not viewed as trash or waste but as valued commodities, and innovation extends beyond the manufacturing process. In a fully circular economy, an entirely new relationship can be fashioned between product and producer, one that redefines the lens through which we view objects—not as disposable goods, but as potential resources.

Action IV: Advance public policies that incentivize producers to internalize the environmental costs of the products from which they profit.

As we move toward a circular economy, the marketplace itself will need to be supported by progressive public policy that extends beyond individual product bans and instead incentivizes and motivates demonstrable improvements in production and manufacturing. Moving toward a circular economy will require public policies that entice and reward market leaders and punish those market laggards who refuse to do so. Embracing policies like Extended Producer Responsibility (EPR) is one way to achieve this. EPR places some responsibility for a product's end-of-life environmental impact on the original producer and retailer of that product (Walls, 2006). These policies incentivize producers to innovate around design changes that reduce waste, including improved recyclability and reusability, reduced material usage and downsized products. A diverse range of policies can be considered under the EPR umbrella, but at the core each acknowledges the real cost of products in the marketplace, accounting for end-of-life impacts and resource-intensive manufacturing, packaging and transport processes.

At present, society only pays for the economic value of a product's consumptive use. Whether through producer take-back mandates or combined fee/subsidy approaches, an EPR framework applies an intrinsic value to the goods that remain once their immediate use has been exhausted. Once these costs reflect the true value of a product, both pre- and post-consumer, the precious resources we've previously viewed as trash will simply become too valuable to toss.

Action V: Invest in the science needed for better decision-making.

Robust science must underpin effective decision-making. At present, there is an opportunity for a wider set of scientists to embrace ocean plastics as an important topic of scientific inquiry. While there is enough scientific understanding to justify societal action now, additional scientific inquiry will be useful as we refine private and public-sector strategies moving forward. Because ocean trash originates from a variety of sources, identifying the primary origins of plastics will boost our ability to implement effective mitigation strategies that address plastics at their source. It is imperative to more accurately determine how much harmful debris is in our ocean, more fully explore the impacts of marine debris on marine species and ocean economies, and determine the impacts of marine debris on human health and local economies. In particular, analyzing the risk of marine debris across multiple levels of biological organization is a prerequisite to understanding which species function as indicators of ocean health. New science will also be indispensable in identifying the most prominent sources of plastic debris for which individual behavior and/ or industry-based solutions can be implemented. In total, a new interdisciplinary research agenda can help better elucidate the scale and scope of the impacts of plastics on marine ecosystems now, and inform policy to better confront these risks moving forward. Advancing this science requires a commitment from funders who recognize that controlling toxic inputs to ocean ecosystems is critical to the ability of oceans to provide the services upon which we depend in the long term.

Action VI: Shift the burden of proof to producers and manufacturers.

The current body of science, combined with anecdotal evidence, is more than sufficient to justify action to abate the impacts of plastics on marine ecosystems. The core issue, however, is more than just plastics in our environment; it is about shifting the burden of proof from society and scientists to industry and others who profit from plastics. Plastics that are safe for human use might not be safe for the ocean—and therefore humans—but this thinking is not currently part of the original calculus. Industry should therefore be required to demonstrate that each product sent to the marketplace is safe for human consumption and the environment, both during and after consumer usage. Employing such a precautionary approach would instill a "benign by design" philosophy in the manufacturing process that holds manufacturers accountable for designing products that are safe throughout their life cycles. These principles, when applied to goods and products most commonly found littering beaches and waterways, will make certain that the products pose minimal risk to marine animals and ecosystems.

Conclusion: A New Ocean Ethic

The ocean impacts each of us every day. It provides the air we breathe, the water we drink, the food we eat, and the whales, seals and polar bears we love. Ocean places like the North Pacific Gyre and Midway Atoll are the final "away," the ultimate resting places for the plastics from our disposable culture. The plastic debris challenge facing these environments is immense, but solutions built on the actions of individuals, companies and elected officials are at hand. What remains is the will to build a collective movement to make a lasting difference. Doing so will not be easy, but enhanced individual responsibility, new industry leadership, innovative science and smart public policy represent the needed components of a comprehensive solution to the ongoing challenge of marine debris *(Fig 3)*.

The time is now for a commitment to collective action. If we succeed, then in a not-too-distant September, we can all gather at the beach for the International Coastal Cleanup© only to realize that there is no trash to pick up.

(Fig 3)

10 THINGS YOU CAN DO
FOR TRASH-FREE SEAS

❶ CAN IT
use a trash can with lid

❷ TAP IT
drink tap water in
a reusable bottle

❸ STOW IT
be a green boater

❹ BUTT IN
write your legislator asking
for policies that address
ocean trash

❺ REMOVE IT
clean up with the
international coastal cleanup
www.signuptocleanup.org

❻ BUTT OUT
use an ashtray so cigarette
butts don't reach waterways
and the ocean

❽ REUSE IT
take along your reusable
coffee mug, picnic supplies
or shopping bag

❾ REFUSE IT
buy less to reduce the
amount of manufactured
items winding up as trash
in the ocean

❿ REINVENT IT
send emails to companies
asking them to reduce
packaging and create new
ocean-friendly materials

Adapted from designs and data created by Ocean Conservancy.

CHINA · CHINA · NEW ZEALAND · HONG KONG

TAIWAN/CHINA · JAPAN · ASIA* · * · ASIA*

TAIWAN/CHINA · HONG KONG · ASIA* · CANADA · CHINA

ASIA* · ASIA* · KOREA · JAPAN · CHINA

CHINA · UAE/JAPAN · KOREA · JAPAN · RUSSIA*

ASIA* · INDONESIA · JAPAN · TAIWAN · UNITED STATES

*SPECIFIC AREA UNDETERMINED

REFERENCES

Baird, R.W., and Hooker, S.K. (2000). Ingestion of plastic and unusual prey by a juvenile harbour porpoise. Marine Pollution Bulletin. 40(8):719-720.

Balazs, G.H. (1985). Impact of ocean debris on marine turtles: entanglement and ingestion. In: Shomura, R.S., and Yoshida, H.O. (Eds.). 1985. Proceedings of the Workshop on Fate and Impact of Marine Debris, November 27-29, 1984. NOASS Technical Memorandum. NMFS, NOAA-TM-NMFS-SWFC-54.

Barnes, D.K.A., Galgani, F., Thompson, R.C., and Barlaz, M. (2009). Accumulation and fragmentation of plastic debris in global environments. Philosophical Transactions of the Royal Society Bulletin. 364:1985-1998.

Carr, A. (1987). The impact of persistent plastics on the developmental ecology of sea turtles. Marine Pollution Bulletin. 18(6):352-356.

Cawthorn, M.W. (1985). Entanglement in, and ingestion of, plastic litter by marine mammals, sharks, and turtles in New Zealand waters. In: Shomura, R.S., and Yoshida, H.O. (Eds.). 1985. Proceedings of the Workshop on Fate and Impact of Marine Debris, November 27-29, 1984. NOASS Technical Memorandum. NMFS, NOAA-TM-NMFS-SWFC-54.

Colabuono, F.I., Barquete, V., Domingues, B.S., and Montone, R.C. (2009). Plastic ingestion by Procellariiformes in Southern Brazil. Marine Pollution Bulletin. 58:93-96.

Convention on Biological Diversity (2012). Impacts of Marine Debris on Biodiversity: Current Status and Potential Solutions. CBD Technical Series No. 67.

Ellen MacArthur Foundation (2013). Towards the Circular Economy: Opportunities for the consumer goods sector. Executive Summary. Plastics Europe. Plastics – the Facts 2012. Analysis of European plastics production, demand and waste data for 2011.

Endo, S., Takizawa, R., Okuda, K., Takada, H., Chiba, K., Kanehiro, H., Ogi, H., Yamashita, R., and Date, T. (2005). Concentration of polychlorinated biphenyls (PCBs) in beached resin pellets: Variability among individual particles and regional differences. Marine Pollution Bulletin. 50(10):1103-1114.

Florida Department of Natural Resources. (1985). Summary of Manatee Deaths—1985. Results of the Manatee Recovery Program. Bureau of Marine Research. St. Petersburg, Florida.

Freinkel, S. (2011). Plastic: A Toxic Love Story. New York: Houghton Mifflin Harcourt. Print.

Gomercic, M.D., Galov, A., Gomercic, T., Skrtic, D., Curkovic, S., Lucic, H., Vukovic, S., Arbanasic, H., and Gomercic, H. (2009). Bottlenose dolphin (Tursiops truncatus) depredation resulting in larynx strangulation with gill-net parts. Marine Mammal Science. 25(2):392-401.

Gorzelany, J.F. (1998). Unusual deaths of two free-ranging Atlantic bottlenose dolphins (Tursiops truncatus) related to ingestion of recreational fishing gear. Marine Mammal Science. 14(3):614-617.

Hardin, G.J. (1968). The Tragedy of the Commons. Science. 162(3859):1243.

Jacobsen, J.K., Massey, L., and Gulland, F. (2010). Fatal ingestion of floating net debris by two sperm whales (Physeter macrocephalus). Marine Pollution Bulletin. 60:765-767.

Klavitter, J. (2010). Wildlife Biologist, U.S. Fish and Wildlife Service. Personal communication, February 2010.

Laist, D.W. (1987). Overview of the biological effects of lost and discarded plastic debris in the marine environment. Marine Pollution Bulletin. 18(6) Supplement 2:319-326.

Laist, D.W. (1997). Impacts of marine debris: entanglement of marine life in marine debris including a comprehensive list of species with entanglement and ingestion records. pp. 99-140 in: Coe, J.M., and Rogers, D.B. (Eds.), Marine Debris: Sources, Impacts and Solutions. Springer Verlag, New York, New York.

Lazar, B., and Gračan, R. (2011). Ingestion of marine debris by loggerhead sea turtles, (Caretta caretta), in the Adriatic Sea. Marine Pollution Bulletin. 62(1):43-47.

Levy, A.M., Brenner, O., Scheinin, A., Morick, D., Ratner, E., Goffman, O., and Kerem, D. (2009). Laryngeal snaring by ingested fishing net in a common bottlenose dolphin (Tursiops truncatus) off the Israeli shoreline. Journal of Wildlife Diseases. 45(3):834-838.

Rochman, C.M., Hoh, E., Hentschel, B.T., and Kaye, S. (2013). Long-term field measurement of sorption of organic contaminants to five types of plastic pellets: implications for plastic marine debris. Environmental Science & Technology 47:1646-1654.

Ryan, P.G. (2008). Seabirds indicate changes in the composition of plastic litter in the Atlantic and south-western Indian Oceans. Marine Pollution Bulletin. 56(8):1406-1409.

Stamper, M.A., Whitaker, B.R., Schofield, T.D. (2006). Case study: morbidity in a pygmy sperm whale (Kogia breviceps) due to ocean-borne plastic. Marine Mammal Science 22:719-722.

Teuten, E.L., Saquing, J.M., Knappe, D.R.U., Barlaz, M.A., Jonsson, S., Björn, A., Rowland, S.J., Thompson, R.C., Galloway, T.S., Yamashita, R., Ochi, D., Watanuki, Y., Moore, C., Viet, P.H., Tana, T.S., Prudente, M., Boonyatumanond, R., Zakaria, M.P., Akkhavong, K., Ogata, Y., Hirai, H., Iwasa, S., Mizukawa, K., Hagino, Y., Imamura, A., Saha, M., and Takada, H. (2009). Transport and release of chemicals from plastics to the environment and to wildlife. Philosophical Transactions B. 364:2027-2045.

Thompson, R.C., Olsen, Y., Mitchell, R.P., Davis, A., Rowland, S.J., John, A.W.G., McConigle, D., and Russell, A.E. (2004). Lost at sea: Where is all the plastic? Science. 304(5672):838.

Walls, M. (2006). Extended Producer Responsibility and Product Design: Economic Theory and Selected Case Studies. Resources for the Future. DP 06-08.

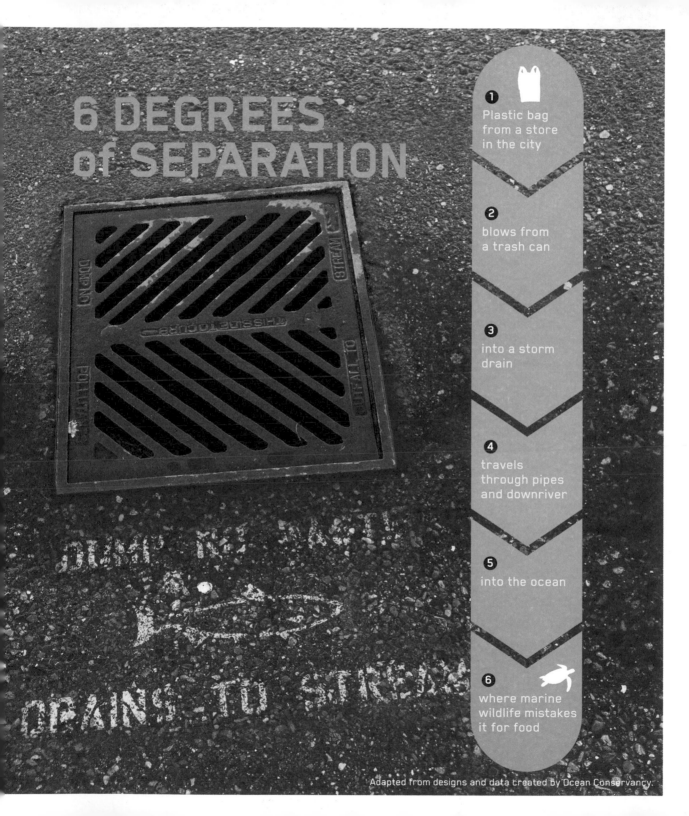

6 DEGREES of SEPARATION

1 Plastic bag from a store in the city

2 blows from a trash can

3 into a storm drain

4 travels through pipes and downriver

5 into the ocean

6 where marine wildlife mistakes it for food

Adapted from designs and data created by Ocean Conservancy.

PLASTIC
BEACH

Donovan Hohn

In 1992, a container of bath toys, marketed under the brand name Floatees, fell off a cargo ship into the North Pacific. Oceanographers turned the toy spill into an accidental drift experiment, tracking the toys and using a computer model to predict where in the world the currents would carry them. In 2005, journalist Donovan Hohn set out to follow the trail of the toys wherever it led, from a factory in China, to the high Arctic, to the heart of the North Pacific Subtropical Gyre. The following essay is adapted from Hohn's best-selling book about his travels, Moby-Duck: The True Story of 28,800 Bath Toys Lost at Sea and of the Beachcombers, Oceanographers, Environmentalists, and Fools, Including the Author, Who Went in Search of Them.

THE SOUTHERNMOST EDGE OF HAWAI'I is also the southernmost edge of the United States of America and feels like the southernmost edge of the world. In the fall of 2007, I traveled there to see a wonder I'd heard about, Kamilo Beach, known to some as Plastic Beach. I stayed in Na'alehu, the southernmost town on the Big Island, and for frugal reasons I took a room at the Shirakawa Motel, the southernmost motel and quite possibly the cheapest one on the entire Hawaiian chain.

The windward side of the Big Island is not what most of us imagine when we dream our Hawaiian dreams. Downtown Hilo, once the capital of a booming sugar trade, reminded me of cities in the American Rust Belt, only with palm trees and rain, lots of rain—a sun-baked, rain-soaked, tropical Sandusky. To get to Na'alehu from Hilo, you drive over the Kilauea volcano, which is active but tame, the lava bubbling forth in a steady simmer but never, in recent history, shooting forth a shower of fire and brimstone. You travel through dilapidated towns made derelict by the collapse of Hawai'i's sugar industry, past bungalows with corrugated metal roofs, past a barn-size movie theater with a sea turtle painted on its corrugated metal roof and a closed sign hanging in its dark entrance even on Saturday nights (or at least on the

STYROFOAM FOUND ALONG GORE POINT, ALASKA
Photograph by Kip Evans

particular Saturday night I drove past it), and past walls of lava rock stacked in the manner of fieldstones in rural New England.

Then at the southern edge of the southernmost town you reach the Shirakawa Motel, advertised by a rusty metal sign protruding out of the foliage. The Shirakawa Motel is a rundown compound of buildings also roofed in metal and encircled by a jungle of banana trees, palm trees, and monkeypod trees, and ti plants, which have big droopy leaves and resemble the sort of tropical flora one encounters in the waiting rooms of dentists. The sky there is smoky gray and the rain falls in torrential outbursts, loud as drumsticks on the canopy of leaves.

***

The rain stops. Within moments, butterflies emerge to suck nectar from the flowering bushes, the flowers of which resemble little red starbursts. From outside my little room come the sounds of insects—cicadas, perhaps, or crickets, or some tropical variety of noisy insect. A dog barks. The striated world visible through the slanted jalousies above the queen-size bed is bright and green. Someone is playing Hawaiian reggae. Chickens run wild here. This is their native habitat, after all. I think of chickens as animals indigenous to a Nebraskan farmyard, but here they emerge from tropical forests all around the Shirakawa Motel. Every so often, a rooster crows. The flora and fauna here are as lush as the economy. But, the architecture is moribund. If the residents left, it wouldn't be long before the motels and movie theaters vanished into the foliage. Yes, this feels very much like the edge of the world. It feels much farther from the tourist-infested boulevards of Waikiki than it is.

One morning I drive farther south still, to the stretch of coastline known as South Point. The lush jungle gives way to sprays of sugarcane. Then to ranchland. The sun comes out. The road is cracked. Horses and cattle graze on windswept pastures over which loom rows of derelict windmills—an alternative energy plan gone bust. I drive on, until the pavement ends, at which point I park my rental car and continue on foot down a red dirt road that branches and splits among green hills carved by storm surges and rain. Every now and again an SUV or pick-up rattles past. At the terminus of the land, blue breakers obliterate themselves against gnarled tumors of black igneous rock. I keep walking, searching, combing, stumbling over the crumbled lava rock. I follow the shoreline, the sun beating down.

I begin to see what I've come looking for—the colorful confetti of plastic debris. In almost every cove there are drifts of it, piled up in crescents many feet deep. There's fishing gear, shattered fishing floats, and tangles of nets. If I stop and stoop down and look closely, I can pick out more commonplace objects—detergent bottles, Nestlé lids, golf balls. The coves sort the plastic. In one there's an abundance of jar lids. In the next is an abundance of nets. In others, there are dozens of plastic popsicle sticks. Do fishermen like popsicles? Or did these formerly belong to children on a seaside holiday? I stumble upon the top of a garbage can on which I read the word RUBBERMAID. I don't find any Floatees, but I do find a green plastic soldier aiming his rifle at a pebble of pumice, and then a few feet away the wreckage of a plastic jeep that by the look of it has been terrorized by an albatross. On and on I walk, under the subtropical sun, and on and on the lava rock is littered with wrack. In one cove, the colorful confetti of plastic comes in on the blue waves.

The next morning, I station myself in the motel courtyard, where a peace pole, a little obelisk inscribed with pacifistic messages in many languages, tilts amid an island of flowers from which butterflies sip. A silver pick-up truck arrives. At the wheel is Bill Gilmartin, a retired, pony-tailed biologist formerly employed by Fish and Wildlife. On the door of his truck is a green sign that reads HAWAII WILDLIFE FUND. His truck isn't your ordinary truck. Gilmartin paid mechanics to turn his pick-up truck into a dump truck. The bed, hoisted by some sort of hydraulic mechanism, can tip. You wouldn't know it looking at it. I climb into the passenger seat, and we zoom south, past the lava rock walls, toward South Point. "I started out in debris collection on the Northwestern Hawaiian Islands in 1982," Gilmartin says. "You get into this business in your gut and your heart and it's hard to back out. I got into this business because of the first monk seal pup I rescued."

In the Northwestern Hawaiian Islands, whose shores are washed by the southern edge of the North Pacific Subtropical Convergence Zone, locus of the so-called Garbage Patch, federal agencies have been staging one of the biggest marine debris projects in history. Since 1996, using computer models, satellite data, and aerial surveys, the National Oceanographic and Atmospheric Administration (NOAA), the Coast Guard, and the U.S. Fish and Wildlife Service had by 2007 located and removed more than five hundred metric tons of derelict fishing gear in hopes of saving the endangered Hawaiian monk seal from extinction.

TWENTY TONS OF TRASH WASH UP AT SOUTH POINT, HAWAI'I, EVERY YEAR.

Pam Longobardi,
DRIFTERS
2006
Fufi crystal archive digital print,
33x50 in.

Administrators at NOAA's Marine Debris Program point to the project as an example of success, but the results have been mixed at best. NOAA incinerates the debris at a power plant on the outskirts of Honolulu, converting it into electricity. But unless they're supplemented by a metropolitan supply of garbage, such incinerators operate at a loss. In places that cannot support them, like maritime Alaska, the only option is to bury debris in landfills, and in many coastal communities, landfill space is already running short. Furthermore, although wildlife biologists are now finding fewer monk seals entangled in debris, they are also finding fewer monk seals, period.

Like the threats facing the Laysan albatross, the poster bird of plastic pollution, the threats to monk seals, biologists explained to me, are legion. There's the increase in shark predation caused in part by the dredging of lagoons. There's the loss of breeding grounds to the rising, warming seas. There's the toxic waste dumped by the U.S. military, the toxoplasmosis contracted from cat pee, and the spread of West Nile virus. Of all the perils monk seals face, the most memorable one to my mind is this: changing phocine demographics have led to a shortage of females and, in response to this shortage, horny bull seals have grown murderously aggressive, drowning and suffocating female pups while attempting to mate with them, and thereby reducing the female population further still.

Although the number of entanglements has fallen since the cleanup efforts began, the rate of entanglement in 2004 was actually seven times higher than in 2000. What accounts for the spike? During El Niño years such as 2004, the boundaries of the North Pacific Subtropical Convergence Zone shifted south, engulfing monk seal habitat. Even in more typical years, the ocean deposits an estimated fifty-two tons of debris on the Northwestern Hawaiian Islands.

South Point is far south of the North Pacific Subtropical Convergence zone, the heart of garbage, and still, according to Gilmartin's calculations, twenty tons of trash wash up there every year. "This coast is so bad," he says, "debris comes up faster than you can keep it clean. It gets continuous onshore winds and it's in the way of the easterly currents. Even if everything stopped today, it would keep washing in." Gilmartin doesn't expect to triumph in this Herculean labor he's chosen to undertake. He just can't think of a better way to spend the weekends of his retirement than this—hauling debris in his truck.

We pull up to a gate and I clamber out to open it, noticing beside it, lashed to a post, a yellow sign commanding me not to approach monk seals. We ramble along the red dirt road, slowly, jouncing, and soon enough we've traveled farther, I can tell, than I made it the day before on foot.

The clouds this morning are gray and low. Out the window, through the shrubbery, I catch glimpses of ocean. We come to a big pile of bright blue bags, left here by a cleanup group. Gilmartin and I hurl them into his truck. Then we come to a big mess of derelict net, which Gilmartin hooks to his winch, mounted just behind the cab of his truck. The engine whines, and slowly, the cable hauls the heavy net in.

At last, we arrive at the edge of Kamilo Beach, which is everything I'd been led to expect: a beach of plastic, finely ground. There are twigs of driftwood, and lava rocks, and a few errant coconuts, but they're far outnumbered by the shrapnel of debris. This is where the flotsam I saw yesterday ends up. Washing in and out, the surf and the sun grind it down and the currents deposit it here. Until a flood, tide, or a storm surge sweeps it out to sea, the plastic sand remains.

It's almost beautiful, all the unnatural colors and shapes in such a natural landscape, beautiful because incongruous. It occurs to me now, as it has before, that this is what I have been pursuing these past months, this is what I found so spellbindingly enigmatic about the image of those plastic ducks at sea—incongruity. We have built for ourselves out of this New World a giant diorama, a synthetic habitat. But, travel beyond the edges or look with the eyes of a serious beachcomber, and the illusion begins to crumble like flotsam into sand. Incongruities emerge, and not just visual ones.

In 1878, nine years after its invention, a sales brochure promoted celluloid as the salvation of the world. "As petroleum came to the relief of the whale," the copy ran, "so has celluloid given the elephant, the tortoise, and the coral insect a respite in their native haunts; and it will no longer be necessary to ransack the earth in pursuit of substances which are constantly growing scarcer." Ninety years later, in the public mind, plastic had gone from miracle substance to toxic blight. In 1968, at the dawn of the modern environmental movement, the editor of *Modern Plastics* argued that his industry had been unfairly vilified. Plastic was not the primary cause of environmental destruction, he wrote, only its most visible symptom. The real problem was "our civilization, our exploding

population, our life-style, our technology." That 1878 sales brochure and that 1968 editorial were both partly, paradoxically right. Petroleum did save the whale, in the short term. And plastics did save the elephant, not to mention the forest, for a while. Modern medicine would not exist without plastic. Personal computing would not exist either. Safe, fuel-efficient cars would not exist without them. Besides, plastics consume fewer resources to manufacture and transport than most alternative materials do. Even environmentalists have more important things to worry about now. In the information age, plastics have won. With the wave of a magical iPhone and a purified swig from a Nalgene jar, we have banished all thoughts of drift nets and six-pack rings, and what lingering anxieties remain, we leave at the curbside with the recycling.

Never mind that only 5 percent of plastics actually end up getting recycled. Never mind that the plastics industry stamps those little triangles of chasing arrows into plastics for which no viable recycling method exists. Never mind that plastics consume about 400 million tons of oil and gas every year. Never mind that so-called green plastics made of biochemicals release greenhouse gases when they break down. What's most nefarious about plastic, however, is the way it invites fantasy, the way it pretends to deny the laws of matter, as if something—anything—could be made from nothing; the way it is intended to be thrown away but chemically engineered to last. By offering the false promise of disposability, of consumption without cost, plastic has helped create a culture of wasteful make-believe, an economy of forgetting.

At Plastic Beach, I crouch down, scoop up a handful of multi-colored sand and sift it through my fingers. This then is the destiny of those toy animals that beachcombers fail to recover: baked brittle by the sun, they will eventually disintegrate into shards. Those shards will disintegrate into splinters, the splinters into particles, the particles into dust, the dust into molecules, which will circulate through the environment for centuries. The very features that make plastic a perfect material for bathtub toys—so buoyant! so pliant! so smooth! so colorful! so hygienic!—also make it a superlative pollutant of the seas. No one knows exactly how long a synthetic polymer will persist at sea. Five hundred years is a reasonable guess. Globally, we are currently producing 250 billion tons of plastic every year, and no known organism can digest a single molecule of the stuff, though plenty of organisms try.

No one—not environmentalists, not oceanographers—will tell you that plastic pollution is the greatest man-made threat our oceans face. Depending who you ask, that honor goes to global warming, or overfishing, or agricultural runoff. In a way, plastic's greatest threat may be symbolic, which is not to say that it is empty or cosmetic. Most pollutants are invisible. Saturated with CO_2, our oceans have begun to acidify. Our scientists tell us this, though—you can't discern pH levels with the human eye. But unlike many pollutants (mercury, for instance, or CO_2), there is no natural source of plastic and therefore no doubt about how to apportion blame. We're to blame. And because we can see it, plastic is a powerful bellwether of our impact on the earth. Where plastics travel, other, invisible pollutants—pesticides and fertilizers from lawns and farms, petrochemicals from roads, sewage tainted with pharmaceuticals—usually follow. There is no such thing as natural plastic, and because it is so visible, it provides a meaningful—and alarming—example of our impact on the earth. As numerous conservationists have told me, the plastic problem when compared to other environmental problems, should be easy to solve. And yet we show no sign of solving it.

Not long before I traveled to South Point, Sylvia Earle, formerly NOAA's chief scientist, delivered a speech on marine debris at the World Bank in Washington, DC. "Trash is clogging the arteries of the planet," Earle said. "We're beginning to wake up to the fact that the planet is not infinitely resilient." For ages, humanity saw in the ocean a sublime grandeur suggestive of eternity. No longer. Looking at the debris at Gore Point or South Point, we see that the ocean, vast as it is, is perhaps smaller and more vulnerable than we'd thought; that we have, perhaps, taken dominion of the watery wilderness, too.

With his truck brimful of plastic debris, Gilmartin and I head from the edge of the world to the nearest dump.

Pam Longobardi, **PLASTIC WORLD**
2008

Fufi crystal archive digital print,
50x33 in.

OCEAN CONSERVATION:

FACTS, FORESIGHT AND FORTITUDE

Howard Ferren, Alaska Sealife Center

IN THE 1950S, I WAS A YOUNG BOY who loved the beach. I watched the vast horizon stretch to the sky and let the reckless ocean surf chase my sunburned feet. I dug in the sand of the East Coast beaches for mole and sand crabs. A few years later, as a surfer, I evaluated wave sets, felt the buoyancy of saltwater, and anticipated storms and the long shore drift, undertow, and force of the water.

At that time, I wasn't thinking about climate change and sea level rise, coastal erosion or the changing beach gradient and orientation. I wasn't thinking about the impacts of trawlers and draggers. I wasn't aware of the relationship between fossil fuel combustion and increasing carbon dioxide concentrations in our atmosphere. And I didn't even know what an ecosystem was. I didn't appreciate how vital healthy oceans were to our lives and prosperity.

In the 1960s and 1970s, countering conservation discussions and advocacy to end water pollution, the catchy slogan "the solution to pollution is dilution," suggested limitless oceans. This view made it easy to ignore how our personal actions had growing impacts on our ocean.

We are now beginning to understand the many impacts of human behavior on our marine ecosystems. We stand before a battery of monumental challenges that will require foresight and fortitude to confront. Ocean conservation is the protection and preservation of ecosystems in oceans and seas. It is a multidisciplinary action designed to integrate biological, chemical and physical oceanography, and to evaluate human impacts, including growing populations and food security, economic enterprise models, fisheries management policy, and emerging strategies such as marine protected areas and marine spatial planning. Ocean conservation is designed to advance ocean health.

One of the many monumental challenges we face is ocean acidification. We know that oceans absorb carbon dioxide. Human activity, including combustion of carbon-based fuels, has elevated the carbon dioxide concentration in our atmosphere, which has a direct

TRASH BARREL ON OCEAN FLOOR
Photograph by Kip Evans

relationship to the absorption of carbon dioxide in our ocean. Dissolution of carbon dioxide in water creates carbonic acid that transforms to carbonate and predominantly bicarbonate ions, which means less carbonate is available for shellfish to generate shells. Some of the shells of concern are those of pteropods, which are small planktonic mollusks at the bottom of the marine food chain and that are a key food source for many other species in our oceans. Since the start of the industrial revolution, oceans have absorbed over 120 billion tons of carbon dioxide.[1]

Oceans might seem limitless when standing on a beach viewing the horizon toward space but, with the growing human population, consumption, waste, and technology, they are a finite resource. Instead of thinking about our oceans as separate water bodies based on bordering landmasses, we must think of our oceans as one volume of water—a global ocean. Activities in one part of the world, either in the ocean or the atmosphere, can contribute to outcomes in another part of the world. This is an important concept when discussing marine debris as a global ocean conservation priority.

We must also understand human population scale and growth in order to tackle ocean resource sustainability. In the last 200 years, the global human population has experienced exponential growth. This growth was fueled by technological advances and improved health standards, which led to increased human survival, industrialization of food supplies and food distribution, and increased extraction and use of natural resources. We see over that time the demand a growing global population has had on extracting protein from the global ocean. Our record of large fish harvests is a record of depletion. Only 10% remains of the biomass of all large fish species such as tuna, swordfish, marlin, and large ground fish such as cod, halibut, skates, and flounders.[2] Sharks have been swimming the global ocean for 400 million years, yet 32% of the open-ocean or pelagic shark species are threatened with extinction largely due to overfishing and by-catch.[3] The depletion of large apex predators could have significant cascading effects on marine ecosystems. The record of depleted fish species is also exemplary of cropping down the food chain. As we eliminate or reduce large species, we shift to harvesting smaller species nested further down the food chain or food web. Our capacity to continually extract fish (and historically, mammals) from the sea exceeds the rate, and hence capacity, of the sea to reproduce on our demand timescale.

Effective fishery regulation and management, such as the Magnuson-Stevens Fishery Conservation and Management Act, encourages sustainable fisheries practices at the national and regional levels. Still, biodiversity continues to diminish.[4] Species that once thrived with larger spawning adults have been selectively harvested so that now only smaller fish are found, resulting in an up to 35% decrease in stock biomass and, in many cases, increased predatory mortality.[5] We decimate benthic habitats and species by drag fishing.[6] In areas of the global ocean where fish protein is in demand, dynamite has been used to harvest fish, which also damages habitat, impairing the area to support fish and invertebrate populations.

With the increased demand and utilization of resources, comes an ever-increasing waste stream. We have sufficiently polluted regions of the world ocean through watershed runoff of various pollutants to create dead zones. In 2004, the United National Environmental Program reported 146 dead zones in the world's oceans. In 2008, that number had increased to 405. Dead zones are caused by an increase in chemical nutrients, a process called eutrophication, that boosts production and decomposition of phytoplankton leading to a depletion of dissolved oxygen. Not all dead zones are caused by human activities. Some dead zones are the result of natural upwelling of nutrients, although chemical fertilizer runoff and sewage discharge are increasingly responsible.

Pollution or nutrient runoff is also contributing to the destruction of the earth's coral reefs. Coral reefs are structures made from calcium carbonate secreted by colonies of tiny animals. These reefs are found in areas where nutrient concentration is low. Siltation and algal growth caused by human activities, watershed runoff and nutrient waste can smother coral. Additionally, coral mining, dynamite blasting to kill fish, sea temperature increases associated with climate change, sea level rise and ocean acidification all can play a role in coral reef impairment or destruction. Scientists estimate 10% of the world's coral reefs are now dead and 60% are at risk due to human activities. We also know that coral reefs are home to more than 25% of all marine species, which are then also at risk.

10% OF THE WORLD'S CORAL REEFS ARE NOW DEAD, AND 60% ARE AT RISK.

Given these facts and competing forces, we must step up our efforts to moderate actions that damage the health and balance of marine ecosystems and their functions. It is reassuring to know that many nations, organizations, and individuals are engaged in this effort to examine the causes of the many threats to the global ocean commons. Across the spectrum of battlefronts, efforts to advance global polices on managing behaviors and ocean resources continue to mature—everything from improvements and innovations in technology to target harvested species, to reduction of by-catch of less marketable or harvest restricted species,[7] to scientific advances to assist wise resource management decisions such as ecosystem-based fisheries management.[8] Even in impoverished economies, where people once overexploited local marine resources, people now embrace their local marine ecosystems as sustainable treasures, rather than pillaging them for short term and finite gain.[9]

While progress is being made on some fronts of ocean conservation, new threats emerge—most notably, marine debris. Defined by the National Oceanic and Atmospheric Administration (NOAA), marine debris is any persistent solid material that is manufactured or processed and directly or indirectly, intentionally or unintentionally, disposed of or abandoned into the marine environment or the Great Lakes. Resulting in global and diverse impacts, marine debris as a converging topic provides a framework to discuss many facets of ocean conservation.

Marine debris is predominantly composed of plastic. It is generally acknowledged that marine debris is now 60-80% plastic, reaching 90-95% in some areas.[10] Marine debris is a generic term covering items such as liquid containers, cigarette butts, monofilament line, plastic bags, needles, flip-flops and the thousands of other products and by-products of our invention. Marine debris also includes derelict fish and crab traps, munitions dumped at sea, abandoned fishing nets and fish aggregating devices. In addition to individual items lost or discarded that are found as debris, it has been estimated that less than 1% of cargo containers shipped annually are lost at sea—not a large percentage, but, in actual numbers, up to 10,000 cargo containers[11] are lost annually from ships.

The scope of issues we face with marine debris parallel and complicate other ocean threats. Debris may contribute to entanglement and trapping of many species of crustaceans, mammals, fish and birds already depleted through directed harvest, by-catch, or loss of habitat. For example, ghost nets may continue to ensnare, trap, and kill numbers of fish long after the nets are lost or discarded. According to the Institute for European Environmental Policy (2005), Baltic Sea ghost nets may be responsible for 4-5 percent of the commercial level harvest after 27 months.[12] In more severe cases, data about deep water fisheries in the northeast Atlantic suggests that the catching efficiency of ghost nets stabilizes at 20-30 percent of commercial catch rates after 45 days and that some nets may continue to catch lesser amounts for more than eight years after being lost. They also report that in the deepwater fishery in the northeast Atlantic, "around 25,000 nets may be lost or deliberately discarded each year, with a total length of around 1,250 km." In a study of derelict blue crab traps, 25,000 derelict crab traps were removed and documented from Virginia waters between the years 2009-2011, many still actively killing crabs.[13] With annual trap losses estimated at 30% in that fishery, an additional 100,000 derelict traps may be added to those already lost and actively killing not only blue crabs, but Atlantic croakers, oyster toadfish and white perch. Millions of organisms are potentially lost each season given that experimental traps show 50 crabs captured per season.

Marine debris is both macro and micro in scale, so the mechanisms of impact vary from large-scale entanglement to micro-scale plastic items that are ingested, causing injury and death. Birds, fish, sea turtles and marine mammals are all impacted by entanglement in plastic products and ingestion of plastics. As we learn more about plastics in the marine environment, new areas of concern emerge including nanno plastics and manufactured micro plastics used as exfoliants in cosmetics. Research is beginning to shed light on micro plastic particle impacts[14] and how high concentrations of hydrophobic organic contaminants are known to be associated with plastics in the marine environment, which may impact animals upon ingestion.[15] Ultimately, humans are a top consumer of marine organisms and may also be the final repository of many of the accumulating plastic by-products and associated chemicals.

We must confront the challenges of plastic, the expanding waste of our culture that enters the global ocean. Plastics are synthetic, and they are aggregating on our beaches and in our global ocean at an astonishing rate and with high volume. Human population scale, global economic growth, universal adoption of plastic as an inexpensive, durable, lightweight, versatile material for thousands of products, adoption of many single-use products, and few repurposing or recycling options globally, results in monumental production of plastic waste. Much of this plastic is finding its way directly or indirectly into our global ocean.

People of our global ocean are mobilizing for these challenges. The 5th International Marine Debris Conference held in 2010 is evidence of both the problem and the emerging global efforts to stem the tide of plastic marine debris. Representatives from more than 40 nations were present at the conference convened jointly by the National Oceanic and Atmospheric Administration (NOAA) and the United Nations Environmental Program (UNEP). As a result of the conference, the Honolulu Strategy was developed, which serves as a framework for a comprehensive and global effort to reduce the ecological, human health, and economic impacts of marine debris globally.[16]

We need to sustain the global ocean for future generations. Marine debris is a solvable problem. Human foresight and fortitude are needed to enter a more hopeful future.

1 CNRS (2008, Ma 29). Ocean Acidification and Its Impacts on Ecosystems. Science Daily.
2 Myers, R.A., Worm, B. 2003. Rapid Worldwide Depletion of Predatory Fish Communities. Nature 423: 480-483.
3 Dulvy, N.K. et al. 2008. You can swim but you can't hide: the global status and conservation of oceanic pelagic sharks and rays. Aquatic Conserv: Mar. Freshw. Ecosyst. DOI: 10.1002/aqc
4 Worm, B., et al. 2006. Impacts of Biodiversity Loss on Ocean Ecosystem Services. Science 314: 787-790.
5 Audzijonyte, Asta, et al. 2013. doi: 10.1098/rsbl.2012.1103 Biol. Lett. 23 April 2013 vol. 9 no. 2 20121103.
6 Bottom Trawling Impacts on Ocean, Clearly Visible from Space. ScienceDaily. http://www.sciencedaily.com/releases/2008/02/080215121207.htm
7 Lewison, R. L., et al. 2004. Understanding impacts of fisheries by catch on marine megafauna. Trends in Ecology and Evolution vol. 19 no. 11.
8 Pikitch, E. K., et al. 2004. Ecosystem-based Fishery Management. Science 305: 346-347.
9 Aalbersberg, B. et al. 2005. Village by Village: Recovering Fiji's Coastal Fisheries. World Resources Institute. http://www.girda.no/wrr/050.htm
10 Moore, C. J. 2008. Synthetic polymers in the marine environment: A rapidly increasing, long-term threat. Environmental Research. 103 (2): 131-139.
11 USA Today Report. August 8, 2006. http://usatoday30.usatoday.com/money/world/2006-08-03-cargo-problems-usat_x.htm
12 Brown, J. et al. 2005. Ghost Fishing by Lost Fishing Gear. Final Report to DG Fisheries and Maritime Affairs of the European commission. Fish/2004/20. Institute for European Environmental Policy / Poseidon Aquatic Resource Management Ltd joint report.
13 Havens, K. J., et al. 2008. The Effects of Derelict Blue Crab Traps on Marine Organisms in the Lower York River, Virginia. North American Journal of Fisheries Management 28: 1194-1200.
14 Brown, M. A., et al. 2008. Ingeted Microscopic Plastic Translocates to the Circulatory System of the Mussel, Mytilus edulis (L.). Environ. Sci. Technol. 42: 5026-5031; Andrady, A. L. 2011. Microplastics in the marine environment. Marine Pollution Bulletin. 62: 1596-1605.
15 Teuten, E. L. et al. 2007. Potential for Plastics to Transport Hydrophobic Contaminants. Environ. Sci. Technol. 41: 7759-7764.
16 http://www.google.com/#hl=en&sclient=psy-ab&q=Honolulu+strategy&oq=Honolulu+strategy&gs_l=hp.3...289140.293134.3.293466.17.14.0.3.3.0.423.2749.0j1j4j2j2.9.0...0.0...1c.1.8.psy-ab.Hn1h2gvSN2k&pbx=1&bav=on.2,or.r_qf.&bvm=bv.44770516,d.cGE&fp=1fbe153d2657d67d&biw=1707&bih=1209

BUOY FOUND ALONG THE COAST OF MONTAGUE ISLAND, ALASKA
The island, in the Gulf of Alaska and at the entrance to Prince William
Sound, has been subject to unprecedented amounts of ocean trash
transported by wind and currents from Japan's March 2011 tsunami.
Photograph by Tim Remick

NOWHERE IS REMOTE:

VOYAGE TO THE NORTHWESTERN HAWAIIAN ISLANDS

Susan Middleton

Laysan Island

IN THE SUMMER OF 1999, I HAD THE GOOD FORTUNE to visit Laysan Island and camp there for six days, in what would be my first exposure to the Northwestern Hawaiian Islands (NWHI). I was working on a project focusing on rare and endangered native plants and animals of Hawai'i, with my collaborator David Liittschwager, and we wanted to represent the Leeward Islands as well as the main Hawaiian Islands. After consulting with the U.S. Fish and Wildlife Service (USFWS), which was the overseer of all of the Northwestern Hawaiian Islands except Kure Atoll (managed by the State of Hawai'i), we were advised to visit Laysan since it has the richest terrestrial ecosystem in the NWHI. Passage would be arranged for us by ship on one of the routine field camp resupply missions. The USFWS supported our work on the island by supplying camp gear and food, as well as the expert guidance of their field personnel.

Before departure, I underwent training in quarantine procedures, National Oceanic and Atmospheric Administration (NOAA) ship protocol, health guidelines and requirements, and emergency medicine techniques. I was embarking on an adventure, one that would take me to a place distinctively different from any of my previous field locations on the main Hawaiian Islands. The packing alone was an enormous ordeal. Laysan's quarantine requires that all soft goods, including clothing, backpacks, camera straps, shoes—anything that is not hard and smooth-surfaced—must be new, straight off the shelf, and frozen for 48 hours. These rules intend to prevent alien seeds and insects from hitchhiking to the island on visitors' gear. All "hard" items, including cameras, cases, and tripods, had to be carefully inspected and cleaned. Even though I was accustomed to the rigors of packing for fieldwork, these strict quarantine regulations and the remote location added several complicated layers of mindfulness. Once established on Laysan, I would be simply out of luck if I discovered I had forgotten something. I knew I must arrive with exactly what I needed, plus backups in case

LAGOON AT KURE ATOLL, NORTHWESTERN HAWAIIAN ISLANDS
Photograph by Susan Middleton

something broke. At the same time, I couldn't pack excessively, since everything would be transported by Zodiac from the ship to the island, often in rough seas, and then hand-carried to the campsite.

For me, complying with the rigorous quarantine procedures began a process of understanding the uniqueness and fragility, and indeed the value, of the Northwestern Hawaiian Islands. In the past, when I worked in museums, I exercised a similar care and attention in the handling of precious cultural objects; I realized that the assemblages of life on these islands were no less precious and no less a part of our heritage.

Never before had I been to a place where wildlife so clearly reigned supreme. I knew of the USFWS refuge mission of placing "wildlife first," but there I actually experienced it. Every decision was guided by its potential impact on the resident island community: the birds, seals, turtles, and the native plants. The mission affected every move I made, from the food I ate (nothing with seeds that might sprout, like tomatoes) to the places I walked (on the beach I could disturb resting monk seals, and inland I ran the risk of crushing the ubiquitous nesting burrows of various bird species). I had the overwhelming sense that I was a visitor in someone else's home.

At the same time, I recognized the necessity for human intervention on the island to help correct our past and present blunders. In the past, Laysan suffered from a series of disastrous human activities, beginning with guano mining and exploitive feather hunting in the late 1800s, and the 1905 release of rabbits as a food source. The rabbits did as rabbits do, multiplying at their fabled rate and devouring vegetation. By 1920 they had transformed Laysan into a wasteland, and the once thriving ecosystem had crashed. The long process of restoration began with the elimination of the rabbits by the Tanager Expedition in 1923; it continues to this day under the management of the Fish and Wildlife Service. Much of the native vegetation is now restored, while alien weeds continue to be eradicated. What started as a tragedy has become a success story, and the rich native flora and fauna of Laysan today bears witness to a painstaking restoration program, repairing the extensive damage inflicted by human activities.

I photographed throughout my six days on the island, focusing on the rare Laysan ducks and Laysan finches, as well as native plants, many species of seabirds,

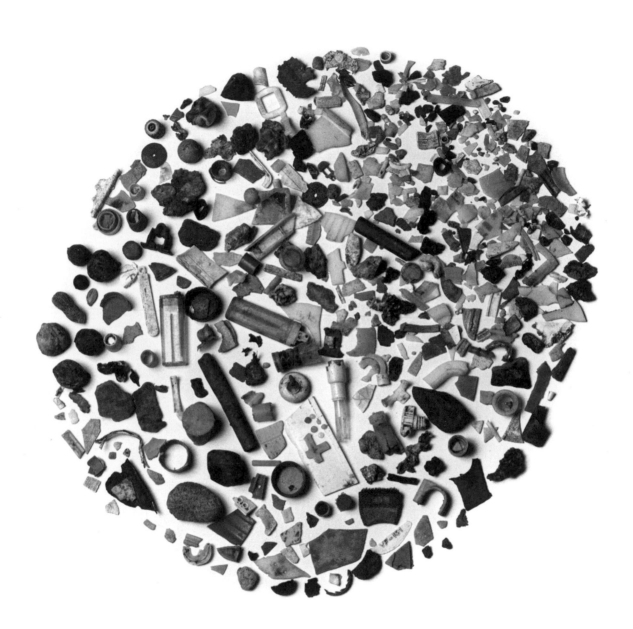

THE ENTIRE STOMACH CONTENTS OF 'SHED BIRD'
Photograph by Susan Middleton

and landscapes and seascapes, much of them littered with marine debris. I was shocked to see massive amounts of marine debris strewn across the beach: floats, plastic lighters, plastic shoes, toys, thousands of liquor bottles, television tubes, laundry baskets, light bulbs, plastic containers of all sizes and shapes, medical waste – the flotsam and jetsam of civilization. Ropes, nets, and lines presented entanglement hazards to wildlife, including seals, turtles, and birds; everyone on the island systematically gathered this debris and placed it in piles to be transported back to Honolulu for proper incineration. I knew I was in one of the most remote places on earth, but suddenly civilization seemed pressingly close. This was my first exposure to marine debris in the Northwestern Hawaiian Islands, and it would not be my last. I visited Laysan in July—albatross fledging time—and I witnessed many outstretched wings in the wind, practicing for flight. I also watched chicks die and witnessed the mute testimony of their rotting carcasses, the exposed rib cages containing plastic disposable lighters, bottle caps, toothbrushes, toys, and other bits of plastic mixed with squid beaks and pieces of pumice. Sadness and outrage set in, and I suddenly sensed that this remote island was not all that remote.

The refuge management protocols taught me to live lightly on Laysan and changed the way I think, adding an unexpected bonus to the whole experience. Every action had to be accompanied by conscious awareness of its effect on wildlife and an effort to minimize that effect. This was not our place; we were only there to make it better for the species that do belong. If we could not do that, we had no business being there at all, and everyone permitted on Laysan bears that responsibility. I found it reassuring that places like Laysan still exist on the planet, but of course this is only because it has been designated for protection. People are not the dominant species here, but our human will—in this case, the will to protect—prevails nonetheless. What a different reality from the main Hawaiian Islands, where humans are indeed the dominant species. On Laysan, surrounded by the strange and exuberant energies of the wildlife, by the sounds and cycles and vibrant forms of the island residents, my soul felt nourished in a new way, being in a place that is wildlife-centered, not human-centered.

This experience on Laysan Island inspired an entirely new project focused specifically on the Northwestern Islands involving many subsequent visits over several years.

The Hawaiian Archipelago

The world's most remote chain of islands, the Hawaiian archipelago, emerges in splendid isolation from the middle of the Pacific Ocean. One by one, the islands of Hawai'i were born from the volcanic hot spot that still fires eruptions on the Big Island. In conveyor-belt fashion, the relentlessly moving Pacific plate has carried the islands to the northwest, while the forces of time and the sea have reshaped and leveled them into volcanic remnants, atolls, and shoals. Larger and geologically younger, the islands to the east—Kaua'i, O'ahu, La-na'i, Moloka'i, Mau'i, and the Big Island of Hawai'i—are known as the main Hawaiian Islands and collectively represent what people generally think of as Hawai'i. These islands have been inhabited by people for over a thousand years, first by the early Hawaiians from Polynesia, and, after the arrival of Captain Cook in 1778, by waves of immigrants from around the world attracted to the natural and cultural beauty of Hawai'i.

But there is another Hawai'i, lesser known and unseen by most people. Extending northwest from Kaua'i are ten smaller and geologically older islands and atolls, often referred to as the Leeward, or Northwestern Hawaiian Islands. Comprising only one-tenth of one percent of the Hawaiian archipelago's land area, and yet extending for two-thirds the length of the chain, they provide refuge for vibrant natural communities including monk seals, sea turtles, vast numbers of nesting seabirds, plants, and insects. Human culture is not the dominant presence here. Wildlife reigns. The surrounding marine environment contains nearly 70 percent of our nation's coral reefs—altogether, one of the most intact coral reef ecosystems left in the world.

Like their famous sister-islands to the southeast, the Northwestern Hawaiian Islands have been graced with one of the most spectacular natural environments on Earth; ironically, this environment is also one of the most threatened. Through a succession of protective actions, beginning with Teddy Roosevelt establishing a bird refuge in 1909, President Bill Clinton's creation of the NWHI Coral Reef Ecosystem Reserve in 2000, and most recently the designation of the Papahānaumokuākea National Marine Monument in 2007, the Northwestern Hawaiian Islands have become virtually off-limits to people, with the exception of authorized research and conservation expeditions. Their inaccessibility and need for protection means that few people will be able to see and experience these islands and reefs directly. For me, this presented a unique challenge—the importance of sharing this national public treasure to help create the awareness and the appreciation that will be critical to its future protection. My hope is to reveal the richness and value of the Northwestern Hawaiian Islands through photographs that bear witness to what I saw and came to understand. My approach was partly documentation—at times almost forensic—balanced with my subjective response, driven by imagination and compassion.

Midway Atoll

For the last hundred years, Midway has been a story about people as well as about wildlife, and in this way it differs significantly from the other Leeward Islands. Tern Island, in French Frigate Shoals, and Kure Atoll each supported Coast Guard LORAN stations, but they do not have the extensive and complex history of human occupation that Midway has experienced.

Midway's saga of human contact begins with shipwrecks and castaways during the last half of the 19th century, eventually leading to the formal establishment of a population whose goal was to link and maintain the first trans-Pacific cable in 1903. Most of the handsome cable buildings still stand, though in an advanced state of disintegration. During the mid-1930s, Pan American Airways developed the Clipper seaplane operation on Midway, which was soon followed by the U.S. Navy and the construction of a Naval air station. All this activity brought over ten thousand people to the island, and a rush of civilization.

Military operations there changed after World War II. Although Midway remained an important base during the Korean and Vietnam Wars, the population declined to around 3,000 servicemen and their dependents. Final withdrawal of military personnel occurred in 1997, when Midway was officially designated a National Wildlife Refuge and National Historic Site, and authority for the island was transferred to the U.S. Fish and Wildlife Service (USFWS). Midway's current population fluctuates between thirty and fifty people, depending on seasonal activities.

Almost like a ghost town, Midway has a general air of dilapidation. Once a thriving one-company town, it's now a skeleton operation with two primary goals: to manage Midway for the benefit of the wildlife, and to keep the airport open for emergency landings. In effect, this airport functions as the only gas station in the middle of the Pacific. Much of the infrastructure departed along with the Navy, but many buildings remain: barracks, officers quarters, airport facilities, power plant, movie theater, gym, infirmary, library, and the All Hands Club—a bar and pool hall. Some buildings are used and maintained; others are abandoned. Some have historical significance, including the cable station buildings, seaplane hangar, and gun emplacements. Several memorials commemorate the Battle of Midway and pay tribute to those who lost their lives during World War II.

During my time on Midway, it struck me that the "gooneybirds," as the albatrosses are affectionately called, have reclaimed the island and have truly won the battle for Midway. Roughly one million albatrosses arrive in the fall to dance, breed, build nests, lay eggs, and raise their young, a process that culminates in successful fledglings leaving the atoll the following July. Between July and October, the island seems quiet and lonely—some think calm—and it's a good time, in fact the only time, to work on the grounds before the next wave of albatross nesting.

Over the past century, the human inclination to alter places eroded Midway's native terrestrial ecosystem. With no quarantine protocols in place, planes, boats, and people came and went. The native species that survived hopelessly mixed with numerous exotics, including canaries, myna birds, and a plethora of alien plants and insects. Since the focus of my work was on native flora, fauna, and habitat, I had not expected Midway to be fruitful, and I was surprised to discover quite the opposite. Thanks to the eradication of rats, which had been introduced during World War II, ground-nesting birds have returned to Midway, especially Bonin petrels. The USFWS has made significant progress in making Midway once again hospitable to native wildlife by creating good seabird nesting habitat; working on the removal of destructive alien species like verbesina, or golden crownbeard, which crowds out the native vegetation; and cultivating indigenous plants in key areas.

Midway affords certain human creature comforts—a roof over your head, electricity, hot and cold running water, telephone and Internet service, and, of course, convenient access provided by the airport. All of this helped facilitate my work since I devoted less time to survival tasks. I decided to use Midway as

A GOLDEN PLOVER FOUND AND PHOTOGRAPHED ON MIDWAY ATOLL, who starved to death trying to free itself from the death grip of a plastic ring caught between its beak and around its neck. Photograph by Susan Middleton a base for much of my seabird work, some of the plant work and a good deal of marine work—as much as I could do that would remain representative of the Northwestern Hawaiian Islands.

One day, Sak Phosri, the Water Plant manager, responsible for the collection and dissemination of all the fresh water on Midway, brought me something he thought I would be interested in photographing. Sak had lived on Midway longer than any other person—for over thirty years—and he knew the island better than anyone. As I opened the cardboard box and unwrapped its contents, I recognized a dead bird. Then I saw that it was a Golden Plover with a weathered red plastic ring caught in its beak, circling around its neck and caught between the top and bottom beak, gagging the bird. It was obvious it had desperately tried to free itself because the plastic was worn almost halfway through its diameter as the bird attempted to chew through it, to no avail. The bird died, unable to free itself from the grasp of this deadly plastic ring and unable to eat. Sak told me he found the bird on the side of the airport runway and collected it. I worked late into the night photographing the plover; it struck me as a sad testimony of human carelessness and the lethal consequences of plastic debris.

Kure Atoll

Two months on Kure Atoll became my deepest experience of the Northwestern Hawaiian Islands, due to the length of time I lived there and the total immersion in nature. Sleeping on the ground for two months, surrounded by noisy seabirds; helping to band birds and weed out invasive alien plants; and making frequent boat trips into the atoll to explore the flourishing coral reefs. These experiences provided me with an intimate connection to the place, with time and guidance to get to know it a little. I collected many wondrous marine animals and plants in plastic buckets of seawater, placed them in aquariums to be photographed, and then returned them to their reef homes. On Kure, I came to fully understand the perils of marine debris.

Kure is the oldest island in the Hawaiian archipelago, over 28 million yeas old, and the farthest from Honolulu. It is the last gasp of the archiplelago keeping its head above water. Further to the northwest are the Emperor seamounts, sunken islands worn away by erosion and the subsidence of the Pacific plate. Kure is the end of the line.

Getting there is not easy, since the old Coast Guard airstrip is no longer functional. That leaves boat transport and, as Kure is situated at the end of the chain, a boat must be destined for it, not just "passing by." I was able to get berth space on a NOAA research vessel that was bringing field personnel and provisions to the island. The vessel would return for pick-up two months later.

As I approached Kure, I began to make out a tiny turquoise line of blue water in the distance with a bright-white line resting above it, and, eventually, some green on the white. Zodiacs were dispatched from the ship to navigate through a break in the surrounding reef. Suddenly I was in what appeared to be the world's largest swimming pool—luminous, pale blue-green water with a white-sand bottom and occasional patch reefs. We pulled up on the white sand shoreline and proceeded to haul our gear in wheelbarrows up to camp.

I immediately dove into work, setting up aquariums for marine photography in a tool shed that provided shade and shelter from the rain. I was guided into the atoll to the pristine patch reefs, where I snorkeled and collected marine creatures and algae for portraits, placing the specimens in white plastic buckets full of fresh seawater. Solar panels provided enough power to clean and aerate the aquariums and the "holding" buckets containing the subjects of the portraits, all of which were later returned to their reef homes.

There were seven of us on the island: Cynthia Vanderlip, Refuge Manager, and her daughter, Amarisa Marie, as well as Michael Holland, Rob Marshall, Tracey Wurth, David Liittschwager, and myself. Rob and Tracey were researching and monitoring monk seals, and the rest of us helped with wildlife sanctuary work: banding birds, pulling out alien plants, removing marine debris, and assisting with spinner dolphin surveys. All of us contributed to chores such as cooking, collecting and hauling water, washing dishes, and general cleaning tasks. We lived in tents and shared kitchen space, complete with propane burners, located in a cinderblock structure dating from the Coast Guard Loran station which closed in 1993. Cooking tested our ingenuity, especially when the fresh food ran out and we found ourselves staring at shelves of canned goods. Our solar-powered freezer was a real luxury; it contained cheese, tortillas, meat, and other delicacies, which we doled out sparingly. Our small supply of garlic was as good as gold.

Camp life was lively with our entertaining camp mates, the albatross chicks. We watched them grow, and found them endlessly engaging. Fed by their parents—who fly thousands of miles to find prey in mid-ocean gyres created by currents, which they later regurgitate into their chicks' mouths —these youngsters soon become fat and begin to lose their baby down, often appearing hilariously awkward in their adolescent phase. When adult plumage grows in, they start to appear sleek; they still can't fly, however, and they are just beginning to feel the power of their wings as they stretch them out and balance in the wind. Next to our tents we each had albatross chick neighbors, and we came to know them as individuals. They behaved like toddlers, putting everything in their mouths, yanking on tent lines, pulling on tent flaps, biting shoes and socks left outside the tents and sometimes moving them to new locations. Cynthia discovered her red bikini top missing one day, later to find it had been snatched off the laundry line by an albatross.

Weather could be fierce on Kure, and a particularly thrilling thunderstorm nearly blinded me with lightning; the flash actually penetrated the skin of my tent and my eyelids, and I could feel the earth shake beneath me, followed by a heavy downpour of rain. Storms were always welcomed on the island; they not only dazzled us with fireworks, but also provided a fresh supply of water. We hurriedly mobilized during every rainstorm, positioning open buckets and barrels in strategic places. Though we brought sufficient drinking water with us in five-gallon jugs, we used rainwater for laundry, doing dishes, and taking luxurious solar-heated showers; a lack of rainwater meant we had to make do with sticky seawater—a poor substitute.

I appreciated the shelter the tool shed provided for our makeshift marine studio, even though it was often unbearably hot and muggy inside. I measured 92 degrees with no breeze, and I took to wearing bandanas around my head and neck to keep sweat from dripping onto the equipment and specimens. We had a fan, which helped cool us down; it also dispelled the fumes from the stored fuel barrels, and discouraged the wasps who built nests in our strobe lights. For several weeks, I divided time between the shed and the relief of the reefs. I swam on my stomach, skimming over the intricate corals where a vibrant community flourished: fishes, invertebrates, algae, even the occasional curious monk seal. Here I would look for subjects to collect, bring them to the shed for their portraits, and then return them to the coral reefs. I developed a great respect for these reefs, the largest biogenic structures made by any organism (including man) on Earth, constructed through the combined effort of countless individual coral polyps—tiny translucent bodies—over time. Impressive and often immense, the reefs are as delicate as porcelain and particularly vulnerable to human clumsiness. I quickly learned how to move gracefully around the corals.

One day I walked out to the shed and saw David sitting in a shady spot with an albatross I recognized. It was "Shed Bird," a chick we had watched since our arrival almost six weeks before. It had hatched near the shed, and, as albatrosses do, stayed close by to be fed by its parents, to grow, and eventually to fledge. It had become our companion and we were fond of it. David looked concerned. He explained that he had noticed Shed Bird having a hard time, panting in the hot sun; when the bird tripped over one of our plastic shower bags bulging with water, it didn't have the strength to pick itself up. David moved the bird into the shade, sprinkled water on it, and cooled it with our fan. Finally, Shed Bird seemed to revive. Relieved, we went back to work in the shed, occasionally checking on the bird, who seemed to be doing fine.

The next day we found Shed Bird dead. Cynthia decided to do a necropsy, and we watched and photographed. As she opened the bird we could see a bulging stomach with the skin stretched tight, revealing protrusions from hard, sharp bits inside, and two ulcer-like perforations. She pressed the blade through the taut skin and it split open, exposing brightly-colored plastic—a sharp rectangular piece causing one of the perforations, two disposable cigarette lighters, several bottle caps, an aerosol pump top, shotgun shells, broken clothespins, toys—hundreds of plastic bits. "It's like opening a piñata," Cynthia said, "but so depressing...."

We were all emotional, and I could not hold back tears. Shed Bird was stuffed with plastic, which had led to dehydration, malnutrition, and ultimately starvation. The bird couldn't pass its stomach contents; it was severely impacted and could not accept food. What a horrific experience for Shed Bird to have endured, and how sturdy it was to survive as long as it did. David photographed the bird with its open stomach, and then I spent several hours removing every item from the gut. I used gloved hands at first, then tweezers for the small pieces, and in the end I arranged everything on a sheet of white plastic, four feet wide by eight feet long. It was an exciting event for the island flies, who swarmed the putrid innards. I was nearly overcome by the powerful stench, and by my sorrow for Shed Bird, who we had seen just a few days earlier, standing with outstretched wings, testing the wind.

LAYSAN ALBATROSS CARCASS ON MIDWAY ATOLL
WITH EXPOSED RIBCAGE REVEALING PLASTIC
Photograph by Susan Middleton

FROM PRISTINE TO PLASTIC:

THE CLUTTERING OF ALASKA'S COAST

David Gaudet, Alaska Marine Stewardship Foundation

WHEN MOST PEOPLE THINK OF THE ALASKAN COAST, the image that comes to mind is one of pristine, wild beaches, free of the ugly debris found on beaches elsewhere in the world. This is simply not accurate. Unfortunately, Alaska's coast—44,5000 miles in total—is littered with debris, a lot of which is plastic washed in from faraway places.

Marine debris has existed for as long as the human race has been building shelters, tools and goods. This debris is transported to the ocean via lakes, rivers, floods and wind. Until the last century, marine debris was made primarily of natural materials such as wood, glass, cloth, leather, earth (bricks and pottery), and ferrous materials. This debris could be reused, and it would eventually decompose, causing little or no harm to the environment.

Today, our marine debris situation is very different and extremely dire. Not only is the world population larger, the consumption of goods is greater—and, more than anything, the kind of goods consumed has changed.

The incorporation of plastics into everyday life has had a major impact on our marine debris over the past century. The first important plastic, celluloid, was discovered in the late 1860s. A form of this material persists today, used to make cigarette filters. Plastics were incorporated into industrial use in the early 1900s with the introduction of Bakelite, used for handles on pots and pans and for plastic enclosures such as for telephones and even bowling balls.

From then on, plastics have been incorporated into almost all manufactured items. Most dangerous and alarming about this development is plastic's persistence after the lifespan of its intended use. Put simply, plastics do not decompose—or not quickly enough. And with the birth of plastic came the manufacturing of plastic single-use items such as water bottles, packaging and disposable products designed to serve a short time period—even though the plastic by which these items would be made would not disappear for centuries or more.

Where is all this marine debris coming from today? Some of it comes from careless disposal practices, but other sources include poorly managed landfills, manufacturing facilities with inadequate controls, and recreational use of coastal areas. The United States Environmental Protection Agency estimates that 49% of all marine debris comes from land-based activities. Other estimates have gone as high as 80%.

Marine debris from ocean-based sources is also a major hazard. These sources include commercial fishing operations, recreational boating, shipping and offshore drilling. According to the World Shipping Council, an estimated 675 containers are lost at sea every year.

Fishing gear and equipment from other maritime activities make up a large portion of the marine debris along the coast of the Gulf of Alaska and the southern Bering Sea. Prior to 1976, the Alaska territorial sea boundary was 12 miles and the United States had little interest in fishing in that area. But many foreign countries fished in those waters. The National Marine Fisheries Service (NMFS) reported an average of 697 Japanese and Soviet vessels fished off the coast of Alaska in the late 1960s and 1970s. Most of these were large ships with crews that trawled for fish.

Additionally, Alaska is on the great circle route for shipping between North America and Asia. Alaska received a large influx of people, ships and planes during World War II. The majority of military bases were in Alaska's maritime areas. Due to expense, most of these bases were abandoned after the war, leaving buildings to decompose and debris to be spread by the winds. Military activities also contributed to large and often poorly located landfills, some of which are now eroding back into the sea.

Perhaps the greatest source of debris for the Alaska coastline comes from the North Pacific Gyre. This great gyre is estimated to be 800 nautical miles (nm) by 3,500 nm, with a circumference of 6,800 nm. It travels at a speed of approximately 6.8 miles per day, with an estimated orbital period of 3 years. Debris can be transferred from one gyre to another and, as a result, marine debris may come to Alaska from any portion of the North Pacific and from as far away as Indonesia. One of the chief characteristics of today's marine debris is its persistence. In a table from the Pocket Guide to Marine Debris by the Ocean Conservancy, plastics and glass have some of the longest decomposition rates or 'persistence.' *(Fig 1)* These are of course only estimates of persistence. Plastic and glass have not been in existence

(Fig 1)

BREAKDOWN RATES

These are of course only estimates of the persistence of these materials. Plastic and glass have not been in existence long enough to confirm these estimates.

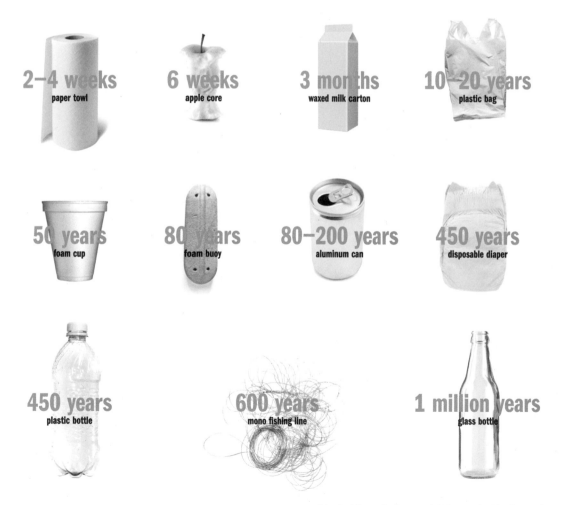

2–4 weeks
paper towl

6 weeks
apple core

3 months
waxed milk carton

10–20 years
plastic bag

50 years
foam cup

80 years
foam buoy

80–200 years
aluminum can

450 years
disposable diaper

450 years
plastic bottle

600 years
mono fishing line

1 million years
glass bottle

Adapted from designs and data created by Ocean Conservancy.

GULF OF ALASKA KEEPER CLEANUP PROJECT
Photograph by Ted Raynor

long enough to confirm the estimates. And, even though glass has the longest estimated persistence, it poses fewer threats than plastic.

The EPA estimates that the United States generated 64,000,000,000 pounds of plastic in 2010, only 8% of which was recycled. This included almost 14 million tons of plastics in containers and packaging, 11 million tons in durable goods, and 7 million tons in non-durable goods. The general negative impacts of plastic marine debris are: entanglement, ingestion, economic woes, social concerns and human health safety.

Entanglement is perhaps the most visible of these problems. Marine mammals and birds are most susceptible to entanglement. In the North Pacific and Bering Sea, there are 11 species of mammals listed under the U.S. Endangered Species Act (ESA) or are under review for protection or special management under the Marine Mammal Protection Act (MMPA). Five seabirds also meet this criterion.

Two of the major complications of entanglement are the limitation of the animal's mobility and starvation due to suffocation. In a place as large and as remote and sparsely populated as Alaska, it is safe to assume that the majority of entanglements go unseen.

The northern fur seals found along Alaska's coastline were first seen entangled in marine debris following World War II. In recent years, the most common types of entanglement debris have been net webbing, plastic packing materials, and monofilament line. One study suggested that, while land-based entanglement rates were too low to explain the seal population decline, the unrecorded number of animals entangled and killed at sea may be a potentially significant factor.

Ingestion of small or degraded plastic items is devastating to seabirds. Death from obstruction or false satiation often results after birds have mistaken plastic for food. Many seabirds succumb to this, and many cases are likely unrecorded due to the remoteness of the sea and seabird habitat.

Not all marine debris is floating, either. An untold amount of debris travels below the surface of the ocean, washes up on beaches, or even sinks to the bottom of the ocean where it may damage the habitat through abrasion or smothering. Plastic marine debris has been implicated in the absorption of pollutants and the transportation of them. Ultimately, these pollutants enter the food chain. There is also growing concern that marine debris could be instrumental in the introduction and spread of alien species.

The economic impacts of marine debris include ghost fishing and lost fishing gear. This impacts fisheries because 'ghost nets' or lost nets continue to kill targeted species and other species. This may result in economic harm as well as limitations to fisheries. There are also navigational hazards that occur as a result of marine debris. Equipment can be damaged due to blocked water intake. Immobilization of the rudder or propeller of boats can also occur.

The social impacts of marine debris are more difficult to evaluate. Possibilities include humans avoiding beaches and the ocean due to the debris—particularly the dangers of medical debris. Also, the public may become less interested in purchasing ocean resources such as seafood due to potential contamination and health hazards.

There are several major marine debris cleanups each year. The Alaska Marine Science Foundation (AMSF) has been sponsoring cleanups since 2003, beginning on St. Paul Island and eventually expanding statewide. The Center for Alaskan Coastal Studies (CACS) has sponsored small community Challenge Grants throughout Alaska as well as coordinated the Ocean Conservancy's International Coastal Cleanup. NOAA has sponsored cleanups through its Marine Debris Community Grant program. Additionally, there are many good Samaritan groups throughout the state that have sponsored volunteer cleanups.

AMSF compiles statistics on the number of pounds of debris removed and the coastline mileage cleaned each year. Based on an analysis of currents, wind patterns, human activity and other factors, the state was divided into 14 groups. Data were compiled from various groups for each region. Through 2011, records indicate that a total of 2,453,242 pounds of marine debris was removed from 1973 miles of Alaska coastline. (Fig 2)

This data reflects only a fraction (approx. 4%) of the current amount of Alaska marine debris, because Alaska has 44,500 miles of coastline. Many obstacles make it difficult to clean up Alaska's immense coastline. Not only are the beaches difficult to access, transporting the debris to be properly disposed can be a monumental challenge. A large boat that may be used to transport laborers and debris must anchor offshore if weather permits, and this often requires smaller boats to get to and from shore.

On March 11, 2011, a powerful 9.0 magnitude earthquake occurred 81 miles off the coast of Japan. A large tsunami, with wave heights up to 33 ft., washed over three prefectures (Iwate, Miyagi and Fukushima) inundating approximately 459

(Fig 2)

2011 MARINE DEBRIS REMOVED IN ALASKA

TOTAL
2,453,242 lbs/**1,973** miles

The number of pounds of debris removed and number of miles of coast cleaned through 2011.

NORTHERN BERING COAST
76,556 lbs/**174** miles

ST. LAWRENCE ISLAND
121,592 lbs/**100** miles

NORTON SOUND
469,766 lbs/**245** miles

CENTRAL BERING COAST
25,955 lbs/**61.8** miles

PRIBILOF ISLANDS
266,722 lbs/**54** miles

BRISTOL BAY
236,331 lbs/**106** miles

ALEUTIANS
68,020 lbs/**8** miles

COOK INLET
14,086 lbs/**77** miles

PRINCE WILLIAM SOUND
391,874 lbs/**569.2** miles

YAKUTAT
41,807 lbs/**60** miles

SOUTHEAST ALASKA INSIDE
308,655 lbs/**72** miles

CENTRAL GULF OF ALASKA
328,665 lbs/**371** miles

SOUTHEAST ALASKA OUTSIDE
103,213 lbs/**76.8** miles

KATMAI TIDAL FLATS, ALASKA
Photograph by Kip Evans

square miles. The tsunami—termed the Tohoku Tsunami—created more than 20 million tons of debris, of which 5 million tons was estimated to have washed into the ocean. The Japanese Ministry of the Environment estimated that 70% of this debris sank, leaving 1.5 million tons adrift in the ocean. The debris fields were so dense that they were traceable via satellite photos until April 14, 2011. This tsunami debris only added to the already dense and dangerous amount of debris in our ocean.

Scientists predicted that the tsunami debris would make landfall on the west coast of North America in the spring of 2013. However, possible tsunami debris was sighted as early as December 2011. Soon after, other sightings of tsunami debris were reported in Washington State and the Province of British Columbia. Dr. Curtis Ebbesmeyer noted that this could be expected from debris that had a high 'windage'[1] factor.

Following these reports, AMSF established a monitoring program for Alaska. AMSF reasoned that tsunami-generated debris would originate from south of Alaska and that the pattern of landfall would be from south to north and west (first southeast Alaska followed by the Prince William Sound region and then the Kodiak area).

From this tsunami debris, uncommon items such as large heavy plastic and fabric-covered buoys were seen along with fuel and other containers with Japanese writing. AMSF was more limited in wintertime but, in summer, a call-in program facilitated by NOAA and AMSF confirmed that debris from the tsunami had reached Alaska.

Whether from the increased use of plastic in our world, or the debris washed up on the coastlines from the Tohoku Tsunami, Alaskans face a major cleanup task. The volunteer programs that work so well in other areas are not as feasible in Alaska because of its vastness and remoteness. It will take a large amount of resources and tireless and ambitious work groups to clean and dispose of the volumes of debris from Alaska's coastline—a part of our global ocean.

---

1 Windage is defined as the sum effect of the wind on the movement of an object in water. A high windage factor results from a large sail area and a low drag, such as a piece of styrofoam or a buoy with no lines attached. A small windage factor results with a low sail area and a high drag, such as a piece of wood.

FISHING GEAR AND MARITIME DEBRIS MAKE UP A LARGE PORTION OF THE DEBRIS ALONG ALASKA'S COAST

GHOST NETS:

MODERN WASTE AND AN ANCIENT CULTURE

Sue Ryan and Trish Barnard, GhostNets Australia

FOR THOUSANDS OF YEARS, nets have been used to harvest resources from the sea. Although once made from natural fibers that would decompose in the environment and constrained in size by material characteristics and the limits of human strength to cast and haul them, nets are now made of synthetic materials. Durable and of immense size, these modern nets are deployed and hauled by powerful ships. Nets can be lost in storms, deployed but not retrieved; when worn or damaged, they may be discarded at sea, ghost nets adrift to follow ocean currents. Drifting nets or those bound to structures such as reefs may persist for decades, their entangling mesh bringing death and destruction to marine habitats.

Given the recent introduction of synthetic materials, we don't know for sure how many individual nets cast shadows over marine ecosystems during their ghostly travels, or the volumes of prey that may fall victim. To address this crisis, GhostNets Australia is the voice of Indigenous people in a confrontation of spirit and respect for nature with modern technology and environmental impacts. GhostNets Australia transforms waste into important contemporary art and artifacts, using it for outreach and activism.

Indigenous Australians inhabiting coastal regions refer to themselves as 'Saltwater People.' As an alliance of saltwater Indigenous communities from across the top end of Australia, GhostNets works to find and remove nets that have washed up along beaches. With funding from the Australian Federal Government, the program has supported Indigenous rangers to remove over 12,000 ghost nets—some so large they required heavy machinery to move them. Removal of nets has resulted in the recovery of trapped wildlife, particularly marine turtles.

Less than 10% of these nets have been attributed to Australian fisheries; most of them originated from various parts of Southeast Asia. Data related to the type, size, location and probable origin of each net recovered is recorded and collated by GhostNets Australia, and this program has assisted Aboriginal communities to fulfill aspirations of stewardship for their traditional lands and adjacent marine environments.

The conundrum of what to do with the number of ghost nets and other marine debris retrieved from these far-flung shores engendered considerable thought and discussion during the semi-annual meetings of ranger representatives. Some not entirely satisfactory solutions included burning marine debris or burying it in a landfill. Given the remoteness of many shores, recycling ghost nets has never been a viable option. Using ghost nets as material for craft or art was a positive way to address the challenge.

In 2006, Design for a Sea Change was a competition that challenged participants to create products incorporating ghost nets. The result was a strong range of innovative designs. Buoyed by success, the program expanded into the Cape York and Torres Strait Indigenous communities, and contemporary artists were invited to conduct workshops with local artists and weavers in various Indigenous communities where ghost nets were a significant problem.

The first workshop was in June 2009 with artists and weavers at the saltwater Aboriginal community of Aurukun on the western side of Cape York Peninsula. The weavers initially struggled with the ghost nets, unhappy with the stiffness and untidiness, but, as time went on and the baskets grew, the artists began to develop a fondness for the material and an excitement for the project. Unlike the traditional delicate baskets, these ghost net baskets were colorful, knotted, and lumpy. The baskets were displayed at the inaugural Cairns Indigenous Art Fair in August 2009. They were new and inspiring, attracting considerable attention and selling quickly to collectors at surprisingly high prices. Invitations to exhibit works followed, and the *Ghost Net Art Project* gained momentum, with galleries wanting to host exhibitions and institutions expressing interest in acquiring artworks.

Workshops featuring Indigenous artists have been effective in alerting mainstream Australians to the grave problem of marine debris and the threat it poses to Australia's marine fauna. The saltwater people already know what the ghost nets are doing to their reefs and beaches. For an urban-dwelling mainstream Australian to hear about it from someone who is directly affected makes it personal in a way not otherwise possible. Ghost net artworks are now regularly included in exhibitions of Indigenous art in major city galleries, and they have been acquired by organizations including the National Gallery of Australia in Canberra, Parliament House Collection in Canberra, Australian

GHOST NET AND ROPE COLLECTED BY INDIGENOUS
RANGERS FOR USE IN THE GHOST NET ART PROJECT.
Mapoon Land and Sea Ranger Base, Mapoon,
Cape York, Queensland, 2012

Museum in Sydney, Queensland Art Gallery in Brisbane, University of Queensland in Brisbane and the Australian art lending institution Artbank. Even the British Museum in London acquired one of the works.

An Indigenous artwork made from synthetic marine debris contains an environmental message. People who buy the work feel they are supporting the artist, the community and the environment. Institutions see it as the beginning of a new art movement and as a historical reference to a changing world.

Indigenous people interviewed said that they could not remember ghost nets or plastics on the beach in any quantity prior to the early 1990s. Saltwater people spend a lot of their time on the ocean. It is their heritage, their place, and their home. They rely upon it for food and for travel between communities, and they observe marine life being killed and wasted by ghost nets.

The Indigenous communities are relatively small, many with populations of only a few hundred people. Most of the inhabitants in these communities are related to each other in some way, and everyone in the community is aware of someone making art from net and exhibiting the work. Community members out fishing find nets and ropes to bring back for their artist relatives. The marine debris and ghost nets now have value. Kids keep a lookout for special colored ropes and nets and interesting plastic objects for their sisters, aunts or grandmothers to use. Money from the sale of artwork filters back through the community, so everyone benefits.

These artworks contain the whole ghost net story—from the net's initial use for fishing, to being discarded at sea, to the destructive force in the ocean, and finally when it washes ashore and is made into something beautiful by a saltwater Indigenous Australian.

The *Ghost Net Art Project* has not provided the ultimate answer to the question of how to dispose of the tons of retrieved ghost nets in an ecologically sound manner, but it has delivered many surprising and unexpected benefits. The project has been embraced by Indigenous artists from twenty-two coastal communities. For all Indigenous Australian cultural groups, the spiritual relationship to land and sea is omnipresent, and ancestral creation stories govern the understanding of life and meaning from everything in the natural environment.

Sea management programs assist by focusing particularly on sustaining the dugong and marine turtle populations, an endeavour to improve public understanding of the dangers of abandoned nets and the impacts of marine debris. Many of our communities have entered into 'Traditional Use of Marine Resource Agreements' (TUMRA) with the Great Barrier Reef Marine Park Authority (GBRMPA) and government to protect and conserve marine creatures and manage traditional hunting practices. Ghost net debris and marine plastics deposited along our jagged coastline not only counter and challenge our efforts, but they affect the relationship and balance between nature and the natural order of our environment and serve as a reminder of the threats of commercial industry.

Today large rocks along the remote shorelines stand like sentinels bearing witness to the pollution of our once pristine coasts. This is in direct contravention to the teaching of Ancestral spirits that knowledge and respect for the land and sea is essential to our people's survival and the survival of all living things within an environment.

We have been bestowed with custodial responsibilities for the sea, but cleaning the ocean rubbish is escalating beyond reasonable control. The marine creatures affected by the discarded and abandoned ghost nets have totemic associations to traditional owners and are essential to our identity, cultural behavior and custodial responsibilities. Dugong and turtle were once hunted only by senior initiated men. Although some traditional laws have been relaxed to allow other men to hunt, cultural laws still reinforce the cultural continuum of taking only what is needed. One dugong will be strictly apportioned according to custom and will feed around 30 people so there is no wasteful excessive harvest of these creatures. It is an affront for our people to see their natural seagrass habitat polluted and creatures entrapped in nets when, for generations, we have respectfully managed these resources.

We continue to depend upon marine resources as a valuable part of our diet, particularly for the Torres Strait Islanders living in smaller and more remote areas who use more than 450 species of marine animals. The depletion of certain sea creatures demonstrates a lack of respect for the Indigenous system of resource management.[1]

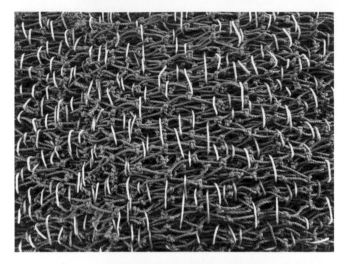

GHOSTNETS AUSTRALIA

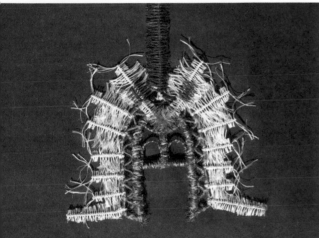

The clean-up work by GhostNets not only recovers entangled lacerated dugongs, turtles, stingrays, dolphins, sharks and even crocodiles from ghost nets, it retrieves a large quantity of plastics and other debris that can be ingested by our marine life or smother our mangrove and shallow reef systems. According to Nicolas Peterson and Bruce Rigsby, throwing meat and fatty substances into the sea fouls the waters and angers the spirits.[2] Aboriginal people and Torres Strait Islanders spiritually associate all creatures as 'kin,' so it therefore perplexes us to see other cultures display no apparent moral or spiritual consciousness towards sea creatures. It distresses us to see the ocean willingly contaminated with discarded ghost nets and other consumables. This is in disappointing contrast to traditional times, when there were established ramifications for not respectfully caring for the ocean.

In some communities, traditional owners continue their custodial responsibilities and practice ceremonies to perpetuate the ocean supply for future generations. Such rituals may employ songs, sacred artifacts, dance performances, or conciliatory offerings to appease the spirits and ensure the recurrent supply of all resources. Some Indigenous groups have been known to hang turtle heads in trees to bring abundant supply. Torres Strait Islanders in the eastern group on the small island called *Dauar*, next to *Mer* (Murray Island) acknowledged their successful turtle catch by placing it upside down on the beach and performing a ritual involving highly decorated *zogo baur* (turtle poles), rhythmically beating a drum and chanting a song.[3] Notable Australian archaeologist Ian McNiven noted many mounds of dugong bones were found throughout the Torres Strait. They were thought to be graves or lookouts, or remnants of increase ceremonies.[4] Increase ceremonies unite spiritual beliefs and custodial responsibilities to maintain the balance and order to everything in nature. Anthropologist Noni Sharp once aptly explained that the relationship of saltwater people to the sea is, "ontological rather than technical. It is about how you spiritually relate to the sea and engage with spiritual forces that create it and you."[5]

Torres Strait Islander people also associate themselves with the winds and four seasons. These spiritual beliefs are fundamental to their sense of identity and cultural obligations for customary marine tenure. At one time, these winds also supported economical relationships with our saltwater people. The south-easterly winds once brought Macassan traders to collect beche-de-mer (sea slugs) from Australian waters, returning sail with the northwest winds to sell the culinary delicacy in Asian countries.[6] Currents, winds and tidal effects from two ocean systems that once delivered coconut husks, driftwood, bamboo and other organic debris to our coastline, now bring a destructive array of modern man-made consumables. McNiven has referred to the spiritual energies and belief systems associated with different currents throughout the seas hugging northern Australia, and she noted that spirits had 'created strong currents running through Prince of Wales Channel to discourage outsiders from venturing into the Kaurareg area.'[7] No doubt the spirits are watching the sea changes and disrespectful human behavior more closely too.

As we continue to clean our coastlines, artists transform this debris into a new medium for modern cultural expression that attracts national and international attention to this serious issue. Exhibitions of art produced through the *Ghost Net Art Project* provide Indigenous Australians with a platform to voice their discontent and encourage support to address the problem.

Not long ago, all our Indigenous material culture was created from organic natural fiber grown in our country, such as grasses, bark fiber or palm leaf used for baskets and vessels, or from naturally grown trees used for the carved artifacts and effigies. Artists still use natural fibers, but, with seasonal obstacles, access challenges, and family responsibilities, it can become a time-consuming and arduous task. It is therefore noteworthy how artists have adventurously embraced the nylon ghost nets and turned a negative into a positive. In one way, the strong long-lasting nylon fiber can be interpreted as a metaphor for the resilience of Aboriginal people and Torres Strait Islanders who refuse to let their culture deteriorate. Ironically, the green and blue colored nylon used to blend the ghost nets into the sea, also references the colors associated with Torres Strait Islander unity and identity symbolised on their official flag—the green represents the land and the blue represents the sea. Male and female artists have used their traditional weaving techniques of knotting, twining, coiling and looping to transpose the introduced material into innovative works of art. Gaining confidence, artists who began with utilitarian objects such as baskets, mats and jewelry, are now creating larger and often abstracted forms that present a visually arresting display.

In 2012 GhostNets artists demonstrated their skills and ingenuity at the Cairns Indigenous Art Fair. Seated on mats under a tree with a cool gentle sea breeze, artists from various communities shared techniques, stories and laughter in a relaxed atmosphere that epitomised the communal sharing of knowledge for all Aboriginal people and Torres Strait Islanders. Various forms of this eco trash were scattered across the grass, inspiring artists to make marketable turtle brooches for the visitors or large-scale jellyfish and dance headdresses created from re-purposed polystyrene foam, ghost net remnants and other random materials.

The large mounds of discarded ghost nets indicate the magnitude of this problem. Many recent erratic weather patterns and systems convey a stern message from our Ancestral Creation Spirits about the blatant disregard for the natural environment and the destruction that follows.

1 McNiven, I.J., 'Saltwater People: Spiritscapes, Maritime Rituals and the Archaeology of Australian Indigenous Seascapes', World Archaeology, Taylor & Francis Ltd., Vol. 35, No. 3, Seascapes (Dec., 2003), pp.329-349.
2 Denham, P., 'Not to give away, not to die away' in 'Story Place: Indigenous art of Cape York and the Rainforest', Seear, Lynne, Gunning, Judy, Were, Ian, (eds). Queensland Art Gallery, Brisbane, 2003, p.65.
3 Robinson, B., and Mosby, T., 'Ilan Pasin (this is our way): Torres Strait Art' exhibition catalogue, Cairns Regional Gallery, Cairns, 1998, p.91.
4 McNiven, I.J., 'Saltwater People: Spiritscapes, Maritime Rituals and the Archaeology of Australian Indigenous Seascapes', World Archaeology, Taylor & Francis Ltd., Vol. 35, No. 3, Seascapes (Dec., 2003), pp.329-349.
5 Sharp, N., 'Saltwater People: The Waves of Memory', Allen & Unwin, Crows Nest, 2002.
6 Mulvaney, J. and Kamminga, J., 'Prehistory of Australia', Allen & Unwin, Crows, Nest, 1999, p.412.
7 McNiven, I.J. and R. Feldman, 'Ritually Orchestrated Seascapes: Hunting Magic and Dugong Bone Mounds in Torres Strait, NE Australia', Cambridge Archaeological Journal, Vol. 13, Issue 2, October 2003, pp.169-194.

PHOTOGRAPHS PAGES 154-155 LEFT TO RIGHT, TOP TO BOTTOM
LINE 1
1. Hammond Island workshop, Torres Strait, Queensland 2012. Photo - Nalda Searles
2. Saibai Island workshop, Torres Strait, Queensland 2010. Photo - Cecile Williams
3. Hammond Island workshop, Torres Strait, Queensland 2012. Photo - Nalda Searles
4. Moa Island puppet performance, Saint Pauls community, Torres Strait, Queensland 2010
LINE 2
5. Aurukun workshop, Cape York, Queensland 2009. Photo Sue Ryan
6. Moa Island puppet performance, Saint Pauls community, Torres Strait, Queensland 2010. Photo - Dujon Newie
7. 'Ghost Net Dari' Darnley Island Headdress by Jimmy Thaiday. Courtesy Erub Erwer Meta. Torres Strait, Queensland. Photo - Lynnette Griffiths
8. Gumurr Marthakal Ranger collecting net. Elcho Island, Arnhem Land, Northern Territory
LINE 3
9. Saibai Island workshop, Torres Strait, Queensland 2010. Photo - Cecile Williams
10. 'Ghost net basket' by Angela Torenbeek. Moa Island workshop, Saint Pauls community, Torres Strait, Queensland. Photo - Sue Ryan
11. 'Ghost net crocodile' at Sculpture by the Sea - Bondi, Sydney, New South Wales, 2012
12. 'Saltwater Immigrants' by Lynnette Griffiths, Cairns, Queensland, 2012, Photo - Lynnette Griffiths

Sue Ryan
GHOST DOG
2012

Synthetic ghost net, beach thongs, wire,
poly cotton thread
Courtesy-Martin Browne Contemporary
Sperone Westwater Gallery

MARK DION AND ALEXIS ROCKMAN:

ARTISTS AT THE END OF THEIR ROPES

A Conversation Between Alexis Rockman and Mark Dion, 2013

Alexis Rockman:

Mark, I want to talk about our outlook on art and how it may have changed in terms of things that we care about in our work and in our lives. *Do you feel more or less hopeful about ecology, conservation and biodiversity than you did when we both started our careers in the mid 1980s?*

Mark Dion:

I fear the trajectory of our thoughts about wild lands and wildlife conservation has been parallel. It is a long train of ideas that terminates in pessimism and melancholy. If I had to categorize my thoughts and feelings about ecology over my development as an artist, it would form a list like this:

Amazement/Wonder

Curiosity

Outrage/Anger

Hope/Activism

Disillusionment

Pessimism/Melancholy

We were both fascinated by a wonder and love for animals and wild places. This became the motivation for reading about natural history and zoology in particular, which led to our understanding of the challenges of wildlife conservation issues. At one point I became convinced that environmental issues were really information problems. I believed that if people knew the damage their way of life caused to the natural world, they would change. I believed that people would opt for environmental sanity over ecological suicide. My early work tended to be quite informational and didactic since I was literally attempting a kind of sculptural documentary practice.

BEACH LITTER FOUND AND ARRANGED BY ARTIST MARK DION
at Gore Point, Alaska, during the Gyre project expedition, 2013
Photograph by Kip Evans

After a while it became apparent that access to knowledge wasn't the problem. Ecological knowledge was readily available. The main issues were questions of political will, ideology, capitalism and psychology. It is hard to say that people don't know about the crisis in biodiversity, because the information is everywhere.

For me it is clear that we will continue our disregard for other living things and the degradation of the environment, to suicidal extremes. This leads me to a perspective of pessimism. However, I would love to be proven wrong. Dark conclusions and complex positions that end in ambivalence are difficult to articulate in various forms of culture. You cannot always express these sentiments in politics, in activism, perhaps even in journalism. Art is an excellent place to express complexity, paradox, uncertainty, ambivalence, and hopelessness. The role of the artist as witness can be as valuable as the artist as catalyst.

Don't you find a great deal of push back from the environmental community when it comes to issues of pessimism and doubt?

Alexis Rockman:

Yes, there is a lot of pushback from the scientific and environmental activist communities. They might confess privately that they are despairing, but they often feel that if they articulate this in public, people will flee as if from a burning building and bury their heads in the sand. Well, the state of the world's resources and ecology is like a building on fire, and it's terrifying. I'm grateful to have art as a way to cope. One of my jobs as an artist is to show how we can't afford to be ambivalent about human activity.

Obviously, it's easy to be confused by what fuels our behavior and motivation. Knowledge just isn't enough. Our behavior has as much to do with the Pleistocene as it does with the 21st century. What I mean is we are tribal, territorial animals who are afraid of mortality. We really can't imagine what the world will be like one hundred years from now let alone two years. This is an unfortunate cocktail of paradoxes for everything else alive on this planet. I often try to imagine what the person who cut down the last tree on Easter Island was thinking around 1600 AD.

Like you, I used to believe that knowledge and information would open our eyes to the environmental issues and create radical change in behavior and save the world. I made art to teach a lesson. But I learned the lesson from Al Gore's *An Inconvenient Truth* that people, even if they listen, just don't have the collective will to do much. The engine of capitalism is too powerful.

How do you think future generations will perceive this period in history, now that our impact on the planet is an undeniable and acknowledged fact?

Mark Dion:

I guess we could look at how we feel about those who made selfish, corrupt and unforgivable choices in the past. How do we feel about those who clear-cut the entirety of New England? How do we feel about the agriculturalists who killed the last Carolina parakeet, or the market hunters who raided the last passenger pigeon nest site? How do we feel about those who administrated the Trail of Tears and other schemes of genocide? How do we judge those who brought buffalo and wolves to the very border of extinction?

If it is true that we are the last generation who can significantly change the course of environmental degradation, and we do little or nothing, then I imagine our place in history will be as the enablers of shaping the planet into a crummier place.

I am not sitting on the moral high ground and wagging my finger. I am very much implicated in the problem. I am far from a paragon of environmental sainthood. While we need some leadership and models of a positive culture of nature, it seems to me very much a question of values under capitalism.

We live in a world of contradictions and compromises, and artists are certainly not immune from the everyday life conflicts of anyone living under capitalism. It is hard to participate in the global art world and not have a significant carbon footprint, for example. Some of the staunchest environmentalists I know, board a lot of jets.

You depict a good deal of trash in your work. What does it mean to you? How does it function in your iconography?

Alexis Rockman:

When I first started to paint natural history landscape paintings in the 1980s, trash was a big thrill. It was something that hadn't really been included in the history of painting and seemed like a taboo. I don't mean the formalist relationship to trash like Duchamp or Rauschenberg, but the socio implications of trash. There was something perverse about painting trash in a loving and careful way. Trash was also a way to stake out my own territory. I was aware that one can't make a painting about ecology in the 20th or 21st century and not include it. It's everywhere, whether visible on a beach or on a microscopic level, and it's the reality of the state of the planet.

One of my earliest memories of trash was being in Lima, Peru, and seeing what looked like mountains of trash clogging the river. To add insult to injury, it seemed as if the trash was covered in vultures. It terrified me particularly because at home I lived near the East River in NEW YORK CITY, and I was afraid those mountains of trash might happen there too.

You have traveled to as many 'dream' destinations as anyone I know. Is there a place you have yet to go that is at the top of your list?

Mark Dion:

I have been to some remarkable places—both remote and natural, and highly populated and cultured—but what makes traveling fulfilling is the company I've shared. The GYRE expedition to the trash-strewn beaches of Alaska was extraordinary, not merely for the rich wildlife and stunning landscape, but also for the assembly of artists, scientists and documentarians. Traveling with people who shared my passion for wild places and commitment to conservation, but who came with such different sensibilities and strategies, was amazing.

Artists and scientists are obvious allies when it comes to environmental justice and wildlife issues, but they speak different languages and employ entirely separate tool boxes in their approach. The Alaska GYRE expedition was a model of my ideal kind of travel. The team was relaxed, yet highly committed and remarkably intelligent and thoughtful. I had not imagined that the expedition would be so productive and that we would all get along so well, but of course it makes sense given we all share the same concerns.

Needless to say, there is always a sense of urgency in nature travel today since so many wild places are under pressure. It is easy to get caught up in "the last chance to see" mentality. Places you and I traveled to in the 1990s have become drastically degraded. Many of the forests you visited in Madagascar are gone forever. For me, the importance of travel is that it affirms my connection with wild places and it recharges my batteries, and it makes me give a damn. It is easy to lose a sense of what we're fighting for, so I find visiting wild places essential to keeping my focus.

The notion I mentioned earlier about the artist as a witness is also an important dimension of conservation travel. Artists were important to the process of documenting new animals as they were first identified to science. Now they are equally important in documenting their disappearance.

Mark Dion, **FLOTSAM AND JETSAM (THE END OF THE GAME)**
1995

Installation De Vleeshal, Middleburg, Holland
Courtesy of the artist and Tanya Bonakdar Gallery, New York

Mark Dion, **A TALE OF SEAS**
1996

Mark Dion and Stephan Billemuth's Journey along the coast
of the North Sea and Baltic Sea and what they found there

Eel Grass
(Zostera nana)

Mixed
Algae and
Eel grass

Algae
(Fucus serratus)

WILDERNESS AND INVASION

PLASTIC PLACE-MARKERS OF THE ANTHROPOCENE

Pam Longobardi

(Portions excerpted from forthcoming chapter in "Framing the Ocean, 1700—present: The Sea as Social Space," Ashgate 2014)

THE SPLASHDOWN LANDING ON THE BEACH happens in a furious rush lest a particularly vigorous wave grounds the *Jubatus*, our open-hulled metal-bodied landing boat. Jumping off in knee-deep water, we run through the small wavelets onto the pebble beach and immediately spot the heavy hand of human presence that has now permeated even our most remote and pristine places: dozens of water bottles, a large plastic float colored survival orange, and surprisingly, an unbroken full-length fluorescent light bulb.

The potential mercury that may leak from the bulb is troubling, but the real danger here is the myriad of plastic objects that dot the beach. A few steps further, after cresting the berm that serves as a breakwater from furious winter storms, we see a massive array of thousands upon thousands of colored plastic ocean voyagers, from as far away as Japan, Russia, and Costa Rica. This is what we are here for.

Traveling expanses of space and time, ocean plastic is a material that can unleash unpredictable dynamics. I am interested in plastic in particular, as opposed to all garbage, because of what it reveals about us as a global economy and what it reveals about the ocean as a type of cultural space and a giant dynamic engine of life and change. As a product of human consumer culture that exhibits visibly the attempts of nature to reabsorb and regurgitate it, ocean plastic has profound stories to tell us about the interconnectedness of the fate of the planet and our impact on it.

My initial contact with plastic—the archaeological marker of our time—happened in 2006 when I stumbled upon vast fields of plastic that the ocean vomited onto the far shores of Hawai'i. The enormity of this first sighting revealed itself to me in the form of a horrifying truth: we have filled the ocean with plastic, and, in the process of trying to clean itself, the ocean communicates with us through the plastic objects of our own making.

Pam Longobardi, **BLACK TSUNAMI FLOAT**
2013
found plastic debris from Gore Point, Alaska

Five thousand miles north of Hawai'i's arc of islands is the twin curve, the upper parenthetical bracket of Alaska's tail of islands that bend inward to its crenelated coastline where the research vessel *Norseman* now takes us. These parentheses frame the entire basin of the Pacific Ocean and its swirling Gyre, now home to a continental-sized miasma of parti-colored plastic. These two outstretched arms of the United States colonial empire contain the yin and yang of Romantic possibilities: Hawai'i is Paradise, and Alaska is Wilderness. However, the invading army of plastic now populates all physical spaces of the planet and, symbolically, the furthest reaches of the mind.

In the *Drifters Project*, I centralize the artist as cultureworker/activist/ researcher, and I employ forensics as an aesthetic mode of inquiry. Before touching or moving anything, I photograph the sites as I find them. I examine and document the deposition as it is—as if already installed by an artist. I have a system of identifying the date and location of the collection as part of the study of its transport. Then I begin collecting, sometimes making constructions and installations on site, and other times carrying the debris away to recombine it in larger works later. I prefer to keep it in a transitive form as installation, so the work can be dismantled and reconfigured. The objects are presented as specimens on steel pins, recombined into large installations or constructions, or as highly detailed photographic portraits.

Plastic objects are the cultural archeology of our time, spun and exchanged on the global lubrication of currency to be transported on the conveyor belt of the ocean. These objects form a portrait of global late-capitalist consumer society, mirroring our desires, wishes, hubris and ingenuity. These are objects with unintended consequences that become transformed as they leave the quotidian world at the end of their useful life and collide with nature to be mutated, transported and regurgitated out of the shifting oceans.

The plastic elements initially seem attractive and innocuous, like toys, some with an eerie familiarity and some totally alien. We are largely ignorant of plastic's true impact, both to our own bodies, to the bodies of the creatures of the earth and sea, and to the very earth itself. From death by entanglement or ingestion, to life-altering endocrine disruption and estrogen mimicry, plastic is implicated in a host of damaging and destructive outcomes.

ARTIST PAM LONGOBARDI SORTS THROUGH OCEAN TRASH
on the deck of Norseman off the coast of Wonder Bay, Alaska,
during the Gyre project expedition, 2013
Photograph by Kip Evans

We have made the most versatile material substitute imaginable: plastic can go anywhere, and it can do or be anything. With the ocean as our accomplice, plastic is now everywhere on earth. The International Commission on Quaternary Stratigraphy[1], a worldwide committee that decides the structure of the Geologic Time Scale, has set 2016 as a goal date for the addition of an entirely new epoch, the Anthropocene.[2] The Anthropocene Era marks the intensification of human-borne geo-engineering, from the trapping of nitrogen through advanced industrial farming techniques of fertilization for mass-scale food production,[3] to the present day externalization of the earth's oily core. Oil drilling goes further and deeper now in more extreme environments. It is also the raw ingredient of every component of the plastic army now laying siege. The orphan plastic object exists in a nether world, functionless, unwanted and in many ways invisible. But the plastic that has invaded our surroundings will never disappear. It is not of this earth in the same way that other materials are. It's a completely new substance with this chilling truth: every piece of plastic ever made on earth is still on earth. It will be all that will remain in a future fossil layer.

More so than any other substance, plastic absorbs and reflects the pure notion of Karl Marx's 'commodity fetishism.'[4] In my project, the process of re-absorption of plastic into commodity fetishism begins at the collection sites. I often find, keep and reuse objects in their original use-value function. I have found many usable items, including nearly always, a plastic bag or bucket to transport the collection. In this way, I re-enact a past and future hominid activity of hunter-gathering tools from my environment. These objects transcend their status as lost or rejected by returning to the social world in the same form they left it—as re-useful objects.

More often the things I collect follow an elaborate and circuitous route by transcending their original status as commodity to become pure fetish, being marked by the ocean's colonization. Ocean plastic is a new type of commodity, one that has illuminated nature's role in the creation of capital. The bryozoan-encrusted pair of superhero legs from Midway Island, the haunting and exquisitely cracked smiling clown mouth, now separated from the rest of the hapless face, or the shark-chewed Japanese bleach bottle on a beach in Resurrection Bay, all become

Pam Longobardi, GHOSTS OF
CONSUMPTION/ARCHEOLOGY
OF CULTURE (FOR PIET M.),
2012

110" x 75" x 8"
found ocean plastic from
Hawai'i, Costa Rica, Alaska,
steel pins, silicone

supreme fetish commodities as they sit in the social space of high culture. This transformation process from consumer commodity fetish (useful or desirable plastic object), to status-less lost object (ocean plastic) to recovered, re-fetishized commodity and portent-wielding toxic symbol (art capital) qualifies this material as a new type of commodity. It is a new supreme commodity because it expresses the 'amount of labor' that nature bestows, wrought by ocean forces, and it carries readable knowledge of nature's powers of material production, transport and transformation. It also carries with it messages of fragility and limitations.

I see the plastic of my collections also as a magic encyclopedia.[5] Going to extreme lengths and physical exertion to scour far-flung locations, deep inside of sea caves in Greece, along remote shorelines of Alaska, Hawai'i, Costa Rica, or Alabama, and free diving subsurface seas from Italy to Taiwan, I feel that I am not only a collector, but a divinator, culling out the magic encyclopedia that may tell us our fate.

I pause to bend down and pick up a small round cerulean blue dome. It is an unidentifiable piece of plastic that painfully reminds me of the beautiful Aleutian symbol of the blowhole, the blue eye in abstracted animal sculptures I saw at the Anchorage Museum. The blue blowhole, the breathing hole of our ocean-borne cousin the whale, symbolizes interconnection of the human world and the spirit world that animals also inhabit. Can this plastic surrogate reawaken this understanding that Native Alaskans have, but that we have forgotten? The latent futility of collection is not lost on me, but intervening in plastic's horrifying omnipresence is not unlike willfully turning to face the monster in a dream, to examine its features in close detail. It is an attempt to re-gather what has been lost, to understand the position of humans within the encompassing world, and to see the future in the prophetic objects of our recent past.

By staring into the face of plastic, we see that it can be both supreme commodity fetish and siren of grave consequences. It can be both waste material and future fossil storehouse of the raw material of oil. It can be the vehicle on which we sail into our own extinction, or the ringing alarm that wakes us into action to turn the ship of our fate.

1 Subcommission on Quaternary Stratigraphy, "Working Group on the Anthropocene," http://www.quaternary.stratigraphy.org.uk/workinggroups/anthropocene/

2 "A Man-made world," May 26, 2011, *The Economist*, http://www.economist.com/node/18741749

3 Zalasiewicz, Jan, Mark Williams, Will Steffen, and Paul Crutzen. 2010. "The New World of the Anthropocene," *Environmental Science and Technology*, 44:7: 2228-2231.

4 Marx writes: "To what extent some economists are misled by the Fetishism inherent in commodities, or by the objective appearance of the social characteristics of labour, is shown . . . by the dull and tedious quarrel over the part played by Nature in the formation of exchange value. Since exchange value is a definite social manner of expressing the amount of labour bestowed upon an object, Nature has no more to do with it, than it has in fixing the course of exchange" (Marx, 1915, 93-94). Marx, Karl. 1915. *Capital: A Critique of Political Economy*, Vol.1. Translated by Samuel Moore and Edward Aveling. Edited by Frederick Engels. Chicago: Charles H. Kerr & Company.

5 Taussig, Michael. 2012."Fieldwork Notebooks" from *100 Notes – 100 Thoughts*, No. 001. Catalog of dOCUMENTA (13). Kassel: Hatje Cantz Verlag.

Pam Longobardi, **CYCLOPTIC VISION**
2013
Collaboration with Petra Matuskova, Czech Republic

144" x 65" x 18"
found ocean styrofoam collected from sea caves of Kefalonia, carved stone.
Installation in ENDLESS, exhibition at ionion Center for Art and Culture, Kefalonia, Greece

DRIFTERS OBJECT PORTRAITS
2006-2011

found ocean plastic collected from Hawaii
L to R: mayanbead, dragoncastle, blueleg, plutohead, pinkblob, fossiljaw, flowerballs, clawtong, camelnub, textsrip, INRI, meltcolor, universalgun, armymanblue, smallbrain, starsofdavid.

EMBEDDED

Andy Hughes Edited by Martina Heintke

WALKING ALONG THE SAND DUNES AT SKER POINT, SOUTH WALES, with a surfboard under my arm, I suddenly felt a sharp pain in my left hand. I noticed that some sort of splinter had embedded itself into my palm. It hadn't bothered me while I was surfing, concentrating on catching that wave. After a long soak in a hot bath, I had a go at digging out the offending article with a needle. When the tiny fragment finally made it to the surface, I wondered how anything so tiny could cause so much pain. After close inspection, it turned out to be 'just' a small shard of plastic.

It was a minor incident, yet now permanently stored in my memory, popping back up into conscious thought decades later as the bigger picture emerged: the world's oceans are littered with man-made waste in devastating abundance.

Pollution and floating waste are not new or unique to the 21st century. My own experiences as a young surfer in the late 1980s surfing at Sker Point gave me an early awareness of human consumerist detritus. Sitting astride my board in the brown, dirty sea waiting for the right wave, it was not uncommon to see all manner of unpleasant things floating past: the odd panty-liner or condom, or even excrement.

Regular surfers suffer from a host of infections, no doubt caused by all sorts of pathogens present in the seawater. This part of the Welsh coastline, and indeed many other parts of the British Isles, suffers mightily from ocean pollution. In the 1980s and 1990s, many European countries labeled Britain 'the dirty man of Europe' due to its air pollution, as industrial power plants emitted high levels of sulphur dioxide into the atmosphere. Carried away by the wind, these emissions came down on other, mostly Scandinavian countries, as acid rain, destroying trees and aquatic life further afield. This began the environmental age and the realization that pollution knows no boundaries.

Andy Hughes, **HERMOSA BEACH, LOS ANGELES**
2004

On Sker Beach, large amounts of coal particles washed up from the nearby steelworks, interspersed with other debris. The coal tended to render the beach black, which made the brightly-colored plastic waste stand out like jewels presented on a black velvet cushion. Having grown up in a blue-collar mining community in Yorkshire, I had grown accustomed to industrial pollution and how detrimental it can be to human health. My coal miner grandfather died at age 63 of emphysema. Slag heaps, power station smoke stacks and cooling towers were the backdrop to my youth. The coast, on the other hand, had always appeared to me to be a place of unadulterated beauty, with pristine air and waters. It was a place to go on holiday, and it was a place to rejuvenate and rejoice.

In 1995, I moved to Cornwall, coined the "Cornish Riviera," as it is warmed by the Gulf Stream and boasts a temperate microclimate. The sand on the beach is white, and the seas are clear blue. Millions of holidaymakers flock there each summer to enjoy sand, sea and surf. Since the days of Whistler and Turner holidaying and painting in St. Ives at the beginning of the 20th century, many artists also made their way to Cornwall, such as Barbara Hepworth, Ben Nicholson, Naum Gabo and Mark Rothko. Art practice became important in this part of Britain.

But I quickly found that all was not as pristine as it seemed. Local surfers had started a campaign called "Surfers against Sewage," as they found themselves contracting viral illnesses from exposure to the water. A place where people paid to come on holiday was consumed by flotsam and jetsam and washed-up waste—nearly all of which was plastic.

My daily journeys across the dunes and beaches at low tide have followed a certain pattern: short walks, long walks, dog walks, and so on. Land and sea appear like a curtain in continuous motion. During these walks, it was not the organic forms or matter that stood out to me. Instead it was the abject matter of humanity that punctuated the experience of the walks and which left a lasting impression. These plastic objects were first made, then desired, and, finally, rejected by humans and have found their way into natural settings. In my photographs, rubbish is rendered as part of the contemporary sublime. The use of scale and

Dominica Williamson, **GULF STREAM**
2013
Mixed Media

Dominica Williamson, SKER BAY
2013
Mixed Media

saturated colors help to draw the eye to the subject. The viewer's response is one of ambiguity: in the first instance the mind is seduced by a beautiful aestheticism absolved from contextual meaning, followed by the secondary reaction of repulsion, when the mind recognizes the object as rubbish on a beach and realizes it should not be there.

Wherever we go in the world, waste is all around. But as waste is transported on large container ships away from one nation or continent to another to be treated, used, and ultimately manufactured into new waste, the oceans' currents do their bit to transport all other 'unorganised' waste streams around our planet to wash up where it will. Traces of plastic are found everywhere. This is no longer a mere local problem; it is a global concern

Plastic waste is the ultimate Kristevian abject matter—once desired, then discarded and reviled. What we can't see may not bother us, but imagine the ultimate effect of plastic flotsam. As nature exerts its abrasive forces, plastic items break into smaller pieces over time—small enough to be embedded splinters.

Max Liboiron
NORTHERN TOPOGRAPHY VI: ENVIRONMENTAL MONITORING, YUKON RIVER (CAVERN)
2010
Styrofoam from river dock, pollutants, salt

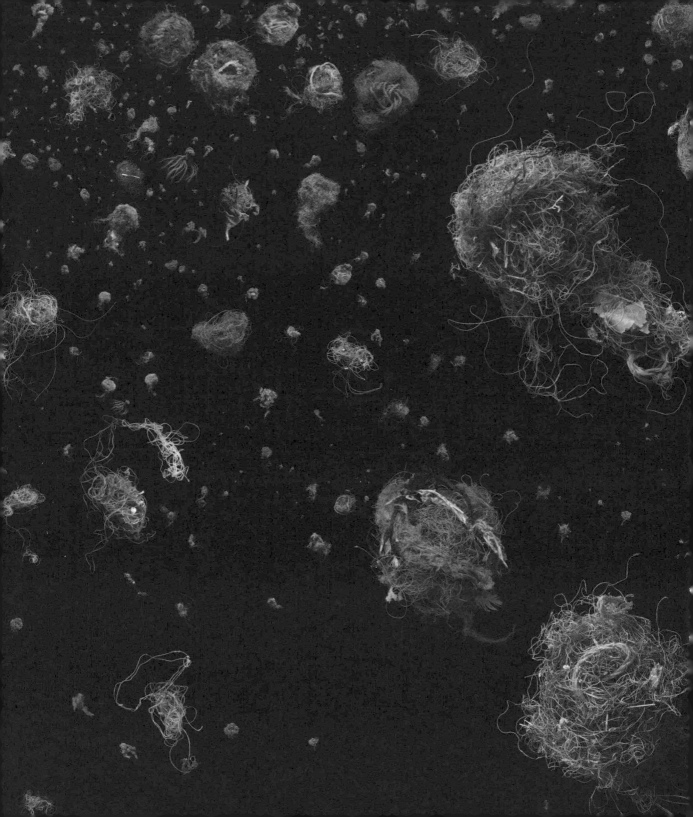

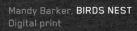

Mandy Barker, BIRDS NEST
Digital print

Alexis Rockman, **GOLF COURSE**
1997, Envirotex, digitized photo, trash, Astroturf, golf balls,
golf club, soil, cast plastic human femur, and oil paint on wood,
40 x 32 x 4.25 in.

Judith Selby and Richard Lang, **WREATH SOLDIERS**

Joan Wadleigh Curran, **NET – BALLLYCASTLE**
Gouache on paper

ACKNOWLEDGEMENTS

GYRE: The Plastic Ocean is a project organized by the Anchorage Museum and the Alaska SeaLife Center, in collaboration with many organizations, including the National Oceanic and Atmospheric Administration (NOAA), the Ocean Conservancy, the Blue Oceans Institute, National Geographic, and others. This publication is an accompaniment to the Anchorage Museum's *GYRE* exhibition (2014), which was generously funded, in part, by the Surdna Foundation, Paul G. Allen Family Foundation, Robert Rauschenberg Foundation, and NOAA. Publication support was provided by the Elizabeth Firestone Graham Foundation. Many thanks to the essayists and to other key contributors to this project and publication, including Howard Ferren, Tara Jones, Ryan Kenny, Carolyn Kozak, Don Mohr, Jane Rabadi, Tim Remick, and countless others. Publication design provided by Karen Larsen of Creative Space. Special thanks to Hannah Moderow.

TRISH BARNARD has considerable experience as a collections interpreter and exhibition curator. She has conducted research on historical Indigenous collections held in all major Australian museums and has a sound knowledge of contemporary arts, and new developments and innovations within the arts and crafts industry. She is a descendant of the Yambina people of central Queensland and is committed to assisting Aboriginal communities to develop their keeping places or museums. As an accredited mentor, she provides work placement opportunities for skill development. Barnard currently works as Senior Curator of Indigenous Studies at the Queensland Museum.

JULIE DECKER, Ph.D, is the Chief Curator at the Anchorage Museum. Decker has authored numerous articles and publications on the art and architecture of Alaska, including *Quonset: Metal Living for a Modern Age, Modern North: Architecture on the Frozen Edge* and *True North: Contemporary Architecture of Alaska.*

MARK DION was born in New Bedford, Massachusetts in 1961. He received a BFA (1986) and an honorary doctorate (2003) from the University of Hartford, Hartford Art School, in Connecticut. He also attended the prestigious Whitney Museum of American Art's Independent Study Program. Dion's work examines the ways in which dominant ideologies and public institutions shape our understanding of history, knowledge, and the natural world. The job of the artist, he says, is to go against the grain of dominant culture, to challenge perception and convention. Appropriating archaeological and other scientific methods of collecting, ordering, and exhibiting objects, Dion creates works that question the distinctions between 'objective' ('rational') scientific methods and 'subjective' ('irrational') influences. The artist's

spectacular and often fantastical curiosity cabinets, modeled on *Wunderkammen* of the 16th Century, exalt atypical orderings of objects and specimens. By locating the roots of environmental politics and public policy in the construction of knowledge about nature, Mark Dion questions the authoritative role of the scientific voice in contemporary society.

He has received numerous awards, including the ninth annual Larry Aldrich Foundation Award (2001), the Joan Mitchell Foundation Award (2007), and the Smithsonian American Art Museum's Lucida Art Award (2008). He has had major exhibitions at the Miami Art Museum (2006); Museum of Modern Art, New York (2004); Aldrich Museum of Contemporary Art, Ridgefield, Connecticut (2003); Tate Gallery, London (1999); and the British Museum of Natural History in London (2007). "Neukom Vivarium" (2006), a permanent outdoor installation and learning lab for the Olympic Sculpture Park, was commissioned by the Seattle Art Museum. Dion has recently completed a major permanent commission, 'OCEANOMANIA: Souvenirs of Mysterious Seas,' for the Oceanographic Museum in Monaco. He is the co-director of Mildred's Land, an innovative visual art education and residency program in Beach Lake, Pennsylvania. Dion lives with his wife and frequent collaborator Dana Sherwood in New York City and works worldwide.

HOWARD FERREN is Director of Conservation at the Alaska SeaLife Center (ASLC) based in Seward, Alaska. He has been with the Center for ten years, serving first as Assistant Director for Research Operations. He is currently responsible for establishing the ASLC Stewardship programs including seeking solutions to marine debris and preventing marine invasive species from impacting marine ecosystems of Alaska. He has been instrumental in developing citizen science conservation programs including BioMap Alaska and the Alaska Corps of Coastal Observers (AkCCO). Ferren holds a MS degree in biological oceanography from the University of Alaska, Institute of Marine Science, where he studied marine mammal physiology. His career has spanned an array of for-profit and non-profit businesses, with a focus on conservation. Ferren also serves as a Board Director with the Kenai Watershed Forum.

DAVE GAUDET earned a BS degree in Fisheries Management from the University of Wisconsin, Steven's Point in 1973 and a MS degree in Fisheries Science from the University of Washington in 1980. He worked for the Alaska Department of Fish and Game (ADF&G) in the Division of Commercial Fisheries from 1981 to 2003. His first assignment was to implement assessment of fish populations using sonar. The assignment involved travel to all regions of Alaska to determine if sonar would be a useful tool for fisheries management. In 1989, he moved to the Southeast Region to become the management biologist for the Commercial Salmon Troll fishery. During this time he became Alaska's co-chair for the Pacific Salmon Commission's (PSC) Chinook Technical Committee as well as represented Alaska's interests in Endangered Species Act (ESA) activities. In 1999, he became the Special Assistant to the Commissioner for the PSC. He was involved in the 1999 negotiations that resulted in the implementation of abundance-based management in salmon fisheries under the PSC's jurisdiction.

Gaudet retired in 2003 and has since worked for the University of Washington's Bristol Bay field program and LGL Consulting. As an independent consultant, he participated in the Marine Stewardship Councils' (MSC) review of the California salmon fishery, provided analysis for renegotiation of the Pacific Salmon Treaty to the ADF&G in 2008, and he worked with the Alaska Seafood Marketing Institute and Alaska Fisheries Development Foundation to certify Alaskan salmon and Pacific Cod as sustainable in the MSC program. In 2009, Gaudet contracted with the Marine Conservation Alliance Foundation as the Marine Debris Program Coordinator. He currently is the Director of the Alaska Marine Stewardship Foundation (formerly the Marine Conservation Alliance Foundation) in Juneau and manages their marine debris program. He has also operated a commercial troller in the Southeast Alaska salmon fishery and currently drift gillnets for salmon in Bristol Bay.

DONOVAN HOHN's first book, *Moby-Duck: The True Story of 28,800 Bath Toys Lost at Sea and of the Beachcombers, Oceanographers, Environmentalists, and Fools, Including the Author, Who Went in Search of Them* (Viking, 2011), was a national bestseller, a New York Times Notable Book of the Year, a finalist for the New York Public Library's Helen Bernstein Book Award for Excellence in Journalism, runner-up for the 2012 PEN/E. O. Wilson Literary Science Writing Award, and a finalist for the 2013 PEN / John Kenneth Galbraith Award for Nonfiction. Hohn is the recipient of a Whiting Writer's Award, an NEA Creative Writing Fellowship in nonfiction, and a Knight-Wallace Journalism Fellowship. He has written for such national publications as *The New York Times Magazine*, *Harper's*, *Outside*, and *Popular Science*. A former high school English teacher, senior editor of *Harper's*, and features editor of GQ, he is now Associate Professor of English at Wayne State University and lives in Ann Arbor, where he has begun work on a second book—about the history, natural and otherwise, of America's inner coast.

ANDY HUGHES' photographic depictions of plastic and other human waste along the coastal fringes explore the tension between attraction and repulsion. They are photographic expressive visions that find beauty and humanity in our throwaway society. Born in 1966, Hughes grew up in the North of England in the mining town of Castleford, West Yorkshire. He attended Art College in Wakefield before being awarded a First Class Honors Degree in Fine Art at Cardiff University and then an MA at the Royal College of Art, London in 1991. While studying in Cardiff, he learned to surf, and for over twenty years he has made visual works related to the littoral zone. He was an early and active member of the Cornish-based NGO Surfers Against Sewage. He moved to Cornwall in 1993 as the first artist in residence at the Tate Gallery St. Ives. His work has been published by Booth-Clibborn Editions in London, and Abrams, New York. Various photographic works are in a number of public and private collections in Britain and America. His two dogs, Lily and Maui, spend many hours with him walking the beaches and coastal paths in Cornwall, England.

PAM LONGOBARDI has had over 40 solo exhibitions and 65 group exhibitions in galleries and museums in the US, China, Italy, Spain, Finland, Poland, Japan and elsewhere. Her artworks are in numerous collections, including commissions for Benziger Winery, the Hyatt Corporation, the Atlanta Hartsfield International Airport, Fulton County Medical Examiner's Facility and First Tennessee Bank, Memphis. Her large installation, "1614-1914," was included in the 2004 exhibition Birdspace at the New Orleans Contemporary Art Center, and it traveled for 2 years to the Norton Museum of Art, Hudson River Museum and four other US museums. She received a

SAFNEA Visual Artist Fellowship in Painting, a Tennessee Arts Commission Visual Arts Fellowship, and was artist in residence with the BAU Institute in Otranto, Italy, in Kasterlee, Belgium, and in Beijing at NY ARTS/Beijing during the 2008 Olympics. In 2005, Longobardi was named recipient of Georgia State University's Outstanding Faculty Achievement Award, where she is Professor of Art.

Longobardi currently lives in Atlanta, Georgia. She created the *Drifters Project* in 2006, addressing global plastic pollution and the changing ocean. Working solo or with communities, she has made scores of interventions, cleaning plastic from beaches all over the world, and removing thousands of pounds of material from the natural environment and re-situating it within the cultural context.

NICHOLAS MALLOS is a Conservation Biologist, Marine Debris Specialist at Ocean Conservancy. He received a BS degree in Biology and Marine Science from Dickinson College where he focused his research on the efficacy of marine protected areas and migration patterns of lemon sharks in the Turks and Caicos Islands. Mallos holds a MS degree from Duke University's Nicholas School of the Environment with a special concentration in Coastal Environmental Management. He has traveled around the world studying marine debris including ocean plastics research in the North Pacific Gyre and fieldwork on Midway Atoll to examine the impact of plastics on native marine fauna. Following the devastating earthquake and tsunami in Japan, Mallos traveled to prefectures on the northern coast to assess the cleanup effort and to speak with experts about debris projections for U.S. coastlines.

Mallos oversees a diverse range of projects in Ocean Conservancy's Trash Free Seas

Program including ocean plastics and beach litter research, a marine debris working group at the National Center for Ecological Analysis and Synthesis (NCEAS), International Coastal Cleanup data analyses, and strategic partnerships targeting collaborative debris research and marine wildlife conservation. Science communication also plays a major role in his work at Ocean Conservancy. Mallos is a diehard surfer who works hard to catch a wave wherever his travels take him.

SUSAN MIDDLETON has been dedicated to the documentation and portraiture of rare and endangered animals, plants, sites, and cultures for the past 30 years, inspired by the earth's biological and cultural diversity and motivated by the need to protect it. She is a photographer, author, producer, curator, lecturer and educator. A graduate of the University of Santa Clara, she chaired the California Academy of Sciences department of photography from 1982 to 1995, where she currently serves as a research associate. She has worked extensively in Hawai'i and West Africa. In 1985, she worked for a year with photographer Richard Avedon in New York City. Susan is an effective communicator on behalf of biodiversity preservation, combining art and science in a unique approach to reach a diverse audience and raise public awareness. This effort has resulted in numerous publications, exhibitions, public presentations and media coverage.

For thirty years, **CARL SAFINA** has studied the ocean as a scientist, stood for it as an advocate, and conveyed his travels among sea creatures and fishing people in lyrical non-fiction writing. Dr. Safina has helped lead campaigns to ban high-seas driftnets, overhaul U.S. fisheries law, achieve a United Nations fisheries treaty, and reduce albatross and sea turtle drownings on commercial fishing lines. Along the way, he became a leading voice for conservation. Safina is author of 6 books and more than 100 scientific and popular publications. Founding president of Blue Ocean Institute, Safina is also a professor at Stony Brook University on Long Island, NY where he co-chairs the new Center for Communicating Science. Safina has received many honors that range from a MacArthur "genius" Prize to a James Beard medal. Audubon magazine named him among "100 Notable Conservationists of the 20th Century." His television series, Saving the Ocean with Carl Safina, will premier this fall on PBS stations around the country.

RUTH PELZ, senior writer and exhibit developer for the Burke Museum of Natural History and Culture, has several decades of experience as a writer of educational materials, which have included: social studies and science curricula for Seattle Public Schools and other institutions; elementary and secondary textbooks for national publishers; newsletters, research articles, and additional publications for the University of Washington; exhibit labels, school curricula, and public educational materials for the Burke Museum. The exhibitions she has developed and written for the Burke include *Plastics Unwrapped, Coffee: The World in Your Cup, Wolves in Washington State*, and *The Big One: Earthquakes in the Pacific Northwest*.

Painter **ALEXIS ROCKMAN**'s canvases present a darkly surreal vision of the collision between human civilization and the natural world. His art draws from a diverse range of inspirations, including old master painting, science fiction and above all, natural history. In researching his paintings, Rockman has undertaken extended expeditions into the Amazon Basin, Tasmania, Madagascar, South Africa and Antarctica. He has worked not only with other artists, but also with leading scientists, including paleontologist Peter Ward on the book *Future Evolotion*, famed naturalist Stephen Jay Gould, who wrote an extended essay for the 2004 monograph *Alexis Rockman*, and NASA climatologist James Hanson. This last collaboration resulted in the 8 X 24 foot mural *Manifest Destiny*, commissioned by the Brooklyn Museum, a post-apocalyptic vision of a city submerged as a possible consequence of climate change.

Rockman recently completed work for Ang Lee on his film, *Life of Pi*, where he served as "Inspirational Artist." Rockman's work has been featured in *Wired, The New York Times* and *The Wall Street Journal*, and is in the collections of museums such as LACMA, the Guggenheim and the Whitney Museum of American Art. He was recently the subject of a major 2010-11 retrospective at the Smithsonian Museum of American Art, entitled *Alexis Rockman: A Fable for Tomorrow*, which traveled to The Wexner Center for the Arts.

SUE RYAN is a North Queensland based artist who works across a range of mediums including printmaking, painting, drawing and sculpture. Since her initial studies at the Queensland College of Art, where she majored in printmaking, Ryan has been immersed in the arts as a practicing artist and arts worker. Throughout her career, Ryan developed a deep involvement with North Queensland Indigenous artists, nurturing and promoting their art both nationally and internationally. After her time with Lockhart River Art Centre as Art Centre manager from 2001 to 2007, she was appointed to conduct a study investigating the potential for developing artwork from 'ghost nets' - discarded fishing nets. Subsequently, Ryan took on the position of Art Project Director for GhostNets Australia and continues to work in collaboration with Indigenous and non-Indigenous artists to facilitate environmental community arts projects, exhibitions and workshops.

NANCY WALLACE is the Director of the National Oceanic and Atmospheric Administration's Marine Debris Program, where she oversees federal efforts to research, prevent, and reduce the impacts of marine debris in the United States. Ms. Wallace has 10 years of experience in ocean policy, and her work has ranged from resource conservation with the National Park Service, to developing sustainable catch limits for fisheries off the U.S. East Coast, to efforts to improve water quality in the Gulf of Mexico. She holds a MS degree in Marine Affairs and Policy from the University of Miami and a BS degree in Biology from Fairfield University.

Max Liboiron, **SEAGLOBE**
2012
Ocean plastics collected in New York City,
water, glass, wood, mixed media

Evelyn Rydz, GULF PILE #4
12 x 17" (unframed)
Pencil and color pencil on drafting film

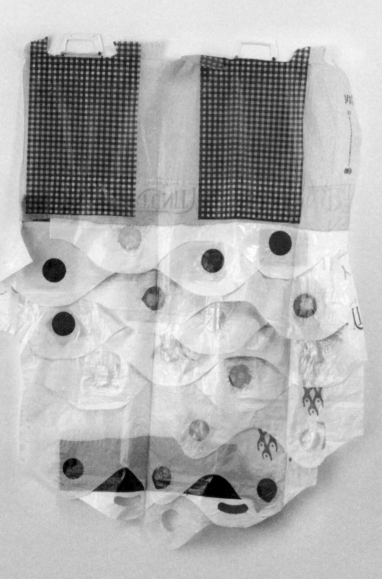

Dianna Cohen, **LE POISSON**
Plastic bags, handles and thread

This bag is made from
50% recycled material

Sainsbury's
Try something new today

sainsburys.co.uk

bag and
nectar poin

recycle